Interpreting American Military History at Museums and Historic Sites

Interpreting History

Series Editor: Russell Lewis, Chicago History Museum

About the Series

The American Association for State and Local History publishes the *Interpreting History* series in order to provide expert, in-depth guidance in interpretation for history professionals at museums and historic sites. The books are intended to help practitioners expand their interpretation to be more inclusive of the range of American history.
Books in this series help readers:

- quickly learn about the questions surrounding a specific topic,
- introduce them to the challenges of interpreting this part of history, and
- highlight best practice examples of how interpretation has been done by different organizations.

They enable institutions to place their interpretative efforts into a larger context, despite each having a specific and often localized mission. These books serve as quick references to practical considerations, further research, and historical information.

Titles in the Series

Interpreting American Military History at Museums and Historic Sites

Marc K. Blackburn

ROWMAN & LITTLEFIELD
Lanham • Boulder • New York • London

Published by Rowman & Littlefield
A wholly owned subsidiary of The Rowman & Littlefield Publishing Group, Inc.
4501 Forbes Boulevard, Suite 200, Lanham, Maryland 20706
www.rowman.com

Unit A, Whitacre Mews, 26-34 Stannary Street, London SE11 4AB

British Library Cataloguing in Publication Information Available

Library of Congress Cataloging-in-Publication Data

Names: Blackburn, Marc K., author.
Title: Interpreting American military history at museums and historic sites /
    by Marc K. Blackburn.
Description: Lanham, Maryland : Rowman & Littlefield, 2016. | Series: Interpreting history |
    Includes bibliographical references and index.
Identifiers: LCCN 2015044499 (print) | LCCN 2016002250 (ebook) | ISBN 9781442239739
    (cloth : alk. paper) | ISBN 9781442239746 (pbk. : alk. paper) | ISBN 9781442239753
    (Electronic)
Subjects: LCSH: Military museums—United States. | Historic sites—Interpretive
    programs—United States. | Museums--Educational aspects—United States. |
    Military parks—United States.
Classification: LCC U13.U6 B55 2016 (print) | LCC U13.U6 (ebook) | DDC
    355.0074/73—dc23
LC record available at http://lccn.loc.gov/2015044499

Printed in the United States of America

To my loving family

Contents

Preface

Misunderstanding of the present is the inevitable consequence of ignorance of the past. But a man may wear himself out just as fruitlessly in seeking to understand the past, if he is totally ignorant of the present.

Marc Bloch[1]

Why should we care about military history? In the American narrative, we are a country born of a violent revolution. Our society was remade in a great Civil War. We helped make the world safe for democracy in World War One and World War Two. We went on the offensive against perceived threats in the global war on terror. While we are not a society of warriors, we are certainly a country made by war. Cultural institutions with large military history collections and exhibits are certainly not established to glorify war or downplay its ultimate costs. Warfare on any scale can be seen as a catastrophe—the loss of men, women, and children; the breaking of families; the physical and mental damage it causes, whether it is the burning of a town in the far past or the psychic wounds that soldiers carry today. We live, however, in the shadows of these events. As a profession, it is our collective responsibility to not only embrace the complexity of these events, but also take a thoughtful and nuanced approach to telling the stories our historic sites, museums, and archives can share. *Interpreting American Military History* will provide a useful guide in relating the stories of our martial past to contemporary audiences.

The work of presenting narratives of military history that reach beyond, and challenge familiar public conceptions of the field is an immense task. This book is not meant to be an in-depth explanation of American military history, but it will do two things. First, it will act as a primer for those unfamiliar with academic trends of the last forty years. Historiography of American military history, like that of other sub-fields, shifts as new information surfaces or as perspectives change. Since the 1960s, tectonic shifts have occurred across every field of American history, so this will at least provide the groundwork for further explorations. Each chapter provides a summary of events, personalities, and policies to help interested readers formulate the questions they need to ask in programming and media that relate to American military history. Second, case studies, real and hypothetical, will explain how to take this information and start thinking about how to create programs, interpretive media, outreach strategies, and mission goals that are relevant to the public and the institutions charged with serving them.

A LIFE IN HISTORY

Interpreting American Military History is also a personal journey. For most authors, I imagine that the origins of a book, novel, or otherwise, are complicated and difficult to conceptualize in one "aha" moment. As I think about the genesis of what you are about to read, it is the result of many different influences in my professional and personal life. As long as I can remember, I have been drawn to military history. I grew up in Palo Alto, California, home of Stanford University and the epicenter of the high technology industry. As a twelve-year-old kid, I was captivated by the city's children's library rather than the emerging high technology industry that would make the area famous. My mother would plop us in the car so that we could spend the afternoon in the library. I often found myself drawn to the modest history section and, in particular, a series of illustrated books on World War Two published by American Heritage. There books were filled with colorful art, maps, and vintage black and white photographs. I was enamored by the action in the illustrations and the stories of struggle between the Axis and Allied forces.[2] From the children's library, I graduated to the city's main library and discovered so much more. The library was an easy walk from home, so I would make excuses that I had to do my homework and the library was the only place I could go to. Instead of cracking open a text book, I would pull the most recent volume of Jane's Fighting Ships and devour the contents. In short, military history became part of my life. While some would comment that I never grew out of playing with plastic soldiers, I just laughed and dismissed the remarks. I knew that military history was going to be part of my future.

I pursued a history degree as an undergraduate at the University of Puget Sound in Tacoma, Washington, taking a smorgasbord of classes, exploring topics related to military history when the situation warranted it. At the end of four years, it was inevitable that I would continue on to graduate school and plunge into a specialized degree in American military history. It was in graduate school, guided by my advisor Dr. Russell F. Weigley that I really began to understand that there is value to the study of conflict and military history. Under Dr. Weigley's tutelage, American military history became the standard narrative of not just battles and leaders, but of bigger ideas and broader questions that govern our military institutions.

Rather than an academic career, public history and interpretation captured my imagination. Although I did have the privilege of teaching at a community college in Puget Sound, Washington, I eventually turned toward the National Park Service (NPS). I was exposed to many NPS sites as a kid. Whenever my parents saw a sign with the park service arrowhead, they would veer toward it. While I attended Temple University in Philadelphia, from 1986 to 1991, I worked as a seasonal interpretive ranger at Independence National Historical Park. For five summers I had the opportunity to work at the various buildings and exhibits that make up Independence. While guiding visitors through the old state house, now known as Independence Hall and the pavilion that housed the Liberty Bell, I experienced first-hand the ability to connect the meanings of

Figure P.1 Author having a military history moment at Fort Worden, Washington. *Source*: Author photograph

these famous icons to the interests of the park's visitors. There seems to be a degree of synchronicity between the fields of history and interpretation that continues to fascinate me. Factual information pulled from primary source material can be re-examined and re-interpreted by new generations of historians, deriving new meanings from familiar stories. Visitors from around the country would flock to see the Liberty Bell not to see an old cracked bell, but its symbolism and diverse meanings. My fascination with interpretation and the mission of the NPS came together with a permanent job at the Seattle unit of Klondike Gold Rush National Historical Park in 1994. As my career in the National Park Service blossomed, it brought into sharp focus the role public historians and interpreters have in being stewards of objects, places, and

Figure P.2 Author in 1987 in Independence Hall, Philadelphia, Pennsylvania. *Source*: Author photograph

historic structures of our military past. From 2002, to 2015, I served in a variety of capacities at Nez Perce National Historical Park in north central Idaho. In the heart of Nez Perce country, I have the unique opportunity to interpret battlefields of the so-called Nez Perce War of 1877, but more importantly, connect the public to the ancient stories of a people who have lived among the hills of Palouse and Camas Prairie since the beginning of their existence.

As you can see, from an early age I was fascinated with military history. That fascination went far beyond a hobby or a casual interest. While the study of war is tangentially about death and destruction, I would rate my own experiences as positive and fulfilling. I would not be honest, however, if I did not admit that I do struggle between the utility and futility of violence. Internalizing public opinion pieces when the nation considers war certainly gives me pause and, at times, a crisis in confidence, yet I always come back to relevancy. Our military past provides a window to examine the present with a more critical eye. When I look beyond my own personal knowledge about the subject, and look to the wider world, there seems to be a large, captive audience for materials related to military history. Moreover, I would argue that there are more materials now than ever before. Many aficionados are not academically trained historians and are often described as buffs, but in reality they are amateur historians. The needs of the amateur, buff, and casual observer are readily met by a robust publishing industry. A search of online book retailers shows tens of thousands of titles that relate to American military history in print and accessible to the public.[3] While many are published by academic presses, larger printing houses publish dozens of titles a year to meet the public's appetite for military history. There may be some who question the value of books for history buffs and hobbyists versus those that come out of academic publishing houses, but there is something for everyone in this field.

The United States is fortunate to also have many of the battlefields of its various wars preserved at the national, state, and local levels. At the federal level, the National Park Service manages several dozen sites connected to the American Revolution, the War of 1812, the Civil War, and World War Two. Gettysburg National Military Park and Valley Forge National Historical Park, both located in Pennsylvania, play host to over 1,000,000 visitors a year.[4] At Pearl Harbor, a unit of Valor in the Pacific National Monument, the *USS Arizona* also attracts over 1,000,000 visitors a year.[5] The museums of the Smithsonian Institution in Washington, DC, in particular the National Air and Space Museum and the National Museum of American History, have several permanent exhibits with military themes and have audiences that surpass those of Valley Forge, Gettysburg, and the *USS Arizona* combined. In 2013, the National Air and Space museum alone counted over 8,000,000 visitors to its two facilities. Visitors come to these places because these museums and historical sites hold some intangible quality that is relevant to the experiences and values of the visitors that frequent them.[6]

There is a tendency to see the practice of history confined to the academic and public history world, but the use of history in hobbyist groups and popular culture cannot be completely dismissed. There are hundreds of re-enactor groups across the country, representing every time period, made up of individuals who are as passionate about history as a tenured university professor. Personal experience indicates that a musket demonstration is always a crowd pleaser and a visceral reminder of the connection between technology and warfare. Hollywood blockbusters such as *Saving Private Ryan*, the Home Box Office Mini Series' *Band of Brothers* and *The Pacific* attracted millions of dollars in revenue and fans, suggesting a more than casual interest in modern American history.

While these attendance numbers do not reveal the motivations of visitors, they seem to indicate that American military history is alive and well in the public's mind. If there is such a large audience that voraciously reads books on military history, and visits historical sites by the thousands, then to tell these stories in a responsible manner is the duty of every manager, historian, volunteer, and field personnel that staffs our historical institutions across the country. Museums, historical sites, research libraries, and local historical societies are, for many, the most accessible place to be exposed to history. Whether in the largest national museum or the smallest historical society, every staff member and volunteer should be charged to tell personal stories within the context of modern scholarship.

Regardless of whether you work in a museum with a specific mission that revolves around military history or in a historical society with a modest collection of military items, there is one universal principle that is understood by the entire profession—the meanings assigned to historical events and objects are not static. Factual information may remain constant, but meanings change. There seems to be a disconnection between the great narratives of wars and conflicts that are widely known and appreciated by the public, and trends of recent academic scholarship. One example of this dichotomy regards the issue of combat performance of the US Army in

World War Two. Max Hastings, a popular and prolific author, argues in his book on the invasion of Normandy in 1944, *Overlord: D-Day and the Battle for Normandy*,[7] that the successes of Allied armies generally, and the Americans specifically, was not finesse and sophistication on the battlefield, but overwhelming and massive firepower and mountains of supplies and materials. By implication, it is the Germans who should be admired for their skillful, but costly defense of the Normandy beachhead. In the last ten years, various historians have challenged Hastings' arguments. Michael Doubler's *Closing with the Enemy, How GIs Fought the War in Europe*[8] and Peter Mansoor's *The GI Offensive in Europe*[9] argue that the US Army learned from its past mistakes, adapted quickly to changing conditions, and became more proficient in combined operations than its German counterparts. It is far too easy to remain comfortable with an existing narrative. Rather than revising the standard narrative, we avoid taking a chance for something that's safe and comfortable. If museums are to remain relevant, they must be true to the nature of presenting history; revising a master narrative is the norm rather than an aberration.

I have had unique opportunities in my life to visit battlefields, military museums, and historic sites across the United States and Western Europe. From touring one of the forts of the Maginot Line in northeastern France, to spending time walking in the footsteps of Major General George E. Pickett's charge at Gettysburg, Pennsylvania, I walked away with a special appreciation of what these places meant. When I visited the World War One battlefield at Verdun, France, I was

Figure P.3   Pennsylvania Memorial, Gettysburg National Military Park. *Source*: Author photograph

drawn to the ossuary that dominates the site. As I approached the monument, it gave me pause. While the upper floor memorializes the fallen, the basement of the building is peppered with galleries filled with the bones of the dead taken from the battlefield. It was a sobering moment for me. Despite my enthusiasm for military history, I was reminded that this was a place where men died by the thousands. For a brief moment, I questioned my interest in anything having to do with military history, American or otherwise. In the end, I came out of that experience with a more finely tuned sense of responsibility to the past. Those who study military history, or manage objects and sites related to the same, do not revel or celebrate the ultimate cost of war. They are not warmongers for dedicating their careers to these places, objects, and stories—these are stories of collective history, perhaps even of our families, and deserve to be remembered.

AN OVERVIEW

Interpreting American Military History is not meant to be a survey of American military history but to serve as a guide to interpreting our military's past. The first chapter takes a close look at the process of interpretation. A guide such as this is of no use to historical institutions without first defining interpretation as a process of communicating meanings to the public and then examining the components of the said process. When set against changing trends and current historiography in American military history, we have a handy guide that will empower institutions to create programs, media, and strategies interpreting these new trends to the public.

Chapter 2 begins the discussion of military history with a close look at the state of the field in the United States and some of the broad concepts in American military history, providing a primer on how we construct our knowledge of our military's past. The countervailing forces of the American military tradition are, on the one hand, the need and support of a permanent standing military and professional military institutions and on the other, a deep distrust of those same institutions. This tension manifests itself in what amounts to a dual history of the army—the militia tradition and citizen soldiers versus the need for a standing professional army. The dichotomy between citizen soldiers and a standing army is as old as the republic. Similarly, historians continue to explore whether or not Americans had a unique way of prosecuting wars and other types of conflicts. Thrust into the North American continent, institutions and practices evolved toward what can perhaps be described an American way of war. Admittedly, it is difficult to apply labels to every conflict and clash of arms from 1607 to the present day, but whether or not there is an American way of war is certainly worth exploring.

Chapters 3 through 13 are really the bulk of *Interpreting American Military History*—a linear chronology of America's military past broken down into appropriate and digestible time periods. Beginning with the founding of Jamestown, chapters 3 through 10 will take the reader to the present. Rather than providing an in-depth discussion of each conflict on the American timeline, each chronological chapter will have a brief overview of the events and personalities involved. This is not meant to be a text book of American Military History, so the narratives regarding the development of the armed forces and the wars they fought are summaries. Where appropriate, personal experiences, site visits, and hypotheticals of museums and historical sites will explore practical solutions on how to use military history. I think history professionals understand that history never stands still. Where space allows, there will be some space devoted to understanding how the master narrative of American military history has changed and evolved over time.

The book's final chapter serves as an object lesson on what not to do, summarizing the notion that small institutions can accomplish big things with a little planning and foresight. Interpreting military history can be challenging, in particular if we move beyond simple narratives and embrace complexity. If we want new generations to remember the stories of our military past, we have to not only know how these stories evolved over time, but also connect stories to objects that make sense for modern audiences. To do this, it is helpful to review the process of interpretation and its individual elements and explore what constitutes success.

NOTES

1. Marc Bloch, *The Historian's Craft*, trans. Peter Putnam (New York: Vintage Books, 1953), 43.

2. I still keep one around, Stephen W. Sears' *Desert War in North Africa* (New York: American Heritage Publishing Co., Inc., 1967).

3. Using the search term "American Military History" in Amazon.com and Barnes and Noble.com revealed 39,154 and 48,416 titles respectively (accessed 20 April 2014, http://Amazon.com and http://www.barnesandnoble.com).

4. Visitor statistics for the National Park Service can be accessed at https://irma.nps.gov/Stats/. Gettysburg National Military Park, accessed April 20, 2014, https://irma.nps.gov/Stats/SSRSReports/Park%20Specific%20Reports/Annual%20Park%20Recreation%20Visitation%20(1904%20-%20Last%20Calendar%20Year)?Park=GETT. Valley Forge National Historical Park, accessed April 20, 2014, https://irma.nps.gov/Stats/SSRSReports/Park%20Specific%20Reports/Annual%20Park%20Recreation%20Visitation%20(1904%20-%20Last%20Calendar%20Year)?Park=VAFO. Because of Valley Forge National Historical Park's proximity to Philadelphia, many visitors use the park as a recreation site. The park's statistics do not make a distinction between those visiting purely for recreation versus those wanting to experience the history of the site.

5. Valor in the Pacific National Monument, accessed 20 April 2014, https://irma.nps.gov/Stats/SSRSReports/Park%20Specific%20Reports/Annual%20Park%20Recreation%20Visitation%20(1904%20-%20Last%20Calendar%20Year)?Park=VALR.

6. Smithsonian Institution Visitor Statistics, accessed 20 April 2014, http://newsdesk.si.edu/about/stats. The figure for the National Air and Space Museum includes the main building on the mall and the Steven F. Udvar-Hazy Center located at Dulles International Airport in Chantilly, Virginia.

7. Max Hastings, *Overlord: D-Day and the Battle for Normandy* (New York: Simon & Schuster Touchstone Edition, 1985).

8. Michael Doubler, *Closing With the Enemy. How GIs Fought the War in Europe, 1944–1945* (Lawrence: University Press of Kansas, 1994).

9. Peter R. Mansoor, *The GI Offensive in Europe. The Triumph of the American Infantry Divisions, 1941–1945* (Lawrence: University Press of Kansas, 1999).

Acknowledgments

In the fall of 2013, I had the distinct pleasure of sharing three weeks with an outstanding group of museum professionals in Indianapolis, Indiana. The origins of this book began on the first day of the Seminar for Historical Administration (SHA), the intense three-week management course sponsored by the American Association for State and Local History (AASLH). Bob Beatty, Chief Operating Office of AASLH asked if any of us would pitch a proposal for this book series by Rowman and Littlefield. Bob's passion for interpretation convinced me to throw my proverbial hat in the ring and see what might happen. Without Bob's enthusiastic encouragement and guidance, this project would not have happened. Special thanks also goes out to the SHA class of 2013. It is rare that a person is granted three weeks to leave one's daily responsibilities to spend time with one's peers in an intensive and compelling learning environment. The class of 2013 has cheered this project on since the first chapter. The camaraderie of this special group has inspired me to move forward. In those deep moments of frustration that are common to many book projects, the giving spirit of the group has propelled me forward. My mentor and graduate advisor, the late Russell F. Weigley, gave me the courage to pursue a career in public history and provided the tools to translate those passions into compelling history. Finally, without the assistance of my family, in particular, my wife, Cheryl, this work would not have been possible. The narrative voice that guides this work is as much hers as mine. Without her critical eye, this book would never have happened. Thank you for your love and support after all of these years.

Chapter 1

Interpretation

"The chief aim of interpretation is not instruction but provocation"[1]

Freeman Tilden

When you are an interpreter interacting with an audience, you often do not know what the end result will be. Will you connect with the audience? Will the program be a bust? Without the benefit of a social scientist doing focus groups and literature reviews, it is hard to know what the visitor "gets" when he or she leaves your institution. That being said, sometimes there is a vibe that you feel, that cannot be measured, but you know in your heart that you have made a connection, and it was meaningful. That is the power of interpretation—facilitating a connection between the resources that we are charged to protect and the interests of the audiences who visit the places where we work. Audiences visit our institutions and sites because they crave something more than absorbing facts and figures. Visitors want a meaningful experience. They want an experience that connects with their deepest-held values and attitudes. Admittedly, that is a hard nut to crack, but with practice and study, virtually any visitor that comes in contact with an interpreter can walk away with something of value. If institutions that we care so much about are to remain relevant, a thorough understanding of how interpretation facilitates connections to our visitors is a vital prerequisite for working in the field that we dedicate our lives to.

Ever since human beings mastered the spoken word, sharing stories and experiences with one another has become a constant force that shapes our history, culture, and identity. Story tellers occupied important roles in extended family groups, using stories to pass along the information concerning ancestors, the intricacies of language, gender roles, spirituality, and history. The traditions of story-telling continue in the museums and libraries that populate our modern landscape and we call it interpretation. As a profession, what we understand as interpretation has roots that stretch back to the late nineteenth and early twentieth centuries. The eloquent nature writing of John Muir and the guided walks of Enos Mills in the Rocky Mountains, established a precedent of revealing greater meanings through their personal experiences and observations. A generation later, philosopher Freeman

Tilden began defining interpretation as a particular mode of communication.[2] Building on Tilden's work, other social scientists, communication experts, and public employees established the profession of interpretation. Today, there are thousands of people who work at the local, state, and federal levels who classify themselves as interpreters.

DEFINING INTERPRETATION

The very essence of a profession is expressed as an agreed upon definition of the work that is commonly pursued by everyone associated with that field of work. As in many professions, definitions change over time as attitudes change and subject matter expertise expands. The first attempt to define interpretation began in the mid-1950s, when Freeman Tilden published his seminal book *Interpreting our Heritage*. Since Tilden, the definitions of our core work have continued to evolve. Despite variations between organizations whose mission is interpretation, there are common elements that will become clear as we examine the evolution of these definitions. In 1957, Freeman Tilden defined interpretation thus:

> An education activity which aims to reveal meanings and relationships through the use of original objects, by firsthand experience, and by illustrative media, rather than to simply convey factual information.[3]

Figure 1.1   Freeman Tilden. *Source*: National Park Service

Tilden identifies interpretation as an educational activity rather than a process of communication. Despite his word choice, it appears that Tilden implicitly acknowledges that this activity could be understood as a particular process of communicating information to a visitor. The key to Tilden's definition of this activity is how information is communicated to the visitor. Rather than concentrating on factual information, the interpreter facilitates a relationship or connection between an object, a photograph, or a place that reveals meaning for the visitor. Sam Ham, a well-respected professor of interpretation suggests that the key to the process lies on the shoulders of visitors. Each visitor attaches meanings to the objects and places he or she is seeing that are relevant to himself or herself.[4] Tilden provided a key breakthrough in conceptualizing interpretation as a means to move beyond what is provided in a classroom. Instead, it opens a new realm of understanding by speaking to the visitor's heart rather than his or her head.

Beginning with Tilden's principles, over the last fifty years, both the National Park Service (NPS) and National Association for Interpretation (NAI) have developed very similar definitions for interpretation that build on Tilden's conceptualization. Founded in 1916, the NPS has provided interpretive services in one form or another for a century. NAI is the professional organization for interpreters. Using materials from the NPS's interpretive development program, NAI has created a certification program to serve the profession. Both organizations recognize interpretation as a process of communication. Both organizations recognize that this process allows for emotional and intellectual connections to resource meanings. Defining interpretation as a process has allowed both organizations to build training programs and curricula that break down the elements of the said process into something that can be taught and mastered. The NPS definition for interpretation suggests:

> The interpretive presentation is successful as a catalyst in creating an opportunity for the audience to form their own intellectual and emotional connections with the meanings/significance inherent in the resource.[5]

As with Tilden, interpretation is not about factual information, but rather about meanings that are formed by the audience. The presentation is a catalyst between the interpreter and the audience; it can create change within the audience. That change can manifest itself as an interpretive opportunity (IO) that can assist in the creation of an emotional connection (something that the visitor can feel) or an intellectual connection (something that the visitor can understand) to the meanings that each resource has. David Larsen, a training specialist at the NPS's Mather training center in Harpers Ferry, West Virginia, and an extraordinary interpreter, spent a great deal of his career exploring the process of interpretation. He understood that the audience wanted more than information: "If information and learning were the primary goal of most visitors, they would never need to visit. Audiences want something more. They seek meaningful experiences."[6] If this is what visitors want—experiences—it is critical that we understand the process of interpretation.

The final definition to consider comes from Dr. Sam Ham, professor emeritus at the University of Idaho. Ham defines interpretation thus:

Figure 1.2   David Larsen. *Source*: Author Photograph

a mission-based communication approach to communication aimed at provoking in audiences the discovery of personal meaning and the forging of personal connections with things, places, people, and concepts.[7]

Ham recognizes that the process of interpretation is used not only to provoke meanings, but to meet the needs of the organization providing the interpretive service. Ham also acknowledges the core concept that is carried through each of the definitions—that interpretation is a facilitated experience between the resource in question and the needs of the audience.

Each one of these definitions is different and each one continues to have relevance in attempting to understand the process of interpretation. One of the common threads is that interpretation is more than a resuscitation of facts. It is a facilitated conversation that connects the interests of the visitor to the meanings that reside in the resources we protect and serve. Regardless of which definition moves an individual interpreter, we can see that interpretation is a process that can be learned and understood by everyone in an organization, from management to volunteers. It allows us to move beyond simple facts and figures to exploring the meanings behind the resources we protect. Too often, the mastery of a story is called interpretation. While it is a critical part of the issue, I think that David Larsen, put it best: "Interpretation does not tell people how it is, it reveals personal significance."[8]

THE INTERPRETIVE EQUATION

If we recognize that interpretation is a process of communication, we can make that process work for us and our visitors, allowing for sharper interpretive messages, programs, and media. A process implies that there are many steps or elements required to make the process work. For employees unfamiliar with interpretation, David Larsen's team of experts broke down the process of interpretation into an equation. This would not be a real equation, but an analogy that allows to identify what success should look like. Stated simply, the process is:

$$(KR + KA)\, AT = IO$$

or

(**K**nowledge of the **R**esource + **K**nowledge of the **A**udience) **A**ppropriate **T**echnique = **I**nterpretive **O**pportunity.[9]

For those of us who are mathematically challenged, it can also be expressed as a Venn diagram.

Each one of these elements works together with the others to produce an IO for our visitors. Leave one of these out, and we fail. Overemphasize one to the detriment of another, and we fail. Each element of the equation flows to the next, and they all work together to create an opportunity we can suggest to our audience.

As someone who came out of a rigorous academic environment, knowledge of the resource (KR) is to me one of the most meaningful elements of the interpretive equation. Every interpreter should have a basic mastery of the facts that govern a historical site or comprehensive collection of objects and papers. Even re-enactors have the responsibility of not only knowing why and how the various elements of

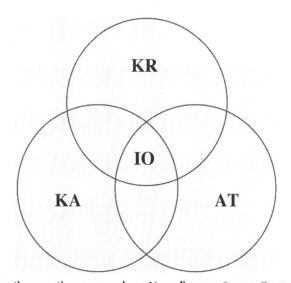

Figure 1.3 Interpretive equation expressed as a Venn diagram. *Source*: Created by author

their costumes work, but also mastering the personality of the characters they are portraying. This information is more than likely readily available in secondary sources, institutional histories, or training materials. For those who have access to primary source materials, all the better. Every interpreter can master the basics rather easily. However, history is more than facts. It is interpretations; it is about finding meanings. As stated earlier in the introduction, the way we conceptualize and understand the information of a battle or an event changes over the course of time. To be true to the mission of your institution, it is necessary to understand not only what the information is, but also how the meanings associated with your place of work have changed over the course of time.

One of the keys to successful interpretation is recognizing that every event along a historical timeline generates multiple points of view. Therefore, if we want to act as a facilitator between the interests of our audience and the meanings of our sites, collections, etc., we must understand and internalize these multiple points of view. Despite the notion of a historian writing objective history, we are the sum total of our beliefs. In a profession that defines success as objectivity, personal views are recognized as bias, yet they define who you are and how you write about an event. A left-leaning historian, for example, may be more inclined to acknowledge the influence of economic forces on events. A combat veteran may understand the stress and terror of combat that a historian cannot even begin to fathom. A group of historians may agree on or argue over the forces that exerted themselves over any particular event. What is more valuable is the perspective that a view brings, adding a layer of sophistication and context that perhaps you did not know existed because of limited reading. Understanding our resources, then, is more than reading a few books; it is a sophisticated and thorough knowledge of not only facts, but also how a story evolves over time.[10] With that knowledge, an able interpreter can respond to any visitor question put before them. Understanding how a story evolves over time acknowledges there are always multiple perspectives to our collective past. Those multiple perspectives could influence the choices that we make on how to engage the visitor.

How does a sophisticated knowledge of the resource work? One of the mainstays of any archival or artifact collection are letters and items that relate to a person's service in the World Wars of the twentieth century. Each individual has a story to tell. A small collection of personal letters and objects reveals information not only about that individual, but also about his or her own place in the community he or she is from. How, then, are these experiences integrated with the contextual knowledge that is generated by the community of scholars? How does that individual collection of letters fit into our wider understanding of a soldier's motivations, hopes, and fears?

Let's look at our hypothetical collection of letters and objects and see how it connects with current academic trends. Our understanding of motivations and attitudes of soldiers serving in Europe and the Pacific during World War Two is changing. The view conditioned by popular culture and books is that the men and women who went overseas banded together and fought for one another rather than some high ideal. While every soldier had a unique experience, you can make some generalizations. For a long time, there was a consensus about the GIs' general attitudes and motivations toward their peers and their adversaries.[11] The title of Stephen Ambrose's popular book *Band of Brothers*[12] telegraphs his meaning to the reader without even cracking open the book—these young men got through tough times by depending upon one another.

A new study by historian Christopher Hamner challenges this notion. By taking a longer view and comparing battles of the American Revolution, the Civil War, and the Second World War, Hamner sees a different pattern. Due to the limitations of flintlock and rifled muskets, the linear tactics of the 1770s and 1860s put men in close proximity to one another. By the 1940s, because of the lethality of weapons, men were dispersed and much more divided as a result of larger units and individual specialties. They depended not only upon comrades, but also upon pilots in the air, artilleryman to the rear, and tank operators who remained wedded to their metal steeds. They were connected, but yet very much alone.[13]

When you connect current scholarship to the collection of letters and artifacts, it allows you to look at these materials with several perspectives in mind. How close was this individual to his buddies? Are there indications that he felt alone or did he build ties to the people around him? How do these experiences reflect or challenge the notion of comradeship? A command of the sources places the information of that one soldier into a much richer and more diverse historical context. Disagreements between historians are not so much a challenge as an opportunity. The various ways historians approach a historical problem allow the interpreter to ask the same questions of his or her visitors—how did you experience the military? What's more important to you in your work environment, the relationships you have to your co-workers or to the mission of the organization? It takes time and effort to master the complexities of a story. That effort, though, gives you the tools to connect to any given audience's needs in a thorough and responsible manner.

The second part of the interpretive equation is the knowledge of the audience (KA). Before any audience can be dissected, there is one tenet that must be understood—the visitor is sovereign. A guide, docent, or museum professional may possess expansive knowledge of a subject. He or she may be passionate about his or her views on a particular topic. He or she may have mastered the art of crafting an interpretive talk. Despite these skills, it is ultimately in the hands of the audience to connect their own interests to your institution. All we can do is to meet the visitors where they are and hope that we can facilitate a meaning that is responsive to the visitors' needs.[14] If interpretation, then, is supposed to facilitate meanings to our audiences, it is vital that we know their needs. If we cannot connect to the audience's needs, or if we misjudge their needs, interpretation does not happen.

Understanding what the audience needs runs the gamut from visitor surveys and focus groups to reading body language and active listening. It is a complicated skill set, but one that is vital in providing quality interpretive services. So, where do you begin? There are many different methods, but the easiest to master is finding out where visitors come from. Basic demographic information can be gleaned from a variety of sources. Many institutions have visitor logs where visitors self-identify their hometown. Anecdotal information from the time-honored question, "Where are you from?" can be helpful. Simply asking a visitor, "What brought you here today?" can reveal what he or she hopes to discover and explore. If your institution serves a local or regional community, census data can reveal more in-depth information that may be helpful in crafting engagement strategies or programs. Social media platforms such as Facebook can provide a host of metrics that paint a fairly complete portrait of who is looking at your page and when. This information can provide clues as to the type of posts you provide your fans and even what time of day to post them for maximum effect.

Besides a look at the readily available data, simple observation can lead to some understanding of visitor needs. A tour bus filled with World War Two veterans is going to have different needs and expectations than a group of fourth grade students. Even the simple observation of body language can reveal whether or not you are connecting to a group. As with knowledge of the resource, even though we have a long tenure at a local institution and instinctively know what we may think the needs of the audience are, without asking them directly, we can only use anecdotal evidence to measure effectiveness.

More sophisticated techniques can be used to evaluate the effectiveness of a program given to a particular audience or to plan new products or programs. By far the most effective and rewarding data is collected through visitor surveys, focus groups, and other intensive survey practices of various cross-sections of our visitor base. It can be done at any point in the interpretive process: at the beginning of an experience (front-end), during the experience (formative), or at the end of the process (summative).[15] Costly projects such as the development of films and interior exhibits often require evaluation to make certain that the designs generated by an institution coincide with the interests of their clientele, but the same techniques can be applied to planning and program development as well. Without the benefit of either in-depth visitor studies or engaging a community of users in a planning process, the end result may still be interpretive, but will it attract the audience that you desired?

Figure 1.4 Re-enactors firing an artillery piece at a Civil War Battlefield. *Source*: Author Photograph

The third element of the interpretive equation is appropriate technique (AT). What do we mean by technique? Think of your last visit to a battlefield. One of the most popular and time-tested techniques is weapon demonstrations. Seeing someone go through the manual of arms for a musket that culminates in pulling the trigger and firing the weapon is a visceral experience that engages the imagination and the senses. When the demonstration includes a piece of artillery, the effect is magnified—the gallop of the horses, the movements of the crew, and the firing of the weapon could make visitors feel as though they are a part of the action. Most audiences, regardless of their age or interests, find demonstrations compelling, engaging, and perhaps even sobering. If the demonstrators have done extensive research into a soldier, then not only can they demonstrate a weapon, but they can also do it by adapting the persona of the individual they have researched.[16]

There are a multitude of considerations that go into choosing an appropriate technique for a presentation. The first consideration is that the technique is closely related to both the knowledge of the audience and resource. Without a basic understanding of the audience or an expansive knowledge of the resource, we are left scratching our heads on how to choose the most appropriate technique to craft interpretive opportunities. The second consideration in this discussion is to focus on the word "appropriate." Whatever the technique that is chosen by an interpreter, it must be suitable and proper for the situation at hand and meet the needs of the audience. If you used a musket demonstration at a documented massacre site, it would be in poor taste and more than

Figure 1.5 World War Two Weapons in situ. While impressive in their own right, something's missing when you can hear, smell, or touch the objects. *Source*: Author Photograph

likely alienate the audience in question. Rather than creating a positive experience, it could sour a visitor from ever coming to your institution again. Similarly, while it may be appropriate to use levity to break the ice with a group of people, humor should be used judiciously. As with the previous example, cracking jokes at a solemn site is not the right technique to use. Just as with the other elements of the equation, a poorly chosen technique could make it difficult to provide visitors with opportunities for interpretation.

The final element of the interpretive equation is the IO. The end result of the interpretive equation will be the creation of an IO, that is, a connection between the audience and the resource. The visitor may seize the opportunity or reject it, depending upon his or her perspectives, but it is offered to him or her, nevertheless.[17] These individual opportunities can be crafted to be either emotional or intellectual, or a combination of the two. As these terms suggest, these opportunities appeal to either the heart or the head of the visitor. A balance between the two will increase the likelihood of a memorable experience.

Independence National Historical Park in Philadelphia, Pennsylvania, plays host to the Liberty Bell. My very first experience as an interpretive park ranger was at the Liberty Bell. The bell becomes a prop, a tangible object that the audience can examine closely. I would point out the features of the bell—you can see who made the bell, when it was made, its size, weight, and the rather large gap that extends across the front of the bell. The basic information about the bell's physical attributes could be absorbed by the audience as an intellectual opportunity. I was connecting the interests of a general audience, unfamiliar with the nomenclature of the bell, to its general attributes and information, thus creating an intellectual opportunity for interpretation. If the way the bell looks was important (it appears to be cracked, but the wide gap at the front of the bell is not a crack but a repair) and the age of the bell was critical (it was manufactured in 1753), then it would be known as the old cracked bell. Fortunately, it is known as the Liberty Bell. At the top of the bell, you can see plainly the words "Proclaim Liberty thro' all the Land to all the Inhabitants thereof. Levit[icus]. XXV. [Verse] 10." After providing examples of how other groups, such as abolitionists and exiles from the Cold War, have drawn meaning from those words, the visitors can then be asked to pause for a moment and draw their own meanings from the bell. Rather than the ranger telling them what to believe, the visitors draw upon their own emotions and find meaning.[18]

Interpretation is the sum of all of its parts. Our enthusiasm for some of the individual elements of the interpretive equation may be appealing, but mere enthusiasm is not interpretation. Given the work that we do, it is difficult not to want to share all of the information that we have absorbed with our public. Providing great detail, but nothing more, could be called *interpretdata*. While many visitors certainly appreciate information, without contextualizing that information, no meaningful connections are made to resource meanings. Visitors appreciate a docent or guide who is engaging and friendly. When a program or interaction with a visitor focuses on the personality of the interpreter, it becomes *interpretainment*. Employees should always engage visitors with a positive attitude, but if a program is more about the docent rather than the resource, then interpretation does not occur. Every topic that is covered in a museum can be told with multiple perspectives. When these various perspectives are ignored to favor a foregone conclusion, this can be characterized as *interpreganda*. If these patterns are present, take a step back and try to see how programs can shift from these definitions to a broader form of interpretation.[19]

The interpretive equation is a helpful tool in understanding that interpretation is a process. It is a process that can be replicated. It is a process that can be learned and mastered. The individual elements of the equation represent the keys to any successful interpretive program, regardless of the size, budget, and scope of an institution.

THE PRACTICE OF INTERPRETATION

Generally speaking, interpretation comes in two broad forms: personal and nonpersonal. Personal interpretive services are programs that require the efforts of a person. Nonpersonal interpretive services encompass the interpretive media that can be found in digital form such as websites and social media, or in more traditional forms such as interior exhibits, interpretive waysides, and publications.

It is beyond the scope of this book to provide in-depth instructions on how to put together a program, but there are resources available that are very helpful. As with any profession, interpretation is constantly evolving to meet the changing needs of the audiences that visit our institutions. That being said, there are many works in print where most people can begin to explore this profession.

Despite its age, Freeman Tilden's *Interpreting our Heritage* is still relevant and meaningful in defining the parameters of interpretation. Tilden conceptualized interpretation as six principles[20] that still define interpretation and provide guideposts for successful interpretation. Tilden's book is not a how-to guide on the mechanics of interpretation, but it is useful in providing a philosophical grounding in understanding the basics of interpretation. In the aftermath of Tilden's work, many authors have built on Tilden, the basic building blocks to effective interpretation. Sam Ham has conducted original research as well as published two books that have become influential guideposts to the field since their publication. Ham's *Environmental Interpretation* and his new book *Interpretation, Making a Difference on Purpose* are indispensable in providing practical guides to the nuts and bolts of personal and nonpersonal interpretive services.[21]

Larry Beck and Ted Cable have taken Tilden's six principles and supplemented them with additional material in their book *Interpretation for the 21st Century*.[22] Beck and Cable's book builds on Tilden's principles, providing information and opinions on new trends in interpretation, especially around technology, something that Tilden could not have forecasted in 1957. A nice beginner's guide to the interpretive profession and a broad overview of the process of interpretation can be found in *Personal Interpretation*.[23] This was published by the NAI, the professional organization for interpreters, whose publishing arm has produced a wide range of books and materials related to the profession. In terms of exploring your personal values and how they relate to interpretation, David Larsen's *Meaningful Interpretation* is outstanding. Using journaling, readers are invited to weigh how they feel about the resources they protect, and knowing what is relevant to their audiences. There are many other resources available that cover public history, museum studies, and interpersonal communications skills, but those listed above are foundational works that should be in any institution's library.[24]

THE PAYOFF

Consistently good interpretation requires time, money, and a skilled group of people. Much like investing in the stock market, when you look after your customers, invest in your employees, and grow your company, eventually there is a payoff. When they take the time to build their knowledge of the resource, understand the needs of the audience, and craft appropriate opportunities, interpreters can facilitate the creation of very memorable experiences. Social scientists have demonstrated that while a typical audience cannot necessarily regurgitate specific factual information, they can remember and recount vivid experiences.[25] In 1990, I had the opportunity to visit Appomattox Court House National Historical Park in Virginia while on a family vacation. One of the ranger programs we attended was conducted by a costumed interpreter telling the story of a paroled Confederate soldier who was on his way home. I do not recall all of the details of the presentation, but the ranger told a riveting, believable account of the thoughts, motivations, and worries of a defeated soldier who wanted nothing more than to go home. In my own mind, Appomattox was always associated with the victory of the Union and the defeat of the Confederacy. After attending the program, I began to understand this as a human story of longing for home and family, perhaps even a new beginning. It was one of the most vivid interpretive experiences I have had at a site administered by the NPS. Imagine, then, how one memorable experience can translate into support for your institution from not only visitors, but also from your local community.

Interpretation can lead to attitudes of appreciation. Thematic interpretive programs in particular can lead to new attitudes. If visitors are presented with opportunities for interpretation that are new to them but do not necessarily challenge beliefs that they already hold, they could formulate a completely new attitude.[26] You are not necessarily challenging a belief, but forming new beliefs that, in turn, can lead to appreciation. In both the public and private world of historic sites and museums, institutions cannot survive without a supportive patronage. To care for a place, you have to care about it. To care about that place, the visitor's beliefs and attitudes should align with each other. Interpretation can provide that alignment.

Interpretation is more than about facts and information. Think about your own personal museum adventures. When I was a kid, my parents drove us across the United States. One of the stops that we made was at the National Museum of the US Air Force at Wright-Patterson Air Force base in Dayton, Ohio. As I wandered through the maze of aircraft, I searched for the World War Two gallery. I knew enough about aircraft at the time, and I knew what to look for. When I found the B-17G, I dragged my mother to the plane and explained every feature that I recognized. It was a memorable experience and one that I still remember. Why? This unique process reveals meanings. When an interpreter facilitates a connection between the visitor's desires and the meanings that reside in a story, object, place, or photograph, it becomes a memorable and lasting experience for that one individual. That one person could walk away and have a

completely new appreciation not only of that story, but also of that place and, by implication, of your institution. That is the power of what we do. When it comes to military
history, be it a battlefield, a story, or object, these things seem to evoke powerful feelings. To put those possible meanings into a framework, the next chapter will examine
the broad themes that have defined American military history for the last fifty years.

NOTES

1. Freeman Tilden, *Interpreting Our Heritage*, 4th ed. (Chapel Hill: University of North Carolina Press, 2007), 59.

2. For a brief history of interpretation, please see Carolyn Widner Ward and Alan E. Wilkinson, *Conducting Meaningful Interpretation: A Field Guild for Success* (Golden: Fulcrum Publishing, 2006), 6–8; and Lisa Brochu and Tim Merriman, *Personal Interpretation: Connecting Your Audience to Heritage Resources* (Fort Collins: Interp Press. 2002), 11–15.

3. Tilden, *Meaningful Interpretation*, 33.

4. Sam H. Ham, *Interpretation: Making a Difference on Purpose* (Golden: Fulcrum Publishing, 2013), 7.

5. David Larsen, *Meaningful Interpretation: How to Connect Hearts and Minds to Places, Objects, and other Resources* (Fort Washington: Eastern National, 2003), 47.

6. Ibid., 49. See also, Theresa L. Goldman, Wei-Li Jasmine Chen, and David L. Larsen, "Clicking the Icon: Exploring the Meanings Visitors Attach to the Three National Capital Memorials," *Journal of Interpretation Research* 6, no 1 (Summer 2001): 3–30.

7. Sam H. Ham, *Interpretation: Making a Difference on Purpose*, 8.

8. David Larsen, *Meaningful Interpretation*, 63.

9. Becky Lacome, "The Interpretive Equation" in David Larsen, *Meaningful Interpretation. How to Connect Hearts and Minds to Places, Objects, and other Resources* (Fort Washington: Eastern National, 2003), 2.

10. Ibid., 3–4.

11. Lee Kennett, *G.I. The American Soldier in World War Two* (New York: Charles Scribner's Sons, 1987), 138; Peter S. Kindsvatter, *American Soldiers: Ground Combat in the World Wars, Korea, & Vietnam* (Manhattan: University Press of Kansas, 2003), 125–133; Gerald F. Linderman, *The World Within War: America's Combat Experience in World War II* (New York: The Free Press, 1997), 263–299. Kennett's book remains one of the best accounts on the experiences of soldiers from the draft board to separation from service. Kindsvatter looks at the twentieth century and Linderman focuses on World War Two, but both are critical looks at the experience of the American soldier in combat. For a contrarian voice, see Paul Fussell, *Wartime. Understanding and Behavior in the Second World War* (New York: Oxford University Press, 1989).

12. Stephen E. Ambrose, *Band of Brothers: E Company, 506th Regiment, 101st Airborne. From Normandy to Hitler's Eagle Nest* (New York: Simon and Schuster, 1992).

13. Christopher H. Hamner, *Enduring Battle: American Soldiers in Three Wars, 1776–1945* (Manhattan: University Press of Kansas, 2011), 173–200.

14. David Larsen, *Meaningful Interpretation*, 81–86.

15. Ward and Wilkinson, *Conducting Meaningful Interpretation*, 226–227.

16. An outstanding resource for exploring appropriate interpretive techniques can be found in Peggy Ann Scherbaum, *Handles. A Compendium of Interpretive Techniques to Help Visitors Grasp Resources* (Fort Washington: Eastern National, 2006).

17. Lacome, "The interpretive Equation," 10.

18. In 1987 I worked as a seasonal park ranger at Independence National Historical Park. This example was the gist of my bell talk.

19. These terms are found in David Larsen, *Meaningful Interpretation*, 70–71.

20. Tilden's six principles are:

    1. Any interpretation that does not somehow relate what is being displayed or described to something within the personality of experience of the visitor will be sterile.
    2. Information, as such, is not interpretation. Interpretation is revelation based upon information. But they are entirely different things. However, all interpretation includes information.
    3. Interpretation is an art, which combines many arts, whether the materials presented are scientific, historical, or architectural. Any art is in some degree teachable.
    4. The chief aim of interpretation is not instruction but provocation.
    5. Interpretation should aim to present a whole rather than a part and must address itself to the whole man rather than any phase.
    6. Interpretation addressed to children should not be a dilution of the presentation for adults, but should follow a fundamentally different approach.

21. Sam H. Ham, *Environmental Interpretation: A Practical Guide For People With Big Ideas and Small Budgets* (Golden: Fulcrum Publishing, 1992) and *Interpretation: Making a Difference on Purpose* (Golden: Fulcrum Publishing, 2013).

22. Larry Beck and Ted Cable, *Interpretation For the 21st Century* (Champaign: Sagamore Press, 1998).

23. Additional titles on a full spectrum of interpretive activities can be found at NAI's website: http://www.interpnet.com/nai/Resources/Publications/InterpPress_Books/nai/_publications/InterpPress_Books.aspx?hkey=de782e09-f72c-43a0-97e6-243e822441a6. NAI also has an interpretive certification program for guides and leaders. The curriculum is fee for service and hosts dozens of workshops around the country every year. Information on NAI's certification program can be found on NAI's website at http://www.interpnet.com/nai/Certification/nai/_certification/NAI_Certification.aspx?hkey=0c08ac07-c574-4560-940f-82fba3a22be9.

24. Two additional books that may be of assistance are Allison L. Grinder and E. Sue McCoy, *The Good Guide: A Sourcebook for Interpreters, Docents, and Tour Guides* (Scottsdale, AZ: Ironwood Publishing, 1985) and Carolyn Widner Ward and Alan E. Wikinson, *Conducting Meaningful Interpretation.*

25. Sam H. Ham, *Interpretation: Making a Difference on Purpose*, 80–83.

26. Ibid., 84–88.

Chapter 2

Introduction to American Military History

A measure of acquaintance with the past may help to dissipate both the
awe and contempt that alternately have hobbled American deliberation upon
military issues.[1]

Russell F. Weigley

The history profession never stands still. It is constantly changing and evolving, considering new ideas and discarding old ones. Change is the very nature of this discipline. For the last generation, there have been several overarching themes in American military history that have guided the development of the field inside and outside of academia. It seems prudent to begin this exploration with a look at the state of the field from the inside out.

THE STATE OF AMERICAN MILITARY HISTORY

Military history has had a long and rich pedigree in the western world—beginning in ancient times with Herodotus, Thucydides, and Caesar, and accelerating in the modern period with Machiavelli, Jomini, and Clausewitz. Writing about and reflecting on military history is part of our collective historical tradition. Beginning in the late nineteenth century and continuing to the present day, American academics, historians, and military officers began writing on military topics and have never stopped. In the aftermath of the Second World War, courses on American military history could be readily found on most large college campuses. In the last forty years, though, the field of military history has changed and evolved for the better, but not without a certain amount of tension and uncertainty. Many of the issues and subsequent tensions that rose in the 1970s are still with us, exerting an influence on the practice of American military history in colleges and universities around the country.

In the aftermath of World War Two, the various publications related to that war, whether in Western Europe or in the United States, came of age. The US Army's publication of its multivolume series on the US Army's various campaigns was typical of the institutional works produced in the decades after the war. Comprehensive in scope, analytical in tone, they marked a new high point in objective history. Beginning in the late 1960s and through the 1970s, perhaps a reflection of the tumult that affected the country, there was a sea change in the way the academy looked at history. Rather than looking at traditional political institutions and the men who ran them, the paradigm shifted to history from the bottom up. In the decades since these dramatic changes, the manner in which we understand American military history and the way it is practiced in academia has been affected. Since the 1970s, there has been a movement to step beyond the details of strategy and tactics, labeled as "drums and trumpets" by the military history community, and, instead, examine institutions, civil-military relations, and the intersection between war and culture.[2] Known as the "new" military history, these new trends found a general acceptance within the community of military historians. In graduate school, one of my peers and I pursued how the US Army adopted the motor truck and tank.[3] How and why institutions accept and reject innovation and new technology is as important as how tanks and trucks are used on the battlefield.

Despite the vitality of the field, there continues to be perceptions both in and outside of the military history community that question the utility and relevance of military history. Nearly fifty years ago, Louis Morton, in an article for the *Mississippi Valley Historical Review* (precursor to the *Journal of American History*), identified a deep prejudice in the history community against the value of military history. The historical profession's collective doubt over the value of military history was due to the utilitarian use of military history by the armed services—"narrow and technical in approach, didactic in character, and unrelated to the broad stream of historical writing."[4] In other words, history was pursued not for the sake of intellectual inquiry, but used as a teaching method to improve the skills of soldiers. Morton also acknowledges that in the United States in particular, our deep historical prejudices may also be reflected in why military history has been largely ignored in the academy. The intellectual tradition of fear and loathing of a standing, professional army has put military history at a disadvantage in understanding the growth of American society.

Morton's prognostications were validated in the 1990s. In 1997, John A. Lynn wrote a scathing article titled "The Embattled Future of Academic Military History"[5] for the *Journal of Military History*. Drawing evidence from the lack of articles on military history in the pages of the *American Historical Review*, the flagship publication of the American Historical Association, Lynn noted that the older disciplines of military and diplomatic history were shut out of its pages almost entirely by the new social history.[6] He continued with personal observations on the decline of tenure track positions at major universities where the professor deals primarily with military history. Despite his tale of gloom, Lynn did advocate pushing for crossover studies in gender and cultural history, both of which can examine old topics in new ways. Twenty years later, John Shy gave the George C. Marshall lecture in military history at the American Historical Association, echoing Lynn's commentary, highlighting four books that came out on military topics from historians who generally worked outside of the field of military history. In every case, Shy lauded their work since they wrote on topics of great interest to the community of military history. Despite their contributions, however, Shy chided them for not engaging military historians. If they had, they would have been richer works. As with any group of people, regardless of their profession, by creating a dialogue between historical fields, you get a richer narrative and more compelling conclusions. There needs to be an intersection between both communities so that each could benefit from the other.[7]

As Shy's article indicates, while there may still be a degree of tension between the various disciplines within the wider historical community, American military history continues to evolve and, in my mind, make a positive impact on the reading public. Nevertheless, the books Shy highlights in his article demonstrate that military history continues to find ways to intersect with what have become mainstream historical currents. As the previous chapter indicated, successful interpretation requires the recognition of multiple perspectives, or, at the very least, the recognition of other voices that have not dominated the narrative held by the dominant population. At Big Hole Battlefield in Wisdom, Montana, the staff was challenged by Tribal elders to tell new stories that had not been featured previously: the stories of the Nez Perce people. Embracing this challenge, the park created an exhibit that honored the stories of both sides, challenging popularly held views of the battle that in the past was often told from just one perspective.[8] Challenging and changing long-held notions in any field of history is a challenge and opens up any institution to criticism for challenging "the truth." When Gettysburg National Military Park built their new visitor center, rather than just telling the story of the battle, the entire exhibit was framed around President Lincoln's Gettysburg address. The battle represents more than a military victory over General Lee's Army of Northern Virginia; instead, it is a new birth of freedom for the future of the Republic. It recontextualizes the notion of the battle as a tipping point into something much more. There continues to be a vitality to the discipline. Long-held ideas about the core concepts of American military history continue to not only define the field, but to be challenged as well.

AMERICAN WAYS OF WAR

There are several overarching themes in American military history, on which you will find general agreement. The first theme is the mythos of the citizen soldier and civilian control of the military. The second is understanding if there exists an American way of war. Robert F. Weigley figures prominently in both ideas and has had a profound effect on a generation of military historians, myself included.

The countervailing forces of the American military tradition are, on the one hand, the need for a permanent, professional, standing military, and on the other hand, a deep distrust of those same institutions. This tension manifests itself in what amounts to a dual history of the army—the militia tradition and citizen soldier versus the need for a standing professional army and civilian control of the military. In the twenty-first century, the armed services are all-volunteer; recruits are not compelled to join by the state, that is a draft—they sign their papers of their own accord. While these are certainly citizen soldiers, there are deep historical roots to this dichotomy that have created a historical tension between creating and maintaining a professional standing military and an expansible force built around citizen soldiers. There are strong partisans on both sides of the equation.

Figure 2.1   Dr. Russell F. Weigley, Temple University. *Source*: Dr. Greg Urwin, Temple University

From colonization until the American Revolution, the militia of the individual colonies was the chief instrument for protecting life and property. Inheriting the tensions between a standing army and a public militia from their English forbearers, Americans saw the militia as a reliable method for enforcing the will of the state. While the ethos of the citizen soldier would be mythologized and romanticized, there has been a continuous historical tension between citizen soldiers and their professional counterparts. In modern times, as the reserve components of the armed services have become integrated into the regular force structure, these tensions have abated, but there is a continual interest in the military history community in works that detail the history of the militia and the National Guard. With intensive deployments of the National Guard to Iraq and Afghanistan, there has been greater attention in the public eye toward their sacrifices. Michael Doubler's *Civilian in Peace, Soldier in War, The Army National Guard, 1636–2000* is a recent overview of the citizen soldier that takes a celebratory tone in recounting the militia tradition and the subsequent growth of the guard. Older overviews are still worth looking at, including John K. Mahon's *History of the Militia and National Guard* and Jim Dan Hill's *The Minute Man in Peace and War.*[9] While many of the issues related to the utility of the militia may have had more credibility with a nineteenth-century audience, they have had a profound effect on how we currently tell the story of our military's past.

To tell a story that is wrought with tension is inherently difficult. Many institutions that deal with military collections or stories will often concentrate on what's easiest, the story of the regular army, marines, etc. Moreover, with the draft playing such a prominent role in the First and Second World Wars, the distinctions between draftees and armed civilians have grown blurred. In the public sphere, the Pritzker Military Museum and Library in Chicago, Illinois, a relatively new institution, celebrates and commemorates the contributions of the citizen soldier to the preservation of democracy. Rather than focusing on the enmity between the idea and ideal of the citizen soldier, they focus on the more positive aspects of this relationship. Museum exhibits, electronic media (in particular, podcasts of popular military historians and historical novelists, and oral histories of citizen soldiers), and Medal of Honor recipients have placed the contributions of these men and women in the public eye. While they have invested in a research library in downtown Chicago, they also use digital media to reach out to audiences that cannot visit the library, but want to enjoy the content. The Pritzker uses podcasting as an outreach tool. In the intervening years, the library has built a robust collection of author interviews in particular, and special interest programming that illustrates the popularity of military history and the citizen soldier.[10]

Russell. F. Weigley, in his groundbreaking book, *History of the United States Army*, outlines his argument succinctly and through the lens of two powerful personalities: Emory Upton and his contemporary John Logan. Upton, a decorated veteran of the Civil War, after spending time in Europe, wrote *The Military Policy of the United States* that castigated the notion of an army dominated by civilian volunteers. Enamored with the Prussian model of a highly trained, professional army, Upton dismissed the militia tradition, in Weigley's mind something completely alien to American political traditions. Published long after Upton's death by Secretary of War Elihu Root, Upton's views held sway over a generation of officers. A regular army, rather than armed citizens, was the only guarantee of a safe and viable democracy. Upton's book was published posthumously by Secretary Root as a means to justify modernization, but at the expense of the citizen soldier. As the United States was poised to build an empire across the Pacific and the Caribbean, the small regular army would not be up to the task. Rather than dependence upon a militia, Root believed, conscription, a regular army, and a General Staff would provide the guidance necessary to properly defend the United States.[11]

Brigadier General John McAuley Palmer in the twentieth century, and his nineteenth-century counterpart, John Logan, a volunteer officer in the Civil War, offered counterpoints to Upton's views. Logan's book, *The Volunteer Soldier of America*, argued that the tradition of a volunteer militia and a small standing army is what gave the United States its edge. In Logan's mind, it was the capacity of the nation's men to answer the call to arms in an emergency that created a force superior to any nineteenth-century standing, professional army. John McAuley Palmer was a vocal advocate of universal military training. Rather than keeping an excessively large regular army, Palmer advocated for a citizen reserve that filled out cadres of regulars. His ideas were not accepted, but they certainly embraced an army built on what was palatable to the American political system.[12] Upton, Logan, and Palmer represented countervailing traditions that had been present since the beginning of the republic.

One of the key themes in Weigley's book is the role of Emory Upton. In Weigley's estimation, it was Upton's work on military policy that colored a generation of policy makers and leaders and has framed the debate ever since. David J. Fitzpatrick reframed Weigley's critique of Upton's influence by reexamining the question. Upton did not reject the efforts of citizen soldiers, but his Civil War experience indicated that civilian soldiers succeeded in almost any task given to them if they had proper training, robust leadership, and consistent discipline. Upton's postwar interests, then, focused on tactics, organization, and military policy. In the context of Upton's era, his observations are not necessarily antidemocratic so much as merely emulating successful examples that just happened to be found in Germany. Rather than antidemocratic and militia-bashing policies, Upton wanted strategies in place that would allow the army to expand quickly to meet any contingency, and have men properly trained to avoid the bloodshed that is often seen when undertrained troops go into battle. Upton could not rationalize a larger, professional army when he was writing in the 1880s because beyond domestic threats, the country was in no danger abroad, mitigating the need for a large standing army, expansible or otherwise.[13]

The roles the citizen soldier played in the country's wars, large and small, are undeniable. Both Weigley and Fitzpatrick offer insightful points of view in recognizing the role of the citizen soldier and the challenge of reform. It is all too easy to embrace historical myths without examining them more closely. The debate over the value of citizen soldiers versus a standing army is something you do not readily see in military museums and exhibitions. Rather than building exhibitions and collections at opposing ends of the spectrum, exhibits, instead, tend to offer a rich panoply of stories that recognize the contributions of both. A post museum, such as the museum at Fort Lewis, Washington, tends to focus on the story of a place and the units, regular and otherwise, who have called it home. State museums, such as the Indiana War Memorial Museum in Indianapolis, focus on the accomplishments of a state, again with the focus on both regulars and citizen soldiers. That being said, there is much to be gained by, at the very least, recognizing the historic tension between a standing, professional military and the citizen soldier.

Like bookends on a shelf, one side of the debate is defined by the historic tension between a standing army and the citizen soldier. At the other end, and no less important, is the question of a unique and distinctive American way of war. Has our tenure on the North American continent created a truly American way of war? Are we distinctive enough to merit that label? These questions have generated a vigorous and ongoing debate in the academic community for a generation. In 1973, Russell F. Weigley published *The American Way of War*. Using definitions supplied by German historian Hans Delbruck, Weigley defined two kinds of military strategy, attrition and annihilation. Attrition is the gradual wearing down of an adversary through a judicious use of force. Annihilation is the polar opposite, the application of overwhelming force and destructive power to destroy an adversary.[14]

Generally speaking, until the Civil War, American strategic thought and policy reflected the paucity of resources available in the developing country. Beginning with the American Revolution and continuing through the nineteenth century, American

Generals and policy makers favored strategies of erosion or attrition. George Washington knew he could not match the British toe to toe. In order to preserve the Revolution, he needed to choose his fights carefully. Preserving the Continental army and fighting pitched battles only when necessary helped the Americans win their independence. A generation later, inspired by the success of Napoleon Bonaparte, American strategic thought gravitated toward wars of attrition. In the decidedly narrow interpretation of Napoleon's victories vis-à-vis the works of Baron de Jomini, there was less of a concern regarding the complete destruction of an adversary. Instead, there was more concern regarding the use of available resources to gradually wear down an enemy's ability to resist. With the lack of a large regular army and the continued antipathy toward a large standing army, this conservative and practical approach matched the traditions established in the republic since the revolution.

The Civil War changed this outlook. President Lincoln spent years looking for a General who could prosecute the war according to the ever changing political and strategic priorities of the Union. With the lack of synchronicity between Lincoln's war aims and a General who could translate them into action, the war against the Confederate States of America progressed slowly. Both Ulysses S. Grant and his protégé William T. Sherman expressed a willingness to annihilate the Confederacies' will to resist. Unable to defeat the enemy in one decisive blow, "Grant became the prophet of annihilation in a new dimension, seeking the literal destruction of the enemy's armies as the means to victory."[15] Whereas Grant took a very direct approach against his opponents, Sherman took the opposite approach—breaking the will to resist by bringing the war to the South's doorstep. Weigley takes this new beginning forward to the Second World War, indicating that the American preference for bringing a second front to Western Europe and destroying the German war machine in a direct assault in Germany was the legacy of Grant.

When Weigley wrote *The American Way of War*, the war in Vietnam was winding down and the stand-off with the Soviet Union was entering its third decade. The last third of his book is devoted to finding a strategic vision that will fit the new reality of the Atomic Age, observing that "the history of usable combat may be coming to an end."[16] Weigley never updated his work after its publication, yet its basic ideas held sway for many years. It does raise the question: Can we, indeed, neatly categorize the nation's military past into broad classifications? There are certainly other authors who contend that the prosecution of a war is influenced by historical trends particular to that society, such as a Western or German way of war.[17] There are some who say "no" to Weigley's assertions.

Dr. Brian Linn, in a 2002 critique of Weigley's work, argues that *The American Way of War* thesis is perhaps the beginning of a conversation on American ways of war rather than the end. Linn challenges Weigley with four points of argument. First, there is confusion over the terms annihilation-attrition/exhaustion. Second, the book does not accommodate other forms of national strategy, in particular deterrence and limited wars. Third, if the Civil War is characterized by annihilation, there is no accommodation for what was really a more ambivalent understanding of the aftermath of the war. Finally, from 1865 to 1943, peacetime thought and wartime performance was geared toward practicality rather than annihilation.[18] Linn's analysis is persuasive, however, of the four issues mentioned; the notion that deterrence and limited wars are not accommodated by Weigley's views is a criticism that has the greatest resonance given our adventures in southwest Asia since 2001.

One of the most consistent themes that we see in American military history is continental defense, a strategy that occupied the army well into the twentieth century. A small navy and an expandable, professional army was the basis for American defense policy for generations. The intense focus on engineering at the Military Academy and the penchant for fixed fortifications around the country are visible reminders of the commitment to defending our ports and shores. Similarly, the development of modern fortifications and a steel navy in the waning years of the nineteenth century acted as a deterrent to quick and indiscriminate action along the Atlantic and Pacific seaboard. Similarly, American expansion into the Caribbean and Pacific during the Spanish-American War is difficult to contextualize within Weigley's argument.[19]

If Weigley's treatment is incomplete, Linn conceptualizes his own notion of an American Way of War by concentrating less on strategy and more on how the army conceives ideas. Linn observes that American military thought and policy emerges from three distinct voices or martial philosophies within the American military tradition. The first, the Guardians, manifested themselves in continental defense through the study of engineering. By applying scientific principles to a problem, a possible solution will guarantee success. Linn brings a modern analogue of ballistic missile defense. The second group, labeled as Heroes, brings in a very simple notion of war: the application of violence to meet a certain goal. The final group constitutes Managers who have an outlook that seeks the complete destruction and annihilation of an enemy through what Linn calls the rational application of resources. These distinctive groupings have affected the manner in which the country pursues defense policy in times of peace and fights its wars in times of strife.[20] Linn's notions of these broad groupings certainly offer an alternative to Weigley that is more nuanced and allows for more flexibility in understanding how the choices made by Generals and Presidents were influenced by circumstance and how people understood the problems before them.

Is there an American way of war? A new survey text on American military history captures the essence of this debate: "No one way, concept, or type of war can fit every conflict in American history. Rather, there have been many complex and sometimes contradictory ways of war."[21] Can this rich and compelling debate be incorporated into the stories that are told at a battlefield or in a museum? Certainly. As with any historical pursuit, the debate will never end, but will perhaps allow for a much more expansive and nuanced view of an American way of war. It is the responsibility of all historical institutions to look at the context of the events in which they are telling.

For example, there are many forts scattered along the Atlantic and Gulf coasts. In many cases, there is a mix of nineteenth- and twentieth-century fortifications in one location. By moving beyond a technical description of weapons and structures and conceptualizing the story in terms of the wider narrative of national defense and deterrence, a local fortification acquires a greater significance. By linking the idea of deterrence to what the visitor sees in the news, you can facilitate an IO that brings greater national significance to a site that is currently only understood in local terms. Additionally, if you point out the fascination with a technology that can defeat ballistic missiles, the visitor will see that the country is pursuing a time-honored defense policy that goes back to the beginning of the republic.

BRANCH HISTORIES

We can recognize that American military history has several omnipresent themes that manifest themselves in how we relate this history to a larger audience. These themes should, in turn, add the necessary context to the stories that we tell in our historic sites, museums, and other cultural institutions. Academics and military history experts, however, do not have a monopoly on interpreting the historical record. History plays an important role in each of the branches of the armed services and produces works that also add to our understanding of our military's past.

Whereas the academic world produces works to advance the state of knowledge, history is frequently used by the armed services in a more utilitarian approach. History is often used as a tool to discern lessons from previous campaigns or activities to inform present policy makers or soldiers on the ground. Each service has its own traditions and narratives that are used not only to commemorate its activities, but also to provide a tool for recruitment and retention. While institutional histories can be prone to self-promotion, the works produced by the armed services are subject to the same rigor of critical review as their academic peers. When it comes to gathering resources for exhibit development or to gain insight on a particular subject, works produced by the various historical agencies of the armed services are welcome additions to standard academic works.

The US Army's primary historical agency is the Center of Military History in Washington, DC. It has a host of administrative responsibilities for the Army's museum and history program and produces several monographs a year on a host of topics, which are available to the public. The United States Army Heritage and Education Center in Carlisle, Pennsylvania, is on the campus of the US Army's War College and administers a rich collection of manuscripts, oral histories, and records related to the college. While they do not have a publication program, their research library and manuscript collections are world class and an important stop when conducting research on topics related to the history of the Army. Technical publications, photographs, and other official Army publications are also available through a searchable database. It is a treasure trove of information. In addition, the United States Army Combined Arms Center at Fort Leavenworth, Kansas, produces publications on a variety of topics that often feature historical themes related to issues of war fighting and offer insight into the Army's performance in more modern conflicts.[22]

The US Navy's Naval Heritage Center is located in Washington, DC. As with the Army, it supports historical activities across the service and has a staff of professional historians. It supports a publications program and updates the ongoing Dictionary of American Naval Fighting Ships. Similarly, the US Marines History Division is the Marine Corps history arm. It is located in Quantico, Virginia, as part of the Marine Corps University. The US Air Force hosts its historical agency at Maxwell Air Force Base in Montgomery, Alabama. As with its sister historical services, it hosts professional historians supporting history activities within the Air Force. It also has organizational records and other resources available to people doing research. The Air Force Historical Studies Office in Washington, DC, is the publications arm of the Air Force and provides original research regarding Air Force activities.[23]

Museums often address certain specific constituencies. Military museums are no different. The flagship of the Marines is the National Museum of the Marine Corps in Triangle, Virginia. It is in close proximity to the Marine Corps base in Quantico and is part of the Marine Corps University. Besides being a museum that commemorates the sacrifices of its men and women, it also tells a story of the Marines across the national timeline. As an institutional museum, its pivotal role is in recruiting, retaining, and educating Marines. Rather than taking a strict, institutional approach, it provides a non-Marine insight into the Corps. Using interactive exhibits, videos, and experiential vignettes, visitors are provided an institutional overview.

It is difficult for military museums to provide insight into the sights and sounds of service. The director of the museum, Lin Ezell, characterizes this choice of technique as "'every clime and place' where Marines saw action; we put the visitors' shoes literally in the boot prints of Marines."[24] This manifests itself as dioramas that are vignettes of Belleau Wood in World War One, the Chosin Reservoir in the Korean War, and Khe Sanh in Vietnam, providing a telling experience for large artifacts. While these exhibits are not interactive per se, they, nevertheless, provide a powerful backdrop for large artifacts. By lowering the temperature of the room in the Chosin Reservoir diorama, and raising the room's heat in the Vietnam, the visitors are provided the experience of finding themselves caught in the moment. The visitors, in particular those who have not entered into service with the Marines, are offered a view of boot camp, including an indoor rifle range, to bring home the institutional values of the Corps.

Figure 2.2   National Museum of the Marine Corps. *Source*: Author Photograph

Opened in 2006, the management of the Marine museum are constantly evaluating their audiences and planning to meet the needs of the visitors. Using social science and focus groups, exhibits are introducing diverse voices into the museum, in particular those of women and African-American Marines. While they continue to engage the Marine community, rather than just meeting the needs of their institutional audience, they have also engaged the local education community, creating a plethora of curriculum-based education programs that serve 45,000 students annually. What the staff of the museum demonstrate is that an institutional museum can remain relevant not only to its core users, but also to other visitors by engaging those users on a regular basis. The visitor numbers suggest that many repeat visitors are families who are not associated with the Marine Corps. Repeat visitors are drawn to museums for many reasons, but if we recognize that people come to places because it is relevant to them, the museums are doing something right. While those familiar with military museums will find recognizable techniques in use, the museum uses its collections to create exhibits and experiences that meet the needs of multiple audiences while still staying true to the mission of the Marines.[25]

American military history is a tool that is used by the academic community, the military branches, and other historic institutions across the country. When consensus is found, ultimately, it is tested, challenged, and modified to meet the demands of a new generation of historians. This chapter has spoken of themes that define the entire spectrum of American military history. The story of our military's past also occurs when

Figure 2.3 Vietnam Fire Base Vignette, National Marine Corps Museum. *Source:* Author Photograph

we look at the passage of time from colonization to the present. The broad sweep of the American narrative continues to change. The remaining chapters of this book will offer a critical examination of individual events, allowing practitioners of the field the opportunity to reexamine how their institutions tell the stories of our military's past.

NOTES

1. Russell F. Weigley, *History of the United States Army* (New York: Macmillan Publishing Co., 1967), xiii.

2. Allan R. Millett, "The Study of American Military History in the United States," *Military Affairs* 41 (April, 1977): 58–61. John Whiteclay Chambers II, "The New Military History: Myth and Reality," *The Journal of Military History* 55 (July, 1991): 395–406. Edward M. Coffman, "The New American Military History," *Military Affairs* 48 (January, 1984): 1–5. For a rebuttal to the turn away from operational history, see Dennis E. Showalter, "A Modest Plea for Drums and Trumpets," *Military Affairs* 39 (April, 1975): 71–74. A precise summary of the concerns of modern military historians can also be found in John Southard, "Beyond 'A Company, B Company' History: A Military History State of the Field," *The American Historian* (August, 2014): 20–23. A dated but concise summary of military history in the American academic world can be found in Ronald H. Spector, "Military History and the Academic World," in *A Guide to the Study and Use of Military History* (Washington, DC: Center of Military History, US Army, 1982), 431–37.

3. Marc K. Blackburn, "A New Form of Transportation, the Quartermaster Corps and the Standardization of the United States Army's Motor Trucks, 1907–1939" (Ph.D dissertation, Temple University, 1992); Robert S. Cameron, "Americanizing the Tank: U.S. Administration and Mechanized Development with the Army, 1917–1943" (Ph.D Dissertation, Temple University, 1994).

4. Louis Morton, "The Historian and the Study of War," *The Mississippi Valley Historical Review* 48 (March, 1962): 612–13.

5. John A. Lynn, "The Embattled Future of Academic Military History," *The Journal of Military History* 61 (October, 1997): 777–89.

6. From Lynn's narrative, it appears he examined issues of the review for a twenty-year time period, one can assume from 1977 to 1997, and noted very few articles on military history. From 1992 to 1996, nearly every article dealt with race, class, gender, and/or labor.

7. John Shy, "George C. Marshall Lecture," *The Journal of Military History* 72 (2008): 1033–46. For insight into the state of cultural analysis in American military history, see Wayne E. Lee, "Mind and Matter – Cultural Analysis in American Military History: A Look at the State of the Field," *Journal of American History* 93 (March, 2007): 1116–42.

8. The author was present at these meetings. Planning began in 2005 and the exhibit was dedicated in the summer of 2011.

9. Michael D. Doubler, *Civilian in War and Peace – The Army National Guard, 1636–2000* (Lawrence: University Press of Kansas, 2003); John K. Mahon, *History of the Militia and the National Guard* (New York: Macmillan Publishing Company, 1983); and Jim Dan Hill, *The Minute Man in Peace and War. A History of the National Guard* (Harrisburg: The Stackpole Company, 1964.

10. http://www.pritzkermilitary.org/, accessed June 12, 2014.

11. Russell F. Weigley, *History of the United States Army* (New York: Macmillan Publishing Co., 1967), xii, 277–280. See also, Russell F. Weigley, *Towards an American Army: Military Thought from Washington to Marshall* (Westport: Greenwood Press, 1974), 100–26.

12. Weigley, *Towards an American Army*, 222–49.

13. David J. Fitzpatrick, "Emory Upton and the Citizen Soldier," *The Journal of Military History* 65 (April 2001): 355–90 and "Emory Upton and the Army of a Democracy," *The Journal of Military History* 77 (April, 2013): 463–90. See also, Jason Patrick Clark, "The Many Faces of Reform: Military Progressivism in the U.S. Army, 1866–1916" (Ph.D dissertation, Duke University, 2009), 1–60.

14. Russell F. Weigley, *The American Way of War: A History of United States Military Policy and Strategy* (New York: Macmillan Publishing Co., 1973), xxii. See also, John Shy, "The American Military Experience: History and Learning," in *A People Numerous and Armed* (revised edition) (Ann Arbor: University of Michigan Press, Ann Arbor Paperbacks, 1990), 265–94.

15. Weigley, *The American Way of War*, 145.

16. Ibid., 477.

17. John Lynn, *Battle: A History of Combat and Culture From Ancient Greece to Modern America* (Boulder: Westview Press, 2003) critiques this approach for a broader cultural model of warfare around the world. Robert Citino. *The German Way of War: From the Thirty Years' War to the Third Reich* (Lawrence: University Press of Kansas, 2005) does take a more typical approach arguing that the German approach to war was a result of culture and Germany's geographic position.

18. Brian Linn, *"The American Way of War* Revisited," *Journal of Military History* 66 (April, 2002): 502–503.

19. Linn, *"The American Way of War* Revisited," 508–9, 515–17. To understand the importance of coastal defense within the context of Linn's argument, a good place to begin is Emanuel Raymond Lewis, *Seacoast Fortifications of the United States. An Introductory History* (Missoula: Pictorial Histories Publishing Company, 1979). See also, Robert S. Browning III, *Two if by Sea. The Development of American Coastal Defense Policy* (Westport: Greenwood Press, 1983); J.E. Kaufmann and H.W. Kaufmann, *Fortress America: The Forts That Defended America, 1600 to the Present* (Cambridge: Da Capo Press, 2004).

20. Brian McAllister Linn, *The Echo of Battle: The Army's Way of War* (Cambridge: Harvard University Press, 2007), 5–9.

21. Matthew S. Muehlbauer and David J. Ulbrich, *Ways of War. American Military History from the Colonial Era to the Twenty-First Century* (New York: Routledge, 2014), 6.

22. Center of Military History: http://www.history.army.mil/. The United States Army Heritage and Education Center: http://www.carlisle.army.mil/ahec/index.cfm. The website includes access to the military history research catalog and to the digital collections. The research and publications arm of the Combined Arms Center Combat Studies Institute can be found at http://usacac.army.mil/CAC2/CSI/RandPTeam.asp.

23. The US Navy Heritage Center: http://www.history.navy.mil/. The US Marine Corps History Division: https://www.mcu.usmc.mil/historydivision/SitePages/Home.aspx. The Air Force Historical Research Agency: http://www.afhso.af.mil/main/welcome.asp. The US Air Force Historical Studies Office: http://www.afhso.af.mil/main/welcome.asp.

24. E-mail to author from Director Lin Ezell, July 17, 2014

25. Interview with Assistant Director Charles Grow, June 20, 2014 and e-mail to author from Director Lin Ezell, July 17, 2014. See also, Andrea K. Jones, "All Hands on Deck: Toward the Experience History Museum," *History News*, (Spring, 2014): 18–22.

Chapter 3

Colonization and Settlement, 1607–1763

Few men came to America to be soldiers. More likely they came in part to escape soldiering. They would fight when they had to, to preserve their homes and farms and way of life they had crossed the ocean to find.

Russell F. Weigley[1]

Where do we begin our story? In the popular imagination, the traditions and institutions of the United States of America begin with the Declaration of Independence. While these sentiments are understandable, they do not fully explain where our military institutions come from. Between the establishment of English colonies on the Atlantic coast in 1607 and the end of the French and Indian War more than a century later, the roots of our military traditions and practices were established and would continue to evolve. Some works of American military history, both old and new, begin with the American Revolution, overlooking the prerevolution roots of our national military traditions.[2] The tendency, however, to begin an American narrative with Jamestown also overlooks the fact that imperial Spain was the dominant European power in North America for a century before the English established a permanent presence on the continent.

Beginning with the voyages of Christopher Columbus in 1492, Spain would establish outposts across the Caribbean in Hispaniola, Puerto Rico, Jamaica, and Cuba for the next twenty years. With the Cortes expedition to Mexico in 1518, by 1525 Spain was the preeminent European power in the Western hemisphere. For a good portion of the sixteenth century, starting in 1513 and culminating in the 1560s, Spain also attempted to establish a presence on both sides of the Florida peninsula. The founding of St. Augustine in 1565 was the logical extension of that policy. When the English arrived in what would become Virginia, Spain was well ensconced in the New World. Similarly, the Dutch and French became involved in the colonization of North America. The French began exploring the St. Lawrence beginning in the 1530s and the Dutch came to the Hudson River Valley in the 1620s. Spain and France dominated much of North America until the nineteenth century, but it would be English traditions that would shape the military practices of the English colonies emerging along the Atlantic coast.[3]

CONFLICT IN VIRGINIA AND MASSACHUSETTS: 1602–1688

The founding of English colonies at Jamestown on the Chesapeake in 1607 and Plymouth in what would become Massachusetts in 1620 are the two geographic book-ends to the English colonization of the Atlantic seaboard. Both colonies would struggle to gain a toehold on the North American continent and clash with native populations as the colonies expanded. These conflicts would not only lay the groundwork for many of our military traditions, but also provide the pretext for a greater commitment from the mother country as the problems of the old world exerted themselves on the new.

Before we let the narrative take over, let's pause to consider how these stories are told. The native cultures of the northeast, as with their peers across the continent, often would pass on stories and traditions orally. With the drastic downturns in population caused by disease and warfare, and the disruptions in the lives of these tribes and bands, their modern ancestors are left with more questions than answers. While the colonists left a rich written record, attempting to recapture the same level of information for the native peoples of Virginia and New England is daunting. While written records can and do reveal a great deal of information concerning native life ways, they are filtered through an alien culture. When it comes to translating these stories, therefore, we can reconstruct the past, but only to a point.

When Jamestown was established in 1607 on the James River at the southern end of the Chesapeake, the English were strangers to a new land. Backed by the Virginia Company of London, this venture was intended for profit. In order to make a profit, the company took measures to protect their investments. The officers who led the effort at Jamestown, conditioned by the brutal religious wars in Europe, would meet any threats from native populations with force. That being said, conflict between the colonists and native peoples of North America was not set in stone. Lured by profit, the gentlemen who went to North America were ill-prepared to make Jamestown a self-sustaining, colonial outpost. The small colony grew dependent upon the indigenous peoples of the region for food.

Jamestown was established amid a Confederacy of various bands of native peoples known collectively as the Powhatan, which was the name of their chief. Struggling to maintain a basic level of subsistence, both the English and Powhatan attempted to be the dominant partner in this relationship. Tensions rose between the two parties, leading to an outbreak of hostilities in 1609, and would continue intermittently until 1614. Opechancanough, the successor to Powhatan, assaulted the English eight years later in 1622, with the hope of running the English out of the region. Hundreds of settlers lost their lives, which led to immediate reprisals and the militarization of the colony. Hostilities tapered off and would come to an end in 1632. More than a decade later, in 1644, Opechancanough attacked again. In the intervening years, the number of English had increased to the point that there was little hope that another war would force the English out of the Powhatan homeland. This last attack would ultimately lead to the destruction of the Powhatan. Demographics, disease, and the economics of tobacco cultivation were the necessary precursors to the colonists' insatiable desire for land that neither the Powhatan nor other native peoples across North America could defeat.[4]

The last major war in Virginia was a complicated affair that involved not only warfare against the natives that lived on the frontier of the colony, but also political violence against William Berkley, the royal governor of Virginia. In the seventy years since the founding of the colony, the boundaries had stretched further west. In the now familiar justifications for violence, the loss of land and influence created a perfect recipe for violence on the frontier. In the face of expansion and loss of land, in 1675–1676, there were raids against settler homesteads on the frontier. Rather than launching punitive raids and causing problems with the friendly Indians living among the colonists, Governor Sir William Berkley chose to build a picket line of nine forts, garrisoned with a total of approximately 50 men. A cavalry detachment linked each fort. Unaccustomed to sitting still, the frontier homesteaders vehemently disagreed with this chosen strategy. Nathaniel Bacon, a planter and relative of the governor, led a rebellion of sorts. Coming from the militia establishment, Bacon led raids against friendly Indians. Occupying the colonial capital after his victory, Bacon demanded more resources to carry the war further across the frontier. Declared a rebel by the governor, a colonist-on-colonist struggle occurred, culminating with the burning of Jamestown. Bacon died from disease a month later and the rebellion fell apart. Unwilling to lose the wealth of the colony, King Charles II sent 1,300 soldiers to the colony to secure royal authority, and negotiated a Treaty with the Tribes of the Tidewater. Royal authority was restored, the Indians were relegated to small tracts of land, and regulars had entered the scene.[5]

The settlement of what would become New England was, as with their neighbors to the south, fraught with difficulty and violence. Whereas the roots of the colony in Virginia were commercial in nature, the colonists of New England were moved by religious motives. When the Pilgrims arrived off the coast of Massachusetts in 1620, there was a working relationship with the local peoples that occasionally erupted into violence. Despite these episodes of aggression, the settlers became powerbrokers between the various peoples of the region. Many of the native groups had histories of hostility toward one another, making the region ripe for alliances. In the beginning, though, it was less about power and more about leveraging that power with trade. To make the most of the goods brought across the Atlantic, the English settlers developed trading relationships with the Wampanoags and the Narragansetts. When the Narragansetts got into a dispute with the Pequots, the English became involved. In a treaty with the Pequots, the natives ceded land along the Connecticut River, allowing the Puritans to establish a fort and several settlements. As the colony expanded south from Massachusetts Bay, tensions rose commensurately. Despite attempts to come to an accommodation, hostilities erupted in 1636. After several expeditions and raids, in the spring of 1637, colonists in concert with Narragansett Indians attacked a Pequot village on the Mystic River and destroyed it. Conflicts continued through the summer with further attacks in western Connecticut, leading to the Treaty of Hartford in 1638. With the Pequots' power broken, tensions with other native peoples rose.[6]

The outbreak of war in 1675 was complex. Beginning with a fear of new native alliances with the Dutch who had a colony to the south in what would become New York, as well as murmurs of plots against English settlers, trust eroded over time and created a bubble of tension that spread across the Connecticut River Valley. As the population of nonnatives grew in Narragansett territory, traditional hunting and gathering patterns that bands had followed for generations were impeded. Moreover, the establishment of religious communities set aside for natives to inculcate Christianity created internal

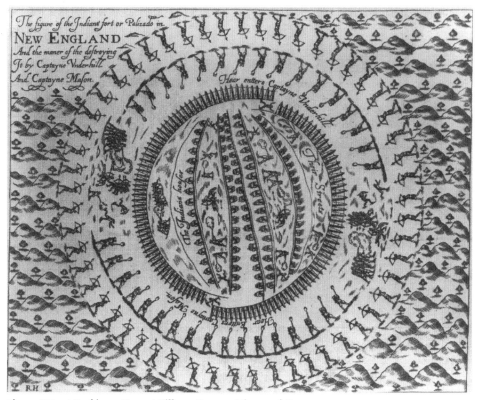

Figure 3.1   Attacking a Pequot Village. *Source*: Library of Congress

divisions as tribal members flocked to these communities, not so much to embrace Christian theology as to stay close to their traditional lands.

These internal and external pressures came to a head in 1675. The leader of Wampanoags, Metacom or King Philip to the English, went to war. His father, Massasoit, had signed a treaty in 1621, but unrelenting pressure to sell land as colonists moved into their traditional lands brought that treaty to an end. When a Christian Indian was murdered, Metacom was blamed, precipitating the bloodiest conflict in the colonial period as well as an inter-colonial alliance between Massachusetts Bay, Connecticut, and Rhode Island. The so-called King Phillip's War would continue to shape New Englanders' views about native peoples for generations. Joined by other peoples, in particular the Narragansett, the natives conducted raids in Connecticut and parts of Massachusetts, including the infamous Great Swamp Fight in December, 1675, where colonial forces attacked a Narragansett settlement. With a force of 1,000 men, the settlement was destroyed, and along with it the food, clothing, and shelter needed to survive through the winter. Fighting would continue into 1676, but with Metacom's death in August of that year, the war would come to a close. Despite the damage done to the economy of New England, the power of King Philip was broken and, by implication, that of the people he had led. The Indian tribes in the heart of New England withered and could no longer fight the growing English colony.[7]

THE ROOTS OF THE AMERICAN MILITARY TRADITION:
THE MILITIA

The clashes between the native peoples of Virginia and New England occurred not between professional soldiers, but between ordinary citizens who took up arms. As stated in the previous chapter, one of the threads of the American military tradition is the role of the citizen soldier. These roots preceded the generation of 1776 to the first colonists in Virginia and Massachusetts. As colonization unfolded in the seventeenth century, the professional armies that would come to dominate North America and Europe in the eighteenth century were, of course, not available. The leaders of both the prospective groups, John Smith in Jamestown and Myles Standish in Plymouth, knew they could only succeed if they had the cooperation of all of the able-bodied men of the colonies. If the colonies were to remain safe from external threats, they could only depend upon themselves—it was the militia that would become one of the pivotal institutions of the colonial era. There would be a great deal of variation within the colonies with each militia company conforming to its community and being suitable for the specific needs of that place and time.

The establishment of the militia did not occur in a vacuum. It had deep roots in the English tradition that had taken root in North America. In Britain, serving in the capacity of a citizen soldier began in Anglo-Saxon England with the *fyrd*, which at its core was an obligation to serve one's community in times of emergency. There was a more select *fyrd* that required ownership of land as a basis for service. Regardless of who served, this established a precedent of a universal military obligation. In 1181, Henry II issued the Assize of Arms that established an obligation of freemen to serve the king when called upon. The weapons they brought with them were what they could afford. The Assize was reaffirmed in 1285 by the Statute of Winchester. The statute reaffirmed the nature of a militia as a means of defense and for keeping law and order. With the ascent of the Tudor dynasty to the throne, the equivalent of a militia, or an obligation to serve, was firmly established in English law and tradition. A mandatory muster of able-bodied males was instituted and it became the responsibility of the local municipality to raise and manage them. The militia was meant to be for the defense of the realm and even local policing, but it was not meant to be used in overseas adventures. The militia system in the first decades of colonization in North America, then, would closely follow the precedents established in the English tradition—universal military service for men, compulsory musters, and strong ties to the local community.[8]

We can see the links between the English system and the evolving American system by looking at some of the larger trends that could be seen in each of the colonies. As mentioned previously, the key to the success of the early militia was a universal obligation for military service. Every colony would develop a set of statutes that determined who would serve. Over time, this obligation would be diluted as exemptions were introduced that, for the most part, were only applicable to the colonial elite. In the first decades of colonization, the perceived threats from the local native populations were at their greatest, requiring regular musters of all able-bodied men for training in the manual of arms and the rudiments of military discipline. The weapons brought from Europe—matchlock muskets, pikes, and body armor—quickly changed as the colonists adjusted their arms and techniques to the conditions found in the Mid-Atlantic colonies and New England. In the opening decades of colonization, when there was a thin veneer of English settlements scattered along the Atlantic seaboard, militia musters required mandatory attendance, with fines levied on those who chose to be absent. The militia was not meant to be a surrogate standing army, but a body of able-bodied men who responded to the needs of the colony and the desires of the leadership. Therefore, in the beginning, the militia was not organized, per se, into units, but into a body of trained men available for emergencies.[9]

While the English traditions informed the importance of a militia, every colony created a militia according to the needs of that particular community or colony. For example, in Virginia, beginning in 1623 and again in 1626, statutes that provided for universal military service for all males between 17 and 60 years of age were introduced. There were exemptions for sickly newcomers and older planters. Moreover, there was compensation for farmers marching off to war with a formula that required other labor, be it close neighbors or hired hands, to work the fields. This safety net allowed for participation in military action without losing economic livelihood. In 1624, the Virginia Company went bankrupt and rule was handed over to the crown. Further legislation created a more viable militia organization with the levy of taxes to pay for arms and equipment, and the growing colony was divided into military districts to better organize manpower. District commanders enforced the muster and had the ability to launch punitive raids relatively quickly. In 1634, Virginia was further divided into eight counties, each with a militia company and officer appointed by the governor to manage it with further fine tuning when the colony waged war against the Powhatan again in 1644. Ongoing conflicts with the local Indians and the perceived threats of other European powers infringing on the Virginia colony led to a highly organized, regional system that expanded as the colony grew.[10]

Unlike the motivations of their peers to the south, those of the colonists of Massachusetts Bay lay in the religious rather than the temporal realm. Known as the Puritans, they had fled religious prosecution in Great Britain for a place they could call their own. Perhaps already conditioned by reports of the conflicts between Virginians and natives, they were searching with caution for a proper place to make landfall. In Massachusetts, faced with unknown and uncertain threats, the Puritans took a wait-and-see approach. Once ashore and established, the settlement built a palisade and established permanent militia companies to protect Plymouth. Even as the colony expanded beyond Plymouth, new communities established militia companies. Beginning in 1634, compulsory military service was enforced by decree. These traditions and rules would form the basis of the trained men mobilized during the conflicts with the Pequot and during King Phillip's War in the 1670s. Moreover, on the basis of manpower, much like in Virginia, larger units were formed that would reach their full maturity in the 1670s. The militia companies also knit communities together during annual musters and training days and served, over time, as a way to attain social and political mobility. Despite the pretense of martial prowess, regardless of the colony that a militia man mustered out of, the key was that these men served as temporary soldiers. When the threat passed, they went home.[11]

The colonial conflicts that marked the period of the establishment of colonies in Virginia, Massachusetts, and in between were fought by citizen soldiers rather than regulars or mercenaries, marking a tremendous difference between North America and the old world. It was in this crucible that not only the citizen soldier arose, but a form of warfare that, while informed by the old world, was perhaps particular to the new.

AN AMERICAN WAY OF WAR?

In the previous chapter, we discussed the debate around the notion of an American way of war. The colonial period brings this issue into focus when we move our narrative from battles and the composition of colonial militias to how they fought and why they made the choices that they did.

The scholars of the last forty years have explored the conflicts of the early colonial period by moving beyond traditional military history and using other fields to understand not only the mindset of colonial leaders, but also the way the New World, gun powder, and the wars of the old world intersected on the shores of the New World. The unyielding brutality of the Indian Wars may have laid a key foundation for developing a distinctly American way of war whose hallmark was overwhelming force to break the will of an adversary to resist. Attacking settlements, agricultural production, and families took away the capabilities required for protracted resistance. With populations decimated by warfare and disease, relegated by treaty to confinement on small tracts of land, resistance was broken. If this disease and warfare led to a demographic disaster, then how did we arrive at this point? It is an important question that deserves a closer look.[12]

Most of the evidence that we have concerning how aboriginal populations fought is from a European perspective. Given that bias, primary source materials are colored by continental perspectives and tend to see the native populations as the perpetrators of unrest. Without a baseline of information before contact, it is difficult to produce a narrative that demonstrates that one form of warfare changed to another, so it is necessary to make informed suppositions. Using New England as an example, Patrick Malone begins his book The *Skulking Way of War, Technology and Tactics Among the New England Indians* with a characterization of Indian warfare in terms that we are undoubtedly familiar with. Intertribal or interband "feuds," akin to low-intensity warfare, were fought by tough, highly mobile warriors using cover and concealment, attacking settlements with bows and stone axes. Another favorite tactic was raids and ambushes against a village. Casualties were light when compared to European bloodbaths and, by implication, the goals of warfare were not total destruction but modest exchanges, that is, acquiring honor and manhood through acts of bravery. While this portrait is helpful and useful, we can never truly know what the extent of native practices was.[13]

The academic debate on how contact changed or altered both Indian and non-Indian warfare is cast from two frames of reference: either as adapting new technology and techniques, or reacting to these changes against a framework that the colonists in particular brought with them, as noted by E. Wayne Carp. Adapting Indian ways of warfare is something that has been recognized for the last thirty years. In New England and Virginia, militia companies as well as Indians adapted the technology and tactics of each other. For Europeans, the intricate drill and massed infantry formations of the continent never entirely went away. While there were varying degrees of success with adapting Indian ways, the so-called skulking way of war, there was always an underlying fear of having to meet competing European powers on the field of battle. The palisades at Jamestown are potent symbols of protecting their investment from a possible Spanish rather than native attack, despite the constant pull against a complete transformation to a force that fought by a skulking way of war. Native populations adapted quickly to the European style of warfare, quickly transitioning to gun powder weapons and blending them to their own ways of war. Europeans quickly understood that despite a shared ethnicity, tribal groups had enemies that could be used as valuable auxiliaries to the European powers. In turn, native confederacies could play the Europeans off against each other, making them powerbrokers in the imperial wars of the seventeenth century.[14]

In chapter 2 we recognized the contributions of Russell F. Weigley in asking the question if there is an American way of war. When examining the early colonial period. This debate reaches back to Jamestown and Plymouth, serving as a reminder that the roots of our ways of war stretch back beyond 1776. How the colonists reacted to native populations is as important as what was adapted or discarded. The mindset of the military leaders who came across the Atlantic was conditioned by the brutal wars of religion on the European continent and, in particular, the English subjugation of the Irish. The Puritans' theology of primitive, uncouth people who needed salvation or had to pay the price for sin also had an effect. The unrelenting pace of the warfare in Virginia and Massachusetts was conditioned by these factors, resulting in near total war and complete dissolution of Indian power in Massachusetts and Chesapeake Bays.[15]

As the previous observations suggest, the early colonial period is a crucible for American military institutions and practices. John Grenier in his book *The First American Way of War: American War Making on the Frontier* offers a synthesis of recent scholarship and a further corrective to Weigley's thesis. Grenier recognizes, as the title suggests, that the early colonial and national periods formulated an American way of war that evolved from the circumstances of settling in North America. From 1607 until the beginning of the nineteenth century, settlers used a mix of unlimited and irregular warfare to best their native opponents. The Indian Wars of the nineteenth century on the Great Plains have their roots in the practices of the early colonial period. The infamous tactic of attacking noncombatants and the villages that sustained them was a common practice in the seventeenth and eighteenth centuries. While underplaying the role of racism in formulating this strategy, Grenier suggests that the unrelenting violence against native peoples in the generations before the Revolution conditioned future generations as "Indian haters." Grenier's book treats the North American continent as a laboratory that brought forth the worst habits of the old world to the new, creating a brand of warfare that was bent on extirpation rather than accommodation.[16]

Where do these themes lead us in terms of interpreting these events to the public? Despite the passage of time, these events are still relevant today. The early colonial period provides the necessary context in acknowledging that the Euro-Americans who would come to dominate the Atlantic seaboard were conditioned by the practices of their forebears. To be fair to this complex and nuanced story, museums and historic sites must endeavor to capture the multiple perspectives of this time period. There are numerous interpretive techniques that could be used to tell this story. There are several that can be engaging, but they must be used with foresight, study, and caution. The first is to use costumed interpreters portraying known characters of these conflicts so that visitors can put a face to these people who may otherwise seem figments out of the past. This technique demands a robust knowledge of the events and the ability to empathize with the people they are portraying. For native roles, it is best to seek out community members who are not only willing to portray people from their past, but are also willing to make this portrayal authentic. Costumed, first person interpretation is an effective tool if done well, but given the relevance of these topics to the headlines that dominate our news outlets, it seems that a more appropriate technique would be a facilitated dialogue. The ways in which the early colonists pursued warfare are relevant to how the country struggles with counter-insurgency warfare and the desire to achieve peace without killing civilians. The relevancy of these events from three hundred years ago is often lost if a narrative concentrates on purely military history, even though that is still a valuable thing to know. If the audience is always seeking something of value in what is being interpreted to them, then perhaps rather than a didactic approach, the colonial wars would be better served through a dialogue with the audience. By allowing the audience to define the parameters of the conversation, events of three hundred years ago come to have relevance and meaning for a twenty-first-century audience.

The historic legacy of how colonial warfare influenced future generations can be handled in an engaging and compelling way in a museum if the focus is less on the events and more on the voice of the story-telling. The Mashantucket Pequot Museum & Research Center in Mashantucket, Connecticut, tells the story of the Pequot War with a native voice. Using a film and traditional exhibits, the museum presents a point of view that is reflective of tribal members. It brings home the point that to bring light to an authentic voice, oral history, archaeology, and engaging audience, emotions are potent tools that can be replicated in institutions of any size. Using a massive diorama of a village that is the centerpiece of the museum, it reminds visitors that the story of New England is a story that extends to long before the Pilgrims ever landed on Cape Cod. While the events of the Pequot War and King Phillip's War took place over three hundred years ago, the lives of current tribal members are still affected by those events. Capturing those voices is critical in providing multiple perspectives of an often-told story.

There are no arguments that the struggles between natives and colonists were bloody affairs. It is undeniable that the practices that came from Europe had an effect on how the old world looked at the new. Each time the colonists clashed with the Indians, it was in different circumstances and rationalized in a different manner. Moreover, as we will see, as North America became the battleground of empire, the tactics that had worked in defeating the power of Indian nations would not work against the French regulars in Canada. Finally, the relationship between colonists and Indians was not completely an adversarial relationship. From the beginning, colonists enlisted friendly Indians as auxiliaries and would continue to do so until the frontier closed in the 1890s.

WARS OF EMPIRE: 1688–1763

The colonization of North America did not occur in a vacuum. As stated previously, Spain, Holland, and France sent expeditions and colonists to the Atlantic seaboard in the sixteenth and seventeenth centuries. Whereas the warfare that occurred in Virginia and Massachusetts could be characterized as internal conflicts, from the late seventeenth century until the Seven Years' War (known in North America as the French-Indian War) in the 1750s and 1760s, warfare took on a more international flavor. While much of the combat in North America was smaller in scale than its equivalent on the European continent, and involved continual clashes with native populations that had aligned themselves with either the British or the French, for the first time, contingents of professional soldiers and sailors would complement the militia and volunteers. Finally, the various conflicts in the colonies did have links to wars fought on the continent, but the clashes that happened in North America between colonists was separate from the events of Europe and tended to blend into each other. The geographic spread was also much wider as the English colonies spread south from Virginia into the Carolinas and north into Canada.

The wars of the 1690s would look very similar to those of the previous generation on inter-colony conflict. This time, the actors were proxies, pitting French interests against those of England. When James II fled the English throne in 1688 under the threat of violence from William, Prince of Orange from the Netherlands, any threat of a Catholic king ruling a Protestant country was put to an end. The ascension of William to the English throne curried English support for the Dutch wars against France, which aligned the English against the French for the next century. The domestic antecedent to this international conflict was the way it affected the relationships of the various tribes that lived in New France and the Hudson River Valley. French interests had curried favor with various Algonquin Tribes who would be used as auxiliaries against the Algonquins' traditional enemies, the Five Nations of the Iroquois (Onondaga, Oneida, Cayuga, Seneca, and Mohawk). With the Iroquois developing a robust trading relationship with the English, French interests in their own fur trade were threatened, creating a great deal of antagonism with the Five Nations. The French sent troops into Iroquois territory in 1683 and again in 1687 to raid Seneca villages. The Indians responded and a low-intensity conflict erupted. When war broke out between England and France in 1689, the two events collided into an intercolonial war.[17]

Beginning in 1689 with the so-called King William's War and continuing until 1713, the struggles of Western Europe spilled into North America. Across New England and the southern colonies, both sides raided communities, disrupting the economies and lives of thousands. In spite of their advantages in population and global reach, the English colonies could not unseat French power in the new world. Caught in the middle, native peoples were splintered as groups and took sides with the powers that made the most promises. In 1713, a treaty was signed in Utrecht, ending the European and North American wars. In the New World, Newfoundland and Nova Scotia went to Great Britain, the French recognized the relationship between the Iroquois and the British, and Spain gained the right to import slaves to the Spanish colonies. France and Spain, however, still remained ensconced in Canada and Florida.[18]

Despite the relative quiet for the next twenty-five years, periodic violence occurred in New England and in the South but did not blow up into larger conflicts. The quiet, however, came to an end in 1738 when Robert Jenkins, a British ship captain, accused Spanish authorities of boarding his ship and cutting off his ear. The incident prompted a declaration of war, and in 1739 and again in 1740, James Oglethorpe led two raids into Florida that led to a siege of St. Augustine that failed. The Spaniards responded with their own advance up the Atlantic coast with no results. The emphasis would shift again when France and Britain went to war, resuming hostilities between the two continental powers.[19]

Once war resumed between the two primary continental powers, the campaign moved back to New England and French Canada. Known as King George's War in North America, New England, and in particular Massachusetts, embarked on an ambitious enterprise. Governor William Shirley, provoked by French privateers attacking fishing boats in Nova Scotia, proposed an expedition to capture the great French fortress of Louisbourg that dominated the approaches to the St. Lawrence River. With support from the Royal Navy, Shirley succeeded in besieging and capturing the fortress in June of 1745. It was, to date, the greatest victory ever achieved by colonial forces over a continental power. Shirley, however, stretched Massachusetts' financial resources to their limits as he lobbied to expand the campaign to conquer the French colony's heartland. The British did not support the operation and canceled it. To add to the insult, riots broke out in Boston when the Royal Navy attempted to coerce New Englanders into serving on board warships of the Royal Navy. The rioting lasted for three days and registered a deep resentment over the British policy of pressing men to serve as crews on naval vessels. North America, from the British perspective, was peripheral to Britain's wider interests and in the 1748 peace treaty of Aix-la-Chapelle, Britain agreed to return Louisbourg to France. After expending a great deal of treasure, New England's grand adventure gained them nothing.[20]

The so-called imperial wars of the eighteenth century serve as a bridge between the Seven Years War and the origins of the American Revolution and the initial period of British colonization in North America. Many of the patterns established in the formative period continued through the 1740s with the use of militia, and then citizen volunteers, to fight the increasingly costly wars. From the point of view of London, violence against the French was justified, but these conflicts were largely sustained on land by colonial resources and at sea by the Royal Navy. While there was certainly resentment against the methods of the British, namely, the pressing of civilians for service in the Royal Navy and scapegoating colonials for problems in the field, these issues do not necessarily foreshadow the American Revolution. Such concerns, however, would continue to grow during the Seven Years War.[21]

THE FRENCH AND INDIAN WAR: 1754–1763

The pivotal event of pre-Revolutionary America was the Seven Years War, also known as the French and Indian War. It is recognized for creating many of the conditions that would lead to the American Revolution. The victorious British toppled French power in North America, and reordered the priorities of Native Americans in the Ohio Valley and New England. It gave Americans the perception of martial prowess when set against the many British disasters that occurred early in the war and, conversely, it made the British dismissive of American forces that were often seen as nothing more than an armed rabble. Many of the officers who would lead the Continental Army to victory in the revolution acquired experience fighting in Canada and along the frontier.

It is a story that is often lost in the long shadow cast by the American Revolution. It certainly deserves our attention.[22]

When hostilities broke out in 1754, for the colonial participants, and in particular a young George Washington, the events that triggered this war could be characterized as a disaster that might have ended Washington's career before it had even started. The spark occurred in the Ohio River Valley. In 1753, French influence was spreading across the Great Lakes and south to the Ohio River Valley. There were many players at work in this complex, imperial struggle. English colonists venturing west over the Appalachian Mountains, the French attempting to block the spread of British power through alliances with Indians, and the Iroquois attempting to assert power collided on the shores of the Allegheny and Monongahela Rivers. It was a recipe for conflict. A small British outpost at the confluence of these rivers was overpowered by the French and, in its place, a large fortification was constructed—Fort Duquesne. The governor of Virginia, Robert Dinwiddie, wanted to re-establish British power in this pivotal region. Led by 22-year-old George Washington, the expedition failed spectacularly. In the initial clash with the French, Washington was successful. Unfortunately, at a critical moment, Washington's Indian allies killed the French commander, bashing his head in. The unsuccessful parlay would lead to a series of events that Washington would carry with him for the rest of his life. Besieged in a poorly sited fort that Washington had named Necessity, Bad weather, demoralized troops, and a large mixed force of French and Indians resulted in Washington's decision to cut his losses and surrender to the French.[23]

The news of Washington's debacle in May, 1754, reached London in September. After debating over a course of action in London, it was decided to send two regiments of British troops to North America. General Edward Braddock was selected to lead the expedition to the forks of the Ohio. After meeting with representatives from five colonies, Braddock was convinced by the group of a more ambitious plan with the promise of the requisite resources to back him up. Not only would British regulars and American volunteers move against the fort on the Monongahela and Ohio, but they would also send columns against Fort Niagara, Crown Point along Lake Champlain, and other forts in the Ohio River Valley. Washington served as Braddock's aide and hoped for a commission in the British Army. The Americans had struggled to find a way to unite their resources through the Albany Plan for union in 1754, just before Braddock's arrival, but had failed to bridge the gap and consolidate colonial resources. Undeterred, Braddock raised additional forces to the two regiments he had, marching west with 2,400 British regulars and colonial volunteers. The expedition carved a rough road through the forests of central Pennsylvania, confident of success. In July 1755, not very far from the forks, Braddock's command met with disaster. Unaccustomed to fighting in the forests of Pennsylvania, the British forces lost any cohesion they had and were decisively routed. Braddock was mortally wounded, and Washington guided the defeated column to safety. The French remained at the forks of the Ohio until 1758. With British power at an ebb, the trans-Appalachian west was open to raiding parties.[24]

Nearly all of the other British plans of 1755 failed as well. The advance to Fort Niagara stopped well short of their objective, and an advance up Lake Champlain was halted at Lake George. However, operations against Nova Scotia were a success.

Braddock's death meant that William Shirley, the governor of Massachusetts, was in command of the British forces, but he was subsequently relieved by the arrival of the Earl of Loudon who came with fresh troops. The year 1756 saw additional planning and French action across the Great Lakes. Emboldened by the defeat of Braddock, the French moved on Fort Oswego, which fell, threatening New York. The subsequent capture of Fort William Henry at the base of Lake Champlain blocked the route north. Despite French victories, changes in London and Montreal would seal the fate of New France in 1757. Marquis de Montcalm, a soldier with a continental pedigree, was mentally equipped to fight a conventional war and frowned upon the use of Indian auxiliaries, an important part of French forces in the Ohio. This predilection toward conventional warfare would contribute to the decline of French power and resources.[25]

The British focus on North America would redouble with other attempts to blunt French power around the world, with the accession of William Pitt to a position of power in June, 1757. As chief minister to the Newcastle government, Pitt made decisions that transformed North American operations from an intercolonial struggle to a world-wide war for Empire. Rather than fighting the war for North America by proxy on the continent, Pitt chose to secure the safety and security of the colonies by asserting the power of the Royal Navy to block French reinforcements, allowing New France to wither. Making the choice to use regular forces from the Royal Navy and Army would also lay the seeds of revolution as provincials were pushed aside for a largely supporting role.[26]

In the 1758 campaign season, Pitt continued to eliminate French power in the Ohio, Lake Champlain, Louisbourg, Fort Duquesne, and perhaps even the heartland of New France—Quebec and Montreal. In June 1758, Jeffery Amherst led 14,000 men up the St. Lawrence and successfully besieged Louisbourg, opening the St. Lawrence. James Abercrombie was ordered to open Lake Champlain but could not break the French defenses. Another expedition from Albany led by John Bradstreet captured Fort Frontenac on Lake Ontario, which was the main supply point for the forts on the Ohio. With supply becoming tenuous, in late 1758 Fort Duquesne was abandoned and occupied by John Forbes. These victories set up the final conflict in New France with Montcalm on the Plains of Abraham in front of the walls of Quebec. Led by the victor of the siege of Louisbourg, in 1759 James Wolfe accompanied his men to meet Montcalm. After scaling cliffs west of the city, Wolfe met Montcalm's forces on the Plains of Abraham, in sight of the walls of Quebec. With a mixed force of militia and regulars, Montcalm's forces could not stand up to the persistent fire of the Redcoats. The city fell as did the commanders—both Wolfe and Montcalm died on the field. Amherst successfully captured the forts at the head of Lake Champlain; Ft. Niagara on Lake Ontario was captured as well. Winter stopped the campaign season, but in 1760, Montreal was surrounded and had to surrender, which ended the war in North America.[27]

The French opened peace talks in 1761 that dragged on until 1763 to culminate in the Treaty of Paris. It was a disaster for the French. Not only did the French lose all of Canada, they gave up all lands they laid claim to the east of the Mississippi River, except New Orleans, which went to Spain. Britain also gained France's Caribbean colonies and those in the Indian subcontinent. It was an unparalleled British victory. It was not the end, however, of hostilities in North America. In the southeast, the

Cherokees took action against the British. In an attempt to blunt French power in the southeast, the British built forts in the heart of Cherokee country. Wary of a British power base in their homeland, the Cherokees launched a series of raids that the British countered with several punitive expeditions. After several skirmishes, the Cherokees signed a treaty in 1761 that left them secure. In the Ohio Valley, it was assumed that with the French defeat, the tribes would be allowed to resume a status quo without much British interference. An Ottawa chief known as Pontiac, emboldened by a prophet that urged the rejection of the British, led violent attacks that spread across the Ohio Valley in 1763. The British struck back. Support for Pontiac wavered as a result and his rebellion ended. To ameliorate the circumstances of Pontiac's actions, in 1763 the British closed the lands west of the Appalachian's to settlement. The British added yet another factor in colonial discontent with the mother country, England.[28]

LEGACY

Why remember the French-Indian War? Historic sites that figure prominently in this story, such as Fort Pitt in Pittsburgh, Pennsylvania, or Fort Ticonderoga in New York, have ties to these events. At Fort Pitt, exhibits certainly acknowledge the long-held view that the French and Indian War did create conditions that would lead to revolution, and they try to remind visitors that we see that from the advantage of hindsight. Exhibits and activities concentrate on the importance of the fort in the development of the region and what its rise and fall meant to a British presence in the Ohio Valley. Anecdotal evidence collected from visitors also suggests that they want to know about the people who served the fort and how they contributed to the story. After moving away from costumed interpretation, Fort Pitt has redoubled its efforts to create family activities around demonstrations and costumed interpretation. These activities engage the visitors, but they also allow the Fort's staff to use them as a "hook" to introduce visitors to the history of the area.[29] These places, then, and the roles they played in the subsequent campaigns in northern New York and western Pennsylvania are undeniably important and should be studied. They remind us that until 1776, the colonies in North America were part of a world-wide empire that would catapult Great Britain to a continental power. Most historians would also agree that in these victories lay the discontentment that would lead to Lexington and Concord in 1775. The threads of this narrative are well known. Burdened with a large debt, Britain passed these obligations on to the colonies through a variety of legislative acts that were ignored or vigorously protested. Douglas Leach, the preeminent historian of this era, has also argued that the road to rebellion lay through the deep resentment of colonial militia and volunteers of their shoddy treatment by officers and men of the British Army. These roots predate the French and Indian War, with origins going back to the first British actions at the beginning of the eighteenth century.[30]

While it is easy to exaggerate the role that deep-seated grudges played, these resentments had the unintended effect of allowing the colonists to think that their own martial skills, whether embodied as militia or volunteers, were equal to those of the professional soldiers that fought in North America. Equally important is the fact that in this period, many of the habits and practices that Americans would come to embody, such as the sacrosanct role of the militia and civil control of the military, were well established. Regardless of how we define it, American ways of war began to express themselves in the near continual conflicts with native peoples in both the North and the South. These trends would continue to express themselves for the next century. In the meantime, as tensions slowly rose across the thirteen colonies in the aftermath of the Treaty of Paris, the generation that fought the French and Indian War would assert themselves again as the colonies proclaimed independence from Britain and struck out on their own.

NOTES

1. Robert F. Weigley, *History of the United States Army* (New York: Macmillan Publishing Co., 1967), 12.

2. Older surveys of American military history, while still having some value, begin at the revolution without acknowledging the richness of our colonial past. These include William Addleman Ganoe, *The History of the United States Army* (New York: D. Appleton-Century Company, 1942); and Matthew Forney Steele, *American Campaigns* (Harrisburg: The Military Service Publishing Company, 1949). A newer work that reflects this same trend is, David W. Hogan, *225 Years of Service. The U.S. Army, 1775–2000* (Washington, DC: Center of Military History, 2000).

3. Ian K. Steele, *Warpaths: Invasions of North America* (New York: Oxford University Press, 1994), Chapters 1 and 2. National Park Service handbooks can provide concise introductions to topics. For Spain in the New World, see the handbooks for Castillo de San Marcos and De Soto, Coronado, and Cabrillo. See also, John Shy, "Armed Force in Colonial North America: New Spain, New France, and Anglo-America," in Kenneth J. Hagan and William R. Roberts, ed. *Against All Enemies: Interpretations of American Military History from Colonial Times to the Present* (Westport: Greenwood Press, 1986). John Ferling, *Struggle for a Continent: The Wars of Early America* (Arlington Heights: Harlan Davidson, 1993), Chapter 1 provides a concise overview of colonization from other European powers.

4. Matthew S. Muehlbauer and David J. Ulbrich. *Ways of War: American Military History from the Colonial Era to the Twenty-First Century* (New York: Routledge, 2014), 17–23. Allan R. Millett, Peter Maslowski, and William B. Feis, *For The Common Defense: A Military History of the United States from 1607–2012* (New York: Free Press, 2012), 6–19. Steele, *Warpaths*, Chapter 3. A concise overview of this period can be found in Douglas Edward Leach, *Arms For Empire: A Military History of the British Colonies in North America, 1607–1763* (New York: The Macmillan Company, 1973), Chapter 2. A dated but still useful essay is Wilcomb E. Washburn, "Seventeenth-Century Indian Wars" in *Handbook of North American Indians*, vol. 4, History of Indian-White Relations (Washington, DC: Smithsonian Institution, 1988), 89–100. For a multifaceted examination of the conflict between both sides, see J. Frederick Fausz, An "Abundance of Blood Shed on Both Sides": New England's First Indian War, 1609–1614," *The Virginia Magazine of History and Biography,* vol. 98, no. 1 (January 1990): 3–56 and William L. Shea, "Virginia At War, 1644–1646," *Military Affairs* 41 (October, 1977): 142–46.

5. Leach, *Arms for Empire*, 56–59, Millett, Maslowski, and Feis. *For the Common Defense*, 18–19, Muehlbauer and Ulbrich. *Ways of War: American Military History from the Colonial Era to the Twenty-First Century*, 23–25.

6. Muehlbauer and Ulbrich. *Ways of War: American Military History from the Colonial Era to the Twenty-First Century*, 25–31, Steele. *Warpaths*, 80–96. See also, Albert A. Cave, *The Pequot War* (Amherst: University of Massachusetts Press, 1996).

7. Despite its age, a classic account of King Philip's War can be found in Douglas Edward Leach. *Flintlock and Tomahawk: New England in King Philip's War* (Woodstock: The Countrymen Press, 1958), Muehlbauer and Ulbrich. *Ways of War: American Military History from the Colonial Era to the Twenty-First Century*, 30–35. Millett, Maslowski, and Feis. *For The Common Defense*, 16–18, Steele. *Warpaths*, 99–108. For a telling examination of the cultural impact of the war, see Jill Lepore, *The Name of War: King Phillip's War and the Origins of American Identity* (New York: Vintage, 1990).

8. Russell F. Weigley, *History of the United States Army* (New York: Macmillan Publishing Co., 1967), Chapter 1, John K. Mahon. *History of the Militia and the National Guard* (New York: Macmillan Publishing Co., 1983), Chapter 1.

9. Louis Morton, "The Origins of American Military Policy," *Military Affairs* 22 (Summer, 1958): 75–82, John Shy, "A New Look at Colonial Militia," *The William and Mary Quarterly* 20 (April, 1963): 175–85.

10. Militia studies are not a dominant part of military history literature. Older works, however, still have great value in understanding how the Virginia militia worked. Michael Doubler, *Civilian in Peace, Soldier in War: The Army National Guard, 1636–2000* (Lawrence: University Press of Kansas, 2003), 10–14. William L. Shea, "The First American Militia," *Military Affairs* 46 (February, 1982): 15–18. See also, William L. Shea, *The Virginia Militia in the Seventeenth Century* (Baton Rouge: Louisiana State University Press, 1983).

11. There is a great deal of older secondary literature on the development and maturation of the New England militia that is still very helpful in understanding the origins and development of the militia. See Douglas Edward Leach, "The Military System of the Plymouth Colony," *The New England Quarterly* 24 (September, 1951): 342–64, Jack S. Radabaugh, "The Militia of Colonial Massachusetts," *Military Affairs* 18 (Spring, 1954): 1–18, Richard P. Gildre, "Defiance, Diversion, and the Exercise of Arms: The Several Meanings of Colonial Training Days in Colonial Massachusetts," *Military Affairs* 52 (April, 1988): 53–55. For the role of the militia in the community, see Morrison Sharp, "Leadership and Democracy in the Early New England System of Defense," *American Historical Review* 50 (January, 1945): 244–60 and T. H. Breen, "English Origins and New World Development: The Case of the Covenanted Militia in Seventeenth-Century Massachusetts," *Past & Present* 57 (November, 1972): 74–96. Views from the militia and native peoples and the continual lackluster performance of citizen soldiers are recounted in Armstrong Starkey, *European and Native American Warfare, 1675–1815* (Norman: University of Oklahoma Press, 1998).

12. T. J. Brasser, "Early Indian-European Contacts" in *Handbook of North American Indians*, vol. 4, History of Indian-White Relations (Washington, DC: Smithsonian Institution, 1988), 78–88. See also, John Ferling, *Struggle For a Continent: The Wars of Early America* (Arlington Heights: Harlan Davidson, 1993), 9–17.

13. Patrick M. Malone, *The Skulking Way of War: Technology and Tactics Among the New England Indians* (Baltimore: Johns Hopkins University Press, 1991), Chapter 1. For an incisive reflection of more recent trends, see Wayne E. Lee, "Early American Ways of War: A New Reconnaissance, 1600–1815," *The Historical Journal* vol. 44, no. 1, (2001): 269–89.

14. Lee, Early American Ways of War, 274. For an older perspective, see John K. Mahon, "Anglo-American Methods of Indian Warfare," *The Mississippi Valley Historical Review* 45 (September, 1958): 254–75. See also, Don Higginbotham, "The Military Institutions of Colonial America: The Rhetoric and Reality," in Don Higginbotham, ed. *War and Society in Revolutionary America: The Wider Dimensions of the Conflict* (Columbia: University of South Carolina Press, 1988).

15. John Ferling, *A Wilderness of Miseries: War and Warriors in Early America* (Westport: Greenwood Press). See also, Francis Jennings. *The Invasion of America: Indians, Colonialism, and the Cant of Conquest* (Chapel Hill: University of North Carolina Press, 1975). Don

Higginbotham critiques Ferling and Jennings in "The Early American Way of War: Reconnaissance and Appraisal," *The William and Mary Quarterly*, 3rd Ser. 44 (April, 1987): 232–34. For Indians as auxiliaries, see Richard R. Johnson, "The Search for a Useable Indian: An Aspect of the Defense of Colonial New England," *Journal of American History*, 64 (December, 1977): 623–51.

16. John Grenier, *The First American Way of War: American War Making of the Frontier* (New York: Cambridge University Press, 2005), 1–19. See also, chapter 1.

17. Ferling, *Struggle for a Continent*, 61–66, Millett, Maslowski, and Feis, *For The Common Defense*, 20–25, Muehlbauer and Ulbrich, *Ways of War*, 38–42. Still useful is Howard H. Peckham, *The Colonial Wars, 1689–1762* (Chicago: University of Chicago Press, 1964), Chapter 1.

18. Ferling, *Struggle for a Continent*, 67–111, Peckham, *Colonial Wars*, 27–73, Muehlbauer and Ulbrich, *Ways of War*, 42–51, Leach, *Arms For Empire: A Military History of the British Colonies in North America, 1607–1763*, Chapters 3–4. For a general overview of the south, see Verner Crane, *The Southern Frontier, 1670–1732*, Second Edition (Tuscaloosa: University of Alabama Press, 2004) and Timothy Paul Grady, *Anglo-Spanish Rivalry in Colonial South-East America, 1650–1725* (London, UK: Pickering and Chatto, 2010).

19. Ferling, *Struggle for a Continent*, 111–17, Muehlbauer and Ulbrich, *Ways of War*, 51–54, Leach, *Arms For Empire*, 206–24.

20. Ferling, *Struggle for a Continent*, 131–42, Muehlbauer and Ulbrich, *Ways of War*, 54–56, Leach, *Arms For Empire*, 224–55.

21. Colonial reactions to British slights are an important factor in the rising tensions between the colonials and British authorities. These resentments are covered in Douglas Edward Leach, *Roots of Conflict: British Armed Forces and Colonial Americans, 1677–1763* (Chapel Hill: University of North Carolina Press, 1986).

22. Beyond the survey texts and monographs that have been previously mentioned, any serious study of the French and Indian War should begin with the works of Fred Anderson. Two of his works on this time period include *Crucible of War: The Seven Year's War and the Fare of the British Empire in North America, 1754–1766* (New York: Alfred A. Knopf, 2000) and the companion volume to a Public Broadcasting Service documentary of the same title, *The War That Made America: A Short History of the French and Indian War* (New York: Viking, 2005). Also from Anderson, *A People's Army: Massachusetts Soldiers and Society in the Seven Years' War* (Chapel Hill: University of North Carolina Press, 1984). An older but still useful overview is Francis Jennings, *Empire of Fortune: Crowns, Colonies, and Tribes in the Seven Years War in America* (New York: W.W. Norton, 1988).

23. Fred Anderson, *Crucible of War* has a brief Prologue to the events that would trigger the war, see also, 42–73. A more complete account can be found in Ron Chernow, *George Washington: A Life* (New York: Penguin Books, 2010), Chapter 3. See also, David Clary, *George Washington's First War: His Early Military Adventures* (New York: Simon and Schuster, 2011). For an overview of the run-up to hostilities, see Muehlbauer and Ulbrich, *Ways of War*, 56–58, Leach, *Arms For Empire*, Chapter 8.

24. Fred Anderson, *Crucible of War*, 86–107, Chernow, *Washington*, 52–62, Leach, *Arms For Empire*, 362–69.

25. Leach, *Arms for Empire*, Chapter 9 and Anderson's *Crucible of War*, 135–208 provide an excellent summary of the tumult facing the British after Braddock's defeat and before William Pitt assumed control of hostilities.

26. Fred Anderson, *Crucible of War*, Chapter 21, Leach, *Arms For Empire*, 415–19, Muehlbauer and Ulbrich, *Ways of War*, 62–65, Maslowski, and Feis, *For The Common Defense*, 37–38.

27. Anderson, *Crucible of War*, 219–414, Leach, *Arms For Empire*, 415–85, Muehlbauer and Ulbrich, *Ways of War*, 65–69.

28. Leach, *Arms For Empire*, 486–510, Anderson, *Crucible of War*, 518–53.

29. Interview with Alan Gutchess, director of Fort Pitt, July 23, 2014.

30. Both *Arms For Empire* and *Roots of Conflict* make this point. That being said, we have the benefit of hindsight. In 1763, war between the colonies and Great Britain was not foreordained.

Chapter 4

The American Revolution, 1763–1781

I believe I may, with great truth affirm, that no Man perhaps since the first Institution of Armys ever commanded one under more difficult Circumstances than I have done.

General George Washington, March, 1776[1]

In the popular imagination, the presence of English colonies on the shores of North America for over a century and the subsequent transplantation of British political and military institutions to the New World matters little because of the violent break with England in the 1770s. Military and political institutions that took root in the eighteenth century diverged from their mother country, rejecting the old, despotic notions of the divine right to rule for a democratic republic of freeholders. The high ideals expressed in Thomas Jefferson's Declaration of Independence defined the new American narrative. Despite the inconsistencies inherent in the new country—the existence of slavery in the south and the steady destruction of native cultures as the country pushed the frontier west—the United States took root and thrived.

The American Revolution and the establishment of a new republic continues to resonate across the American timeline nearly 240 years after the events of the Revolution. The political ideals of the country have deep roots in these events. Unfortunately, the struggle for independence is often reduced to patriotic tropes that are repeated once a year on the Fourth of July, without understanding their meaning and influence upon our past. Even though English colonists had settled in Virginia and New England over 150 years prior to the revolution, it is easy and perhaps forgivable to think of the American Revolution as a new beginning. The colonies did break from the mother country and did form a Republic. The origins of the US Army, Navy, and Marine Corps all have roots in the events of the Revolution; however, in many regards, it was a continuation of many of the practices and institutions of the early colonial period, though with a decidedly American flavor. The act of breaking away from the most powerful Empire in the world is an achievement that we can be proud of and can rightly celebrate. The challenge is in telling the stories of our military past that move beyond our founding myths and, instead, making these events relevant to the needs of the visitor and the latest trends in scholarship.

ORIGINS

The twelve years from the end of the Seven Years War in 1763 to the exchange of shots on the Lexington Green in 1775 can easily be interpreted and understood as an inexorable slide toward war. There seems to be a certain inevitability that the colonists and Great Britain would come to blows. Perhaps violence was inevitable, but the origins and how we understand them are much more complex than a simple linear progression to conflict. Since this work focuses on military history, the origins of the Revolution can be seen through the lens of the British military presence on North American shores and also through the colonial reaction to what some perhaps saw as an occupation.

From an American perspective, it ultimately comes down to a single point. The push for taxes, the quartering of troops in cities, and a growing distrust of British intentions slowly eroded colonist support. Simply put, the intrusion into the affairs of individual colonies was the chief source of discontent. Mistrust led to extralegal bodies, Committees of Correspondence, etc., that questioned the legitimacy of Parliament in ruling the colonies. As Millett and Maslowski define the issue in their survey, *For the Common Defense*, it comes down to who had the right to rule.[2] Whereas the British Army was seen as a coercive arm of the government and as a tool for Empire, for the colonists, it was the militia that protected their local interests. Even though the militia was on the decline, it stood as a powerful symbol and would come to be idealized as a defender of liberty. While the militia would continue to play an important role throughout the war, as the war dragged on, the importance of the militia would decline in favor of a standing Continental Army. In the final analysis, the militia could perhaps be seen as a symbol of community and liberty whereas the British regular was a symbol of oppression and tyranny.[3]

It was within the parameters of who had the right to rule and how it manifested itself that the events leading to the Revolution unfolded. A variety of legislative acts were used to enforce the will of Parliament on the recalcitrant colonists, and their various acts outraged American sensibilities. Dealing with intransigent Bostonians tried the patience of British commanders and Parliament, prompting them to close the port of Boston in 1774. The establishment of the First Continental Congress, also in 1774, brought most of the colonies together for the first time, united in one voice to define their relationship with the mother country. As tensions rose, a flash point would be reached in the spring of 1775, propelling the colonies and Great Britain toward war.[4]

The broad sweep of events that would lead to the Revolution is well known, to the point of being a historical cliché. What can be done to provide compelling opportunities for interpretation? By far the most effective interpretive technique is, simply put, the power of place. Since New England was the center of the discontent that would lead to the Revolution, the National Park Service's Freedom Trail allows visitors to wander through downtown Boston, touching many of the sites that played a role in the road to Revolution. Beginning at the Boston Common and ending at the Bunker Hill monument, visitors can use a variety of guide books, guide services, audio tours, and web-based children's activities which provide the historical context and interpretive opportunities to interact with these sites. While services vary from stop to stop along the trail, there are plenty of opportunities to provide interpretations that connect the sites together. There is no better way to ascribe meaning to the events of the 1770s than walking through the buildings and along the roads that witnessed these events. When you separate yourself from the noise of the traffic and other modern intrusions, you can use your imagination and "see" the past. The power of place is a powerful technique that nearly always provides a tangible link between the past and the present.

Since visitors provide their own meanings to these events, a major key to successful interpretation is providing access to multiple perspectives. The techniques that are used most frequently are stories of the participants, rich and poor alike. Whether using costumed interpretation of real people or composites, it allows the visitor to appreciate that one story can be seen from many different perspectives. For example, the Boston Massacre can be told from both a British and colonist point of view using costumed interpreters, again showing that ordinary people were involved on both sides. These portraits can be compelling, and if they are interactive rather than script-driven, audiences can engage these characters in a dialogue that can be relevant and timely. Visitors are drawn to people's stories because they could very well see themselves in the characters that are portrayed. They see how one person could make a difference.

Figure 4.1   Boston Massacre depicted in a wood print. *Source*: Library of Congress.

Independence National Historical Park in Philadelphia hosts Independence Hall, where the Continental Congress debated and ratified the Declaration of Independence. There is no other place where the events of the day merge with the interests of the visitors. In 1988, I was a seasonal park ranger at the park. At the time, continuing through to the present, rangers guided groups through the building. While it is anecdotal, I recall a palpable feeling of reverence and awe in the Assembly Room as the visitors made personal connections between the events of 1776 and their own interests. If a visitor can experience the complexities and emotions of an event from a single place, can we explain the progress of an event through the eyes of a single participant? Perhaps it is appropriate, then, to explore the most famous person to shape and lead the thirteen colonies to victory: General George Washington.

GEORGE WASHINGTON AND THE CONTINENTAL ARMY

Before we can delve into the events of the American Revolution, the role of George Washington must be addressed. It has been chic for a generation of historians to reject the notion that one man, a hero if you will, can have a profound impact on the progression of events. Given the inherent complexity of any series of events, it is difficult to measure and evaluate the influence of one man or woman on the course of those events. Nevertheless, George Washington's influence on the development of the Continental Army, and his leadership in the field and in the halls of Congress, left an indelible imprint that shaped the Nation's armed forces for a generation. Any consideration of the military history of the Revolution must include Washington and the choices he made.

Washington was well aware of his role in shaping the destiny of the nation and worked hard to cultivate his image of a humble Virginia planter who served his country in a time of need. Born in February, 1732, to Augustine and Mary Washington, he led a life of privilege. His father died when George was 11 and his half-brother Lawrence became his mentor. Lawrence's marriage into the Fairfax family afforded an avenue for patronage and influence that would provide opportunities to go east to the Alleghenies and the Ohio country on surveying missions. From 1754 to 1759, Washington served in a variety of capacities in the Virginia militia that would set his destiny in becoming the commander-in-chief of the Revolutionary forces. Behind this image, though, was a man with as many faults and foibles as any of his contemporaries. He had a volcanic temper that apparently took a great deal of effort to control when provoked. He was a self-educated man who was very sensitive to his inadequacies when compared to his classically trained contemporaries, such as Thomas Jefferson. He made mistakes and he was very aware of his fallibility.[5]

What then of his contributions? Gordon S. Wood in his summary of the American Revolution summed up George Washington best when he declared, "He was never a traditional military hero. He had no smashing, stunning victories, and his tactical and strategic maneuvers were never the sort that awed men. Instead, it was his character and political talent and judgment that mattered most."[6] Washington wanted to create an army based on what he knew and admired—a well-supplied and disciplined army of regulars, supplemented by militia as needed. Given his exposure to British regulars

Figure 4.2   George Washington before the Revolution. Courtesy of Washington and Lee University.

during the Seven Years War, he long admired the professionalism of the British soldier. Even after the Revolution, Washington noted that the British Army had created an army of "near perfection."[7] There was much to be admired in the British soldier's steadfastness under fire, but Washington was also an American and acted accordingly.[8]

The composition of the Continental Army and the strategies that he pursued over the course of the war were a reflection of Washington's experiences and character. In terms of strategy, even though Washington lost more battles than he won, his chief genius lay in his understanding of what was at stake. To sustain the Revolution, and for the colonies to attain their independence, he had to keep his army intact. In *The American Way of War*, Russell F. Weigley identified Washington's ultimate paradox: in order to remove the British Army and attain independence, he had to preserve his own army and remain on a strategic defensive. Washington knew that the Continental Army could never defeat the British and their allies head to head, but they could gradually wear them down. While Weigley calls it a strategy of attrition, he later, and more appropriately, calls it a strategy of erosion. The lengthy supply lines for the British, the lack of a single political or economic center in the thirteen colonies, and the lack of a singular British response all worked in Washington's favor. Washington and his subordinates knew the strengths and weaknesses of their army and men, which resulted in the formulation of a well-crafted strategy that was appropriate for the circumstances of the Revolution.[9]

Do we perpetuate myths when we attribute so much to one man? It is easy to fall into hyperbole and myth by stating emphatically that without Washington, the Revolution would not have succeeded. On the other hand, it is hard to deny that his presence was pivotal to its success. The best way to ameliorate the tendency to credit Washington with everything is to look at the successes and weaknesses of the Continental Army through the lens of local history. By using the resources of a small community that perhaps Washington passed through, stories and documents can be used to see how Washington's decisions impacted the life of a single community. There is hardly a community in New England and the Mid-Atlantic states that does not have an inn or public spot that George Washington either slept in or passed by. Local historical societies can use existing collections to capture either the excitement of the moment or how Washington's decisions impacted the town he passed through. There are many techniques, then, that can be used to acknowledge the General through the lens of the people that he served.

NEW ENGLAND BREAKS THE KING'S PEACE: 1775

As the Revolution unfolded and expanded across the length and breadth of the thirteen colonies, the British used different strategies to end the rebellion and restore order, which was the primary goal of the Empire. If we understand the Revolution in terms of an insurrection, the British certainly had experience in putting down revolts in England and Ireland, but what of North America? Accommodate their interests, or put them down brutally? Grant autonomy, or employ tighter control? How do you sustain an army so far from home? These questions dominated the strategic debate for much of the war and were never satisfactorily answered.

In April 1775, British attempts to quell the rebellion resulted in open hostilities at Concord and Lexington.[10] The aftermath of Lexington and Concord saw a number of moves and countermoves by the Americans and the British, as the Americans consolidated their hold over New England. Ethan Allen and Benedict Arnold conquered Fort Ticonderoga, New York, in May 1775, capturing the fort's significant stock of artillery that would figure in breaking the siege of Boston. The British received help as well. Generals William Howe, John Burgoyne, and Henry Clinton came to Boston with additional troops. The British attempt to break the Rebel line on Breed's Hill came at a price: British casualties were high—over 1,000 dead and wounded. While the British carried the day, the rebellion continued.[11]

With tens of thousands of militia besieging Boston as citizen soldiers under no commitment to remain on the siege line, the Continental Congress took charge. By appointing Virginian George Washington as commander of the "army," they brought support for the Revolution from outside of Massachusetts. Congress could create an army by fiat, but to be truly effective, both Congress and Washington had to create a bureaucracy from scratch to administer and command such an army. As Washington organized his army, a small force under Philip Schuyler launched an invasion of Canada through Lake Champlain. Capturing Montreal, but unable to successively assault Quebec, the invasion ended in failure. Despite failure in the north, in the early spring, William Howe, now commander of British forces in North America after Gage's dismissal, evacuated Boston after the Rebels fortified Dorchester Heights, the highest ground in Boston. With Washington's artillery dominating Boston, rather than risking a bloody fight in the streets of Boston, Howe evacuated all of the troops and sailors in Boston and left in March 1776.[12]

THE STRUGGLE FOR INDEPENDENCE: 1776–1780

The rebellion remained anchored in the northern and central colonies until the war went south in its final campaigns. In spite of their superiority in numbers, the British faced a number of obstacles. Manpower and supplies came from Great Britain. With the supply line stretching across the Atlantic, transport was not cheap. Unwilling to mobilize the numbers of soldiers domestically to put down the insurrection meant a reliance on German allies, popularly known as Hessians. Nearly 30,000 were recruited and paid for by the crown for service in North America. Hopes that colonists loyal to the King, commonly known as loyalists, would provide a reliable supply of manpower with the thirteen colonies also failed to materialize. Throughout the war, the commonalities between the Americans and English created a great deal of sympathy but ultimately, British hubris, an innate sense of superiority and an unwillingness to compromise in a meaningful way, made the job of putting down the rebellion and rebuilding a loyal population difficult. On the other side of the line, as our own adventures in the twentieth century would prove, the colonists fought for ideas. Alan Millett and his collaborators in the survey text, *For the Common Defense*, sum up the ideology of the Revolution succinctly: "The Revolution was no European dynastic squabble, but a war involving an ideological question that affected the population far more than kingly quarrels . . . . Large numbers of colonists ardently believed freedom was the issue, not only for themselves, but for generations unborn."[13]

In the aftermath of the evacuation of Boston, the British set their eyes on New York. The capture of New York City exemplified the martial skills of the British—well trained troops and complete command of the sea lanes up and down the coast, which allowed the British to choose how and when they would attack. As the British began to think about the next steps, certain assumptions and attitudes would plague their planning efforts. Given the size of the North American colonies and their incipient stage of development, even though there were several large cities, there was no center of gravity that the British could hold to either end the rebellion or bring the continentals to the bargaining table. Of greater magnitude, there was a constant push and pull between finding a way to reconcile the Empire's differences with the rebellion and imposing the will of Parliament and the King on the colonists. The campaigns against the Continental Army in 1776–1777 illustrate the challenges of vacillating between conciliation and imposition.[14]

British vacillation between the two extremes resulted in a confused and inconclusive campaign for New York City and New Jersey. For William Howe, New York was an obvious target. In August 1775, through the fall, Washington was forced out of Brooklyn and then Manhattan, allowing the British to occupy most of central New Jersey.

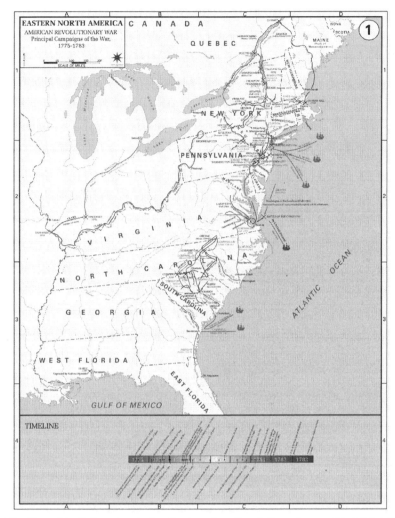

Figure 4.3   Map—North America during the American Revolution. *Source*: West Point Atlas.

With winter approaching and the campaigning season coming an end, Howe halted his forces at the Delaware River. Further to the north, British efforts to descend south from Quebec met with limited success. Benedict Arnold's fleet of gun boats slowed down a British advance at the Battle of Valcour Island on Lake Champlain.[15]

While the British had much to celebrate, Washington's army shrank as enlistments ended and it appeared that the revolution was on the ropes. Opportunities, however, come in unlikely places. The heavy-handed occupation of New Jersey and the scattering of British and Hessian forces across the waist of the state into winter outposts provided Washington with a chance to strike. I am always hesitant to use the phrase "turning point" in describing the effect of any event upon a narrative. That being said, Washington's actions along the Delaware River in December 1776 certainly were a pivotal point in the Revolution. Washington's attacks unnerved the British, making their occupation of New Jersey untenable. Success in the field translated to a fresh infusion of recruits. It underscored the point that as long as the Continental Army remained in the field, the Revolution would continue. Howe's boasts that royalists would come to the British colors proved unrealistic and he still believed he could defeat the Rebels by lancing off New England from the rest of the colonies.[16]

1777

Further attempts to defeat Washington's Continental Army also failed to quell the rebellion. In an attempt to cut the middle and lower colonies off from New England, the primary British commanders in North America, William Howe and John Burgoyne, sought to destroy the rebellion with Howe attacking from the south through Philadelphia and Burgoyne descending from Canada along the traditional invasion route. Neither Howe nor Burgoyne effectively communicated with one another, resulting in two uncoordinated advances that not only failed to destroy the Continental Army, but also ended in a disastrous defeat.

Howe was successfully able to maneuver Washington out of Philadelphia, but was too far south to support Burgoyne, who met with disaster.[17] Burgoyne got underway in May, 1777, with 8,000 troops including German and British Regulars, Canadian militia, some Loyalists and Iroquois warriors. Burgoyne made contact with continentals at Fort Ticonderoga at the beginning of July, a full six weeks before Howe began his march toward Philadelphia. With a long and tenuous umbilical to Canada, Burgoyne's rations were running low. He dispersed some of his force to forage the countryside, where a foraging party of Germans was caught and defeated at Bennington, Vermont, by a large force of militia. In another pivotal clash of arms, Horatio Gates and Burgoyne fought at Freeman's Farm on September 19. Fighting each other to a standstill, the British held the field at the end of the day, but the Americans did not retire. Banking on relief from the New York City garrison, Burgoyne stayed put, fortifying his position. Clinton attacked several fortified positions along the Hudson, moving in a desultory manner, which was of no help to Burgoyne. Unable to re-cross the Hudson to secure reliable supplies to keep his army fed, Burgoyne had no choice but to surrender on October 17, 1777.[18]

The American victory at Saratoga had ramifications that would change the character of the war. Hostilities would continue until 1781 as the British adjusted their strategy, but nevertheless, Saratoga was an important victory that boosted the Americans' morale and brought support from another continental power—France. King Louis XVI and his ministers had already provided some financial aid to the colonies. The arrival of Ben Franklin in Paris in late 1776 proved fortuitous. Franklin was popular and persuasive in court, but the French needed something substantial to ensure an alliance. The American victory at Saratoga provided that. In February 1778, Franklin and the French Foreign Minister signed a trade agreement and alliance. Britain's loss was France's gain. For the Americans, the French could supply loans, provide supplies and weapons, and commit French troops and naval resources to the New World. Britain was faced with new choices.

The Revolution did not divert colonists' attention from the native populations of the thirteen states. The tendency toward total warfare against native populations continued unabated on the frontier. During the Revolution, the Iroquois Confederacy

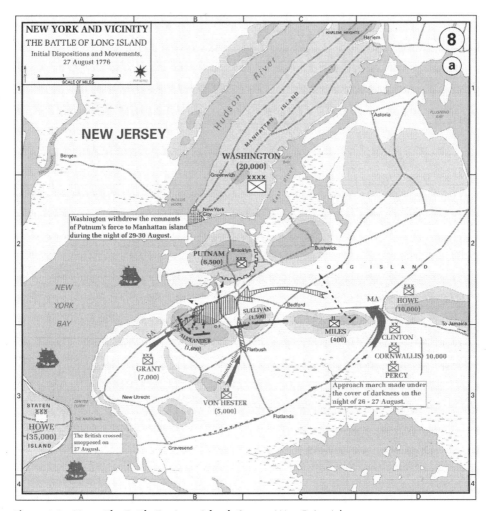

Figure 4.4   Map—The Battle For Long Island. *Source*: West Point Atlas.

split. In 1777, the Cayuga, Seneca, and Onondaga sided with the British. Led by Thayendanegea (Joseph Brant), the breakaway group understood that it was British power that could stop or slow down the incursions of colonists into Iroquois lands. In the Ohio country, British influence and provocations garnered a response from the Americans. In an area claimed by Virginia, George Rogers Clark was ordered by Governor Patrick Henry to take care of the situation. Clark's small force attacked a British outpost in Vincennes in February of 1779, capturing the chief British officer Henry Hamilton. However, the actions in the west, while important in the long run, could not compete with the evolving situation in Pennsylvania.[19]

1778–1780

The period between the end of the Philadelphia campaign and the shift of the campaign to the south saw challenges to Washington's leadership, gradual improvements

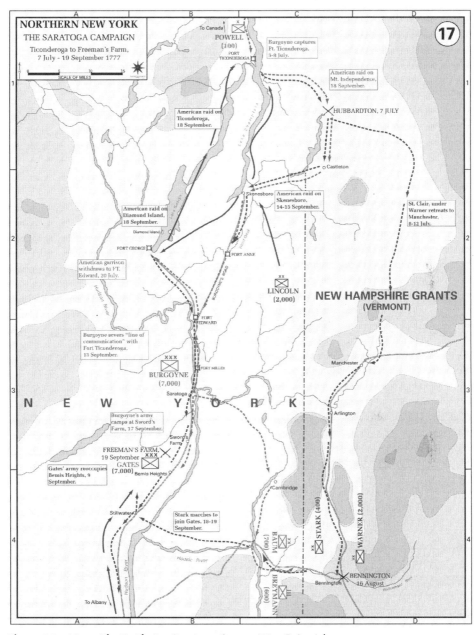

Figure 4.5 Map—The Battle For Saratoga. *Source*: West Point Atlas.

in the performance and capabilities of the Continental Army, and the arrival of French assistance in the form of troops. In the aftermath of the British occupation of Philadelphia and the battle of Germantown, the British moved to their winter quarters in Philadelphia while Washington retired to Valley Forge, a community outside of Philadelphia that allowed him to keep an eye on British activities. The trials at Valley Forge are well known in the popular imagination. By far, the issue at hand was not the weather, but supplies. Dependent upon the states for supplies, the Continental Army's supply system broke down. With the British paying cash, farmers in the area gladly supported British needs. Cold, hard cash was preferable to Continental scripts or IOUs. Practical problems also led to issues—shortages in transportation in particular, an empty treasury, and the lack of expertise at headquarters led to shortfalls. The appointment of Nathanael Greene as Quartermaster General ameliorated these supply issues because of his energetic efforts. Nevertheless, despite improvements in successive years, supply of the army continued to challenge Washington and his staff.[20]

During their tenure at Valley Forge, by far the most momentous occasion was the arrival of Friedrich Wilhelm Augustus von Steuben. Assuming the airs of a baron, which he was not, von Steuben arrived in Valley Forge in February of 1778. He had served on the staff of Frederick the Great and was an accomplished trainer. When he began re-shaping the Continentals, his English was limited but his energy more than made up for it. He organized a group of officers into a training company, which he led himself. These officers, in turn, were sent across the army to inoculate their men on Steuben's methods. His regulations, known as the blue book, would remain as the mainstay for the American Army until the first decades of the nineteenth century. The results of Steuben's efforts depended upon the regimental commanders. Definite improvements occurred across the army, but unevenly.[21]

In 1778 the French entered the war, transforming a colonial insurrection to a much wider conflict. Henry Clinton took over from Howe and would continue in that role until the end of the war. Even though Washington remained in the northeastern states until the Yorktown campaign of 1781, the British began to shift resources south. In preparation for their southern campaign, Clinton ordered Philadelphia to be evacuated. With the British moving troops to New York overland through New Jersey, Washington took advantage of the opportunity to strike. The Battle at Monmouth Court House was inconclusive and would prove to be the last major clash between Washington's continentals and the British in the northern colonies. The British and the Continentals remained watchful as the British went south.[22]

THE CONTINENTAL NAVY

What of the navy during the 1770s? As the siege of Boston unfolded, Washington commissioned several ships to intercept British cargo, including war supplies. Similarly, most of the states also commissioned their own ships that patrolled coastal waters, but certainly did not have the strength to directly challenge the Royal Navy. Whenever they could muster forces, they met with failure. Massachusetts and New Hampshire mounted an expedition in 1776 to Penobscot Bay in what today is Maine, a supply point for timber for the Royal Navy. The expedition failed to root out the British in a fort at the head of the Bay and after some dawdling, a British relief squadron trapped the fleet and destroyed fourteen American vessels; the British captured the rest. A similar effort in 1770 at Charleston, South Carolina, ended in disaster.[23]

Privateering was by the far most successful American maritime endeavor during the war. The Continental Congress and the states provided letters of marque to, in effect, capture enemy shipping and profit from it. Congress authorized over 1,600 privateers. Over the course of the war, these privateers took over 600 prizes valued in excess of $18 million, driving up insurance rates and increasing the cost of supplying British forces in North America. There was one bright spot that would come to symbolize the fighting spirit of the US Navy—John Paul Jones. Jones, with the American sloop of war *Ranger*, raided several communities in England and southern Scotland. When *Ranger* returned to the states, Jones received a converted French merchant ship and turned it into a warship. Naming it the *Bonhomme Richard* in honor of Ben Franklin's Poor Richard, Jones engaged the British frigate *Serapis*. In a bloody battle, Jones captured the *Serapis* at the cost of his own ship and forever enshrined his reputation as the father of the US Navy. While privateers and John Paul Jones succeeded, it was the French who tipped the scales in the Americans' favor. Upon completion of the alliance, a French fleet skirmished with the British in the Caribbean and East Indies. It was the timely intervention of the French fleet that prevented reinforcement of the British forces on the York peninsula, sealing the victory for the Americans. While the American Navy would come of age in 1812, the spirit of John Paul Jones' mantra, "I have not yet begun to fight!" has certainly provided inspiration for future captains.[24]

THE ROAD TO VICTORY LIES THROUGH THE SOUTHERN STATES

The opening years of the Revolution saw British forces campaigning in New England and the Mid-Atlantic states, primarily Pennsylvania and New Jersey. War first came to the south beginning in 1775. In Virginia, royal Governor Lord Dunmore retreated from the colonial capital at Williamsburg to Norfolk where he invited slaves to join him in exchange for their freedom. Disturbed by the consequences of Dunmore's actions, militia drove him out of Norfolk. In South Carolina at the beginning of 1776, at the battle of Moores Creek just north of Wilmington, a force of Loyalists met patriot militia and were defeated, ending British rule in the Carolinas. Finally, in the summer of 1776, Henry Clinton attacked Charleston and was repulsed. For the next two years, the British concentrated upon the North before setting their eyes further to the South.[25]

Moving the fighting to the southern colonies had several advantages. The distance between the main Continental Army in New York and the Carolinas and Georgia in particular was too great to guarantee support coming overland. Savannah, Georgia, was seized in 1778 and after several attempts, Charleston fell in early 1780. The entire Charleston garrison, with around 5,500 men, the largest of its kind in the war, surrendered. The last rebel force in the state was attacked by Lieutenant Colonel Banastre Tarleton's Loyalists in the battle of Waxhaws. As with Charleston, it ended in a defeat for the Rebels and ended the last vestige of a Continental presence in the Carolinas. Unfortunately for the British, despite their victories, the high-handed behavior of Tarleton's men, in particular, would create conditions that would end with the British being seen as predators rather than liberators.[26]

In a scene that would repeat itself with uncommon frequency, the victors turned the local population against them. Burdened with lengthy lines of communication into the hinterland and haughty demands of loyalty on the local population, partisans had ample reasons to take up arms against the British. Attempting to capitalize on the partisans' success, Horatio Gates was sent south but met with defeat at the disastrous battle of Camden, North Carolina, in the late summer of 1780. Washington moved to fix the problem by sending his trusted subordinate Nathanael Greene south. Greene's arrival coincided with a victory of rebel militia over Loyalist militia in the Battle of King's Mountain. Unable to move into the hinterland, Lord Charles Cornwallis canceled his planned invasion of North Carolina and departed to his winter quarters. In January 1781, Greene went on the offensive, and defeated Tarleton at Cowpens. Lord Charles Cornwallis continued to retreat, effectively abandoning Georgia and the Carolinas, allowing the remaining British garrisons to be pushed back to Charleston. Lord Charles Cornwallis was skillful in his retreat north and even though Greene was never able to completely best the British on the battlefield, he maneuvered Lord Charles Cornwallis out of the Deep South to meet his fate at Yorktown.[27]

The British campaign in the South provides ample opportunities to explore current headlines using events from the past. The British waged a counter-insurgency campaign, attempting to not only put down the Revolution, but also convince the local populace that staying loyal to the King was the right thing to do. American operations in Vietnam and southwest Asia provide ample comparisons with both Continental and British activities in the Carolinas. Moreover, many of the battles fought in the South, in particular King's Mountain, saw clashes not between British Redcoats and American Patriots, but between militia companies that fought as Loyalists or Rebels, providing another way to look at the Civil War. Two opposing ideologies clashed in the South eighty years before the War Between the States. These comparisons certainly make current events more relevant to modern audiences by providing historical antecedents. On the other hand, despite the superficial similarities between these events, we must also be careful to avoid overt comparisons. The 1780s was different from the late 1960s or the 2010s. Events must be placed in their proper temporal context. When used with care, the past can inform the present. Many museums and historical sites that deal with the Revolution or Civil War topics can link the two together under the context of Loyalist versus Patriot. Even without the benefit of objects or a battlefield, museums can use these events to initiate provoking conversations about current events under the cloak of the past.

THE END GAME

The siege of Yorktown was the last great clash between American forces and the British and would lead to peace and vindication of the rebellion. Lord Charles Cornwallis arrived in Virginia with his remaining men in May 1781. Prior to Lord Charles Cornwallis' arrival, Virginia had been relatively quiet. In the spring of 1779, the Royal Navy raided communities along the Chesapeake. With no recourse but to abandon the Carolinas, Lord Charles Cornwallis found Virginia the one place where he could regroup and destabilize the largest colony in the south. While waiting for Clinton to provide instructions, Lord Charles Cornwallis' forces raided the interior, nearly capturing Governor Thomas Jefferson. In the meantime, Lord Charles Cornwallis and Clinton bickered over the next steps. Clinton feared that Lord Charles Cornwallis was contravening his orders by communicating directly with confidants in Parliament. Lord Charles Cornwallis in the meantime wanted to make Virginia the center of operations and was exasperated by Clinton's vacillation between protecting New York and providing a vision for the South. Buoyed by the success of raids in central Virginia, but unable to divine clear orders from Clinton, Lord Charles Cornwallis secured a port at Yorktown to serve as a base of operations in order to facilitate any future movements.[28]

Washington, like Clinton, was faced with choices. In the summer of 1780, Comte de Rochambeau arrived in America directly from France. With the addition of Comte de Grasse's fleet and the accompanying soldiers, Washington could attack Lord Charles Cornwallis rather than his initial target of New York. De Grasse outnumbered the British in ships of the line and used his superiority to lead the French to a rare victory over the British squadron at the battle of the Virginia Capes. With the remaining British ships sailing back to New York, Lord Charles Cornwallis was trapped and, in a reversal of fortune, was outnumbered by the combined French and American Army. Backed by French engineers, Washington conducted a siege of Yorktown. They began working their way to the British position on October 6, 1781. On October 14, Cornwallis surrendered his command of nearly 7,000 soldiers and laid down his arms. In a snub to Washington, he sent a subordinate to deliver his sword to the victorious Allies. The war was over. In a communication to Congress, Washington wrote, "I consider myself to have done only my duty and in the execution of that, I ever feel myself happy."[29]

The Treaty of Paris was generous with the Republic's new borders. The Ohio Valley and the interior northwest, including the Great Lakes, was ceded to the United States, increasing the size of the country. Florida remained in Spanish hands to the thirty-first parallel. The American and British delegates wrangled over fishing rights, debt service, and restitution of confiscated property for Loyalists. Wrangling over the terms continued through the beginning of September 1783, when the document was signed. The Americans won independence and substantially expanded their land base. Despite the ongoing debates that would occur throughout the early national period over the utility of the American Army, important precedents established during the Revolution would carry over to the first years of the Republic: an army that could expand and contract depending upon the dangers faced by the Republic; a strong tradition of civil control over the military; the role of the militia and volunteers as supplements to, and checks on, the regular army. With a decentralized government, a dangerous world, and unresolved issues involving native populations, the new government had to chart a route that honored the new path of liberty and freedom, but protected the Republic from its enemies, both foreign and domestic, without betraying the ideals of the Revolution.

NOTES

1. Don Higginbotham, *George Washington and the American Military Tradition* (Athens: University of Georgia Press, 1985), 69.
2. Millett, et al., For the Common Defense, 46.
3. James Kirby Martin and Mark Edward Lender, *A Respectable Army: The Military Origins of the Republic, 1763–1789* (Arlington Heights: Harlan Davidson, 1982), 1–30.

4. There are several introductory texts to the American Revolution that, despite their age, are still very useful for gaining a broad understanding of the events that would trigger a clash of arms. These include Edmund S. Morgan, *The Birth of the Republic, 1763–89*, Revised Edition (Chicago: University of Chicago Press, 1977); Robert Middlekauf, *The Glorious Cause: The American Revolution, 1763–1789* (New York: Oxford University Press, 1982); and John R. Alden, *A History of the American Revolution* (New York: Knopf, 1969).

5. There are many character studies and biographies of George Washington. For an overview of his character and contributions, see Marcus Cunliffe, *George Washington, Man and Monument* (New York: Mentor Books by The New American Library, 1958), Joseph J. Ellis, *His Excellency: George Washington* (New York: Vintage Books, 2004). Washington's mansion, Mount Vernon, is a testament to his character and his accomplishments. It is well preserved and cared for by the Mt. Vernon Ladies Association. A plethora of Washington resources are available on their website: www.mountvernon.org.

6. Gordon Wood, *The American Revolution*, 84.

7. Ron Chernow, *George Washington – A Life*, 293.

8. Don Higginbotham, *The War of American Independence: Military Attitudes, Policies and Practice* (Boston: Northeastern University Press, 1983), 85–88, Martin and Lender, *A Respectable Army*, 40–48.

9. Russell F. Weigley, *The American Way of War: A History of United States Military Strategy and Policy* (New York: Macmillan Publishing Company, 1973), 3–16, Russell F. Weigley, *Towards an American Army: Military Thought from Washington to Marshall* (Westport: Greenwood Press, 1962), 1–9. For the ideological component, see Charles Royster, *A Revolutionary People at War: The Continental Army and American Character* (Chapel Hill: University of North Carolina Press, 1979).

10. One of the best recent accounts on the events leading to Lexington and Concord is David Hackett Fischer, *Paul Revere's Ride* (New York: Oxford University Press, 1994). In terms of how the community was changing in the years before the Revolution and how it would impact the way Concord reacted, Robert A. Gross, *The Minuteman and Their World* (New York: Hill and Wang, 1976) is still a useful work for understanding how Concord met the Revolution.

11. For a traditional military history of these opening events and the subsequent war, Willard M. Wallace, *Appeal to Arms: A Military History of the American Revolution* (New York: Harpers and Brothers Publishers, 1951) is still useful. See also, Martin and Lender, *A Respectable Army*, 34–40, Higginbotham, *The War of American Independence*, 68–77. For a traditional military history of Breeds Hill, see Richard M. Ketchum, *Decisive Day: The Battle for Bunker Hill* (New York: Doubleday, 1974).

12. Weigley, *History of the US Army*, 29–43; Higginbotham, *The War of American Independence*, 81–121; Wallace, 67–87.

13. Millett, et al., *For the Common Defense*, 48. See also, Higginbotham, *The War of American Independence*, 112–47.

14. Millett, et al., *For the Common Defense*, 49–50; Martin and Lender, *A Respectable Army*, 48–58.

15. Ira D. Gruber, "America's First Battle: Long Island, 27 August 1776" in *America's First Battles, 1776–1965*, ed. Charles E. Heller and William A. Stoft (Lawrence: University Press of Kansas, 1986), 1–32, Higginbotham, *The War of American Independence*, 148–65, Millett, et al., *For the Common Defense*, 60–63.

16. A fresh and compelling look at Washington's Crossing is David Hackett Fisher, *Washington's Crossing* (New York: Oxford University Press, 2004). See also, Ron Chernow, *George Washington*, 269–84, Higginbotham, *The War of American Independence*, 165–71.

17. Wallace, *Appeal to Arms*, 134–45; Higginbotham, *The War of American Independence*, 181–88. For an in-depth look at the Pennsylvania campaign, see Stephen R. Taaffe, *The Philadelphia Campaign, 1777–1778* (Lawrence: University Press of Kansas, 2003).

18. Wallace, *Appeal to Arms*, 146–68; Higginbotham, *The War of American Independence*, 188–98. There are many books on the campaign; a well-regarded narrative can be found in Richard M. Ketchum, *Saratoga: Turning Point of America's Revolution* (New York: Henry Holt and Company, 1997).

19. Martin and Lender, *A Respectable Army*, 136–42; Higginbotham, *The War of American Independence*, 319–31.

20. Martin and Lender, *A Respectable Army*, 99–103; James A. Hutson, *The Sinews of War: Army Logistics, 1775–1953* (Washington, DC: Office of the Chief of Military History, 1966), 58–62, Erna Risch, *Quartermaster Support of the Army: A History of the Corps, 1775–1939* (Washington, DC: Quartermaster Historian's Office, 1962), 29–37. A critical resource to understand the local perspective, see also, E. Wayne Carp, *To Starve the Army at Pleasure: Continental Army Administration and American Political Culture, 1775–1781* (Chapel Hill: University of North Carolina Press, 1984). An in-depth look at its effect on soldiers and civilians alike can be found in Wayne Bodle, *The Valley Forge Winter: Civilians and Soldiers in War* (University Park: Pennsylvania State University Press, 2002).

21. Weigley, *History of the US Army*, 63–67.

22. Martin and Lender, *A Respectable Army*, 118–26; Higginbotham, *The War of American Independence*, 245–51; Wallace, *Appeal to Arms*, 180–91.

23. Millett, et al., *Provide For the Common Defense*, 72–74, Kenneth J. Hagan, *This People's Navy: The Making of American Sea Power* (New York: The Free Press, 1991), 1–10. For general accounts on the war at sea during the Revolution, see Nathan Miller, *Sea of Glory: The Continental Navy Fights for Independence, 1775–1785* (New York: David McKay and Company, 1974); William M. Fowler, *Rebels Under Sail: The American Navy during the Revolution* (New York: Charles Scribner and Sons, 1976). For the British perspective, see John A. Tilley, *The British Navy and the American Revolution* (Columbia: University of South Carolina Press, 1987).

24. Stephen Howarth, *A History of the United States Navy, 1775–1998* (Norman: University of Oklahoma Press, 1991), Chapter 3, Hagan, *A People's Navy*, 18–19.

25. Wallace, *Appeal to Arms*, 88–96, 204; Higginbotham, *The War of American Independence*, 351–55.

26. Wallace, *Appeal to Arms*, 204–11. For an overview of British successes, see David K. Wilson, *The Southern Strategy: Britain's Conquest of Georgia and South Carolina, 1775–1780* (Columbia: University of South Carolina Press, 2005).

27. Wallace, *Appeal to Arms*, 211–15, 228–45; Russell F. Weigley, *The American Way of War: A History of United States Military Strategy and Policy* (New York: Macmillan Publishing Company, 1973), 24–39. See also, Russell F. Weigley, *The Partisan War: The South Carolina Campaign of 1780–1782* (Columbia: University of South Carolina Press, 1970).

28. Wallace, *Appeal to Arms*, 245–52; Higginbotham, *The War of American Independence*, 380–83.

29. Chernow, George Washington, 419. For the siege of Yorktown, see Wallace, *Appeal to Arms*, 256–62; Higginbotham, *The War of American Independence*, 376–79.

Chapter 5

The Constitutional Settlement, 1783–1815

Yes Fellow Citizens I admit it—it is a Standing Army, but composed of your brothers and sons. Can you require or conceive a better security. Are they not your natural guardians?

Frederick Steuben[1]

The questions that dominated these decades carried over from before the Revolution and would continue as the United States attempted to define a military policy true to the spirit and intent of its founding. Tensions between settlers and native peoples on the frontier, as well as the ongoing wars between France and various continental powers, created a need to have some sort of military establishment. By instituting a regular army, however, there still remained the underlying concern of a standing army becoming the enforcers of a despotic, centralized government. The establishment of a professional military was the one issue that underlined many of the political debates from the 1780s to the War of 1812.[2]

THE ARTICLES OF CONFEDERATION AND THE RISE OF THE NATIONALISTS

During the Revolution, the Continental Congress established a national government organized under the Articles of Confederation. Ratified in 1781, the articles provided the necessary infrastructure and legislative authority for the central government to function until surpassed by the Constitution. If the main point of the Revolution was to resolve who had the right to rule and by implication a distrust of central authority, the Articles of Confederation reflected the mood of the country. Distrust in central authority is embodied in the articles' military clauses. While the central government reserved the right to make war and represent the states overseas, Congress did not have power over the purse strings.

The articles seemed appropriate, even more so because of the behavior of the Continental Army at the end of the Revolution. Three incidents colored political debate about the future of the Continental Army. In the later years of the Revolution, there was a growing gap between the officers of the Army and the rest of society. There was a palpable feeling of resentment against the society at large and Congress. In 1780, Congress promised to officers serving in the Continental Army an annual pension of half of their pay. Apprehensive about their futures, in 1782, a party of Continental Army officers went to Philadelphia, where Congress was in session, to change the terms to full pay for six years. As the Army's congressional allies struggled to find a solution, several inflammatory letters implied the Army would take action if Congress did not. Washington was aghast and called for a meeting where he denounced the actions of his men and humbled his officers. Congress voted full pay for continental officers for a period of five years and enlisted men for four months. Further heightening apprehensions, in 1783, Henry Knox organized the Society of Cincinnati, an honorary fraternal society for Continental officers. Membership could be passed down and inherited by sons, creating a permanent military aristocracy. Washington was appointed President but he distanced himself from the organization. Finally, Pennsylvania troops in the Continental Army mutinied and marched on Philadelphia demanding to be demobilized and paid. Neither of this happened. It was in this atmosphere that the Army disbanded and the Confederation Congress began to plot a course for the future.[3]

In 1783, Congress formed a committee to look into the military establishment for the New Republic with advice from Generals Washington and Steuben. Promulgated as "Sentiments on a Peace Establishment," Washington's recommendations for an American Army were modest: four infantry regiments and one of artillery and the necessary infrastructure to support them, around 2,600 men, and a mechanism for a more robust militia with something approaching a universal requirement to enroll in the militia for service in case of an emergency. Rounding out Washington's wish list was a military academy and a series of arsenals. Washington's recommendations were summarily rejected. Congress directed that fifty-five men remain on duty at West Point, New York, and Fort Pitt to guard military stores. Given the weaknesses of the confederation government to raise revenue to pay for a regular force as well as an aversion to a powerful central government, the creation of a modest Army was difficult to achieve.[4]

Regardless of the orders to disband the Continental Army, on June 2, 1784, there was still a need for troops to serve. The British continued to garrison forts in what at the time was known as the Northwest (today, the states in the upper Midwest), and with the influx of settlers to areas east of the Appalachians, some semblance of a force was required. The very next day, Congress asked the states for a levy of militia, and the First American Regiment was formed with 700 volunteers to serve for a year. Given the dependence on the states for funding, despite expending the most funds of any department in the confederation government, shortfalls always existed, exacerbating supply and manpower issues. Domestic issues remained a constant source of worry. In 1786, a tax rebellion of sorts led by Daniel Shays broke out in western Massachusetts, threatening the new federal arsenal in Springfield. Massachusetts militia broke up the protest, not before showing how ineffective the mechanisms available to Congress were. Congressman Edward Carrington of Virginia castigated the lack of power of the confederation government: "Here is felt the imbecility, the futility, the nothingness of federal powers."[5]

There is no museum that explores the Confederation period that I am aware of, but it is a pivotal transition time between the joy of success and the reality of rule.

A small, professional army, the capacity for a regulated militia that stands as a ready reserve, and the tradition of civilian rule are all a bridge between the practices of the Revolution and the founding of the Republic. While the trials and tribulations of the Confederation Congress would provide fodder for Nationalists hoping to create a stronger central government, the issues of balancing security needs within the abilities of a government to fund them are issues that still resonate with modern audiences. Interpretive techniques of facilitated dialogue, historical documents, and artifacts from the Confederation period can be used to explore the issues of that era, as well as their relevance to our own lives. After every major conflict, beginning with the Revolution and stretching across time to the twentieth century, questions regarding the size and missions of the military dominate the political sphere. In the aftermath of the fall of the Berlin Wall and the more recent drawdown of troops in southwest Asia, these historical parallels in terms of what our national security establishment should look like are here. The public asks the question of how much is enough. It was from the tumult of the Confederation that the Constitution arose.

THE CONSTITUTION AND THE MILITARY POLICY OF THE REPUBLIC

The Constitution, upon its ratification in 1788, would provide the political mechanisms that corrected the weaknesses of the Articles of Confederation. If you recall your civics classes, there are three branches of government—legislative, executive, and judiciary. The President is the titular head of the Armed Forces as Commander-in-chief, but only Congress can declare war and provide the necessary appropriations to fund the Army and Navy.[6] Within the subsequent addition of the first twelve amendments to the Constitution, citizens were guaranteed the right to bear arms in support of the militia. The delegation of power to the government and the states created and institutionalized a dual military tradition with a professional army controlled by the government and citizen militia enrolled in at the state level. The wariness, however, of anti-Federalists over the requirement for a standing army would become one of the differences that would crystallize in the decade of the Republic and formation of the Federalists and Jeffersonian Republicans.[7]

In 1789, George Washington was elected the first President of the United States. In his two terms, he brought the Constitution to life, translating the words on the parchment into actions. Henry Knox carried over from the confederation government and took the post of Secretary of War, establishing the War Department and working with Congress to establish a framework for the standing army. In the background of establishing the Army of the United States, the situation on the frontier began to move toward war. Tensions between the government and the Miami and Shawnee had been increasing beginning in the 1780s. Two campaigns met with failure. The defeat of Brigadier General Josiah Harmar's and Major General Arthur Sinclair's forces led to the creation of the Legion of the United States under the command of Major General "Mad" Anthony Wayne. The legion, a combined arms force of infantry, cavalry, and artillery, was a reflection of Wayne's grim determination to succeed. After negotiations failed in 1792, Wayne marched west and in 1794 defeated the Indians in what became known as the Battle of Fallen Timbers. It broke the back of the native resistance and opened up the northwest to permanent American settlement. Moreover, the Army's presence on the frontier established another important precedent that would carry on until the end of the nineteenth century. The Army not only enforced the will of the national government at the edge of civilization; it was also an important force in opening the frontier and kick starting local economies as they supplied the far-flung frontier posts of the army.[8]

The relative success of Wayne's Legion in securing the old northwest was the result of a fruitful application of force and a demonstration in the minds of the Federalists of a military policy that worked. In the meantime, the Washington administration worked on legislation to rationalize the militia into a more coherent force through greater federal control. Rather than accepting full control, the act passed by Congress provided no federal money for state militias to purchase standard equipment, and relied on the states for oversight. States not complying with the law were not punished, making it difficult to incorporate the militia as a reserve force to supplement the Army. The militia bill was symptomatic of the increased partisanship as like-minded politicians began to coalesce into what would become the Federalists and Democratic- or Jeffersonian Republicans. The mobilization of the militia in response to the so-called whiskey rebellion in 1791 also created a division of opinion over the use of force. No shots were fired, several organizers were arrested, two were tried but both pardoned by the President. For the Federalists, the mobilization of the militia was a successful use of force in a national emergency. The opponents of the policy saw the use of force as excessive and unnecessary and despite the ratification of the underlying premise of the Constitution, the Federalist tendency to err on the side of force would prove to be the undoing of the Federalists.[9]

JOHN ADAMS, THOMAS JEFFERSON, AND THE END OF THE FEDERALISTS

When Adams took office in 1797, his administration would be beleaguered with issues dealing with the war between France and Britain. The Washington administration had attempted to mollify the British in 1794 with the passage of the Jay Treaty. It got the British out of forts that they had occupied since the end of the Revolution, but was only a temporary respite from the blow back of the ongoing wars with France. Fearful of the growing centralized power of the state, which included a larger Army and the beginnings of a Navy with the passage of the first naval act in 1794, John Adams was faced with bitter fights in the hall of Congress and overseas.[10]

With French passions afire as a result of the Jay Treaty, followed by blatant attempts to extort money from an American delegation sent to France to negotiate with the government to smooth out relations (the infamous XYZ affair), Adams was effectively engulfed in an undeclared war. Known as the Quasi-War, it would prove to be the undoing of his administration. In the aftermath of the French Revolution, the provisional government continued to evolve into a more radical form. Regardless, news of the Jay Treaty was perceived by the French as a repudiation of their alliance with America forged during the Revolution, and as a new relationship with Great Britain.

Lashing out, French privateers began to prey on American commercial shipping. Adams' attempt to defuse the situation through diplomatic channels was rebuffed. There would be no negotiations until the delegation paid a substantial bribe. News of this inflamed American public opinion and prompted a demand for action.

Adams took action at sea and on land. Adams inherited a nascent navy that had been created in the Washington administration. Independence from Great Britain meant that American commerce was no longer protected. With the continental powers engulfed in war and the various kingdoms and sultanates of North Africa preying on American commerce in the Mediterranean, something had to be done. In 1794, a naval act was passed to provide for the construction of six frigates to combat the Barbary powers of North Africa. In 1797, three frigates were funded—the *United States*, *Constitution*, and *Constellation*. These ships would become legends in the nascent navy, protecting commerce against the privations of the Barbary States and the predatory practices of British and French commerce raiders. Of equal importance was a decision to expand the army.[11]

As tensions with France increased, it created a frenzy of activity that played a large part in limiting John Adams to one term, marking the end of the Federalist reign in the Executive Mansion. In 1798, the Federalist-dominated Congress passed the Alien and Sedition Acts. Signed by President Adams, the Alien and Sedition Acts for all intents and purposes stifled dissent of foreign-born critics in the press and led to arrests, and would become a key issue in the election of 1800. Congress also authorized the creation of several volunteer armies that, while never established, were seen by Jefferson's legislative allies as a tool to stifle dissent.[12] The most infamous, the so-called New Army, was largely the creation of Alexander Hamilton and his legislative allies. In a lapse in judgment, George Washington accepted the command of the New Army with Hamilton as his second. With a deep dislike of Hamilton, Adams charted his own path and commissioned another peace delegation to France, negotiating an end to the clash. As a result, the Treaty of 1778 was abrogated, and the French reaffirmed American neutrality. Adams had certainly demonstrated his fortitude in ending the conflict, but it came too late to save his administration. He lost the election of 1800 and Thomas Jefferson became the third President of the United States.[13]

Thomas Jefferson knew how to exercise power. He was not a soldier. During the Revolution, he was the author of the Declaration of Independence and the war-time governor of Virginia. Given his experiences, education, and personality, he was cognizant of the fine line between despotism and liberty. Despite his inclination toward using citizen soldiers on land and at sea (including gunboats to guard the coast), he understood the utility of the military and used it as needed. Given the politics of the New Army formulated by the Federalists, Jefferson did not dismantle the Army nor the Navy, but he did insure its loyalty to him. Congress passed the Military Peace Establishment Act that did not reduce the Army per sè, but aligned its authorized strength with the men already serving in uniform. By matching the number of men in uniform to what Congress would allow by law, Jefferson could more easily eliminate officers who were Federalists by legislative fiat. Jefferson wanted an Army that was loyal not only to the administration but also to republican principles. Given his own interests in education, he established the United States Military Academy at West Point, New York, to also provide a path for those with republican values to serve in the Army. Given Jefferson's interests in natural philosophy, in the aftermath of the

Louisiana Purchase, it is no surprise that the Army took a leading role in exploration—Captains Meriwether Lewis and William Clark journeyed up the Missouri, across the Rocky Mountains to the Columbia River and back, and Lieutenant Zebulon Pike charted the central and southern portions of the purchase. While Jefferson was successful in depoliticizing the Army and creating institutions that made the officers in particular more egalitarian, the Army and administrative infrastructure remained small, which would have an effect on Jefferson's successor, James Madison, as he prepared to go to war with Great Britain in 1812.[14]

Jefferson's challenges extended beyond the shores of the United States to North Africa and Europe. Between 1801 and 1805, a naval squadron did battle with the Pasha of Tripoli. Rather than paying more tribute to the Pasha, which he demanded when the previous treaty broke down, Jefferson ordered the navy to blockade Tripoli and stop the depredations against American commerce. From 1801 until 1803, American naval squadrons forced the issue with the Barbary States, using force to stop the raiding of American merchant ships in the Mediterranean. The professionalism of the Navy was apparent, but it could not deter the British from interfering with American commerce carrying goods to neutral ports, the so-called Orders in Council. With Napoleon's control of Western Europe complete and the British Navy effectively blockading ports around the French Empire, as the largest neutral carrier, American ships faced being boarded by British vessels. With the British frustrated over the difficulties of enforcing the Orders in Council as well as the rash of desertions that occurred in American ports, the British Frigate *Leopard* fired upon the American frigate *Chesapeake*, crippling the ship and killing three sailors. The incident was regrettable and the British attempted to apologize, but they would not back down from impressing sailors.[15]

The Adams and Jefferson administrations offer unique opportunities for museums. Beyond providing a time line of the events of the late eighteenth century, illustrating the partisanship of the 1790s as unbridled, dirty, personal politics provides a bridge to our twenty-four hour news cycle. By comparing and contrasting the actions of John Adams and Thomas Jefferson with those of our current leaders, despite the vitriol displayed by the twenty-first-century political process, these comparisons could provide the basis for a discussion on how partisanship and perceptions shaped national defense policy. Jefferson was ready to use force to protect American interests. It is easy to lose sight of the fact that the United States came into being in an increasingly dangerous world through which, luckily, it was able to navigate. For Thomas Jefferson, however, despite his successes, many of the international irritants of his two terms would come to the surface in a big way for his successor, initiating a new conflict with Great Britain.

THE WAR OF 1812

The year 2012 marked the beginning of the bicentennial commemoration of the war of 1812. After two centuries, historians still have much to say about the war. There has been a modest increase in monographs about the War of 1812, as well as many commemorative events at historic sites and battlefields in Canada and the United States. Regardless of the increased coverage, at least in the United States, the particulars of the War of 1812 are largely unknown to the public. Moreover, the war's origins and legacy are contested. There is little agreement in the historical community over the war's origins. There are many issues to consider, some that grow in importance and subside depending upon who says what and when. In Canada, the unmistakable popular perception of the war is the beginning of Canada as a nation distinct from its American cousin.[16]

Whether you are a professional historian or the general public, the opaque reasons for war allow historians and museumgoers alike to explore the complexities of the war and come up with their own conclusions. Often called the second American Revolution, a sentiment that is debatable at best, the war offers a transition from the era of the Revolution and early Republic to continental expansion that would define most of the nineteenth century.[17] It is a conflict that marked the beginning of the professionalization of the US Army and the roots of a competent and skilled Navy. While not as momentous as a second war for independence, it marks a clear end of the transition to an independent republic to an expanding nation, insular in its outlook to the world beyond its shores.

It is fair to say that there is no agreement on any one single cause. Any time an exhibit or piece of interpretive media delves into the root causes of a conflict, it should be up to the visitors to make their own decision based upon the evidence provided to them. In the case of the War of 1812, there were both domestic and international pressures that worked in concert with each other, forcing the issue for President James Madison and a declaration of war against Great Britain. The individual issues that contributed to the decision for war can be summarized as follows:

- American maritime rights, as a neutral power. Ever since the onset of the wars with Napoleon Bonaparte, the right of the United States to carry goods had been infringed upon, in particular by the British. With the destruction of the French and Spanish fleets at the Battle of Trafalgar in 1805 and the subsequent closure of European markets to neutral carriers who touched English shores, it was clear to all that Britannia ruled the waves. The United States was caught in the middle and subjected to seizures by the British, which touched on American rights.
- Impressment of American sailors. The Royal Navy was desperate for the experienced sailors. Admittedly, British deserters could blend in with merchant and American naval crews with relative ease. The lack of conclusive identity documents made it difficult to distinguish deserters from either native born or naturalized citizens. The previously mentioned incident with the American frigate *Chesapeake* was provoked by this very issue.
- The War Hawks and Western Interests. Henry Clay, Speaker of the House from Kentucky, led the effort for war. Impatient over diplomatic wrangling and economic warfare, Clay led the effort for war and was a symbol for Western interests. With the defeat of Shawnee at Tippecanoe in 1811, British material and weapons were found, enflaming the passions of nonnative populations moving into the old northwest. Conditioned by what was perceived as British interference along the frontier, many western politicians voted for war and stood with President Madison. There is no doubt that some westerners may have expressed strong views of moving the borders of the United States at the expense of British Canada, but this was a minority view and wishful thinking.

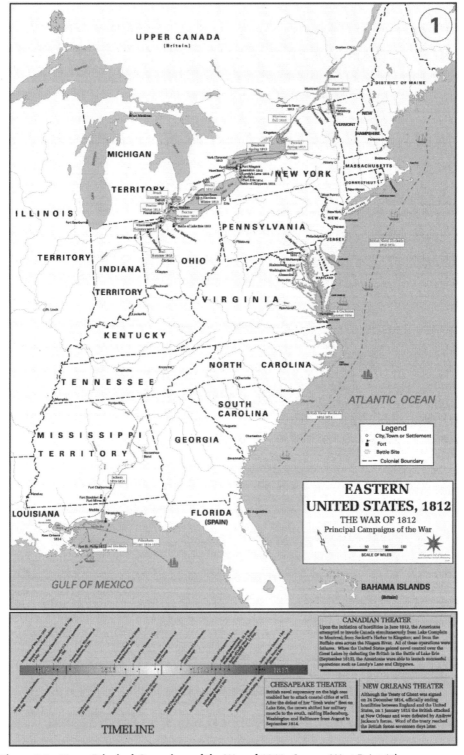

Figure 5.1 Map—Principal Campaigns of the War of 1812. *Source:* West Point Atlas

- Ideology and domestic policies. Since the election of Thomas Jefferson, the Republicans held power for over a decade. In the vote for war, Federalists, representing the commercial interests that lost the most in the decline of trade with the British, were decidedly against the war and voted as a block. Balanced against the Federalists' domestic interests was the Republicans' continued distrust of British power. There were some Republicans who felt that a more aggressive stance against Britain was necessary.

Each of these points alone cannot fully explain why the United States went to war with Great Britain. It seems reasonable, however, to assume that each one of these points contributed to the decision of war.[18]

1812–1814: THE WAR BEGINS AND UNRAVELS

The United States was unprepared for war. The army was authorized to expand to 60,000 but barely reached a quarter of that before the war came to an end. As in the Revolution, the volunteer militia had a pivotal role to play, but many states did not allow citizen soldiers across the international border into Canada because of constitutional scruples. Moreover, the New England states, stolidly Federalist and against the war, were not interested in contributing militia.[19] War planning was also in disarray. Political resistance from New England forced most operations to track further west. Other operations would occur in the South and along the Chesapeake, but most American efforts took place in the upper Midwest, buoyed by the fact that Canada had a small population base and 7,000 British Regulars and Canadian volunteers spread over a lengthy frontier that was in excess of 1,000 vulnerable miles. The greatest irony in all of these preparations is that, as Madison prepared his war address, Britain was willing to mitigate the blockade by granting licenses to American shipping, ameliorating one of the stickiest issues between the two countries.[20]

In the first two years of the war, the Americans went on the offensive to take the war into British Canada. Rather than seeing a resounding success, they met with failure. In 1812, Henry Dearborn, a veteran of the American Revolution, planned a complicated, three-pronged assault into various parts of British Canada, all of which failed.[21] In 1813, British forces and their Indian allies led by Tecumseh, lunged south into the Ohio Valley while Americans assaulted British forts on Lake Erie and Ontario.[22] The spectacular naval victories against a British flotilla by Commodore Oliver H. Perry on Lake Erie cut the supply line to British forces operating to the south. When Tecumseh and his British counterpart retreated, William Henry Harrison went north as the British forces retreated. In a pitched battle on the Thames River, Tecumseh was killed, which secured the northwest for absorption into the United States. As spring fell away, skirmishes with British forces and mediocre leadership would force the Americans to abandon their gains by the end of the year. The last major action along the Northern border was another attempt at Montreal. A two-pronged assault was beset by personality clashes between the principal American commanders James Wilkinson and Wade Hampton. Moving late in the campaign season, after two battles, both sides retired to their respective winter camps.[23]

As the British blockade grew in effectiveness, American exports and imports crashed, virtually eliminating a vital income stream in the form of import duties. Moreover, the British raided communities along the Chesapeake with impunity. With British ships in close proximity to slave-holding states, some slaves voted with their feet and joined the British. Rather than pursuing the British, local militia companies remained watchful over the potential of a slave rebellion. Further to the south, Andrew Jackson gained the attention of the national press with his destructive war against the

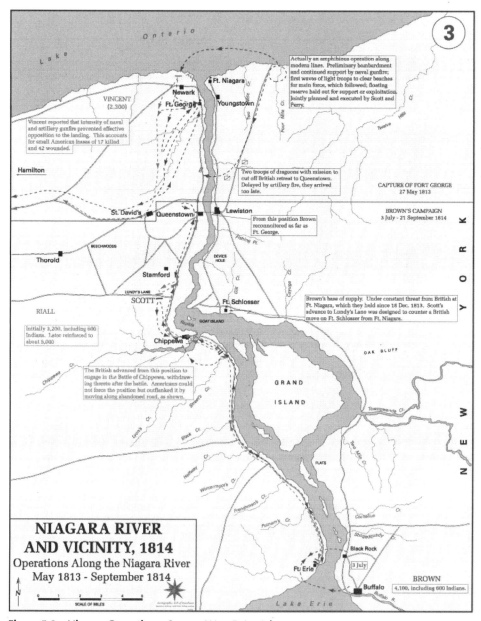

Figure 5.2   Niagara Operations. *Source*: West Point Atlas

Creeks. The Creek bands split among those who wanted to fight the Americans and those who wanted peace. As war parties struck against settlements, Jackson struck back, in March 1814, breaking the back of the Indian resistance. Despite the fact that some Creeks had remained loyal, Jackson called a Treaty Council, stripping *all* Creeks of their lands, opening up the southeast to settlement. Perceived as a success, Jackson emerged from the Creek war a hero, securing a promotion and assuming command of all American forces in the southeast.[24]

The relative successes of 1813 meant little as the New Year rolled around. The year 1814 saw some success along the Niagara River where British forces were met by well-trained American regulars led by Jacob Brown and Winfield Scott. In the subsequent battles along the Niagara peninsula—Chippewa and Lundy's Lane—the Americans fought the British toe to toe, though the final result was a draw.[25] To the south, British command of the sea lanes allowed the Royal Navy to move up and down the coast, raiding communities from New England to the Chesapeake with impunity. By far, Britain's greatest effort was along the Chesapeake Bay. Vice Admiral Alexander Cochrane, Rear Admiral George Cockburn, and Major General Robert Ross led troops up the Potomac. Brushing aside American resistance at Bladensburg, the British reached Washington, DC, and burned public buildings. Unlike their successes at Washington, the British could not capture Baltimore. Fort McHenry successfully kept the British fleet at bay, and the local militia stopped a British column that had landed outside of the city, resulting in the death of General Ross. Despite the repulse of the British, the successful destruction of Washington demonstrated how thin American resources were. Concentrated upon the northern frontier, the Army was unable to muster enough forces to protect the Capitol.

Figure 5.3   Battle For Lundy's Lane. *Source*: Library of Congress

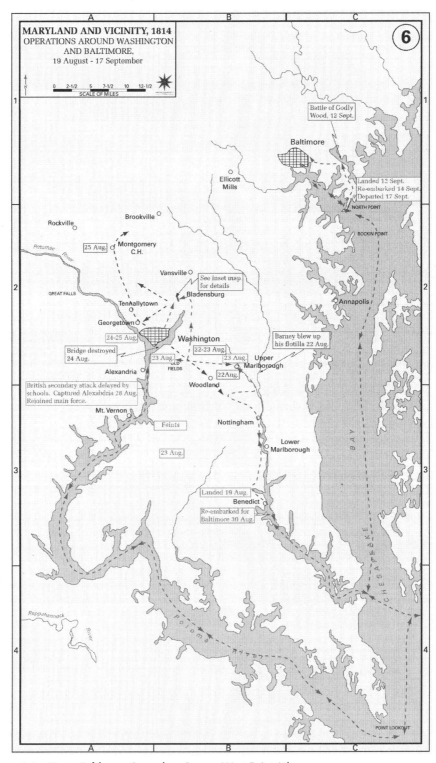

Figure 5.4 Map—Baltimore Campaign. *Source*: West Point Atlas

The battles that took place along the northern frontier with Canada and the Mid-Atlantic States are commemorated and interpreted by Americans and Canadians. Generally speaking, the fact that Americans never conquered a Canadian province, let alone convince the Canadians to join the American cause, in popular memory the War of 1812, triggered the first stirrings of Canadian nationality and identity. For Americans, Lundy's Lane and Chippewa show that Americans could best British troops, just as they had in the Revolution. National myths may have been born in these battles, but it gives interpreters several opportunities to not only speak to the traditional narrative of what took place but also to speak to the interaction between history and memory. At times, national myths are difficult to overcome, but using techniques that deflate myth with factual information, the visitor is given the opportunity to make up his or her own mind, regardless of what he or she has learned previously. For Americans in particular, there is no better place to examine these national myths than what took place on the high seas.

NAVAL ACTIONS ON THE HIGH SEAS

After the dismal performance of the Army and militia along the border in the opening stages of the war, the Navy provided the only glimmer of good news. While the British ruled the seven seas, with so many commitments around the world, the resources available to North America could be described as thin. On the American side, as with the Army, the small Navy Department was overwhelmed as it prepared to mobilize whatever ships it had at its disposal. Knowing that British commerce was the key to the Empire, as in the Revolution, the government commissioned independent privateers to prey on British shipping around the world. While a small American flotilla of five ships went to sea early in the war (it was largely unsuccessful in either disrupting British commerce or its fleets), what captured the public's imagination was the success of individual ships. The *USS Constitution* under the command of Isaac Hull, defeated the 38-gun frigate *HMS Guerrière* in August 1812, and William Bainbridge captured the 38-gun frigate *HMS Java* in December 1812. Despite impressive victories in single ship combat, the Royal Navy effectively shut down American trade and whatever warships the Republic had remained bottled up in port. Unfortunately, after the successes of ship-to-ship combat, they were of no help for the rest of the war.[26]

The victories on the Great Lakes and on the Atlantic Ocean continue to elicit a great deal of popular interest, considering that the *USS Constitution* is still a commissioned ship in the United States Navy. The museum and ship are part of Boston's Freedom Trail and can be found in Boston's Charleston Navy Yard, now a unit of the National Park Service. The ship is a vivid touchstone to the past and, given its association with the War of 1812, an ideal platform to explore the ambiguities of the war's origins and legacies. The U.S.S. Constitution Museum is not a traditional naval museum. The staff works very hard to not only engage family groups with activities and exhibits related to life at sea, but the exhibits are also designed to provoke discussion, engaging young and old alike on the origins of the war and the successes of the Navy. The US Navy still operates the *Constitution* with a Navy crew, and it remains a commissioned ship. The museum is an independent foundation. The Navy is a key partner and they have

Figure 5.5   U.S.S. Constitution at War. *Source*: Library of Congress

an amicable relationship. The museum has the luxury of its own fabrication shop, so they can constantly test new ideas and see how they work with the audience. The moment you enter the museum you can see that children and families are their primary audience. Using learning labs, groups can use gaming to explore the origins of the war and its legacy by choosing the winners and losers in the war. The primary exhibits on the bottom floor that explore the history of the *Constitution* use hands-on exhibits to explore the art and science of ship building and explore the history of the ship in a friendly and approachable way. The second floor of the exhibit focuses on the crew. Using cutouts of contemporary actors playing the roles of officers, crew members and families, the exhibit gives the audience plenty of opportunities to build a relationship with crew members that appeal to their sensitivities and backgrounds. Interactive exhibits allow the audience to unfurl a sail, go through the motions of firing a cannon, crawl into a hammock, and explore the cuisine of a warship. Finally, they explore the darker side of service on a warship—death and dying, in a very tasteful and compelling way, reminding everyone that there is a price to pay for service.[27]

The museum succeeds because it constantly evaluates the interests of their audience. Curators and interpreters too often make assumptions on what the audience wants based on their expectations and knowledge. Curators and interpreters are, by their nature, dedicated to understanding the resources they protect, and will often make assumptions on what the audience would want based on their own expectations rather than the audience. The U.S.S. Constitution Museum is more than a traditional maritime museum. It is a place for intergenerational learning and dialogue about a war that even today is not well known and largely ignored. The ship is manned by a

Figure 5.6 The Costs of War laid bare at the U.S.S. Constitution Museum. *Source*: Author Photograph

detachment of sailors who volunteer for service on the *Constitution*. On a visit to the museum, the ship brings the exhibits alive by connecting the events in the museum to the ship itself. The crew is friendly, approachable, and very knowledgeable.[28]

END GAME AND LEGACIES

While the war was raging in North America, American and British diplomats were struggling to find common ground. Unable to communicate instantaneously, when the British repealed their orders in council, Madison was moving forward to declare war. In March 1813, the Russians offered to mediate between the two parties, and in response the Americans sent a peace delegation to Europe. The British rejected mediation but made a counter offer that demanded a response. In March 1814, the President sent another delegation to Europe and the British assembled a delegation in May. In North America, the British focused on the Gulf Coast of the United States and, in particular, New Orleans. After the victory against the Creeks, Andrew Jackson responded to British moves. Jackson advanced against a combined British and Spanish garrison in Pensacola and was ready to move on to Mobile, when it became apparent that New Orleans would be the next target. The British began their approach to

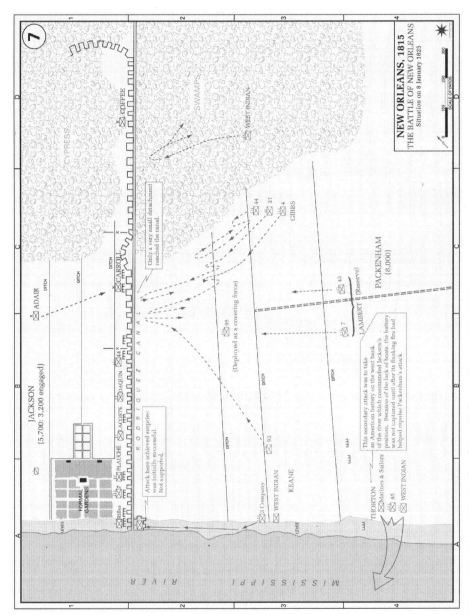

Figure 5.7   Map—The Battle of New Orleans. *Source:* West Point Atlas

Figure 5.8   Battle of New Orleans. *Source*: Library of Congress

New Orleans in January 1815, attacking Jackson's main position in a frontal assault. It was a blood bath with the British suffering 2,000 casualties. The attack on New Orleans was futile. While the British attacked, peace terms had already been agreed to. The British wanted security for Canada; the Americans wanted to make certain the circumstances that led to the American declaration did not reoccur. With British public opinion wanting to end the war and not wanting to incur a larger debt from a war in North America, both sides agreed to turn back time and restore the status quo, that is, return captured land and honor the international borders as they existed in 1812. American land occupied by the British would be returned. With the war in Europe now over, the issue of neutral rights and impressment were null and void. The United States and Canada retained their territorial integrity. But the question Was it worth it? remains.[29]

From the perspective of our national narrative, the War of 1812 has a mixed legacy. On the one hand, 1812 was the last armed conflict between Great Britain and the United States. Tensions would certainly ratchet up during the Civil War, but never again would the two powers go to war. As a result of this peace, the United States turned inward, devoting its considerable energies to internal developments and expansion. Spain lost control of Florida, and Britain ended support for Indians south of the Canadian border, securing the old northwest and the Ohio country. The very expansion that would propel the United States reminds us of the one people who paid the ultimate price for American success—the native peoples in the Mississippi River basin and beyond, who were unable to depend upon the British for support. A cycle of broken promises and violence would continue across the country until the closing of the frontier in 1890.

NOTES

1. Richard H. Kohn, *Eagle and Sword: The Beginnings of the Military Establishment in America* (New York: The Free Press, 1975), 283.

2. For a concise overview of the challenges of this period through the lens of the officer corps, see William B. Skelton, *An American Profession of Arms: The Army Officer Corps, 1784–1861* (Lawrence: University Press of Kansas, 1992), Chapter 4. See also, Robert Wooster, *The American Military Frontiers: The United States Army in the West, 1783–1800* (Albuquerque: University of New Mexico Press, 2009).

3. Richard H. Kohn, *Eagle and Sword*, 17–39, Russell F. Weigley, *History of the United States Army* (New York, NY, 1967), 74–79, Millett, et al., *For the Common Defense*, 77–79, Skelton, *American Profession of Arms*, 68–70. For those who served as officers but who could not be considered part of the land-holding elite of the former colonies, gained social status due to their service in the revolution, something that cannot be discounted in the struggle to gain legitimacy in the years after the revolution, see Derrick E. Lapp, "Did They Really 'Take None But Gentleman'? Henry Hardman, the Maryland Line, and a Reconsideration of the Socioeconomic Composition of the Continental Officer Corps," *Journal of Military History* 78 (October, 2014): 1239–61.

4. Weigley, *History of the US Army*, 78–81, Kohn, *Eagle and Sword*, 40–53.

5. Quoted from Kohn, *Eagle and Sword*, 75. For confederation military policy, see also, 54–72 and Weigley, *History of the US Army*, 80–84.

6. The preamble of the Constitution implies that the new national government will provide for the common defense. Article 1, Section 7 gives Congress the authority to raise revenue. Article 1, Section 8 delegates various war-making powers to Congress such as granting letters of marque, raising and supporting armies, providing for a navy, regulating land and naval forces, and providing for the militia. Article II, Section 2 names the President of the United States the commander-in-chief of the Army and Navy and the militia when called into federal service.

7. Kohn, *Eagle and Sword*, 73–88, Weigley, *History of the US Army*, 84–88.

8. Kohn, *Eagle and Sword*, 91–127 and 141–57, Weigley, *History of the US Army*, 90–93. See also, Alan D. Graff, *Bayonets in the Wilderness: Anthony Wayne's Legion in the old Northwest* (Norman: University of Oklahoma Press, 2004). For an exploration of the army on the frontier, beginning with Wayne's campaign, see Robert Wooster, *The American Military Frontiers: The United States Army in the West, 1783–1900* (Albuquerque: University of New Mexico Press, 2009).

9. Kohn, *Eagle and Sword*, 157–73. For the legislative battle over the militia act, see Michael Doubler, *Civilian in Peace, Soldier in War, The Army National Guard, 1636–2000* (Lawrence: University Press of Kansas, 2003), 66–69.

10. Kohn, *Eagle and Sword*, 193–218.

11. Hagan, *This People's Navy*, 21–53, Harold and Margaret Sprout, *The Rise of American Naval Power, 1776–1918* (Princeton: Princeton University Press, 1944), 24–38, Ian W. Toll, *Six Frigates: The Epic History of the Founding of the U.S. Navy* (New York: W.W. Norton & Company, 2006), 1–62. For a detailed look at the legislative battle over naval legislation, see

Craig L. Symonds, *Navalists and Anti-Navalists: The Navy Policy Debate in the United States, 1785–1827* (Newark: University of Delaware Press, 1980.

12. There is often a variety of terms used to describe the various components of the New Army. The existing or old army had four infantry regiments, born out of the dissolution of Anthony Wayne's Legion. The New Army approved by Congress in 1798 would have allowed for twelve regiments of infantry and four of mounted infantry or dragoons. In May 1798, the ability to raise volunteer companies as well as a 10,000 man provisional army was authorized. In 1799, the eventual army was authorized to appoint officers but not men for a force that could repel an invasion. Despite the authorization, with the exception of the New Army, none of these plans saw any follow-through. Foot note, Kohn, *Eagle and Sword*, 229.

13. Richard Kohn provides the most extensive coverage of these episodes. See Kohn, *Eagle and Sword*, Chapters 10–13. For Washington's part in this affair, see Ellis, *His Excellency*, 248–54. For Adams' view of Hamilton, see Joseph J. Ellis, *Passionate Sage: The Character and Legacy of John Adams* (New York: W.W. Norton & Company, 2001), 62–63, 76–78. For an in-depth look at naval operations, see Michael A. Palmer, *Stoddert's War: Naval Operations During the Quasi War with France* (Chapel Hill: University of North Carolina Press, 1987).

14. The most useful book for this time period is Theodore J. Crackel, *Mr. Jefferson's Army: Political and Social Reform in the Military Establishment, 1801–1809* (New York: New York University Press, 1987). For the Federalist view, see Donald R. Hickey, "Federalist Defense Policy in the Age of Jefferson, 1801–1812," *Military Affairs* 45 (April, 1981): 63–70. See also, Weigley, *History of the US Army*, 105–115, Francis Paul Prucha, *The Sword of the Republic: The United States Army on the Frontier, 1783–1846* (Lincoln: Bison Books, 1986), Chapters four and five.

15. Ian W. Toll, *Six Frigates*, Chapters 5–9; Hagan, *This People's Navy: The Making of American Sea Power*, 54–71; Thomas G. Paterson, J. Garry Clifford, Kenneth J. Hagan, *American Foreign Policy: A History to 1914* (Lexington: D.C. Heath and Company, 1983), 39–42.

16. Journalist and popular Canadian historian Pierre Berton wrote many books on various aspects of Canadian history in his long career, including the war of 1812. His books on 1812 provide an easy narrative from a uniquely Canadian perspective, Pierre Berton, *War of 1812* (Anchor Canada, 2011). Compendium of *The Invasion of Canada* and *Flames Across the Border*. For a more academic look at the Canadian perspective, see John R. Grodzinski, "Opening Shots from the Bicentenary of the War of 1812: A Canadian Perspective on Recent Titles," *The Journal of Military History* 76 (October 2012): 1187–1201.

17. A well-respected historian of the War of 1812, Donald Hickey dismisses the threat to America's independence as "more imagined than real. It existed mainly in the minds of thin-skinned [Jeffersonian] Republicans who were unable to shake the ideological legacy of the Revolution and interpreted all British actions accordingly." From Donald Hickey, *The War of 1812: A Forgotten Conflict* (Chicago: University of Illinois Press, 1990), 300. The same sentiment is expressed in an abridged edition of the above book, *The War of 1812: A Short History. Bicentennial Edition* (Chicago: University of Illinois Press, 2012), 115.

18. For a good place to begin to understand how historians parse out the origins debate, see Jasper M. Trautsch, "The Causes of the War of 1812: 200 Years of Debate," *Journal of Military History* 77 (January 2013): 273–93. For the global context, see Jeremy Black, "The North American Theater of the Napoleonic Wars, Or, As It Is Sometimes Called, The War of 1812," *Journal of Military History* 76 (October, 2013): 1053–66. See also, Hickey, *War of 1812*, 1–28. To see how trade figures into war planning for President Madison, see Donald R. Hickey, "American Trade Restrictions During the War of 1812," *The Journal of American History* 68 (December, 1981): 517–38.

19. Weigley, *History of the United States Army*, 117–26, Coles, *The War of 1812*, 38–45.

20. Hickey, *War of 1812: A Short History*, 17–26.

21. Hickey, *War of 1812: A Short History*, 26–32. See also, Theodore J. Crackel, "The Battle of Queenstown Heights, 13 October 1812" in Charles E. Heller and William A. Stofft. *America's First Battles, 1776–1965* (Lawrence: University Press of Kansas, 1986), 33–56.

22. Hickey, *War of 1812: A Short History*, 40–43.

23. Hickey, *War of 1812: A Short History*, 40–51, Cole, *The War of 1812*, 107–148. For the Battle of Lake Erie, see Hagan, *This People's Navy*, 82–88, Stephen Howarth, *A History of the United States Navy, 1775–1998* (Norman: University of Oklahoma Press), 105–113. See also, Harry L. Coles. *The War of 1812* (Chicago: The University of Chicago Press, 1965), 121–29, 163–71, Hickey, *The War of 1812*, 130–35, 189–93. The National Park Service manages Perry's Victory and International Peace Memorial, a site that not only tells the story of Perry's victory over the British, but is also a symbol of a lasting peace with Canada. See http://www.nps.gov/pevi/index.htm for more information on the park and its mission.

24. Hickey, *War of 1812: A Short History*, 51–59, Francis Paul Prucha, *The Sword of the Republic: The United States Army on the Frontier, 1783–1846* (Lincoln: University of Nebraska Press, 1969), 112–118.

25. Hickey, *War of 1812: A Short History*, 60–66, Weigley, History of the United States Army, 126–33.

26. Hagan, *This People's Navy: The Making of American Sea Power*, 71–90, Sprout, *The Rise of American Naval Power*, 73–85, Ian W. Toll, *Six Frigates*, Chapters 10–15.

27. August 6, 2014 interview with Robert Kiihine, Exhibit Designer, U.S.S. Constitution Museum, Boston, Massachusetts.

28. Kiihine interview. For information on the Constitution's career, crew, and accomplishments, there are a variety of resources available. Some of the most useful are Charles E. Brodine Jr., Michael J. Crawford, and Christine F. Hughes, *Interpreting Old Ironsides: An Illustrated Guide to the USS Constitution* (Washington, DC: Naval Historical Center, 2007), Matthew Brenckle, Lauren McCormack, Sarah Watkins, *Men of Iron: USS Constitutions War of 1812 Crew* (Boston: USS Constitution Museum, 2012).

29. Hickey, *War of 1812: A Short History*, 78–82, 103–13.

Chapter 6

The Antebellum Period, 1815–1860

War is an art, to attain perfection in which, much time and experience, particularly for the officers, are necessary.

John C. Calhoun[1]

One of the issues that museums and historic sites face when it comes to telling stories of institutions over time is that they are not "sexy', or easily told with the tools that we have available. There are no easy solutions. Far too often, stories of inherently bureaucratic institutions such as the Army and Navy are avoided because of the difficulties in interpreting something one cannot see, touch, or feel. Just because a story is hard to illustrate or tell does not warrant skipping over it. The end of the War of 1812 set forces in motion that laid down the basis for a professional ethic for both soldiers and sailors. The men who served in the Trans-Mississippi west or on the high seas made the military their career and began the process of building a professional ethos around their attitudes, work, and mission. In spite of the nation breaking apart in 1861, the Army and Navy's journey was a remarkable one. It all started with the reforms of John C. Calhoun.

JOHN C. CALHOUN AND HIS QUEST FOR EFFICIENCY

In the years that followed the restoration of peace between Great Britain and the United States, a wave of nationalism swept across America. John C. Calhoun was well positioned to take advantage of the support garnered for the Army. Appointed Secretary of War in 1817 at the age of 35, Calhoun can best be described as a young man with great responsibilities. Over the course of his tenure as Secretary of War, Calhoun instituted reforms that would become institutionalized for the remainder of the nineteenth century.

Calhoun accomplished much. Besides paying down debts incurred during the War of 1812, his key reforms were administrative. The War of 1812 demonstrated the weakness of a small bureaucracy that was asked to do everything, from supervising the mobilization of manpower to securing the necessary armies to be deployed along the border. Rather than delegating responsibilities to others, previous secretaries had taken on too many burdens. Legislation passed in 1816 and 1818 created the necessary staff structure to correct the deficiencies that had overburdened the administration of the Army during the War of 1812. As a result of these legislative reforms, a Subsistence Department was established, focusing on issues of feeding the Army, as well as the appointment of a chief medical officer, whose duties revolved around coordinating medical services throughout the Army, and, finally, an inspector general to regulate the field army.[2]

As part of these reforms, Calhoun attempted to address command issues that needed some resolution after the disasters of 1812. The Constitution identifies the President as the commander-in-chief, but this is a titular role. The President, his cabinet, and the Secretary of War provided strategic direction, but there was not a field officer who could command field forces. Toward the end of Calhoun's term as Secretary of War, he took steps to create a commanding general who would command the field forces in peace and war. These reforms were necessary, but had unintended consequences. While providing the necessary technical expertise required for these specialized duties, the reforms created a divide between staff officers serving in administrative capacities, and line officers serving units in the field. The heads of the bureaus had direct access to the Secretary of War; line officers did not. Specialized departments could define requirements for policy, procedures, and equipment that went against the advice of field commanders. Long-serving officers could use their offices to create fiefdoms in the War Department, making coordination by a central authority difficult to achieve. The other unresolved issue that would linger for the remainder of the nineteenth century was the office of the Commanding General of the Army. The bureaucratic reach of the commanding general was subject to the forcefulness of the person holding the position. Yet, despite the friction between bureaus, the Secretary of War, and the commanding general, the creation of specialized bureaus would create the administrative infrastructure and knowledge necessary for a modern army.[3]

The penultimate legacy of Calhoun was the idea, or should I say ideal, of an expansible army. When the war with Great Britain ended, the US Army was reduced in size to an authorized peace establishment of approximately 12,000 men. As the decade went on, in light of economic issues, and the emerging trends of Jacksonian democracy and egalitarianism, Congress pushed forward legislation in 1821 to cut the authorized strength of the Army in half. Calhoun responded with a plan to provide for a system that allowed the Army to expand in times of emergency, that would honor the dual system of regulars and militia, but with greater efficiency. With the regular army spread along the frontier, there was no threat to liberty. The threat lay in the inability to create a necessary force to meet an emergency that might open the door to a despotic regime, using extreme measures to mobilize the nation for war. To meet this demand, regular army units would be akin to a skeleton in peacetime. In times of emergency, the regular units would absorb men, fleshing out the numbers in the existing regiments to full strength, without resorting to expanding the number of regiments and battalions already in service. The idea was ignored and Congress voted to slash the authorized strength regardless of Calhoun's plans. The volunteer militia would continue to be used to supplement the regulars in an emergency, which is what would happen in the war with Mexico. As the war with Mexico went forward, Congress authorized an expansion of the regular army as well as raising 50,000 volunteers from the states. Calhoun established a precedent that would inspire later-nineteenth-century reformers. Russell F. Weigley captures the essence of Calhoun's legacy in emphatic terms: "For the first time a responsible statesman had urged repudiation of the militia tradition, at least for primary military purposes, and a stress upon the professional establishment as the only part of the country's military inheritance to possess unimpeachable military value."[4]

Interpretation works best when the opportunities that are crafted for the public relate to their interests and experiences. It is more than likely a safe assertion that visitors have been exposed to a bureaucracy that is either dysfunctional or works. Telling the story of institutional change can be done in a variety of different ways. By humanizing the process, that is, seeing it through the eyes of the people who are instituting the change, the visitor can gain a certain amount of empathy for the reasoning behind reform. Calhoun was a prolific writer. Telling a story with the words of the protagonists can be a helpful technique to draw the visitors in. Another technique that humanizes institutional change is role playing. By a person playing the role of Calhoun, the visitor can be presented with a problem and either choose among possible solutions or come up with his or her own. The issues facing Calhoun could be reduced to a set of problems—how do you make certain that soldiers are guaranteed a reliable supply of food while on the campaign? The visitor can choose from among various mechanisms and weigh his or her choice against what Calhoun did. The visitor makes choices based on his or her experiences, providing a link between his or her personal experiences, the choices made by a historical figure, and the relevancy of those choices in the twenty-first century. As institutions and bureaucracies change, there are often winners and losers. As Calhoun strengthened the regular army, the militia also experienced change.

Perhaps the biggest loser in this fight was the militia. Committing to a skeletonized army put a premium on the regulars rather than the militia. The militia itself was evolving away from an enrolled militia to a new paradigm that would hold sway for the rest of the century. With the rise of a middle class and greater economic and social stratification, there was little incentive for affluent members of a community to enroll in a militia. In the 1840s, many states abolished the mandatory enrollment requirement, the cornerstone of universal service. Instead, affluent members of the community raised volunteer regiments. Moved by the romance of military service and the sense of community that comes with volunteer associations, volunteer units popped up across the country. In the years immediately preceding the Civil War, these units in their colorful uniforms would become the mainstay of civic pride. The regular army, however, continued to show their disdain for volunteer units, in particular during the Mexican War. Ironically, it was state volunteer regiments accepted into federal service that boosted the number of men under arms without the need to greatly expand the authorized strength of the regular army. Citizen soldiers, not regulars, supplied the manpower to expand the regular army.[5]

There are no soaring Granite monuments or iconic historic sites that commemorate and celebrate the first stirrings of professionalization or something akin to that (with the possible exception of the military academy at West Point). The gradual transformation of the Army from a small, insular institution into something that could be

defined as a professional army is a worthy topic. The rise of both the Army and Navy
as something akin to a profession is a major thematic bridge that links the war of 1812
with the Civil War. The officers, the de facto leaders of the Army and Navy, begin
to display characteristics and behavior that are the hallmarks of a profession. In his
groundbreaking book *The Soldier and the State*, Samuel Huntington provides some
general characteristics that define a profession. The first is expertise. As the word suggests, members are equipped with a special skill that sets that group apart from other
people and professions. The second characteristic is responsibility. Officers perform
their duties and responsibilities according to the expectations of their profession and
society in general. A doctor, for example, who breaks his or her Hippocratic Oath is
not performing responsibly within his or her profession. The final point is corporate-
ness. A group shares a common language and sense of unity that sets its members
apart from those in other fields. These elements begin to appear as the nineteenth-
century progresses. They underline the importance of the emergence of the Army and
Navy academies at West Point, New York, and Annapolis, Maryland, respectively.
While it can be argued that a professional officer's corps does not emerge until after
the Civil War, it is undeniable that by the beginning of the Civil War, the basis of what
could be defined as a profession was already in place.[6]

In the aftermath of the War of 1812, West Point, and later the Naval Academy at
Annapolis, began to build the foundations for young officers to become experts in
their trade. As process and procedure became tradition, and curriculum became standardized, the academy became a reference point that all West Pointers could identify
with. Since the military academies are essentially undergraduate institutions, it would
take the creation of the Army and Navy postgraduate school system to provide the
level of expertise that we know today. Nevertheless, the service academies created a
common frame of reference that all regular officers could identify with and that set
them apart from their civilian counterparts. Unlike today when a majority of officer
candidates enter the service through the Reserve Officer Training Corps (ROTC), in
the nineteenth century, the service academies produced the majority of the officers
serving. As Huntington suggests, the military academies provided a sense of corporate
identity, a necessary ingredient for fostering a professional ethic. What was happening
in the Army and Navy was paralleled in similar trends in larger society. The improved
performance of the Army in the Mexican War would certainly demonstrate that a
sharper focus on the craft of being a soldier paid off, but it by no means mitigated an
underlying distrust of the creation of a genuine military aristocracy and, by implication, a threat to the liberty of the nation. While the Army and Navy were not necessarily professional to their fullest extent, they were mature institutions with their own
unique culture and traditions. As the Army showed improvement over the first half of
the nineteenth century, the one constant that showed little promise of abating was the
clash with native peoples in the interior.[7]

THE FRONTIER CONSTABULARY AT WORK

In St. Paul, Minnesota, at the confluence of the Minnesota and Mississippi Rivers is
Fort Snelling. The fort was completed in 1825 and is a vivid reminder of the role the

Army played in the frontier in the antebellum period. While Fort Snelling is unique for its architectural features, notably a large, round stone tower, there are dozens of frontier forts across the west that are powerful reminders that the Army played key roles in expanding American influence and sovereignty across the frontier. As mentioned in previous chapters, the chief duties and responsibilities of the Army were policing the frontier and serving as the arm of the US government in enforcing American law and carrying out Indian policy on the frontier. In the expansion of national authority into the northwest and southeast, the Army was often the chief institution that not only enforced law, but also built the necessary infrastructure that was a prerequisite to wholesale settlement. This was one of the principal and largely forgotten roles the Army played in the antebellum period. Within the context of the old northwest, regulating Indian trade (in particular, whiskey) and keeping squatters off Indian land was a primary and very necessary role. In a very real sense, building forts, maintaining them, and connecting posts and settlements were critical roles that not only guaranteed communications but also provided infrastructure that facilitated settlement. Certain rations could be produced and sold locally, stimulating the local and regional economy. Balanced against the daily life of routine and tedium were missions and duties that brought the soldiers and their officers into conflict with local native communities.[8]

For staff that has the opportunity to work at an old frontier post, connecting the public to the daily life of the officers and men is a relatively straightforward task. Dressing up as soldiers and telling their stories is a technique that seems to draw the public. There is, however, more to this story, a story with a darker edge that has to be confronted. If the period between the end of the War of 1812 and the beginning of the Civil War could be characterized as insular expansion, the primary victims were the native populations that lived in the Southeast and Midwest.

Three episodes characterized this time period: the first and second wars with the Seminoles, Black Hawk's War, and the removal of the Cherokees. At the center of most of these episodes was Andrew Jackson. Jackson personally influenced the ebb and flow of American Indian relations before, during, and after his presidency. To this day, he continues to be a lightning rod of controversy across history, so portraying him as a villain is rather easy. Jackson was a master politician who embodied the needs and desires of the common man. He bristled at the elites that dominated most of the public institutions, including the Army. Yet, he recognized that as President he was the head of state and needed to use the same institutions to move government policy forward. In decisions regarding Indian peoples, he may have been operating out of a sense of paternalism as well as creating a policy that conformed to the will of the people. He was a complicated man. The decisions he made have to be seen in the context of his time. The nation was expanding and something had to give. Rather than accommodating the needs of native populations, the will of the government was to remove them from their native lands to new locales further to the west. In 1830, Congress passed the Indian Removal Act, allowing the United States to negotiate for the removal of the five tribes (Cherokees, Chickasaws, Choctaws, Creeks, and Seminoles) who lived in the Southeast to lands east of the Mississippi. While the US Army did not go to war during the removal process, it is the most visible role they played in the antebellum period. In spite of the Supreme Court affirming that the Cherokees represented a sovereign entity, the Indian Removal Act forced the tribes of the Southeast to negotiate and move or receive no assistance. The subsequent removal of the Cherokees along the Trail of Tears has become the most memorable symbol of the price native groups paid for manifest destiny. The Army provided logistical support for the move, but conditions were less than ideal and many died. While the use of force was not necessary, the move was not an auspicious moment.[9]

It is within the context of the Indian removal that one of the most intractable conflicts of the antebellum period took place: the various wars with the Seminole Indians of Florida. The gradual assimilation of Florida into American rule, culminating in the treaty between Spain and the United States in 1819, would bring the Seminoles into conflict with the Army. In the years before American rule, American forces had clashed in 1816, and again when Andrew Jackson invaded Florida. The clashes resulted in the destruction of several villages, but given the flux of Spanish rule, there were no immediate repercussions. When Florida became a US territory, a reservation was created in 1823, but a subsequent treaty completed in the aftermath of the Indian Relocation Act ordered the Seminoles out of Florida to lands east of the Mississippi. Quite simply, the Seminoles said no. The subsequent murder of an Indian agent and soldiers in December 1835 triggered a response from the Army that would last until 1842. As a precursor to the long and drawn out campaigns against insurgents around the world, the Army waged a war against the Seminoles, using various tactics to force the Seminoles to relocate. Four separate commanders tried both conventional and unconventional tactics, with various degrees of success. Over the course of the conflict, many Seminoles chose to relocate and many preferred to fight. In 1842, as their numbers diminished and they were forced into smaller enclaves deep in the wetlands of south Florida, the war was declared over.[10]

In this era of Indian relocation, one of the only conflicts to occur in the Old Northwest was the so-called Black Hawk War of 1832. The Sauk and Fox people had negotiated a treaty in 1804 that allowed them to stay in their ancestral homes as long as nonnative settlement did not require movement to the east side of the Mississippi. When the Black Hawk crossed the Mississippi to continue to use their native lands, the militia was mobilized in Illinois, fearful of what this movement might mean. In a flight that went from northern Illinois to southern Wisconsin, the Indians clashed with militia from various states as well as the US Army. Overeager civilian volunteers attacked indiscriminately, at one point firing on a group wanting to parlay, lengthening the hostilities and causing more bloodshed. Volunteer militia from the neighboring states may have played a role in the less than professional handling of the situation, but the regulars were under no illusions and relocated the survivors east of the Mississippi.[11]

By the beginning of the 1850s, the Indian removal had accomplished its goal, largely emptying the Northwest and Southeast of their indigenous peoples. While the Civil War would interrupt the move west, the years after the Civil War would see a redoubling of western expansion. The stories of relocation, in particular for the five tribes that went from the Southeast to Oklahoma, are traumatic stories that continue to resonate with the people. The Trail of Tears National Historic Trail is a multistate trail that covers the major routes taken from the Southeast to Indian Territory. It is a story that touches several states and many tribal, local, state, and federal jurisdictions. More frequently, the stories of the Trail of Tears are told from the point of view of people who were affected by the relocation. Amy Lonetree, in her book *Decolonizing*

Museums, charts a strategy for collaboration among native populations that allows these traumatic stories to be told in a truthful manner, from a native perspective. Using case studies from various museums around the country, she argues that museum are places for building respect and healing in communities traumatized by the past. As decolonizing suggests, the key to moving forward is telling the truth. Throughout much of the Army's history, the officers and enlisted men have served as an instrument of the state, enforcing Indian policy with what is perceived as a heavy hand. Looking through the prism of modern history, the Army can be seen as perpetrators of genocide, or at least conscious symbols of conquest and colonization. For historic sites and museums that deal with stories where native and Anglo-America meet, perhaps it is time for, at the very least, conversations with native partners in looking for truth telling and collaboration in a meaningful way.[12]

THE NAVY

In the decades after the War of 1812, the Navy quietly grew its capabilities and professional ethic. As with their peers on the ground, in the aftermath of peace with Great Britain, the postwar naval establishment grew in the decade after 1815. Legislation created a building plan not only for ships similar to the famous *Constitution*, but also for ships of the line, the equivalent of a battleship in the nineteenth century. The ambitious postwar building plans were ratcheted back in light of the economic issues that plagued the country in the 1820s. Nevertheless, the postwar building program was the first comprehensive attempt at a legislated naval policy.[13]

As the fleet grew, the bureaucracy evolved to accommodate it. As Calhoun strove to provide leadership to the specialized services within the Army, the Navy created the Board of Navy Commissioners to help the Secretary of the Navy supervise administration of the Navy, though their authority was purely advisory. As the Navy gradually moved toward steam-powered vessels, the board was abolished to be replaced by various technical bureaus. In terms of officers, again there are some parallels that can be drawn with the Army. Beginning in the 1790s onward, the technical and leadership skills to lead a Man-of-War into combat were well established and there was an emerging ethic that came to flower during the War of 1812. In terms of emerging as a profession, like the Army, that would also progress slowly. However, given the small size of the Navy, by the end of the War of 1812, a professional ethic was present. The officers shared experiences and values that knit them together as a group.[14]

The creation of the US Naval Academy at Annapolis, Maryland, postdates West Point and was not established until 1845, so its presence across the Navy would not be felt until after the Civil War. In its founding years, however, the academy would serve as an incubator of sorts. Much like West Point, the academy was the beginning of the leveling process for the young men who entered into the Navy. Although they came from different backgrounds, the school provided a curriculum and atmosphere that molded the young men into the beginnings of a cohesive corporate body that had shared values. Prior to the founding of the academy, officer education took place at sea. Young men, boys really, went to sea as midshipmen and learned leadership and tradecraft under the watchful eye of their captain and senior enlisted personnel. The education was uneven and capricious, dependent upon the skill and temperament of the captain. The academy standardized the curriculum that inculcated in the student body the ways of the service.[15]

THE MEXICAN-AMERICAN WAR

The American Civil War casts a long shadow over a good portion of the nineteenth century. Unlike the brutal War Between the States that defined an entire generation, the war with Mexico, in the public's mind, is more obscure. Nevertheless, when you look at a modern map of the United States, you can see that the legacy of this war defined our political geography: California, Texas, and the southwestern states were added at Mexico's expense. Otis Singletary, in his classic account of the war with Mexico, characterized the war as an offensive conflict of conquest. Singletary

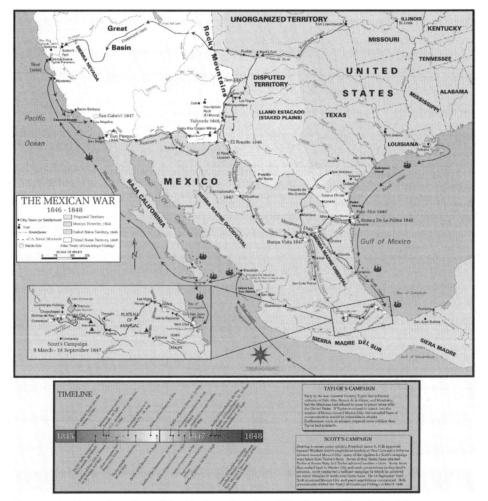

Figure 6.1   Map—Overview of the Mexican-American War. *Source*: West Point Atlas

identified the relative indifference the general population had toward the war in the twentieth century because of our collective guilt. Singletary postulates, "Our indifference to the Mexican War lies rooted in the guilt that we as a nation have come to feel about it. The undeniable fact that it was an offensive war so completely stripped of its moral pretensions that no politician of that era ever succeeded in elevating to the lofty level of a 'crusade.'"[16] It is far too easy in our post-Freudian world to assign guilt to the generations of Americans who benefited from the gains in land from Mexico. Singletary, however, does hit on one of the primary motivations and causations of war with our neighbor to the south: continental expansion.

The war with Mexico cannot be fully understood without putting its causes into the broader context of continental expansion. After the conclusion of the War of 1812, there was a general restlessness and energy that drove the vision of the Republic west to Pacific shores, and south beyond the Rio Grande. Thomas Jefferson thought of this expansion in terms of an Empire of Liberty, stretching from coast to coast, a conglomeration of free states of English-speaking peoples that could create agrarian republics across the continent. As distances became shorter with expanding railroad and telegraph networks, the possibility of expanding from coast to coast became feasible, providing a means for economic expansion and government control over the vast hinterland. The tangible strength of the country was further boosted by a sense of mission and providence that coincided with the clamor for war with Mexico. In 1845, the term Manifest Destiny was coined, presuming a God-given right to the land beyond the Mississippi. With the termination of all Spanish claims to Florida in 1819, the declaration of the Monroe Doctrine proclaiming South America as an American sphere of influence, the opening of the Oregon Trail in the 1840s, and the settlement of the Oregon question with Great Britain in 1846 brought the United States to the Pacific shore. The inexorable expansion of the United States, the boundless empire of liberty, came to a standstill over the question of Texas, Mexico, and the placement of the international border.[17]

If the world view of American policy makers was influenced by something as intangible as Manifest Destiny, there were more tangible issues relating to Texas that proved to be the powder keg for war. In an effort to colonize their northern territories, Spanish authorities provided liberal land grants to American settlers that were honored even after Mexico had won its independence from Spain in 1821. In the tumult of Mexican politics, American settlers and native *Tejanos* were caught up in the Mexican civil war between two factions that wanted central rule for Mexico City versus a federal system that left power to the states. Moreover, the general weakness of the central government meant that most of the power was in the provinces where local authorities built powerful political constituencies that felt more loyalty to local rulers than to the government in Mexico City. The subsequent war between Mexico and Texas resulted in Texas declaring independence in 1836, followed by its formal annexation by the United States a decade later in 1845.[18]

Annexation brought the border issues into tight focus. The Mexican government recognized the historic boundary between the two countries as the Nueces River. The Nueces originates in south central Texas and empties into the Gulf of Mexico at Corpus Christi, Texas. Texans and Americans recognized the border as being located further south, along the Rio Grande, with little precedent to back up their claim, exacerbating an already tense situation. Attempts to negotiate a settlement did not result in any resolution. After annexation, Zachary Taylor was sent into Texas and the Neuces River. With negotiations with the Mexicans going nowhere, Polk ordered Taylor south to the Rio Grande in a hope to ramp up the pressure on the Mexicans to negotiate. The Mexicans responded with surprise and indignation once Taylor arrived and established a presence across from Matamoros in March 1846. After a clash with Mexican cavalry in late April, the clamor for action on both sides of the border commenced. General Mariano Arista crossed the Rio Grande with 6,000 men to attack American fortifications. They held and Taylor attacked to relieve the siege, fighting at Palo Alto on May 8 and Resaca de la Palma on May 9. Taylor's attacks forced the Mexicans back across the Rio Grande and war was declared on Mexico on May 13, 1846.[19]

Polk did not want a lengthy war and preferred to use force as a way to get the Mexicans to the bargaining table. He was the first commander-in-chief to exercise his constitutional authority and oversaw every aspect of the war, both military and political. Conditioned by the thought of a short war, 50,000 volunteers were authorized for a year's service. In addition, there was lobbying for a higher authorized strength for the regular army. The Navy was ordered to blockade Mexico's east coast, and columns were sent into the Northern provinces, using the presence of the Army to force the issue through the bargaining table. What could be characterized as Polk's only territorial ambition, troops were sent into the southwest and naval forces to the California coast with the intent of seizing them for the United States. Support for the war in Congress was by no means unanimous and Polk managed to avoid completely alienating broad sectors of the public, even though sectional differences began to assert themselves over the possible spread of slavery into the new territories. Regardless, prosecution of the war continued as Taylor, waiting for reinforcements, plunged further south, attacking the city of Monterey in September 1846. Taylor succeeded but allowed the remaining Mexicans to leave under an armistice, allowing them to fight again. Two other columns of regulars and volunteers went south and would eventually join Taylor's force at the end of the year.[20]

The origins of the war and the subsequent conflict that occurred along the Rio Grande are, even after nearly 170 years, still emotionally charged events for both sides. At Palo Alto Battlefield National Historical Park, a unit of the National Park Service, the issues of the past and their relevance to the visitors are things that are dealt with every day. Protecting and interpreting the battlefields is an important task of the agency and the park staff, but what the visitors want in terms of programming relates more to the causes and legacies of the war. Most visitors can make an easy comparison of current events in Europe and Southeast Asia and the Mexican War. The park recognizes those connections and certainly provides a hook for the interpreters, but easy comparisons do not reveal much about the events of the war. Rather than making quick and easy value judgments of one country being evil and the other good, the park puts a face to the causes of the war by using the words and stories of the participants on both sides of the conflict. By using the words of those who supported Western expansion or saw the war as evil and immoral, authenticity is given to the past, providing the visitors the space they need to make their own conclusions. The park does not abrogate their responsibility to tell the stories of the battles of Palo Alto and Resaca de la Palma. They tell the story if the audience wants it.[21]

By putting the battles in their larger historical context, larger audiences are drawn in. It is far too easy to interpret historical battlefields at their lowest common denominator with a battlefield narrative that shows movement through space and time. As mentioned previously, the key to successful interpretation is connecting the meanings of the resource to the interests of the visitor. Museums and historic sites that concentrate just on the battlefield narrative risk alienating large sections of a prospective audience that might otherwise have shown interest. The relative successes at Palo Alto battlefield are due in a large part to branching out, by humanizing a story that may be familiar to military historians but not the general public.

Taylor's success along the border was met with good news coming from the west. Stephen Kearney met with success in New Mexico and successfully established American rule before setting his eyes on California. As Taylor's army began invading the city of Monterey in a siege, Kearny continued west to California. The conquest of California was a confusing affair that went through several stages before it was firmly in the control of the United States. John C. Fremont arrived in California in January of 1846 and would remain there, fomenting a revolt of local Anglos. When war was declared, Fremont went south to Monterey and met with the Navy, which took his forces to Los Angeles. A subsequent revolt of locals put the occupation of California in jeopardy, but the arrival of Kearny's column defeated the rebels in southern California, allowing the Americans to once again occupy California. This time the Americans stayed.[22]

As Taylor paused in the interior and the Pacific Coast fell to the United States, there was a pause to consider the next steps. Applying pressure at the peripheries of their empire in order to bring Mexico to the bargaining table did not work. A march on Mexico City, however, in Polk's mind would have the desired effect. As a base of operations, Veracruz proved to be an ideal place to begin. As Polk considered who should take command, Taylor remained in the interior, surrendering many of his men to Scott's expedition. Taking advantage of Taylor's perceived weakness, Mexican General Santa Anna returned from exile, rallied the troops, so to speak, raised an army, and hoped to defeat each American column in detail. The first battle was at Buena Vista against Taylor. Santa Anna failed to break his largely volunteer army but suffered high causalities. Taylor remained in place while Santa Anna went south to defend Mexico City. Despite the political conundrum of finding an apolitical general to lead the campaign against Mexico City (Polk was worried that as a political opponent, Taylor could challenge Polk in an election), Winfield Scott emerged as the general who would lead the Army into the heart of Mexico.[23]

On purely military terms, Winfield Scott's March on Mexico City was a brilliant campaign of maneuver against a determined opponent. Scott needed a secure base of operations and the city of Veracruz met those requirements. It is located on the east coast of the Mexican peninsula, and Scott's route roughly paralleled the route Hernando Cortes had taken centuries earlier. Wanting to get away from the lowlands before fever season set in, and conscious of the impending end of volunteer enlistments, Scott moved quickly. After a brief siege, the city fell at the end of March 1847. Quickly moving west, Scott defeated Santa Anna in a brilliant flanking move at Cerro Gordo in April, but as he got closer to Mexico City, he faced a reckoning. Rather than being burdened with volunteers whose enlistments were about to expire, around 4,000 men, he let them go and waited for additional troops coming from the United States. Resuming his march in August, he found a route flanking the powerful defenses on the outskirts of the city, and he exploited them in two attacks at Contreas and Churubusco. In the heavy fighting that followed, Scott pushed the Mexicans out of their positions and was poised to capture the city when there was a brief armistice before the final battles began several weeks later. In a series of bloody battles on the outskirts of the city, Scott defeated the garrison of Mexican troops at Molino Del Rey and the fortress at Chapultepec, entering the city in September 13, 1847. The occupation of Mexico City brought an end to the fighting in the capital, but not to an immediate treaty. The negotiations would drag on until the beginning of 1848.[24]

The end of the war with Mexico was the first test of Calhoun's system. As commanding general, Scott was hampered by political intrigue, the lack of quick and efficient communications, and an engaged commander-in-chief. Polk understood that the war could catapult both Taylor and Scott into politics, something that Polk did not want to see happen. He trusted Scott more than Taylor, so he received the plum assignment of going to Mexico. Nevertheless, Scott was difficult, bombastic, and had a huge ego that got in the way. The supply services worked reasonably well. Given the distances involved in moving troops and the difficulties in supplying food and clothing in a semitropical environment, the Army did well. The diffusion of expertise into a staff of experts rather than one person proved successful. In spite of these successes, the Americans would remain in Mexico until the issue of a peace settlement was resolved.[25]

Santa Anna resigned and fled Mexico City, and in the chaos that followed there was violence throughout the country. While Scott and Taylor had to deal with attacks on

Figure 6.2   Battle of Chapultepec. *Source:* Library of Congress

supply lines, negotiations moved forward. Although there had been several attempts at negotiations during the course of the war, the occupation of Mexico City forced the issue. The government of Mexico was in no position to demand the restoration of the status quo. After the protracted negotiations had come to a conclusion, the Mexicans renounced their claims to Texas and New Mexico in return for 15 million dollars. The treaty was ratified, but new, unintended problems emerged. The United States had expanded and withdrew from Mexico. Mexican politics would remain stormy for the remainder of the century and into the next. In the continental United States, the seeds of discord that would ultimately lead to the Civil War were sown. In spite of the millions of acres of land added to the Republic, this would be the incubator for disunion. Increasingly, the decade before the Civil War would revolve around bitter debates over the extension of slavery into the new territories.[26]

Is the story of the antebellum Army and Navy worth telling? Yes. In terms of the great American narrative, the origins of the Civil War cannot be understood without a grounding in the events that took place in the years between the end of the country's last war with Great Britain and the beginning of the Civil War. For the story of our military past, the antebellum years provide a bridge between the Army of the Republic and the institutions that we are familiar with in our own time. In the background of the dramatic events that would eventually drive the Union asunder are the quieter trends of institutional change. If the public is ready to handle the complexities of our past, we must strive for a complete picture. There are appropriate interpretive techniques that can be used to tell these stories and provide a lead-in for the most dramatic event of the nineteenth century—the Civil War.

NOTES

1. Weigley, *History of the US Army*, 136.

2 Weigley, *History of the US Army*, 133–138. For sources of reform, see William B. Skelton. *An American Profession of Arms: The Army Officer Corps, 1784–1861* (Lawrence: University Press of Kanas, 1992), 109–19.

3. Skelton, *An American Profession of Arms*, Chapter 12. See also, Richard W. Barsness. "John C. Calhoun and the Military Establishment, 1817–1825," *The Wisconsin Magazine of History* vol. 50, no. 1 (Autumn, 1966): 43–53. To understand the ramifications of individual bureaus, the Quartermaster Corps had some of the widest responsibilities in the army. For the development of the Quartermaster Corps, see Erna Risch, *Quartermaster Support of the Army: A History of the Corps, 1775–1939* (Washington, DC: Office of the Quartermaster General, 1962), Chapter 6. For the issues related to the commanding general, see William B. Skelton, "The Commanding General and the Problem of Command in the United States Army, 1821–1841," *Military Affairs* 34 (December, 1970): 117–22.

4. Weigley, *History of the US Army*, 142–43. See also, Russell F. Weigley. *Towards An American Army: Military Thought From Washington to Marshall* (Westport: Greenwood Press, 1962), Chapter III.

5. Michael Doubler, *Civilian in Peace, Soldier in War*, 90–99; Mahon, *History of the Militia and National Guard*, Chapter Six. A classic work on the martial spirit that permeated the country in the antebellum period can be found in Marcus Cunliffe, *Soldiers and Civilians: The Martial Spirit in America, 1775–1865* (Boston: Little Brown and Company, 1968).

6. Samuel P. Huntington, *The Soldier and the State: The Theory and Politics of Civil-Military Relations* (Cambridge: The Belknap Press of Harvard University Press, 1957), 8–14.

7. Weigley, *History of the US Army*, 145–57. A concise overview of professionalization can be found in Millett and Maslowski, *For the Common Defense*, 117–21 and in Skelton, *An American Profession of Arms*, 166–80. See also, Theodore J. Crackel, *West Point: A Bicentennial History* (Lawrence: University Press of Kansas, 2002). A helpful summary of the army in this time period can be found in William B. Skelton, "The Army in the Age of the Common Man, 1815–1845," in Kenneth J. Hagan and William R. Roberts, ed. *Against All Enemies: Interpretation of American Military History from Colonial Times to the Present* (Westport: Greenwood Press, 1986), 91–106.

8. The classic study that illustrates the important role the army played in developing territories is Francis Paul Prucha, *Broadax and Bayonet: The role of the United States Army in the Development of the Northwest* (Reprint. Lincoln: University of Nebraska Press, 1995). For life on the frontier for officers, enlisted personnel, and families, Edward Coffman, *The Old Army: A portrait of the American Army in Peacetime, 1784–1898* (New York: Oxford University Press, 1986) is an indispensable work.

9. The standard biography of Jackson is Robert V. Remini, *Andrew Jackson* (New York: Harper Row, 1966). For the various views on Jackson's Indian policy, see Ronald N. Satz, *American Indian Policy in the Jacksonian Era* (Lincoln: University of Nebraska Press, 1975) and Francis Paul Prucha, "Andrew Jackson's Indian Policy: A Reassessment," in ed. Francis Paul Prucha. *Indian Policy in the United States: Historical Essays* (Lincoln: University of Nebraska Press, 1981), 139–47. A broad overview of the US Army during this time period can be found in Francis Paul Prucha, *The Sword of the Republic: The United States Army on the Frontier, 1783–1846* (Reprint. Lincoln: University of Nebraska Press, 1986), Chapter 13.

10. Prucha, *The Sword of the Republic*, Chapter 14. A nice summary can be found in Muehlbauer and Ulbrich. *Ways of War*, 152–54. The standard account is John K. Mahon, *History of the Second Seminole War, 1835–1842* (Gainsville: University Press of Florida, 1967). For the Black Hawk War, see Patrick Jung, *The Black Hawk War of 1832* (Norman: University of Oklahoma Press, 2007).

11. Prucha, *The Sword of the Republic*, Chapter 11.

12. Amy Lonetree, *Decolonizing Museums: Representing Native America in National and Tribal Museums* (Chapel Hill: The University of North Carolina Press, 2012).

13. Sprout and Sprout, *Rise of American Naval Power*, 86–104, Hagan. *This People's Navy*, 92–93.

14. Sprout and Sprout, *Rise of American Naval Power*, 92–93. For a very concise summary of navy in this period, see Millet, Maslowski, and Feis, *For the Common Defense*, 108–10.

15. For an understanding of the development of the officer corps in the early nineteenth century, see Christopher McKee, *A Gentlemanly and Honorable Profession: The creation of the US Naval Officer Corps, 1794–1815.* (Annapolis: United States Naval Institute Press, 1991). For the roots of the academy, see Peter Karsten, *The Naval Aristocracy: The Golden Age of Annapolis and the Emergence of Navalism* (New York: Free Press, 1972).

16 Otis A. Singletary, *The Mexican War* (Chicago: The University of Chicago Press, 1960), 5.

17. Thomas G. Patterson, J. Garry Clifford, Kenneth J. Hagan, *American Foreign Policy: A History to 1941, Volume 1* (Lexington: D.C. Heath and Company, 1983), 84–105. For Jefferson's views on expansion, see Joseph J. Ellis, *American Sphinx: The Character of Thomas Jefferson* (New York: Vintage Books, 1998), 251–53. The classic work on Manifest Destiny that still has value is Frederick Merk, *Manifest Destiny and Mission in American History* (New York: Vintage Books, 1966).

18. A nice overview of the events that led to the war and the army's place in those events can be found in Richard B. Winders, *Mr Polk's Army: The American Military Experience in the Mexican War* (College Station: Texas A and M University Press, 1997), Chapter 1. For the Texas Revolution, a good place to start is Stephen L. Hardin, *Texian Iliad: A Military History of the Texas Revolution* (Austin: University of Texas Press, 1994).

19. Singletary, *The Mexican War*, 8–28, K. Jack Bauer, *The Mexican War, 1846–1848* (New York: Macmillan Publishing Company, 1974), 32–66. See also, K. Jack Bauer, "The Battles on the Rio Grande: Palo Alto and Resaca de la Palma, 8–9 May, 1846," in Charles E. Heller and William A. Stofft. *America's First Battles, 1776–1965* (Lawrence: University Press of Kansas, 1986), 57–80. While Bauer's book still remains one of the best narratives of the war, other overviews published recently include John S. D. Eisenhower, *So Far From God: The U.S. War with Mexico, 1846–1848* (New York: Random House, 1989) and David Clary, *Eagles and Empire: The United States, Mexico, and the Struggle for a Continent* (New York: Bantam Books, 2009).

20. Singletary, *The Mexican War*, 28–44, K. Jack Bauer, *The Mexican War*, Chapter 6.

21. E-mail with Douglas Murphy, Chief of Interpretation at Palo Alto Battlefield National Historical Park, September 30, 2014.

22. Singletary, *The Mexican War*, 56–70, K. Jack Bauer, *The Mexican War*, Chapters 10–11.

23. Singletary, *The Mexican War*, 49–54, K. Jack Bauer, *The Mexican War*, 204–26.

24. K. Jack Bauer, *The Mexican War*, Chapters 14–16, Singletary, *The Mexican War*, Chapter 4.

25. Weigley, History of the US Army, 177–82, James A. Hutson, *The Sinews of War: Army Logistics, 1775–1953* (Washington, DC: Office of the Chief of Military History, 1966), 126–54.

26. The juxtaposition of the triumph of nationalism with the completion of the war and the subsequent descent into vicious sectional politics has not gone unnoticed by historians. See David M. Potter, *The Impending Crisis, 1848–1861* (New York: Harper and Row, 1976), Chapter 1 and James M. McPherson, *Battle Cry of Freedom, The Civil War Era* (New York: Oxford University Press, 1988), Chapter 2.

Chapter 7

The Civil War, 1860–1865

In the Civil War and Reconstruction, the United States Army first experienced both the exhilarating potency and the frustrating limitations of modern military power.

Russell F. Weigley[1]

How do we give voice to one of the bloodiest conflicts in American history? Between 2011 and 2015, the United States commemorated the 150th Anniversary of the American Civil War. As we move further away from these traumatic events, the immediacy of the pain and destruction of this great war becomes less palpable, perhaps even less authentic. Yet, everywhere we turn, the reminders of the war still abound. The great stone monuments that are scattered across many of the Civil War battlefields are silent sentinels to how deep the impact was for an entire generation of men and women. If we acknowledge the role that chattel slavery played in the origins of the war, our ongoing conversation about race in the United States will remind us how much work is left to be done. In more recent times, the controversy over the Confederate Battle flag demonstrates that the issues of the 1860s still have resonance in our lifetimes.

The origins, personalities, strategies, tactics, and technologies of the Civil War are subjects that ignite passions across the country. This passion may express itself in raucous debates at the monthly meeting of a Civil War Roundtable or by a hobbyist who spends weekends reenacting battles in either Confederate or Union uniforms. For many who have a casual interest in the war, second guessing the decisions of the Generals seems to be a prerequisite to the many military buffs who hold the events of the Civil War close to their hearts. Of greater importance are the meanings that we divine from the war. For many, the war was a righteous cause to stop the spread of slavery across the West. To others, the war coalesces around the notion of defending a long-cherished culture and way of life. While academia may have come to a consensus on the origins and legacy of the Civil War, there are undoubtedly many who would disagree. Whether we work in the museum world or historic battlefields scattered across the American North, South, and West, it is our responsibility to respect the values of our visitors, and yet present them with accurate information that reflects the meanings that are ascribed to the Civil War.[2]

ORIGINS

Discussing the intricate details of the origins of the Civil War is beyond the scope of this work, but the broad contextual issues should be touched upon. After generations of framing the debate of the Civil War around questions regarding States' Rights, the conversation has shifted to a deeper cause that must be acknowledged. The question that needs to be asked is not how the country descended down the path of secession, for that sequence of events is well known. The question to be asked is this: Why did the North and South choose disunion rather than compromise? The answer is relatively straightforward and simple to comprehend—slavery. We cannot approach any discussion of causes without acknowledging the pivotal role of slavery in shaping the events that led to secession and war. Some will counter this postulate by arguing that not every southerner owned slaves, and therefore, slavery cannot be seen as the chief cause of the war. That may be true, but it was the slave economy that was the source of the region's livelihood and power. The expansion of slavery as an institution was the one constant, reoccurring issue that ultimately could not be compromised away. The economics of the cotton industry was possible through slave labor. No matter what issue is presented, slavery is at the center. In the year 2000, at a symposium on the Civil War sponsored by the National Park Service, James Oliver Horton emphatically stated, "The protection of slavery was the foundation that moved the South toward secession, and it was the underlying reason that the Confederacy was formed. Confederates were willing to take up arms against the United States of America in order to preserve the institution of slavery."[3] There is no other way to conceptualize the origins and prosecution of the Civil War without recognizing the centrality of slavery.

Sectional issues, particularly after 1850, revolve around slavery. In his classic book *The Impending Crisis*, David M. Potter recognized these sectional trends dividing the North and South as being linked to the institution of slavery. Slavery was, in Potter's words, "a transcendent sectional issue in its own right, and as a catalyst for all sectional antagonisms, political, economic, and cultural."[4] James McPherson, who is recognized as one of the most thoughtful and well-known Civil War scholars, has made the same connections. While the forces of nationalism overrode sectionalism until the mid-nineteenth century, when the issues related to slavery overcame the centripetal forces of nationalism, civil war was almost inevitable. In spite of recognizing slavery as the key to understanding the Civil War, there are still those who in twenty-first century America deny the role of slavery in any shape or form. These disagreements range across a wide continuum, from small but vocal groups that take southern nationalism to the extreme, to those who quietly, but respectively disagree with academic trends. As responsible interpreters, we have to accept that we cannot change a person's mind to a deeply held belief, but we can at least provide interpretive opportunities that recognize the central role of slavery in influencing the political elites of the Union and the Confederacy.[5]

We are empowered to provide opportunities for people to weigh the evidence of slavery as the key issue on their own. When introducing the origins of the Civil War into exhibits or personal services, these historical issues cannot simply be tacked on as an afterthought. Deliberate planning and strategizing is required to make a difference in a smart and compelling way. Putting up a small panel in an existing exhibit that

Figure 7.1   Gettysburg. *Source*: Author Photograph

recognizes the role of slavery or providing a short contextual sentence in a museum program just does not cut it. One of the most effective museum experiences that I have had dealing with the role of slavery and the Civil War is at Gettysburg National Military Park. The pivotal battle of Robert E. Lee's second invasion of the North in the summer of 1863 took place in the fields of Gettysburg. It was a key event in the struggle and is recognized as such by the participants, and 150 years later, when set against the backdrop of the entire war.

What sets museum experience at the Gettysburg battlefield apart from others? The museum itself is composed of three experiences: a short film, the museum, and a circular painting from the nineteenth century called the Cyclorama. The movie and the permanent exhibit complement one another. Rather than taking a traditional path with interpretive media that just have a tight focus on the battle, the exhibit and film work together. Gettysburg is often called a turning point of the war. Without putting the story of the three-day battle into context, in my mind, it is just another important battle. The film and exhibit take a cue from the Gettysburg Address and make the battle an important component of the new birth of freedom. Slavery emerges front and center as the primary cause of the war, which connects to the importance of the battle and as a lead-in to President Lincoln's Gettysburg Address. The men buried at the Gettysburg National Cemetery gave their last full measure of devotion to unite the country behind the notion that all men were created equal in a union that was not devoted to sectional interests but national ones. The casual visitor who may not be invested in the minutiae of the battle can come away with a greater appreciation of the meanings that Gettysburg represents. The museum has 22,000 square feet of space, so there is room to tell a more expansive story. While the permanent exhibit that accompanies the film is almost too large, it does point to the importance of context. It is all too easy for a film or exhibit at a battlefield to concentrate solely on the mechanics of a battle. Even in a small exhibit gallery, there should be space devoted to expanding a small story into something much larger and more meaningful.

LINCOLN AND DAVIS CONSIDER HOW TO FIGHT A WAR

For the last fifty years, the historical community has shifted its emphasis from telling stories of our past from the point of view of the so called great men, to the great masses of people who make up most of the population. This technique has proved useful in reimagining our past. That being said, we cannot completely discount the men who led the Union and Confederacy—Abraham Lincoln and Jefferson Davis. Perhaps it is fair to say that history has been kinder to President Lincoln than Davis, but both

Figure 7.2 Abraham Lincoln. *Source*: Library of Congress

men dedicated themselves to winning the war, taking full responsibility for mistakes and promoting their causes when victories dominated the news.

Lincoln was a product of his time. His views on race and slavery changed over the course of his life and he was more egalitarian and ideal than many of his contemporaries. He was pragmatic as a politician but at his core, he was not a friend of slavery. Lincoln started his political career as a Whig, that is, a Nationalist. While his views would evolve over the course of his career, Lincoln was moved by the notion of the right of every individual to improve his or her lot in life. Slavery, by comparison, limited the nation's ability to move in that direction. His Whiggish roots gave Lincoln a certain perspective on the founding fathers. He carried the creed of the Declaration of Independence, that all men are created equal, as part of his world view for most of his life and it undoubtedly affected his views on slavery. As a politician, his views were tempered by the times. In his famous debates with Stephen A. Douglas in the 1858 election, Lincoln moderated his personal views to those of his audience, vehemently arguing against the spread of slavery into new territories, but keeping mute any stark notions of racial equality. Lincoln took the pulse of the nation and stood back until the time was right.[6]

Upon Lincoln's election and the outbreak of war, Lincoln hoped it would be a limited and short conflict. Given his relative inexperience in military matters, he deferred to his Generals. Winfield Scott was the General-in-Chief and recommended what would become known as the Anaconda Plan. As the name suggests, Scott's desire was to squeeze the South by blockading their ports and seizing the Mississippi River, cutting the Confederacy in half. With the Confederacy in the equivalent of a choke hold, the rebels would wither on the vine. While the blockade and cutting off of the Mississippi was being enacted, the public wanted more: a quick march on Richmond, and the war would be over. Elements of Scott's plan remained in place but Lincoln's views evolved. The release of the Emancipation Proclamation indicated that the war was changing. Even though it only focused on the states at the edge of the Confederacy, it marked a distinct shift—the elimination of slavery. This could only be accomplished by destroying the mechanisms of power in the south—the Confederate field armies and their capacity to make war. While we can never know what Lincoln's moves would have been had he lived, what we do know is that his opposition to slavery and hope for a new birth of freedom was what moved him throughout his political career.[7]

Lincoln's counterpart, Jefferson Davis, is a study in contrasts. Prior to his accession to the Presidency of the Confederate States of America, Jefferson Davis had an accomplished military and political career. Lincoln and Davis were contemporaries of one another but each was born into different circumstances. Davis attended the US Military Academy at West Point but resigned his commission after his marriage and became a planter. As a politician he served in the House of Representatives, the US Senate, and as Secretary of War in the Franklin Pierce Administration. His previous experience at West Point put Davis in a position to accept a volunteer commission during the Mexican-American War where he led a regiment. He was an unapologetic supporter of slavery and remained consistent in its defense throughout his tenure as President.[8] As a graduate of West Point and veteran of the Mexican-American War, he came into the Confederate White House with a great deal of experience. He had seen men die; he knew what was at stake. His experiences, however, gave him an inflated

No. 276—Vol. XL]   NEW YORK, MARCH 9, 1861.   [Price 6 Cents.

Our Portrait of the President.

On the eve of the Presidential Inauguration we present to our readers the only correct portrait yet given to the public of Abraham Lincoln, President of the United States. Great labor and care have been bestowed upon its preparation, and we feel assured that as a work of art, and as a life-like portraiture of the man who has been chosen to fill the highest office in the gift of the people at a time of great trouble and difficulty, it will be conceded by all to be unequalled in excellence and truthfulness.

The elegant border which forms the framework of the Portrait contains a series of spirited sketches illustrating incidents in the life of President Lincoln and his father.

JEFFERSON DAVIS,
President of the Southern Confederacy.

Jefferson Davis, lately elected President of the new Southern Confederacy, is the son of Samuel Davis, a Revolutionary soldier, and was born in Kentucky in 1806—8. When a boy he went with his father to Mississippi, where he was educated at Transylvania University, whence he passed to West Point, from which he graduated in 1828, passing at once into service under General Taylor. As the captor of the celebrated Black Hawk he attained an eminent place in the history of our Indian wars. After his marriage, in 1835, to a daughter of General (then Colonel) Taylor, he settled down on a plantation, where he devoted some attention to study, and qualified himself for a Southern political life. In 1843 he entered the campaign on the Democratic side, and with such success as to become one of the

Figure 7.3   Jefferson Davis. *Source*: Library of Congress

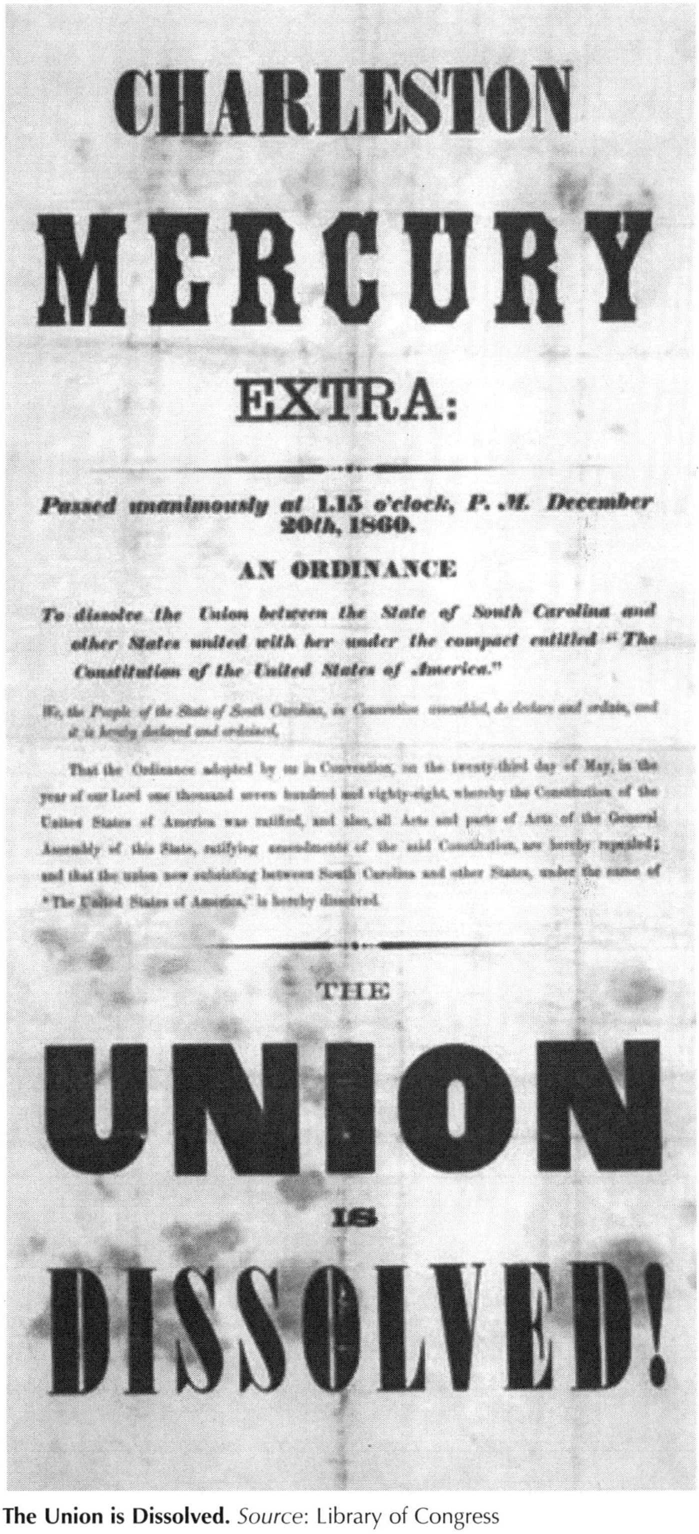

CHARLESTON

MERCURY

EXTRA:

Passed unanimously at 1.15 o'clock, P. M. December 20th, 1860.

AN ORDINANCE

To dissolve the Union between the State of South Carolina and other States united with her under the compact entitled "The Constitution of the United States of America."

We, the People of the State of South Carolina, in Convention assembled, do declare and ordain, and it is hereby declared and ordained,

That the Ordinance adopted by us in Convention, on the twenty-third day of May, in the year of our Lord one thousand seven hundred and eighty-eight, whereby the Constitution of the United States of America was ratified, and also, all Acts and parts of Acts of the General Assembly of this State, ratifying amendments of the said Constitution, are hereby repealed; and that the union now subsisting between South Carolina and other States, under the name of "The United States of America," is hereby dissolved.

THE

UNION

IS

DISSOLVED!

Figure 7.4 The Union is Dissolved. *Source*: Library of Congress notion of his abilities. Rather than building a staff that tended to administrative needs and assisted the President in crafting strategy, Davis took up both the large and small tasks on his own. The perspective that was required to see the forest for the trees was largely absent.[9]

Davis' primary concern was simple: to preserve the Confederacy and secure the new nation's independence. In the opening stages of the war, Davis faced a conundrum. He could withdraw from areas of the Confederacy that were difficult to defend and face the ire of his constituents or defend the entire border of the new Republic. Davis chose to defend everything, adapting a thin veneer of men and fortifications around the perimeter of the new nation. Even though Davis would have to react to Union offensives into the South, by wearing down the attacking columns, Davis could influence Northern public opinion. Throughout the war, there seemed to be a correlation between Confederate success and the swings in Northern public opinion. When the Confederacy was on the offensive extracting huge Union losses, public support for the Lincoln administration waned. It was Davis' fervent hope that he could feed upon the Northern disenchantment and bring Lincoln to the negotiating table. To achieve some modicum of control, Davis chose to divide the South into geographic departments. It was Davis' hope that the Generals who commanded the individual departments would exhibit initiative and flexibility to defend, and when necessary, to attack as the Union moved to assault the South. While Davis' strategy was successful in the East, in particular under the auspices of Robert E. Lee, in the West the Confederates never had the resources to protect everything and this would prove to be the Achilles Heel of the Confederacy.[10]

The one trump card in Jefferson Davis' hand was European recognition and/or intervention of the Confederate States of America. In spite of some sympathy for the South among certain sectors of British public opinion, the strategic calculus of European intervention did not add up. The hope of the South was relatively simple: by withholding the Southern cotton supply from Great Britain, there would be such a deleterious effect on the British economy that they would have to break the Northern blockade and recognize the South. In fact, there was a cotton glut on European markets and much like in the war of 1812, the British would not succumb to economic warfare. Even the heavy-handed interception of a Confederate trade delegation of a British ship, the RMS *Trent*, in late 1861 did not have a marked effect on the Southern strategy. While the relationship between Great Britain and the Lincoln administration could be described as tense, realistically, only a string of stupendous victories on the battlefield would have secured British and French recognition.[11]

OPENING MOVES: 1861–1862

From the beginning of the war until late in 1862, the war was fought in a tentative manner in that there was more of a concern in capturing territory than destroying the Confederates' capability to resist, certainly a reflection of Lincoln's own attitudes. The initial battle at Manassas or Bull Run in July 1861 could be seen as a reflection of the notion that the war would be short. Defeat the army in the field and you are done. In the west, Lincoln and Davis attempted to sway Kentucky, a neutral state,

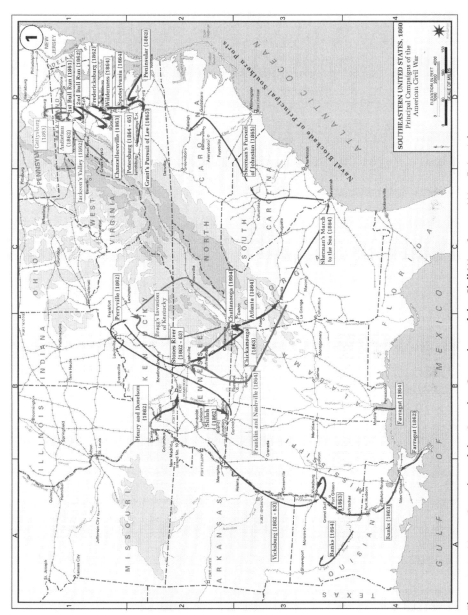

Figure 7.5   Map—Overview of the Opening Campaigns of the Civil War. *Source:* West Point Atlas

without provoking violence. That failed as well. Without a clear path for victory, the war would not be won in 1861.[12]

Even if victory was not decided in 1861, 1862 served as the year of Lincoln's apprenticeship. Beset by victories, defeats, and recalcitrant Generals, as Lincoln gained experience as commander-in-chief, he was provided a sharper vision of what needed to be accomplished to advance the country's aims, even as those aims evolved toward a much sharper and protracted conflict.[13] In the west, with the capture of Forts Henry and Donelson, protecting the Tennessee and Cumberland Rivers, respectively, opened invasion routes through central Tennessee to the Mississippi and Alabama border. After the successful capture of the forts in a joint naval and land campaign led by Ulysses S. Grant in February 6, 1862, Grant continued south down the Tennessee River. In April 1862, Grant clashed with General Albert Sidney Johnston at Pittsburgh Landing, also known as Shiloh. Shiloh was the bloodiest battle of the war and was another indication that this struggle would go for the duration and not come to a conclusion by Christmas.[14]

Far to the south, there were other actions in the western theater of operations of equal importance to Grant and Halleck's successes. Admiral David Farragut and General Benjamin Butler captured New Orleans at the end of April. New Orleans was, by far, one of the most important ports in the Confederacy and in March, at the Battle of Pea Ridge, Union forces defeated their Confederate counterparts, ending overt Confederate influence in Missouri. In spite of a Confederate counteroffensive into Kentucky in the fall of 1862, at least in the West, there was no dramatic change in the strategic situation.[15]

McClellan and Lee

For a good portion of 1862, the two personalities that would dominate the headlines in the battles in the East were Robert E. Lee and George B. McClellan. McClellan was charismatic and a superb organizer of men. In the disarray after Bull Run, McClellan reorganized and trained the Army, inspiring the loyalty and devotion of the troops to him. He was also vainglorious, disrespectful of civilian authority, and prone to exaggerating the numbers of his opponents. As Lincoln's thoughts began evolving over the purpose and aim of the war, it became increasingly clear as 1862 progressed that the two men had very different notions on how to proceed. In McClellan's mind, as his plans for 1862 began to take shape, reunion was the main purpose of the war. Rather than destroying Confederate property and their will to resist, McClellan set his eyes on capturing the rebel capital of Richmond and after much goading by Lincoln, began his march to Richmond in March 1862.[16]

In spite of McClellan's bold move south, the forces left behind to guard the approaches to Washington were neutralized by Thomas "Stonewall" Jackson's famous campaign in the Shenandoah Valley. Overly cautious, McClellan moved far too slowly and was stopped at the gates of Richmond. After the previous Confederate commander Joseph Johnston was wounded, Robert E. Lee assumed command. A career army officer, Lee left federal service only after Virginia seceded from the Union. He held a variety of minor assignments in West Virginia and advised President Davis on military matters. Lee understood his role in protecting the Confederacy as well as in meeting

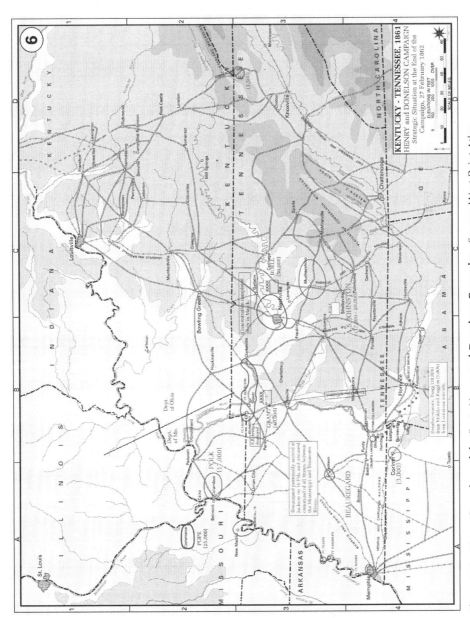

Figure 7.6 Map—Overview of the Forts Henry and Donelson Campaign. *Source:* West Point Atlas

Figure 7.7   George B. McClellan. *Source*: Library of Congress

the President's political aims. In a series of sharp and bloody battles, Lee removed the threat from Richmond and pinned McClellan against the James River. McClellan's gambit had failed and he was relieved of his command.[17]

Not willing to remain on the defensive, Lee turned north. After defeating McClellan's replacement, John Pope, Lee continued north. Lee wanted to bring the war to the North in what could best be described as an extended raid into Maryland. Taking the war north drew union forces out of Virginia, allowing Lee to draw supplies from captured Northern resources and possibly affect the political situation with Confederate forces in a border state.[18] The resulting raid into Maryland failed to meet Lee's expectations. Reappointing McClellan as the commander of the Union Army of the Potomac, they met Lee at Antietam. The battle became the bloodiest single day of the war—the Confederates had casualties of perhaps 13,000 men including three division commanders and nearly half of the brigade and regimental commanders, losses the Confederacy could ill afford. In spite of Lee's losses, the Confederates withdrew in good order. McClellan did not vigorously pursue Lee, which led to his permanent relief in November.[19]

Antietam was a watershed of sorts and offered Lincoln an opportunity to change the focus of the war. Antietam provided Lincoln the opportunity to issue the Emancipation Proclamation. Lincoln chose a symbolic and conservative approach. Slaves were freed in places not yet occupied by Northern troops, preserving support in the border states. Although this was a conservative approach, it was an expression of a new war aim—to end the institution of slavery.[20] In light of the release of General McClellan, Russell F. Weigley captures the revolutionary nature of Lincoln's choices: "If McClellan's unrevolutionary methods of war produced nothing better than stalemate, and indeed

Figure 7.8   Robert E. Lee. *Source*: Library of Congress

opened the war to a season of Confederate offensives, then harsher methods had to be tried. In the light of the Emancipation Proclamation, the departure of McClellan signified the failure of . . . a whole matter of waging war."[21]

At the end of 1862, the war had placed both the Union and the Confederacy at a tipping point. Lincoln's actions suggest that, in just eighteen months, the President's views had changed. The change came because of the battles that took place along the Mississippi, the Appalachians, and Virginia. For Lincoln and Davis, as painful as it was to send men to their deaths, these were the means to an end, a new vision of union or independence to the South. In the story of the Civil War, if the first half of the war tried the patience of the public for the bloodletting and destruction of property, the second half of the war would bring the level of destruction to even greater heights.

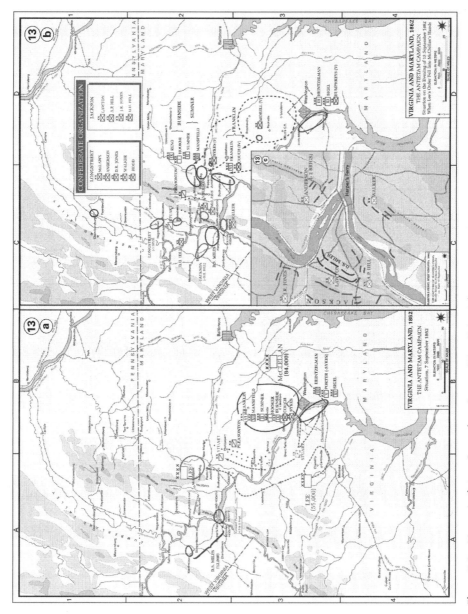

Figure 7.9   Map—Antietam Campaign. *Source:* West Point Atlas

THE WAR ON THE WATER

The Civil War was fought not only on land, but also on the rivers that intersected the South, the coastal waters that extended from Virginia to the border between Texas and Mexico, and on the high seas. James McPherson asserts that the naval forces of the Union contributed much more to the victory over the Confederacy than they are given credit for. Similarly, naval historian Craig L. Symonds says that President Lincoln and his Secretary of the Navy Gideon Welles provided stalwart leadership and also deserve a great deal of praise. As the underdog in the naval fight, the Confederacy leveraged technology such as ironclads and mines to make up for their dearth of vessels, but could never challenge the Union's supremacy on the water.[22]

From the outset of the war with the Confederacy, there was recognition that a blockade was necessary, but that it took time to mobilize the resources to make the blockade effective. However, the most pressing issue revolved around legal matters. Lincoln did not recognize the legitimacy of the Confederacy as a sovereign entity, or a viable nation state, if you will. In his mind, the war with the Southern states was an internal insurrection. Yet, recognizing that a blockade could only be instituted between nations at war put the administration in a bind. The legal situation was ratified by the Supreme Court, but within the Confederacy, the questionable legalities of the blockade provided a justification for either foreign recognition and/or intervention. For the European powers, the question came down to whether it was merely a declaration of a blockade or a real blockade that damaged trade. In reality, the trade, while valuable, was inconsequential. Confederate envoys could convince neither England nor France of the illegitimacy of the blockade. That being said, the only way to truly put an end to blockade runners was to capture ports and close them.[23]

The Confederacy had 189 harbors and coves along their coastline where cargo could be landed. For the first year of the War, the Union blockade could best be described as a sieve. With a limited number of places where Union ships could get coal, provisions, and repairs, keeping an adequate number of vessels on station was difficult at best. Beginning in August 1861, and continuing through the fall, Union forces captured various barrier islands along the Gulf Coast and North Carolina. The next major port to fall was New Orleans in April 1862. The delta of the Mississippi and the bayous that surrounded New Orleans allowed for too many access points to effectively create a blockade. While much progress was made by the end of 1862, several major ports remained open, namely Mobile, Alabama and Charleston, South Carolina.[24]

It is within the context of tightening the blockade that it seems appropriate to mention one of the most well-known naval engagements of the Civil War, the clash between the ironclads USS *Monitor* and the CSS *Virginia* (also known as the *Merrimack*). As General McClellan was preparing for his campaign up the York Peninsula, the CSS *Virginia* sortied from the Gosport Navy Base in Norfolk, Virginia. The Confederates had salvaged the *Merrimack*, rebuilt its engines, and covered the hull in an armored casemate. On March 8, 1862, the *Virginia* created havoc among the Union ships in Hampton Roads. The rebel ironclad sank the *Cumberland* with her ram and attacked the *Congress,* which ran aground and blew up later that evening. In one dramatic moment, the *Virginia* ushered in the era of the ironclads. Union officials were

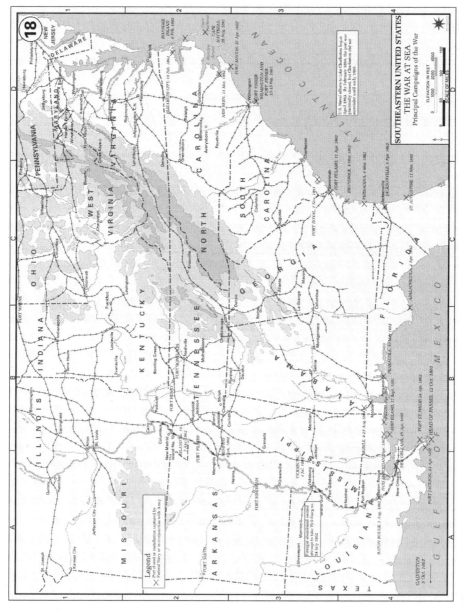

Figure 7.10 Map—War at Sea. *Source:* West Point Atlas

THE GREAT NAVAL VICTORY IN MOBILE BAY, AUG 5TH 1864.

Figure 7.11 The capture of Mobile Bay was typical of the campaigns mounted to close the South's ports. *Source:* Library of Congress

certainly aware of the Confederate plans for the *Merrimack* and planned accordingly. John Ericsson's design of an iron ship with a two-gun turret was selected by the newly established ironclad board. Ericsson's design was constructed and commissioned in time to challenge the *Virginia* on March 9. In spite of the damage to the blockading fleet, the clash between the Monitor and Virginia could best be described a draw. The *Virginia* continued to threaten the Union blockading force, but the presence of *Monitor* was able to deter the wooden ships from further threats. As General McClellan advanced up the York Peninsula, the *Virginia* was bottled up and blown up to prevent the ironclad's capture.[25] It is easy to indulge in hyperbole over the impact of the clash between the two ironclads. As stated previously, I am reticent about labeling a single event as a turning point. In talking about the evolution of technology, the use of ironclads was certainly an important leap forward. The ironclads built for the US Navy could not challenge the Royal Navy on the high seas, but they certainly added value to the Union effort to blockade Confederate ports.

For museums and historical sites that run a tally sheet to bring meaning to the failure of the Confederacy, there is no doubt that the blockade had an impact, but a precise measurement of that impact is not easy. McPherson indicates that the imports of consumer goods and military supplies continued throughout the war, but if the blockade had not existed, the Confederacy would have prevailed. With the constriction of intercoastal and international traffic, the economy was ruined. In cataloging the reasons why the Confederates lost, Beringer and his co-authors completely dismiss the effectiveness of the blockade as a cogent reason for their losing. To offset the access

Figure 7.12   The U.S.S. Monitor after its famous battle with the C.S.S. Virginia. *Source*: Library of Congress

to manufactured goods from the North, the Confederacy was able to develop a modest manufacturing capacity, offsetting the access to the North. Beringer does admit, however, that the expense of importing luxury goods and the general decline in the quality of consumer goods may have affected their morale. In the end, it is fair to say that the blockade played an important role in degrading Confederate ability to keep the economy buoyant.[26]

The greatest success that the Confederate Navy saw was in commerce raiding. Union overseas commerce was certainly affected and created a great deal of drama, but it did not influence the end result. Three ships, the CSS *Alabama, Florida,* and *Shenandoah,* accomplished quite a bit. As had occurred in previous wars when commerce was preyed upon, maritime insurance rates rose. To avoid attacks, American merchants reflagged their vessels to a neutral power to avoid attacks. Because of their relative success in which the *Alabama* alone burned fifty-five merchant ships worth in excess of $4.5 million, Union ships were on the watch for them. As with the blockade runners, the commerce raiders made the headlines and certainly had a disastrous effect on Union commerce as well as increasing tensions with Great Britain who supplied the ships. Yet, in the final analysis, they did not influence the outcome of the war.[27] To understand the complexity of the Civil War, the campaigns that took place on land cannot be fully separated from the actions the Navy took at sea. Lincoln was more cognizant than his counterpart in Richmond of the interplay of actions on the sea, on the rivers, and on land. Regardless of the successes met on the water, the war would be won on the land.

1863–1864: THE BLOODY ROAD TO VICTORY

The Civil War was a drama that dragged on for four years. After the uncertainties that followed secession and the opening campaigns, at the end of 1862, despite their success in the West, Union forces were kept stymied by Confederate counteroffensives. The year 1863 was one that could decide the course of the remainder of the war. For modern audiences, we have the benefit of hindsight, so it is easy to portray the middle portion of the War as an inevitable victory. With war weariness beginning to set in and presidential elections set for 1864, the ebb and flow of the battle lines had the potential of creating repercussions beyond what occurred at the front. One of the most difficult tasks of any institution talking about the Civil War is keeping the story focused on how the people at the time remained engaged in the events going on around them. There was certainly nothing to be cheery about in the first half of 1863.

At the end of 1862, both the Federals and the Confederates had wasted opportunities. The rebel counteroffensives into Maryland and Tennessee had created casualties and put the Union off balance, but in the end did not ease the issue of defending the borders of the Confederacy. Yet, 1863 proved to be critical in blunting the Confederates ability to bring the war north and split the rebel states in half with the fall of Vicksburg.

Vicksburg and Gettysburg

In the east, Lee defeated Union forces at Chancellorsville in an audacious and brilliant campaign. With over 120,000 men at his disposal, General Joseph Hooker' outnumbered Lee's 60,000. Lee did not cooperate. He split his army numerous times, defeating various portions of Hooker's forces in detail. Unfortunately, Lee's most trusted subordinate, Stonewall Jackson, was killed in the fighting. Lee was emboldened, Lincoln fell into melancholy, and Hooker's days were numbered.[28] In the west, from the fall of 1862 until the summer of 1863, Grant attempted to capture Vicksburg and close the Mississippi to Confederate commerce. After several failed attempts, in the spring of 1863, Grant threw caution to the winds and cut himself loose from his supply line, and forced the Confederates back into the fortifications of Vicksburg. After a hard-fought battle, the city fell on July 4, 1863. As Vicksburg's fate hung in the balance, Robert E. Lee's invasion of the North began.[29]

Why raid the North? What did Lee hope to gain? Lee's considerations were practical. First, an extensive raid into Pennsylvania would influence Northern political dynamics and public opinion, perhaps moving fickle voters to support peace with the Confederacy. Second, by keeping the Army of the Potomac busy north of the Rappahannock River, Lee could secure his supply line through the Shenandoah Valley and disrupt any other plans Union forces may have had. Much like Lee's expedition to Maryland the previous year, the move into Pennsylvania is best understood as a large, extended raid. Lee had hoped to battle, and defeat the Army of Potomac on his own terms. With Confederates scattered over south central Pennsylvania, Lee and the Army of the Potomac met at the town of Gettysburg.[30]

The battle at Gettysburg lasted three days, from July 1 to 3, 1863. After a three-day slugfest, the Union line held and Lee withdrew. The campaign failed to meet

Figure 7.13 The field of Pickett's Charge, Gettysburg National Military Park. *Source*: Author Photograph

expectations. Lee suffered 28,000 casualities versus the Union's 23,000. Lee's aggressive style, beginning with the Seven Days battles outside of Richmond and continuing through the battles at Second Manassas, Chancellorsville, and Gettysburg, was creating a butcher's bill of such size and scope that by 1864 he was unable to go on another substantial raid north. Nevertheless, there was enough staying power in the Army of Northern Virginia for the war to last another year and then some.[31]

One of the great blessings of a historic site is that you can put visitors into the exact spot where something happened. With proper preparation, visitors can have a compelling experience because they can witness, in their mind's eye, what happened. When I visited Gettysburg several years ago with friends, we quietly walked the entire length of Pickett's Charge. We did not say a word to each other, we just walked toward the opposite ridge where the Union had established their line. It was one of the most powerful interpretive experiences I have had. Gettysburg, in particular, has an embarrassment of riches in terms of secondary sources, a motion picture, and a historical novel (*The Killer Angels*) that still captivates audiences today. Whether it is Gettysburg or a smaller skirmish site, the inherent power these sites hold to provide meanings to visitors is an immeasurable quality that is easy to lose sight of.[32]

Chickamauga and Chattanooga

With the closure of the Mississippi River to the Confederacy and the blunting of Lee's offensive into Pennsylvania, the Western theater along the Tennessee border was slow in starting but generated success, controversy, and opportunity in 1863. William Rosecrans had been in command of the Union forces in mid-Tennessee since late 1862.

After interminable delays and goading by President Lincoln, Rosecrans went into action in June. In a series of maneuvers, Rosecrans pushed General Braxton Bragg' out of Tennessee into the mountains of northern Georgia, setting up some of the most dramatic battles in the Western theater. In September 1862, the Confederates blunted the invading Union forces with a spectacular victory at Chickamauga. Union forces retreated into Chattanooga, which the Confederates summarily surrounded. In light of the Union reverse at Chickamauga, Rosecrans was relieved of command in October and replaced by Grant, who was given command of all Union forces in the West. Grant broke the siege of Chattanooga in November, 1863. Reinforcements arrived for Grant while Bragg's army shrank as he let go of men for an abortive attack on Knoxville, Tennessee.[33]

1863 is probably one of the most important years of the War in terms of what occurred on the battlefields. Lee's losses in Pennsylvania could best be described as prohibitive, permanently degrading the capacity of the Army of Northern Virginia to take the war into the Union. Lee's army, however, degraded as it was, had survived to fight another day. The victory at Chattanooga opened up the Deep South to invasion, but Bragg's army was not destroyed. In each case, the chaos of these titanic battles made it difficult to follow up a victory with a vigorous pursuit. Moreover, the actions of the various armies remained uncoordinated. The Confederates had the opportunity to shift resources to meet challenges as they emerged. Only with a concerted cross-theater effort could this advantage be nullified. Grant emerged as one of the most effective generals of the Union Armies who would be rewarded when President Lincoln moved him to the East and made him General-in-Chief. 1864 would give Grant the opportunity to crush the Confederacy in one grand campaign. Only time would tell if he could be successful.[34]

BILLY YANK AND JOHNNY REB FACE THE ELEPHANT

Most visitors who come to our institutions have probably not experienced combat. How can we discuss combat from a historical perspective as well as capture the ultimate narrative of any military history, the emotions and consequences of combat? In Bell Wiley's work on the Union Soldier, Wiley captures the essence of combat:

> Battle is the ultimate of soldiering. All else in warfare is but incidental to the vital closing of opposing forces in conflict . . . . Fighting was an intimate, elemental thing, with infantry bearing the brunt, and artillery and horse-mounted cavalry fighting nominally, in near support. The enemy could be seen with the naked eye by soldiers of all branches, and contests usually culminated in head-on clashes of yelling, shooting, striking masses. Closing with the enemy was more than a figure of speech.[35]

Combat is not a romantic affair. It is chaotic, bloody, and exhausting. Too often exhibits and programs will talk about battles and leaders, but with the exception of acknowledging casualties, there is little acknowledgment of the emotional impact of battle. While there may be some disagreement on how men handled the fear of the battle, whether through the bonds of comradeship or other means, it is fair to say that surviving combat with your body and psyche intact is something that most people cannot fathom.[36] It is far too easy to fall into romantic notions of warfare without recognizing the emotional toll and great costs of combat. The Civil War Museum in Kenosha, Wisconsin, embarked on an ambitious film project to look at the impact of the Civil War, and in particular combat, on the lives of three participants.

The Kenosha Civil War Museum focuses on the experience of Union soldiers from the upper midwest—Illinois, Indiana, Iowa, Michigan, Minnesota, and Wisconsin. Their movie titled *Seeing The Elephant* is a unique experience in that it is projected on a screen that is 360 degrees. Knowing that they had to make a movie that would appeal to all audiences, they made a conscious decision not to indulge in gory violence. Although people die on the screen, it is not at the intensity of the first thirty minutes of Director Steven Spielberg's film, *Saving Private Ryan*. Nevertheless, the staff of the museum wanted to provide an emotional experience revolving around the service of three individuals: an abolitionist, a farm hand that was interested in adventure, and a married man who was all for the Union. Together they join the army, experience the tedium of service and the chaos of combat in which one of the characters dies. The words of the characters are genuine, taken from letters written during that time period. In spite of the intensity of the film, audience reaction has been very positive and helps the staff make a tangible connection between its mission, exhibits, and the audience's interests in an effective manner. Conversations with veterans are also positive, particularly in the way in which they replicate the confusion that is so common in battle. While not every museum can build a specialized theater that has the capability to project a film in 360 degrees, a film has the unique capability to capture the sights and sounds of battle and its aftermath. While there are legitimate concerns of showing excessive violence, combat does have a price and people die.[37]

Freedmen Serving in the Blue

When the war began in 1861, given the mindset of the political and military leaders at the beginning of the War, there was not an inkling over the role freedmen would play in the later years of the War. By July 1865, a total of 123,156 African-Americans were serving in the Union Army, making up a good 12 percent of the total number of men in uniform. Their contributions were manifest proof of how far President Lincoln's own attitudes had shifted. Moreover, allowing African-Americans to serve gave them a stake in the fight. With the release of the Emancipation Proclamation in January 1863, the Lincoln administration gave permission to form black regiments. Led by white officers and facing other issues such as unequal pay, those who enlisted fought with determination and vigor.[38]

The response of the Confederate government to the establishment of US Colored Troops (USCT) was blunt. In May 1863, the Confederate Congress decreed that officers leading USCT units could be put to death and the soldiers enslaved. Lincoln retaliated in kind and, for the most part, the Confederates never followed through. However, given the endemic racism in the South, black soldiers faced challenges their white brethren did not. In April 1864, the Confederate Cavalry commander and raider Nathan Bedford Forrest was accused of executing captured USCT soldiers at Fort Pillow in Tennessee. This was symptomatic of the tone that President Davis had set earlier. The first step on the long road to equal rights began when these men donned the blue suit of the Union. Their contributions were necessary as the final act of the Civil War would begin with the hard-fought battles in the East and the West.

THE END GAME: 1864–1865

After Grant came to Washington as Lincoln's General-in-Chief, rather than staying in the Capitol, he went into the field with the Army of Potomac. George Meade was the titular commander, but it soon became clear that Grant was at the helm. Lincoln brought Grant east because the two of them understood what was required to bring the road to a close. Quite simply, Lee's army was to be engaged and destroyed through a coordinated effort. In the West, William T. Sherman was given the task of eliminating the resource base around Atlanta, delivering body blows to the Confederate heartland from which they could not recover. For the first time there is a degree of synchronicity between Lincoln, the movements of the field armies, and the Union's war aims. 1864 was also an election year. It is a fair assertion that even though the Confederacy was fighting for its existence, if there was no progress in either the East or the West, there would be genuine concern over the fate of Lincoln's administration. There was a real possibility that the public would turn against Lincoln at the polls without a measured progress toward victory.[39]

Grant's overland campaign began at the beginning of May 1864. For the next thirty days Grant remained locked in combat with Lee's forces. Unlike his predecessors, after each clash, rather than retiring from the field, Grant continued to pursue the Army of Northern Virginia. The high tempo of operations and the relentless pursuit of Lee produced a consistently high casualty list that labeled Grant as a butcher. It is easy to criticize Grant's handling of the campaign in light of the casualties, but given the state of warfare in the last years of the Civil War, the only way to succeed was to wear away at Lee's freedom of action. During the overland campaign, Grant's armies suffered 52,000 casualities to Lee's 20,000 casualities or 20 percent of Lee's strength. Grant could replenish his army; Lee could not.[40]

As Lee and Grant grappled in Virginia, William T. Sherman began marching toward Atlanta, Georgia. Sherman was given command over three separate armies totaling nearly 100,000 men. Joseph Johnston had just over 50,000. Whereas Lee and Grant were locked in combat, Johnston traded space for time. By drawing Sherman deep into Georgia and lengthening his supply lines, Johnston made Sherman vulnerable, in particular if he was to be drawn into a costly siege around Atlanta. Unfortunately, as wise as Johnston appears, President Davis could not afford the beating he took in the press. Johnston was relieved in July and replaced by John B. Hood. Hood was offensive-minded to the point of being reckless. Hood attacked Sherman several times, but was unable to prevent a siege.[41]

The capture of Atlanta set up the circumstances for Sherman's most memorable campaign. Sherman burned Atlanta and abandoned his supply line for an epic march to the sea. In the simplest of terms, his army of 62,000 marched ten miles a day across a front of 50 miles, destroying railroads, and foraging among the resources available to them. Sherman would repeat his performance in an additional campaign across the

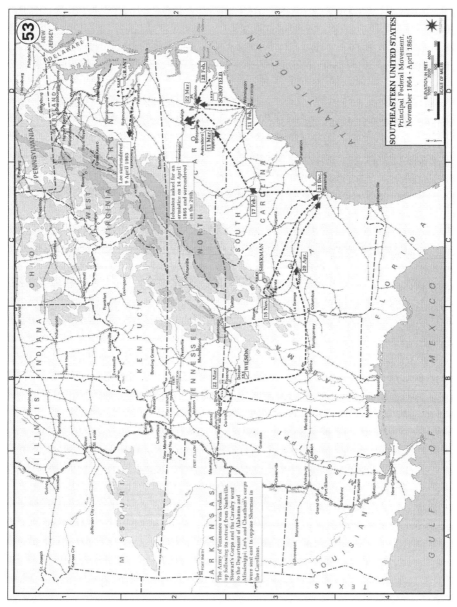

Figure 7.14   Map—The war in the Deep South. *Source:* West Point Atlas

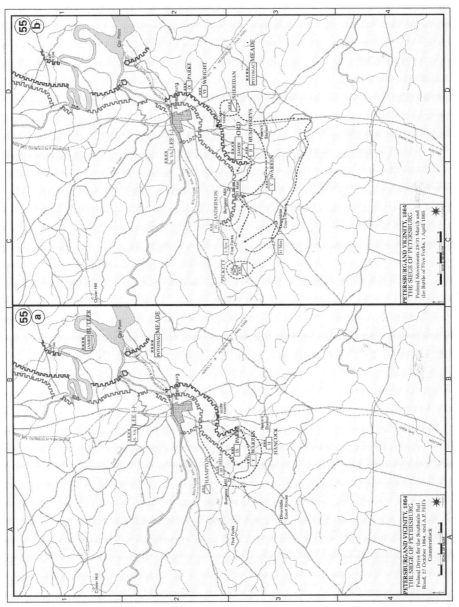

Figure 7.15 Map—Siege of Petersburg. *Source:* West Point Atlas

Carolinas in the spring of 1865. Even 150 years after the event, the event has taken on mythical proportions in terms of the level of destruction and violence. It must be acknowledged, however, for what it was in terms of the Civil War. Telling the story today is challenging but it can be done by acknowledging the controversy and stating the facts as they are known. Concentrating on the voices of those who participated as well as those who were affected is probably the best approach. Sherman was virtually unopposed because Hood had moved his army north to invade Tennessee in October. Hood was defeated by the end of November 1864, and for all intents and purposes, the Army of Tennessee was destroyed.[42]

Besieged by Grant in Petersburg, Virginia, Lee did not possess the manpower to effectively man the 40 miles of siege line. With Sherman running rampant across Georgia and then the Carolinas, desertion grew rampant in all of the Confederate armies, further degrading Lee's opportunities to hold on. In March 1865, Lee was forced to abandon Petersburg and possibly unite with Joe Johnston fighting Sherman in the Carolinas. Lee's retreat to the South was cut off and he was left with little choice but to surrender to Grant. The two men met in the village of Appomattox, Virginia, where Lee surrendered on April 9, 1865. Johnston surrendered to Sherman on April 26, and President Davis was captured at the beginning of May. Unfortunately, in the intervening weeks, President Lincoln was killed by John Wilkes Booth on April 14, 1865. The War was over, but it came at a high price.

WHY DID THE SOUTH LOSE?

Since 1865, when Lee and Johnston surrendered, historians have pondered over how the South failed to win the War and gain their independence. Portraying the military and political results of the Civil War does not do justice to the complexities of the event. The various factors are interrelated to each other and one cannot stand alone without a consideration of the others.

Perhaps the most cogent explanation is that in spite of the brilliant performance of Lee in particular, the South lost the War because its field armies were defeated. Once Lincoln appointed Grant his General-in-Chief, using overwhelming force, Sherman and Grant together not only kept the eastern and western rebel armies occupied, but they wore down the Confederacy's ability to carry out their war aims—securing independence and protecting the territorial integrity of the Confederacy. Davis was able to build a credible war machine despite the challenges brought upon by the blockade. The question, however, revolves around political will rather than the production of rifles. As President Lincoln's war aims changed and he sought to eliminate slavery, Grant's notions of destroying the Confederate will through a march to the sea and wearing down Lee's capacity to resist coincided with Lincoln's aims. Moreover, the Confederate propensity for offensives had a deleterious effect on the South's manpower, a precious resource that could not be replenished without a quick victory. Finally, Davis was never able to develop a cohesive military and political strategy that was able to secure Confederate independence, though he came close in 1862 and early 1864. In the end, one of the chief causes of the Confederate defeat is quite simple: they were vanquished on the battlefield.

One of the issues that is difficult to measure but certainly must be considered is the strength of Confederate nationalism. Can the South's defeat be attributed to internal rather than external changes? In their seminal book *Why The South Lost*, Richard Beringer and his collaborators argue that the principles that underpinned the Confederacy could not stand up to internal dissension and the pressures brought on by the North. In other words, what made the South distinctive could not stand up to the adversities brought upon by war. Other historians argue that Southern nationalism was defined by the military and, in particular, the Army of Northern Virginia. Lee's skill in holding back the northern tide in the East for most of the War, as well as the intense patriotism exhibited by those in the Confederate Army in particular, suggests that at least within the military sector, a strong sense of nationalist identity thrived until the very end. In reality, the truth probably rests between these historical poles. The Confederate central government's inability to protect the hinterland more than likely had a telling effect on morale and belief in a central government. Similarly, we cannot discount the hopes of the rebel republic in disrupting Union public opinion to the point of affecting an armistice that preserved Southern independence. Northern victory hung in the balance until the re-election of Lincoln. Only then can we see the near inevitability of a Confederate defeat.[43]

The memory of the Civil War continues to resonate across time. In terms of sheer numbers, the war produced more casualties than any other conflict the United States has fought in. Until recently, the most widely quoted number of dead and wounded was in excess of 620,000. Poor record keeping, in particular on behalf of the Confederacy, could cause these numbers to be pushed higher. In spite of Lincoln's best efforts, it took another century of struggle to live up to the spirit and intent of abolition of slavery and, it can be argued, that the struggle continues to this day. Small but vocal groups that defend Southern heritage by creating a mythology about the past can be excused as gadflies, but their message still resonates with many people. Until the entrance of the United States into World War Two, the Civil War was the defining event in American history. With the restoration of the Union in 1865, the Army and Navy demobilized and picked up where they had left off in 1861—patrolling the frontier and protecting America's commercial interests overseas. Yet, by the end of the nineteenth century, the United States was poised to play a much larger role in the world as we moved from internal expansion to building an overseas empire.[44]

NOTES

1. Weigley, *History of the US Army*, 233.

2. The passions that the Civil War ignites are ever present. This can be seen in the reaction to film maker Ken Burns documentary on the Civil War that originally aired in 1990. See Jerry Adler, et al., "Revisiting the Civil War: A Stunning Television Documentary Rekindles Enduring Passions," *Newsweek* (October 8, 1990): 58–64. A helpful source to understand the passion behind commemoration can be found in Edward T. Linenthal, *Sacred Ground: Americans and Their Battlefields* (Chicago: University of Illinois Press, 1991), Chapter 3, Gettysburg.

3 James Oliver Horton, "Slavery and the Coming of the Civil War: A Matter For Interpretation," ed. Robert K. Sutton. *Rally on the High Ground: The National Park Service Symposium on the Civil War* (Fort Washington: Eastern National, 2001), 68.

4. David M. Potter. *The Impending Crisis*, 48.

5. James M. McPherson, *Ordeal By Fire: The Civil War and Reconstruction*, Second Edition (New York: McGraw Hill, 1992), 1–2, William C. Davis, *Look Away! A History of the Confederate States of America* (New York: Free Press, 2002), 106–107. For an overview of the historiographical trends in Civil War history, see Francis G. Couvares, et al. *Interpretations of American History*. vol. 1 (New York: Bedford/St. Martin's, 2009), Chapter 10. During the War, soldiers expressed a wide variety of views regarding slavery. See Chandra Manning, *What This Cruel War Was Over: Soldiers, Slavery, and the Civil War* (New York: Alfred A. Knopf, 2007), James M. McPherson, *For Cause and Comrades: Why Men Fought in the Civil War* (New York: Oxford University Press, 1997). There is still some disagreement among historians. Gary Gallagher posits that we are projecting our modern sensibilities onto nineteenth-century soldiers. For the Union soldiers, they were fighting for the restoration and strengthening of the union and emancipation was not a primary motivation. See Gary W. Gallagher, *The Union War* (Cambridge: Harvard University Press, 2011).

6. There are hundreds of works on every aspect of Lincoln's life and political career, too many to mention in an endnote. The works that I have found most useful are Stephen B. Oates, *With Malice Toward None: The Life of Abraham Lincoln* (New York: New American Library, 1977) and by the same author, *Abraham Lincoln: The Man Behind the Myths* (New York: New American Library, 1984). For works more recent than Oates' books, see David H. Donald. *Lincoln* (New York: Random House, 1995) and Michael Burlingame, *Abraham Lincoln: A Life* (2 vols., Baltimore: John Hopkins University Press, 2008). See also, James M. McPherson, *Abraham Lincoln and the Second American Revolution* (New York: Oxford University Press, 1990), Chapter 2.

7. James M. McPherson, *Tried By War: Abraham Lincoln as Commander in Chief* (New York: Penguin Books, 2008), 7–8, Russell F. Weigley, *A Great Civil War: A Military and Political History, 1861–1865* (Bloomington: Indiana University Press, 2000), 90.

8. Jefferson Davis, like Lincoln, has been the subject of many biographies and monographs. William J. Cooper, *Jefferson Davis, American* (New York: Knopf, 2000). For a broad overview of Davis as commander-in-chief, see James McPherson, *Embattled Rebel: Jefferson Davis and Commander in Chief* (New York: Oxford University Press, 2014).

9. McPherson, *Embattled Rebel*, 1–11.

10. Archer Jones, *Confederate Strategy From Shiloh to Vicksburg* (Baton Rouge: Louisiana State University Press, 1991), Chapter 2, Donald Stoker, *The Grand Design: Strategy and the U.S. Civil War* (New York: Oxford University Press, 2010), 26–27, McPherson, *Embattled Rebel*, 28–34. An overview of staff organization can be found in Chapter 5 of Herman Hattaway and Archer Jones, *How the North Won: A Military History of the Civil War* (Chicago: University of Illinois Press, 1983).

11. Weigley, *A Great Civil War*, 77–81; McPherson, *Ordeal By Fire*, 217–21.

12. Weigley, *A Great Civil War*, 49–55, 58–63; McPherson, *Ordeal By Fire*, 157–62. For an overview of the Manassas campaign and battle, see Ethan S. Rafuse, *A Single Grand Victory: The First Campaign and Battle of Manassas* (New York: Rowman and Littlefield, 2002). The classic account of Lincoln's trials and tribulations in the first year of the war are recounted in T. Harry Williams, *Lincoln and His Generals* (New York: Alfred A. Knopf, 1952).

13. The classic account of Lincoln's trials and tribulations in the first year of the war are recounted in T. Harry Williams, *Lincoln and His Generals* (New York: Alfred A. Knopf, 1952).

14. Weigley, *A Great Civil War*, 96–105, 108–15; McPherson, *Ordeal By Fire*, 222–32. As with any Civil War, there are hundreds of works available. A good place to start for these campaigns is Benjamin F. Cooling, *Forts Henry and Donelson: The Key to the Confederate Heartland* (Knoxville: University of Tennessee Press, 1987), Larry J. Daniel, *Shiloh: The Battle That Changed the Civil War* (New York: Simon and Schuster, 1997).

15. Weigley, *A Great Civil War*, 157–60; McPherson, *Ordeal By Fire*, 287–90. For further reading, please see William L. Shea and Earl J. Hess, *Pea Ridge: Civil War Campaign in the West* (Chapel Hill: University of North Carolina Press, 1992), Kenneth W. Noe, *Perryville: The Grand Havoc of Battle* (Lexington: University Press of Kentucky, 2001).

16. Weigley, *A Great Civil War*, 65–67, 81–85, 92–94; McPherson, *Tried by War*, 65–83; Stoker, *The Grand Design*, 52–62. McClellan continues to elicit strong opinions, 150 years after he battled with Lincoln over the direction of the war and his plans. To understand McClellan's place in the history of the Army of Potomac, a good place to begin is Stephen R. Taaffe, *Commanding the Army of the Potomac* (Lawrence: University Press of Kansas, 2006). For an overview of McClellan's life, see Stephen W. Sears, *George B. McClellan: The Young Napoleon* (New York: Ticknor and Fields, 1988).

17. Weigley, *A Great Civil War*, 122–34; McPherson, *Tried by War*, 235–50; Glatthaar, *General Lee's Army*, Chapter 11. For an overview of the Peninsula and Valley campaigns, see Stephen W. Sears, *To the Gates of Richmond: The Peninsula Campaign* (New York: Ticknor and Fields, 1992), Peter Cozzens, *Shenandoah, 1862: Stonewall Jackson's Valley Campaign* (Chapel Hill: University of North Carolina Press, 2008). Thomas "Stonewall" Jackson was one of the most successful generals of the Civil War and his unique personality always attracts interest. His most complete biography is James I. Robertson, Jr., *Stonewall Jackson: The Man, The Solider, The Legend* (New York: Macmillan and Company, 1997). The works dealing with Robert E. Lee's life and accomplishments are too numerous to list here. Glatthaar's work on the Army of Northern Virginia is a great place to start to see how Lee shaped the Army of Northern Virginia.

18. Weigley, *A Great Civil War*, 137–44. For an overview of the campaign, see John J. Hennessey, *Return to Bull Run: The Campaign and Battle of Second Manassas* (New York: Simon and Schuster, 1993).

19. Weigley, *A Great Civil War*, 144–54; Glatthaar, *General Lee's Army*, 163–73; Stoker, *The Grand Design*, 184–91. For an overview of the campaign, see Joseph L. Harsh, *Taken at the Flood: Robert E. Lee and Confederate Strategy in the Maryland Campaign, September, 1862* (Kent: Kent State University Press, 1999). A classic account of the battle that still has value is Stephen W. Sears, *Landscape Turned Red: The Battle of Antietam* (New York: Ticknor and Fields, 1983).

20. Weigely, *A Great Civil War*, 170–76; McPherson, *Ordeal By Fire*, Chapters 16 and 17, Stoker, 191–94.

21. Weigely, *A Great Civil War*, 161.

22. James McPherson, *War on the Waters: The Union and Confederate Navies, 1861–1865* (Chapel Hill: University of North Carolina Press, 2012), 1–9, Craig L. Symonds, *Lincoln and His Admirals* (New York: Oxford University Press, 2008), ix–xiv. McPherson expresses similar sentiments in "The Rewards of Risk Taking: Two Civil War Admirals," *Journal of Military History*, 78 (October 2014): 1225–37. Another helpful overview of the war at sea is Spencer C. Tucker, *Blue & Grey Navies: The Civil War Afloat* (Annapolis: Naval Institute Press, 2006).

23. McPherson, *War on the Waters*, 46–49; Symonds, *Lincoln and His Admirals*, 37–53.

24. The number of 189 harbors is taken from McPherson, *Ordeal By Fire*, 179; McPherson, *War on the Waters*, 36–69.

25. McPherson, *War on the Waters*, 96–111; Symonds, *Lincoln and His Admirals*, Chapter 5. For additional reading, see David A. Mindell, *Iron Coffin: War, Technology, and Experience Aboard the USS Monitor* (Baltimore: John Hopkins University Press, 2012), For the CSS Virginia, see John V. Quarstein, *The CSS Virginia: Sink Before Surrender* (Charleston: The History Press, 2013).

26. Richard Beringer, Herman Hattaway, Archer Jones, and William N. Still Jr., *Why The South Lost The Civil War* (Athens: University of Georgia Press, 1986), Chapter 3.

27. Weigley, *A Great Civil War*, 341–43; McPherson, *War on the Waters*, 201–206, 221–22. For an overview of all of the Confederate commerce raiders, see Angus Konstam and Tony Bryan (Illustrator). *Confederate Raider, 1861–1865* (Oxford, England: Osprey Publishing, 2003). Osprey Press has a host of specialized volumes on the ships of the Confederate and Union navies. Osprey Publishing has specialized in military history titles on technology, battles, Generals, and armies. For a complete list of their catalog, please visit their website at http://www.ospreypublishing.com/.

28. Weigley, *A Great Civil War*, 224–30; McPherson, *Ordeal By Fire*, 315–21; Stoker, *The Grand Design*, 252–59. Chancellorsville is one of the great battles of the Civil War and in American military history. A good overview of the battle can be found in Stephen Sears, *Chancellorsville* (New York: Houghton Mifflin, 1996).

29. Weigley, *A Great Civil War*, 256–70; McPherson, *Ordeal By Fire*, 309–15, 330–31; Stoker, *The Grand Design*, Chapter 15. Grant's moves against Vicksburg are summarized in Michael B. Ballard, *Vicksburg: The Campaign that Opened the Mississippi* (Chapel Hill: University of North Carolina Press, 2003).

30. Stoker, *The Grand Design*, 277–96.

31. Weigley, *A Great Civil War*, 236–56.

32. Michael Shaara, *The Killer Angels* (New York: Ballantine Books, 1974).

33. Weigley, *A Great Civil War*, 271–85; McPherson, *Ordeal By Fire*, 332–40. Chickamauga and Chattanooga are some of the pivotal events of the war and are covered in two books by historian Peter Couzzens, *The Terrible Sword: The Battle of Chickamauga* (Chicago: University of Illinois Press, 1992) and *The Shipwreck of Hopes: The Battles for Chattanooga* (Chicago: University of Illinois Press, 1994).

34. Weigley, *A Great Civil War*, 283–85; Stoker, *The Grand Design*, 330–31.

35. Wiley, *Billy Yank*, 66.

36. Gerald F. Linderman, *Embattled Courage: The Experience of Combat in the American Civil War* (New York: The Free Press, 1987). For a view that is contrary to Linderman, at least for the twentieth century but not necessarily for the Civil War, see Christopher H. Hamner, *Enduring Battle: American Soldiers in Three Wars, 1776–1945* (Lawrence: University Press of Kansas, 2011), see Chapter 2.

37. Interview with Brett Lobello, Curator of Education, Civil War Museum, Kenosha, Wisconsin, October 24, 2014. For more information on the museum, please see http://www.kenosha.org/wp-civilwar/. Their Facebook feed can be found at https://www.facebook.com/CWMKenosha.

38. Dudley Cornish, *The Sable Arm: Black Troops in the Union Army, 1861–1865* (Lawrence: University Press of Kansas, 1987), Weigley, *A Great Civil War*, 185–91. This is a rich topic that continues to grow. Some books that are helpful in exploring this topic are Joseph Glatthaar, *Forged in Battle: The Civil War Alliance of Black Soldiers and White Officers* (New York: Free Press, 1990); Noah Andre Trudeau, *Like Men of War: Black Troops in the Civil War, 1862–1865* (New York: Little, Brown, 1998).

39. Williams, *Lincoln and His Generals*, Chapter 12, Weigley, *A Great Civil War*, 324–30.

40. Weigley, *A Great Civil War*, 330–41; Stoker, *A Grand Design*, 362–73. There are many works regarding this pivotal campaign. There are several good overviews of the campaign, see Mark Grimsley, *And Keep Moving On: The Virginia Campaign, May–June, 1864* (Lincoln: University of Nebraska Press, 1988); William Matter, *If It Takes All Summer: The Battle of Spotsylvania* (Chapel Hill: University of North Carolina Press, 1988); Richard J. Sommers, *Richmond Redeemed: The Siege of Petersburg* (New York: Doubleday, 1981).

41. McPherson, *Ordeal By Fire*, 428–39; Weigley, *A Great Civil War*, 358–78. The Atlanta Campaign, like Grant's Overland Battles, has generated a great deal of attention. Good places to start are Albert Castel, *Decision in the West: The Atlanta Campaign of 1864* (Lawrence:

University Press of Kansas, 1992), Richard M. McMurry, *Atlanta 1864: Last Chance For the Confederacy* (Lincoln: University of Nebraska Press, 2000).

42. McPherson, *Ordeal By Fire*, 459–66; Weigley, *A Great Civil War*, 386–96. A competent introduction to the March to the Sea would be Noah Andre Trudeau, *Southern Storm: Sherman's March to the Sea* (New York, NY; Harpers, 2008) and Joseph Glatthaar, *The March to the Sea and Beyond: Sherman's Troops in the Savannah and Carolina Campaigns* (New York: New York University Press, 1985).

43. Beringer, et al., *Why The South Lost the Civil War*, 64–81; Gary W. Gallagher, *The Confederate War* (Cambridge: Harvard University Press, 1997), Chapter 2.

44. A reexamination of casualty figures is centered on an important journal article, J. David Hacker, "A Census-Based Count of the Civil War Dead," *Civil War History*, vol. 57, no. 4 (2011): 307–48. For a concise overview of the interplay between history and memory in the aftermath of the Civil War, see Michael Kammen, *The Mystic Chords of Memory: The Transformation of Tradition in American Culture* (New York: Vintage Books, 1993), Chapter 4.

Chapter 8

Internal and External Expansion, 1865–1914

Notwithstanding the cudgeling of stress, neglect and hostility that beset the soldier, the army began to be restless for something better. The stir of honest ambition, that lies close to true American hearts, plainly started to transform itself into concrete movement.

William Ganoe, *The History of the United States Army.*[1]

The period between the end of the Civil War and the beginning of the twentieth century is a period of retrenchment, change, and new horizons. As with other time periods that serve as bookends from one momentous event to the next, certain aspects tend to be neglected. In many regards, the end of the Civil War saw the return to business as usual for the Army and Navy. Both shrank and returned to the duties that occupied their time in the decades before the Civil War. Whereas the Navy protected American commerce around the world, the Army returned to its duties policing the frontier. Enforcing Indian policy made the Army an agent for change at the expense of aboriginal populations, paving the way for settlement of the West and, ultimately, the closing of the frontier. As one frontier closed, new possibilities emerged outside of the continental United States in the Pacific Ocean and the Caribbean Sea.

The first task at hand for the Army was reconstructing the South. In the immediate aftermath of the Civil War, until 1877, Federal garrisons remained in the southern states. In 1865, the assassination of President Lincoln left the country without a leader to guide the nation forward. The Republicans dominated Congress and Andrew Johnson, Lincoln's successor, clashed. Johnson wanted immediate reconciliation and the establishment of Southern state governments ready to rule. Grant was put on the spot and came down on the side of Congress, instituting military government. Until the occupation of Germany in 1944–1945, officers were put in uncomfortable situations, protecting public and private property but also acting as the local county government. In what amounted to local police force and municipal authorities, Army officers held a great deal of power at the local level but not a great deal of direction in terms of setting national policy. Despite the overtly political role the Army played in Reconstruction, they were the only Federal institution that had the manpower and authority to carry out the legislative intent of the Republican Congress. For much of nineteenth century, the Army was the only institution that could provide domestic tranquility in uncertain times. However, their chief responsibility was to fall back into the familiar mission of patrolling the frontier.[2]

THE ARMY ON THE FRONTIER

In the decades following the Civil War, there seems to be one topic that generates a great deal of interest—the so-called Indian Wars of the late nineteenth century. As the nation expanded and the last vestiges of open space were set aside for Euro-American settlement, the native populations who had called these spaces home risked expulsion and even extinction. Territorial settlements were regulated through a treaty system, making allowances for the ceding of millions of acres of land in return for small reservations and promises of help and support from the government. Corrupt Indian agents diverted resources to enrich their own pockets at the expense of the people they were charged with protecting. Some tribes accommodated the Indian agents, whereas others clashed with them. Fair access to territorial courts was another irritant. Inequitable or inadequate judicial mechanisms left many native peoples with no avenue to adjudicate disputes, often leading to unresolved grudges that frequently led to violence. Above all else, the inexorable desire for land and settlement left the native peoples of the West (the Great Plains, the intermountain west, the Pacific Northwest, and the Southwest) with few choices: either accommodate the government, or fight it. While there were some successes against the Army, notably George Armstrong Custer's defeat at the Little Big Horn in 1876 and, to a lesser extent, the nearly successful flight of the Nez Perce in 1877, inevitably, the resources available to the Army were seemingly endless in comparison to what most tribes could muster. For example, the Army often mounted campaigns in winter, when the tribes were least active and most vulnerable to starvation. The inexorable process of internal expansion and the Army's role in it has in the past been told from the Army's point of view. In the last twenty years, new strategies have shifted the narrative voice from soldiers to the natives they were fighting. These are stories that must be told, if anything to recognize that there are many voices that need to be heard.[3]

Beginning in the 1860s, as the Civil War was raging in the East, and lasting through 1890, clashes between soldiers and Indians ranged across the West. From Minnesota, across the Great Plains, into the Southwest, and along the border with Mexico, the Army was kept occupied for a generation. There is a great deal of secondary literature available not only on the broad sweep of Indian history, but also on the individual conflicts as well. Rather than re-telling these stories here, it would be more useful to offer strategies for rethinking the master narrative of the Indian Wars. The heart of interpretation is in addressing the visitor's interests. For many who visit battlefields, there seems to be a profound sense of embarrassment over the historical traumas experienced by native peoples as a result of the policies of the US government and perhaps even their ancestors. Rather than laying blame, these sites give license to collaboration with native communities, giving the familiar narrative of these battles a new voice, one that is not often heard by the public. It is possible that some museumgoers may push back at this strategy as revisionism or political correctness. Rather than excluding the voices of soldiers, we are adding to the story by introducing new, relevant voices by collaborating with Native American communities most affected by these battles and skirmishes.

Several National Park Service sites have attempted to incorporate a native voice into their interpretation; most notably, Big Hole National Battlefield, Little Big Horn Battlefield National Monument, and Washita Battlefield National Historic Site have worked hard to incorporate native sensibilities and stories into their programs and interpretation. Big Hole and Washita have engaged native partners to accommodate the stories of contemporary descendants into exhibits and other interpretive media. In a move that generated a great deal of controversy, Custer Battlefield National Monument was renamed in 1991 as Little Big Horn and the installation of a memorial to the fallen warriors marked a drastic change in the narrative voice on the battlefield. What does this add to the interpretation? Robert Utley, a well-respected historian of this time period, argues that while we can certainly judge the actions of the past by weighing them against the values of the present, we still have to view these actions within the context of what was happening in the late nineteenth century. The truth of US Indian policy was fairly straightforward: to assimilate native peoples into mainstream culture. Whether through the actions of missionaries, government Indian agents, or soldiers, assimilation was the predominant theme throughout the second half of the nineteenth century. In spite of their own feelings about the Indians, the Army was left to navigate through the complexities of policy and act in ways they saw fit. In the end, native peoples were left with little freedom of choice: either accommodate or resist. In the twenty-first century, in spite of these challenges, native populations are still here. For institutions that have a Native American component to their story, it is high time to regularly engage their local tribal communities into the interpretive planning process to, at the very least, hear a set of voices that are often excluded from the planning process. We can celebrate the robustness of native culture, but we also have to come to grips with the heavy hand of US Indian policy of the late 1800s. Focusing the narrative on the native voice provides a bridge between the pain of the past and hope for the future.[4]

For thirty years, the US Army served on the frontier, falling into the constabulary role that had occupied the regular army in the decades before the Civil War. Spread out over dozens of posts across the western United States, most officers and soldiers found their lives full of tedium, punctuated by moments of excitement and terror. In 1867, with Reconstruction going full swing, the Army had just over 58,000 men. A decade later, successive reductions had cut these numbers to nearly half. Promotion was stagnant for younger officers entering the service after the end of the Civil War, and Congressional parsimony kept the Army supplied and armed, but only just so. The Army staffed two infantry and two cavalry regiments with African-Americans during this period, the so-called Buffalo Soldiers, providing an avenue of general and begrudging acceptance in a society that was very intolerant. While these regiments were ultimately disbanded in the early twentieth century, like their predecessors in the US Colored Troops, they found a place in the Army. There are several museums throughout the country that honor their service and tell their stories, and provide an excellent way to introduce old stories to new museum patrons.[5] In spite of the difficulties of life in the frontier army, the presence of these scattered garrisons, in particular those found in the more recently organized territories in the southwest, acted as economic anchors, purchasing supplies and services from local communities, providing a boost to local economies and stability to growing communities. As the frontier began to fade along with the threat that Indian peoples represented to some populations, both the Army and Navy began to ask the question, what's next?[6]

REFORM BEGINS

As mentioned in a previous chapter, organizational reform is a topic that is often avoided since it is difficult to mount compelling exhibits and interpretive material that speak to how and why an organization evolves. For the Army, as the Indian Wars began to come to a close, there was a search for a mission. Because of the large role the Army played in Reconstruction and given the rapid economic change and accompanying social problems that characterized the 1870s and 1880s, there was the notion of making use of the Army to control civil unrest. The Army was called out during the great railroad strike of 1877, a number of civil disputes across the West, and strikes in the 1880s and 1890s. In each case the Army provided support to civil authorities in a relatively evenhanded manner. As important as this role was, it was not to be the primary mission of the Army. Instead, they looked overseas for inspiration and found it in Western Europe and, in particular, the new Empire of Germany.[7]

The German victory over France in 1871 brought the formula for their success under intense scrutiny by other Western European powers and the United States. Prussia, followed by the German Army, created a professional officer corps based on a rigorous military education program that fed officers into the Army and the General Staff. As that name suggests, the brains of an Army, or any military for that matter, was embodied in a group of people. Modern warfare was becoming too complex for one person to manage. War planning, mobilization, industrial planning, logistics, and all of the processes that are required could be contained within this highly trained group of general officers. While a US General Staff would not be established for several decades, a number of trends emerged. Drawing lessons from the Civil War, Colonel Emory Upton and others explored ways to mitigate the offensive power of the rifle into tactics that could carry the day. Upton's writings also veered off into policy and politics. His manuscript *The Military Policy of the United States* would fuel further reforms in the first decades of the twentieth century, providing the impetus for the formation of a General Staff. The tone of this work, however, was antithetical to the political culture of the time. Upton scoffed at civilian control of the military, overreliance on volunteers, and the general state of unpreparedness of American arms. Adopting a large, peacetime regular army and establishing a General Staff would ameliorate the defects of the American system. Upton committed suicide, perhaps from the effects of a brain tumor, never seeing his manuscript come to publication. Nevertheless, it would shape the coming debates over creating the proper policy and structure to lead the Army into the twentieth century. Upton's venom against the militia and citizen soldiers was accepted by generations of officers and continues to have an influence on the dichotomy between a regular army and a civilian counterpart. Concurrent with Upton's intellectual efforts, William T. Sherman, now Commanding General of the Army, instituted the first postgraduate education school system, founding the school of application for infantry and cavalry officers as well as encouraging scholarship among the officer Corps. There were other manifestations as well. When Sherman left his post in 1883, his push for comprehensive reform did not become institutionalized, but the emphasis on professional development through postgraduate education brought home the notion that a professional soldier was not solely defined by dedicated service and a degree from the military academy at West Point.[8]

Similar trends occurred in the Navy as well. As with the Army, the Navy shrank in the immediate years after the end of the Civil War. In December 1864, 700 vessels could be counted. At the end of 1870, there were around 200, of which only 52 were in commission. As was the case before the war, ships were scattered around the world in squadrons to protect American maritime interests. The ironclads that defined the Civil War fleet were not ocean-going vessels, but were only suited for riverine service or along the coast. There was little Congressional interest in the Navy and no real threat to induce larger appropriations and modern ships. In terms of personnel, older men remained in uniform, stifling promotion of younger, progressive officers. Beginning in the 1880s, coinciding with interest in the education from their Army peers, change was coming. In the mid-1880s, three new steel warships entered into the fleet: the *Atlanta*, *Boston*, and *Chicago*. This modest flotilla of steel-hulled ships marked the beginning of growing interest in building a modern fleet among the opinion makers in Congress and the White House. Rear Admiral Stephen B. Luce lobbied for and received permission to establish the Naval War College in Newport, Rhode Island, the Navy's first postgraduate school. One of his faculty members, Captain Alfred Thayer Mahan, would use the school as his bully pulpit, producing a text book that would coincide with the first stirrings of empire.[9]

The publication of Mahan's seminal book *The Influence of Sea Power Upon History 1660–1783* provided the intellectual underpinnings for a larger, sea-going Navy. Rather than focusing on the traditional missions of the US Navy, a small fleet that could prey on commerce in wartime and protect commercial interests in peace, Mahan expanded that vision. National power was dependent upon commerce, a merchant marine, that could carry cargo around the world. These commercial vessels needed access to ports, which meant not only colonies to secure the said ports, but also a Navy to protect them. If a merchant marine was the basis of a successful economy, a large Navy was required to protect those interests around the world. Protecting national assets, regardless of where they were located, required command of the seas. Rather than commerce raiders, larger ships, popularly known as battleships, were required in greater numbers to gain command of the seas. The implications for the United States were simple: it meant the building of a battle fleet that could project power around the world. Moreover, Mahan's writings implied that the colonies were needed to base that fleet, providing an impetus to look beyond the shores of the United States. While there were many Mahanian acolytes, not only in the United States but around the world, the Admiral's work did not wholly create the impetus to look overseas. However, Mahan's book came at a time when conditions were ripe for the United States to have its own imperial moment.[10]

THE SPANISH-AMERICAN WAR AND PHILIPPINE
INSURRECTION, 1898–1902

Since the founding of Jamestown and the Massachusetts Bay colony, the inexorable spread of the American frontier came at the expense of the native peoples who inhabited these lands long before the arrival of the Europeans. There are some who call this movement an outright conquest of the continent, others, our national destiny. The difficulty in finding the correct terms to properly characterize internal expansion has also confounded the country's foray into imperialism and colony building in the Pacific and Caribbean. Is it conquest or national destiny, or perhaps something in between? Is it a continuation of the same forces that prompted the settlement of North America? These are difficult questions to address; our movement overseas cannot be reduced to a single cause. The legacy of Spain's defeat is something that we still live with today. As Congress debates the country's role overseas, the wispy willow that is public opinion continues to swing between intervention and isolation. There are many legitimate views on how the country went to war with Spain. Some are less than complementary and others make sense in the context of the time period. Nevertheless, it makes sense to acknowledge that there is more than one way to understand America's imperial moment.

Figure 8.1   Explosion of the USS *Maine*. Remember the *Maine* would propel the United States into a war with Spain. *Source:* Library of Congress

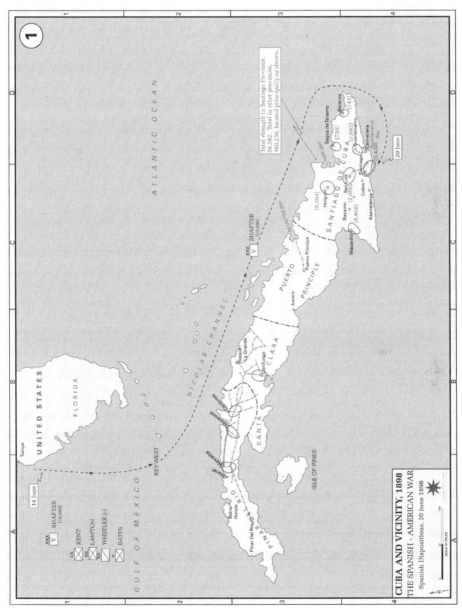

Figure 8.2 Map—Spanish Dispositions in Cuba. *Source:* West Point Atlas

There are many threads that came together to make for America's first push overseas. As with most historical debates, there are many explanations, none of which can
stand alone as *the* cause of the war with Spain, but all contributed to it. Some of the
most prevalent explanations for war originate with economic motives, in particular the
search for new markets for American goods. Securing markets for American goods
in Asia and Latin America may have induced some elites to push for an aggressive
stance in expanding the United States' zone of influence, in particular since European
powers were gobbling up their own empires in Africa and Asia. For other historians, a
rising sense of nationalism and a renewed missionary zeal to export American values
may have stirred public opinion, in particular to intervene and assist the Cuban insurrection against their Spanish overlords. Stories of brutal Spanish practices against the
local population, magnified by the growing mass media market in the form of daily
newspaper conglomerates, may have manipulated the public to support intervention.
The growing attention paid to the expansion of the US fleet, spurred on by the growth
of navalism vis-à-vis Mahan's books and the desire to emulate the great European
imperialist powers, more than likely had an effect on opinion makers. While economics was certainly seen as a major contributing factor in the impulse for empire, a multifaceted approach has more appeal in that it covers all of the influences on decision
makers and public opinion. In the background of all of these forces was the simmering
Cuban Revolution that proved to be the spark that ignited the country into war.[11]

The immediate reasons for intervention were a combination of happenstance and
unfortunate circumstances. Beginning in 1895, the Cuban Revolution had captured
American headlines and the public's interest. Lurid headlines and shrill stories of
the brutality of the Spanish colonial overlords shaped public opinion. American economic interests, primarily the sugar industry, moved the Cleveland administration to
push Spain to stop the revolution and advocate for political reforms. When William
McKinley assumed the presidency, he certainly was not interested in going to war and
urged patience to see if Spain would live up to its commitments for reform. When
rioting broke out in the island's capital of Havana, the USS *Maine* was sent to Havana
in January 1898, to protect American property. On the night of February 15, 1898,
the battleship was destroyed in a massive explosion, killing 250 American sailors.[12]
Newspapers pointed at Spanish culpability in the explosion, inflaming public opinion.
With no hope of a negotiated a settlement, Spain and the United States declared war
on each other on April 25, 1898.[13]

While the war itself may be difficult to characterize, the performance of the Army
and Navy influenced their actions in the years after the war. The Navy's performance
was a successful validation of Mahan's theories and influence. As the decision to go
to war was being debated in Congress, American ships in Asia and the Atlantic moved
to intercept Spanish squadrons in the Philippines and Cuba. An American squadron
led by Commodore George Dewey destroyed Spanish naval power in the Philippine
archipelago. In Cuba, a blockade was instituted around the island to prevent Spanish
reinforcements and the Spanish squadron based in Cuba was bottled up in the harbor
of Santiago de Cuba. After US troops landed and besieged the town, the Spanish
squadron was defeated in a naval battle on July 3, 1898. Spectacular naval victories
and the acquisition of naval bases in the Caribbean and the Pacific seemed to validate
Mahan's correlation between large fleets and naval bases. In the years that would

culminate in the declaration of war against Germany in World War One, political support for a large Navy would expand, allowing it to challenge the supremacy of Great Britain. The Army's experience was far different.[14]

From the moment Congress declared war on Spain, the Army's efforts to mobilize were fraught with problems and missteps. The most glaring difficulties were mobilization, supply, and transportation. Rather than mobilizing National Guard troops, Congress authorized the states to recruit state-based regiments, the last time that this would occur. The peacetime establishment of the US Army was overwhelmed, exacerbating issues related to supply. When they finally left Tampa, Florida, the Army landed on the southeast corner of the island and besieged Santiago. The advance on Santiago would lead to Theodore Roosevelt's famous action on Kettle Hill, propelling his political career forward. The US defeat of the Spanish naval squadron and their subsequent inability to secure reinforcements from Spain or other possessions led to the surrender of the port city, sealing the fate of eastern Cuba, and for all intents and purposes, ending the war on the island. Puerto Rico would fall in a quick campaign at the end of July, bringing the war in the Caribbean to a close. Whereas the war in the Caribbean came and went fairly quickly, the Army's campaign in the Philippines would be long and problematic as well.[15]

Given the public memory of Vietnam and the more recent counter-insurgency campaigns in southwest Asia, the so-called Philippine insurrection continues to be relevant even over a century later. As in Cuba, the Philippines was in rebellion, led by nationalist Emilio Aguinaldo. With the destruction of the Spanish fleet in May, Aguinaldo consolidated his own hold over the islands, forming a provisional government that declared independence. With US forces arriving in August, there was an agreement to assist in the siege of Manila in concert with Aguinaldo's forces. When it became clear that the United States would not honor the independence of the Philippines, Aguinaldo turned against the United States beginning in February 1899. However, even though Aguinaldo's forces outnumbered the Americans, he could not compete with their better organization and leadership, and the conflict transitioned to a guerilla war by November of that year.[16]

For several years the Army remained in the countryside. Leniency, public service projects, and building ties with local political elites were balanced by occasional brutal campaigns against insurgent bands. General Order 100, issued by General Arthur MacArthur (father of Douglas MacArthur), gave officers on the ground a great deal of latitude when dealing with local insurgents by not providing POW protections to captured guerillas and trying them through military courts. When MacArthur returned to the states, his successor Adna Chaffee continued to isolate insurgents using military force, but he was more politically astute than his predecessor. Continuing to use the military to isolate and defeat insurgents, Chaffee turned individual provinces over to civil authority to keep the Army out of providing civil rule. There were several provinces where it became difficult to restore civil rule. In 1901, 48 US soldiers were killed on the island of Samar, triggering reprisals and a hunt for the perpetrators that was reminiscent of what the Spaniards had done, resulting in one of the most brutal campaigns of the war. The harshness of these last campaigns came to symbolize what many thought was a bitterly fought and brutal occupation. Historians are left with coming to their own conclusions, which are often contradictory.[17] Given the tumult of

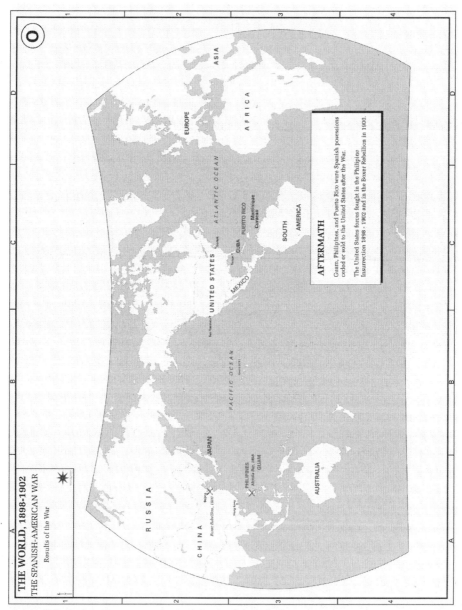

Figure 8.3   Map—The aftermath of the War with Spain. *Source:* West Point Atlas

the 1960s and the failures of Vietnam in particular, and the difficulties encountered in the Near East, it is admittedly difficult to come to objective conclusions. In fact, enough progress had been made to declare the war over in 1902.[18]

The negotiations that would lead to a peace treaty were long and drawn out, concluding with the United States acquiring an overseas empire. Cuba was granted independence, but with close economic ties to the mainland, an American naval base in Guantanamo Bay, and the ability to intervene as necessary, Cuba's status was more of autonomy than complete independence. The United States acquired the Philippines, the island of Guam in the central Pacific, and Puerto Rico.[19] Beyond an empire, there were other ramifications as well. The Spanish-American War and Philippine Campaign, when compared to the Civil War, were short. Overshadowed by the momentous events of the twentieth century, they are largely unknown today. The difficulties encountered in Iraq, Afghanistan, and other parts of the world today are very similar to those at the beginning of the twentieth century. The circumstances are, of course, very different, but many of the challenges faced by the soldiers and their officers today would more than likely ring true to veterans returning from the Philippines a century ago. As has been discussed previously, connecting stories of modern veterans to their contemporaries of a century ago can create compelling and meaningful content. Moreover, the debates that revolve around the role that our country plays in the world, either as an informal empire or as the world's policeman, also have connections to the past.

REFORM

Military history is more than battles and generals; it is the history and evolution of institutions. By far the most influential personality in the reform movement was Secretary of War Elihu Root. Root, who managed the War Department from 1899 to 1904, played a pivotal role in shaping the foundations for the twentieth-century Army. His chief contribution was creating and encouraging the growth of a General Staff. It was perceived that the success of Germany against France in 1871 was possible because of a General Staff. Root thought the time was right for the US Army to have one too.[20]

Determined to correct the well-publicized weaknesses that appeared during mobilization, Root absorbed official reports deconstructing the problems faced by the Army. He read Emory Upton's unpublished manuscript on American military policy celebrating the merits of a General Staff and a standing regular army to the detriment of the militia tradition. He also built a coalition of supporters in Congress and within the Army to test ideas and prepare both bodies for change. Root wanted to abolish the office of the Commanding General of the Army and use the General Staff as a consulting body for the Secretary of War. With no command responsibilities, it gave the Secretary and the President greater freedom of action in making responsible decisions based on well-informed planning. It also provided greater freedom of action in appointing commanding generals that had a distinct chain of command between the President, the Secretary of War, and the field forces. Congress passed the General Staff Act in 1903, and Root went on to establish the Army War College, a postgraduate school that trained officers for service on the General Staff.[21]

The establishment of a General Staff was a milestone, but not without several problems. The key difference between European General Staffs was direct—the Chief of Staff had no direct authority over other branches and bureaus of the Army. The number of officers trained to serve remained small and they had no role in the administration of the Army, allowing the Adjutant General to exercise an unusual amount of control over the day-to-day administrative functions. While this was eventually overcome, until the First World War, the staff remained small and the other bureaus would also retain a degree of independence that would not be brought into the orbit of the General Staff until the Second World War. Weaknesses aside, the creation of a General Staff was an important step in creating a modern military establishment.[22]

In tandem with the creation of a General Staff was a comprehensive reform of the National Guard. Root rejected Upton's pessimistic views on the role of the militia and citizen soldier. Rather than depending upon state-by-state laws regulating militia and a requirement for universal enrollment, Root argued that the Guard would serve as the properly armed and trained chief reserve for the regular Army in exchange for Federal appropriations. Senator Charles Dick worked with the Guard, Secretary Root, and others in Congress to pass the Dick Act in 1903, which ended the militia's independence and tied it closely to the War Department. Guardsmen could be called up for nine months and serve within the continental United States later. Five years later, in 1908, further legislation was passed to end the geographic restrictions and time limit for service. The provision for the Guard to serve overseas was challenged by the Supreme Court and rescinded. It was not until the passage of the National Defense Act of 1916 that a solution was found that basically allowed the guardsman to enlist as individuals rather than as units. There were further attempts by regular army supporters to create an organized reserve separate from the National Guard, but those attempts did not attract the required number of men to make it a viable alternative.[23]

The citizen soldier and the mechanisms that support them today are a direct result of the Dick Act and the subsequent legislation. The National Guard continues to play an important dual role of providing assistance at the state level and serving for all intents and purposes as the primary reserve for the regular forces. Many collections, no doubt, include donations from local, community-based National Guard units. Communities that do not have battlefields associated with them have another historical asset that is often not thought of. Nearly every sizeable community in the United States has a National Guard Armory and, by implication, members who served either recently or in the past in a Guard unit. Papers, oral histories, and artifacts serve as the touchstone to larger national issues from a local perspective. Nearly every state has either a museum associated with the Guard or a military museum associated with another organization. For example, in the Pacific Northwest region where I live, Washington, Oregon, and Idaho all have military organizations as part of the National Guard organization within each state. Other states have additional resources devoted to military history, for example, Indiana, with a Civil War and First World War Memorial with accompanying collections. Often modest in size and limited in hours, these institutions are resources that may prove helpful in highlighting the rich history of the Guard and the communities they serve.[24]

THE END OF THE BEGINNING

In the years before America's entrance into World War One, the primary role for the US Army and its sister service attached to the Navy, the Marine Corps, was imperial defense in the Pacific and Latin America. In the Caribbean, the Army and Marines intervened in Cuba several times and with the completion of the Panama Canal in 1914, there was a permanent military presence to protect the Canal. In many regards, these actions were similar in size and scope to the constabulary mission that the Army in particular had in the American West. While these deployments were modest, they underlined the changes that the Americans experienced. The greatest peacetime deployment of US forces since the war with Spain, however, was not in the Caribbean, but along the border with Mexico.[25]

In 1914, and again in 1916, President Woodrow Wilson sent American soldiers and sailors into Mexico. Ever since the war with Mexico came to an end in 1848, the porous border between the two countries had kept the Army busy fighting revolutionaries, bandits, and Indians for the remainder of the nineteenth century. With the onset of revolution in 1910, Mexican politics saw a revolving door of dictators and weak constitutional governments that created internal chaos. Marines and sailors, later supplemented by the Army, intervened in Veracruz to prevent a German arms shipment from reaching Mexican hands. Americans landed in April and would not leave until November 1914, when a new, albeit weak, administration was established in Mexico City. Revolution would continue and lead to more unrest along the border. Francisco "Pancho" Villa, a warlord in the northern provinces of Mexico, raided Columbus, New Mexico in March 1916, triggering a massive response. Led by Brigadier General John J. Pershing, American Cavalry and Infantry units plunged deep into northern Mexico to capture Villa. President Wilson may have sanctioned the raid, but the Mexican government did not. Its refusal to give Pershing access to Mexican railroads complicated an already difficult situation. While the supply situation was alleviated with the first deployment of motor trucks, the rugged terrain and the dispersal of Villa's forces made the cavalry's mission difficult. Assisting Pershing was the Army's First Aero Squadron, the first deployment of airplanes in the field. The National Guard was mobilized to serve along the border, preventing further incursions, while regular infantry and cavalry units plunged deeper into the interior. After several clashes with Mexican troops in the summer of 1916, Pershing ended the active pursuit and would withdraw from Mexico in February 1917. Villa was not captured, but several of his lieutenants were killed. Villa's power was broken.[26]

The deployment of much of the US Army along the border provided valuable field experience for many of the officers who in just a few months would go to France in the leading elements of the American Expeditionary Force. Concurrent with the intervention in Mexico, Europe was embroiled in a war that, in comparison to the Punitive Expedition, was on a scale that dwarfed the American intervention. Ironically, in spite of the institutional changes that occurred in the first decades of the twentieth century, the Punitive Expedition underlined the point that in the forty years since the end of the Civil War, the Army was still performing constabulary work along the border. This would, of course, all change as the war in Europe grew in intensity and scope. While the United States pursued a policy of neutrality for the first several years of the war, it became increasingly difficult for it to remain on the sidelines. When President Wilson declared war on Germany in April 6, 1917, the United States and its military institutions would be put to their severest test since the American Civil War.

NOTES

1. William Addleman Ganoe, *The History of the United States Army* (New York: D. Appleton-Century Company, 1942), 355.

2. Weigley, *History of the United States Army*, 256–64, Jerry M. Cooper, "The Army's Search For a Mission, 1865–1890" in Kenneth J. Hagan and William R. Roberts, *Against All Enemies: Interpretations of American Military History From Colonial Times to the Present* (Westport: Greenwood Press, 1986), 173–78. Any exploration of Reconstruction should begin with Eric Foner, *Reconstruction: America's Unfinished Revolution, 1863–1877* (New York: Harper & Row, 1988); for the Army's role, see James F. Sefton, *The United States Army and Reconstruction, 1865–1877* (Baton Rouge: Louisiana State University Press, 1967).

3. There are many fine overviews of the Indian Wars that provide a place to start in understanding the details of the various conflicts that occurred in the American West. A good place to start is with two books by Robert M. Utley, *Frontier Regulars: The United States Army and the Indian, 1886–1891* (Lincoln: Bison Books, 1984) and *The Indian Frontier of the American West, 1846–1890* (Albuquerque: University of New Mexico Press, 1984). See also, Robert Wooster, *The Military and the United States Indian Policy, 1865–1903* (New Haven: Yale University Press, 1988).

4. Lonetree, *Decolonizing Museums*, 168–75. For a look at the evolution of the meanings of Little Big Horn, see Edward T. Linenthal, *Sacred Ground: Americans and Their Battlefields* (Chicago: University of Illinois Press, 1991), Chapter 4.

5. There is the Buffalo Soldiers National Museum in Dallas, Texas, (http://buffalosoldier-museum.com/) and at Fort Leavenworth, Kansas, there is a memorial to the Buffalo Soldiers (http://garrison.leavenworth.army.mil/Newcomers---Visitors/Attractions/Buffalo-Soldiers.aspx) that was dedicated by Chairman of the Joint Chiefs of Staff Colin Powell in 1992 as well as the Frontier Army Museum (http://usacac.army.mil/organizations/lde/csi/frontier-museum). There are other exhibits and museums in the United States that feature the Buffalo Soldiers' story; this is only a representative sample.

6. Utley, *Frontier Regulars*, 10–43. A classic work on the soldiers' life in the frontier army is Don Rickey, Jr., *Forty Miles a Day on Beans and Hay: The Enlisted Soldier Fighting the Indian Wars* (Norman: University of Oklahoma Press, 1963). Unsurpassed in its sweep and an indispensable book for understanding the officers and enlisted men of the Army is Edward M. Coffman, *The Old Army: A Portrait of the American Army in Peacetime, 1794–1898* (New York: Oxford University Press, 1986). To explore the effects of posts on local communities, see Robert W. Frazer, *Forts and Supplies: The Role of the Army in the Economy of the Southwest, 1846–1861* (Albuquerque: University of New Mexico Press, 1983) and Darlis A. Miller, *Soldiers and Settlers: Military Supply in the Southwest* (Albuquerque: University of New Mexico Press, 1989).

7. Weigley, *History of US Army*, 272–73. A thorough overview of the Army's role in civil unrest in the nineteenth century can be found in Clayton D. Laurie and Ronald H. Cole, *The Role of Federal Military Forces in Domestic Disorders, 1877–1945* (Washington, DC: Center of Military History, 1997).

8. Weigley, *History of US Army*, 274–81, Cooper, "The Army's Search For a Mission," 183–88. Emory Upton cast a long shadow. A good place to understand his sway is Russell F.

Weigley, *Towards An American Army: Military Thought from Washington to Marshall* (Reprint. Westport: Greenwood Press, 1974), Chapter 7. A short biography that is useful is Stephen E. Ambrose, *Upton and the Army* (Baton Rouge: Louisiana State University Press, 1992). For a discussion of the continued evolution of infantry tactics in the face of the rifle, see Perry D. Jamieson, *Crossing the Deadly Ground: United States Army Tactics, 1865–1869*, (Tuscaloosa: The University of Alabama Press, 1994).

9. Sprout, *The Rise of American Naval Power*, Chapter 11, Hagan, *This People's Navy*, 177–89. A richly illustrated overview of the Navy in this period can be found in John D. Alden, *American Steel Navy: A Photographic History of the U.S. Navy from the Introduction of the Steel Hull in 1883 to the Cruise of the Great White Fleet, 1907–1909* (Annapolis: Naval Institute Press, 1972).

10. Sprout, *The Rise of American Naval Power*, Chapter 13.

11. A nice overview of this time period in terms of diplomacy can be found in Robert L. Beisner, *From the Old Diplomacy to the New, 1865–1900* (Arlington Heights: Harlan Davidson, 1986). For historians who subscribe to the economic determinist school, see Walter LaFeber, *The New Empire: An Interpretation of American Expansion, 1860–1898* (Ithaca: Cornell University Press, 1963). For the role of public opinion, see Ernest R. May, *Imperial Democracy: The Emergence of America as a Great Power* (Harcourt, Brace, 1961).

12. The sinking of the *Maine* was attributed to a Spanish mine by the press and that interpretation held for many years. A revision of that thesis was pursued by Admiral Hyman G. Rickover who concluded from the evidence that it was an internal explosion caused by a simmering fire in the coal bunkers which set off the explosion. Hyman G. Rickover, *How the Battleship Maine was Destroyed* (Second Edition. Annapolis: US Naval Institute Press, 1995). National Geographic magazine revisited this thesis and left it open for interpretation in Thomas B. Allen, "Remember the *Maine?*" *National Geographic*, vol. 193, no 2 (February 1998): 92–111. While we can never know for certain how the *Maine* sank, Rickover's explanation remains the most likely.

13. For an overview of the events that led to a declaration of war, see David Trask, *The War With Spain in 1898* (New York: Macmillan Publishing, 1981), Chapter 1. Given the relative importance of the country's imperial wars in setting the stage for a greater role on the world stage, the Spanish-American war does not garner a great deal of attention. The best survey text remains Trask. Paired with Graham A. Cosmas, *An Army For Empire: The United States Army in the Spanish-American War* (Second Edition, Shippensburg: White Mane Publishing, 1994), the books are excellent monographs to begin. For an overview of logistical issues, see Risch, *Quartermaster Support of the Army*, Chapter 12.

14. Trask, *The War With Spain*, Chapters 5, 6, and 11; Hagan, *This People's Navy*, 209–27.

15. Weigley, *History of the US Army*, Chapter 13; Cosmas, *Army For Empire*, Chapters 4 and 7; Trask, *War With Spain*, Chapters 9–10, and 13. See also, Graham A. Cosmas, "San Juan Hill and El Caney, 1–2 July, 1898," in Charles E. Heller and William A. Stofft, *America's First Battles, 1776–1965* (Lawrence: University Press of Kansas, 1986), 109–48.

16. Trask, *The War With Spain*, Chapters 16–18. A good place to begin for a survey of the Philippine campaign is Brian M. Linn, *The Philippine War, 1899–1902* (Lawrence: University Press of Kansas, 2000), Chapters 2 and 3.

17. The two works that define the debate between a mix of civic engagement and military action are spelled out in John Morgan Gates, *School Books and Krags: The United States Army in the Philippines, 1898–1902* (Westport: Greenwood Press, 1973). The outright conquest of a native people through violence and intimidation is spelled out in Stuart Creighton Miller, "Benevolent Assimilation," *The American Conquest of the Philippines, 1899–1903* (New Haven: Yale University Press, 1982).

18. Linn, *The Philippine War*. Chapters 9 and 14 lay out the challenges of the campaign against the insurgents. The mixed approach to pacification that is advocated by Linn is repeated

in Max Boot, *The Savage Wars of Peace: Small Wars and the Rise of American Power* (New York: Basic Books, 2002), Chapter 5.

19. Trask, *The War With Spain*, Chapter 20.

20. The impetus for reform is a topic that has generated a fair amount of literature. Good places to start are James L. Abrahamson, *American Arms for a New Century: The Making of a Great Military Power* (New York: The Free Press, 1981); William R. Roberts, "Reform and Revitalization, 1900–1903" in Kenneth J. Hagan and William R. Roberts, *Against All Enemies: Interpretations of American Military History from Colonial Times to the Present* (Westport, CT: Greenwood Press, 1986); and Daniel R. Beaver, *Modernizing the War Department: Change and Continuity in a Turbulent Era* (Kent: The Kent State University Press, 2006). For an overview of the development and history of the American General Staff, see James E. Hewes, Jr., *From Root to McNamara: Army Organization and Administration, 1900–1963* (Washington, DC: Center of Military History, 1975). For the German origins and success of the idea of a General Staff, see Robert M. Citino, *The German Way of War: From the Thirty Years' War to the Third Reich* (Lawrence: University Press of Kansas, 2005), Chapter 5.

21. To meet the needs of officers a step lower than the General Staff, the Army's postgraduate school system expanded after 1898 with specialized service schools for the artillery, cavalry, engineers, and signal corps. The school of application at Fort Leavenworth morphed into a two-year program for staff officers and those that would become division commanders. See Timothy K. Nenninger, "The Army Enters the Twentieth Century, 1904–1917" in Kenneth J. Hagan and William R. Roberts, *Against All Enemies: Interpretations of American Military History from Colonial Times to the Present* (Westport: Greenwood Press, 1986), 227–31. Nenninger's essay was derived from his monograph on Leavenworth, *The Leavenworth Schools and the Old Army: Education, Professionalism, and the Officer Corps of the United States Army, 1881–1918* (Westport: Greenwood Press, 1978).

22. Hewes, *From Root to McNamara*, 6–21; Weigley, *History of the US Army*, 314–22; Roberts, "Reform and Revitalization," 207–11.

23. Doubler, *Civilian in Peace, Soldier in War*, 141–59; Mahon, *History of the Militia and National Guard*, Chapter 10.

24. The Washington National Guard Museum, Camp Murray (washingtonguard.org/museum/), the Oregon Military Museum, Camp Withycombe (oregonmilitarymuseum.org), the Idaho Military Museum (museum.mil.idaho.gov), and the Indiana War Memorials (www.indianawarmemorials.org).

25. Max Boot, *The Savage Wars of Peace: Small Wars and the Rise of American Power*, Chapters 4, 6 and 7; Allan R. Millett, *Semper Fidelis: The History of the United States Marine Corps* (New York: Macmillan Publishing, 1980), Chapters 6 and 7. An excellent overview of the Army's role in the Pacific can be found in Brian M. Linn, *Guardians of Empire: The U.S. Army and the Pacific, 1902–1940* (Chapel Hill: The University of North Carolina Press, 1997).

26. A complete account of the US intervention in Mexico can be found in Clarence C. Clendenen, *Blood on the Border: The United States Army and the Mexican Irregulars* (New York: Macmillan Publishers, 1969), in particular Chapters 8–19. For a personal account of the expedition's actions in Mexico, see Colonel Frank Tompkins, *Chasing Villa: The Story Behind the Story of Pershing's Expedition into Mexico* (Harrisburg: The Military Service Publishing Company, 1934). For Pershing's role, see Donald Smythe, *Guerilla Warrior: The Early Life of John J. Pershing* (New York: Charles Scribner's Sons, 1973), Chapters 15–17. An exploration of trucks and airplanes can be found in Roger G. Miller, "Wings and Wheels: The 1st Aero Squadron, Truck Transport, and the Punitive Expedition of 1916," in *Air Power History*, vol. 42, no. 4 (Winter 1995): 12–29.

Chapter 9

On The World's Stage, 1914–1939

Once realizing their obligations, the American people willingly sent their sons to battle; with unstinted generosity, they gave of their substance; and with fortitude bore the sacrifices that fell their lot. They, too, served, and in their service inspired the armies to victory.[1]

General John J. Pershing

It is often difficult to measure the effect of one event across time. To illustrate that concept, my favorite word picture is visualizing what happens when you throw a rock into a still pond. The ripples continue long after the rock has sunk to the bottom. In many regards, I see World War One and the interwar period as just such a case. Even though these events were eclipsed by World War Two, the actions of 1914 and beyond continue to ripple across time. It was a cataclysmic war that killed millions of soldiers and civilians alike. Moreover, it is fair to say that without World War One, the Second would not have followed. The year 2014 marked the beginning of the centennial of the Great War. For many, the First World War is the deep past; yet, the legacy of the war is all around us—tensions in the Balkans, Russia's jittery relationship with the West, the constant tumult in the Middle East, all have historical roots that begin with the first great war of the twentieth century. The United States was involved in fighting the Central Powers from April 1917 to November 1918. In those seventeen months, approximately 50,000 Americans were killed in battle and over 200,000 wounded.[2] Although the war was of relatively short duration for the American Expeditionary Force (AEF), we cannot discount the impact of the First World War.[3]

THE ROAD TO WAR IS PAVED WITH GOOD INTENTIONS

As the twentieth century unfolded, American soldiers and civilians would eventually serve around the world, leaving behind a rich record of experiences. World War One was the first that saw millions of men and women deployed overseas. Even though the battlefields are not located in the continental United States, the soldiers that ventured

149

overseas left a legacy for us to consider. The American Battle Monument Commission (ABMC) administers the network of cemeteries around the world that tend to the American dead buried overseas. They administer the cemeteries, providing services to the next of kin and relatives. Given the general interest in World War One for more general audiences, the cemeteries and memorials are places that also focus on commemoration and remembrance. Providing resources for both mourners and casual visitors, the ABMC is largely successful in providing resources for both. They are adding value to their commemorative mission by including interpretive resources on their website. Guide books, short videos, and cemetery personnel have the ability to connect an entire new generation to the sacrifices of the First World War generation in a meaningful and compelling way.[4]

There are many ways to explore American contributions to the Allied victory in Europe. In 2014, Congress designated the National World War One Museum at Liberty Memorial in Kansas City, Missouri, the United States' national museum on the Great War. Originally built as a memorial to those who fell as well as those who served, it has adapted to a wider mission as the country's primary place to tell the story of the War. To their credit, the American experience is put into the wider context of the War itself. Using artifacts, video stations, film, and interactive digital technologies, the museum provides an immersive museum experience for those who want to understand the War in total or dip into the time line to explore issues of importance to them. It is a unique institution with a mission that encompasses the entire country. Yet, in terms of the American experience, it is fair to apply the label of the War as an obscure event for contemporary audiences. There are several approaches, though, that can still be effective in unlocking the meaning of this cataclysmic event. Nearly every community, even those of modest size, played a role. Local history can provide a sharp focus of stories and words of participants, whether serving on the front lines or working on the home front. These are just as compelling as large, well-funded exhibits. The ongoing American involvement in various actions around the world in our own time provides a unique opportunity to explore the meaning of what the war means in light of the conflicts we are involved with now.[5]

When war broke out in Europe in the summer of 1914, it was a European war. While it did spread to other parts of the world, the United States remained neutral. In spite of the country's economic and cultural ties to Europe, in particular England, President Woodrow Wilson was not compelled to intervene. He was his own man and kept close control of policy. If anything, he was more interested in finding a solution to the conflict than mobilizing American military resources. While understanding the utility of force (he had mobilized a good portion of the US Army to intervene in Mexico), Wilson was reluctant to use violence to meet national ends. He despised imperialism and was a steady advocate of self-determination, which added to his reluctance to intervene on behalf of European powers that had created exploitive empires across the world. Nevertheless, the political elites of the country were inclined to support France and Great Britain. The balancing act between public opinion, the sentiments of political elites, security concerns, and the uncertainties of modern warfare was difficult to maintain. The force of events would compel Wilson to make a decision for war.[6]

Woodrow Wilson is the key to understanding the United States' road to war. In pursuing a policy of neutrality, Wilson wanted to protect the rights of the United States to lead its own destiny and make policies that met the needs of the nation and its people, but he also had to be steadfast to protect those rights. In order to protect those rights, Wilson was willing to stand up to both British and German infringement of the rights of the United States to trade with both sides. Unfortunately, the intermittent but steady erosion of American commercial rights through attacks by German submarines (known as U-boats or *Unterseeboot*) forced Wilson's hand to make a decision for war. Given the balance of trade with Great Britain and France, Wilson would have been hard pressed to force the point by engaging the Royal Navy on the high seas. However, Wilson's administration did want both sides to honor the right of American ships to carry cargo free from interference. When the Germans attempted to blockade Great Britain with its submarine fleet in 1915, the resulting sinking of the ocean liner *Lusitania* strained relations between the Central Powers and the United States. While the Germans ultimately backed off, as victory for Germany became tenuous, unrestricted submarine warfare was unleashed in 1917, resulting in the deaths of American citizens. In addition to the off-and-on German attacks, the British were able to play on American sympathies. However, with substantial German and Irish lobbies, not to mention advocates for peace that desired a negotiated settlement, Wilson had to tread carefully. Although he was cognizant of these opinion makers, Wilson's main goal was to preserve American freedom of action.[7]

In the election of 1916, in spite of the *Lusitania* disaster and public pressure, Wilson kept the United States out of the War, securing a second term. Although the Germans were unwilling to test Wilson's patience, in January 1917, the German government decided to unleash unrestricted submarine warfare against all shipping. Wilson could have pursued an aggressive policy of armed neutrality, but going to war allowed Wilson to pursue his goals with more vigor. Moreover, given the exhausted state of the Allies and the Germans, a negotiated peace in 1917 would have given the Germans more of what they wanted and would have validated the aggression of the Central Powers. British code breakers intercepted a telegram from State Secretary of German Foreign Affairs, Arthur Zimmerman, which turned out to be a message to Mexico promising German support for a Mexican rebellion. The communique certainly inflamed American public opinion and added to the rift, but did not figure prominently in the decision for war. In the final analysis, Wilson went to war to protect American rights, the country's security, and what amounts to the high ideal of making the world safe for democracy. Unlike his successors, though, Wilson never really espoused a set of war aims around which a still divided public could coalesce. The protracted run-up to war left the United States unprepared to meet its obligations once war was declared in April 1917.[8]

MOBILIZATION

World War Two overshadows the stories of its progenitor. For the general audience, the preparations that took place in the United States and Europe in 1917–1918 are largely unknown but critical in understanding World War One. The relatively short amount of time that the United States was involved meant that mobilization, in particular for industry, was rapid and chaotic. Mobilizing the necessary manpower was also fraught with issues. Given the problems that beset the mobilization of the country's war economy and the mobilization of the AEF, it makes the Wilson administration's achievements that much more impressive. In terms of command, Wilson preferred to take a hands-off approach. Secretaries of War and Navy Newton Baker and Josephus Daniels, respectively, their staffs, and the commanding general of the AEF John J. Pershing, would oversee the actual war. Pershing was the man of the hour. Having just returned from Mexico, he was held in high esteem by the President and his peers. He left for France with a small staff in June 1917, and began the lengthy preparations and plans for building an American Army in France. His chief accomplishment after arriving in France was his insistence in keeping the American Army together and not as a manpower pool to staff depleted French and British formations. While exceptions were made in emergencies, such as the German offensives in the spring of 1918, Pershing held his ground and refused to give up his men.[9]

To staff the AEF, the country federalized the National Guard and restored conscription. Wanting to avoid the draft riots that had occurred fifty years earlier during the Civil War, the government put a great deal of thought into the process. Rather than accepting volunteers, manpower was conscripted through a lottery system. No substitutes were allowed, though there were exemptions. There were no draft riots and by the end of the war, nearly 24 million had registered, and 2.7 million men served. As for the National Guard, it was completely federalized by July 1917. The creation of larger infantry divisions than what the Guard organized meant breaking up and re-designating units, eliminating the unique geographic distinctions that many units brought into the Army. In spite of these identity issues, the guard divisions that did make it to the line fought with distinction. Moreover, the draft touched even the smallest of communities, again providing a means for a small museum to mount an exhibit regarding the community's interaction with the draft.[10]

The Army was not the only branch of the armed forces preparing for action. The Navy envisaged a role for themselves as well. The Royal Navy was the dominant force in terms of heavy units, that is, battleships, so the primary role the US Navy could fill was to insure that American troops and supplies could get across the Atlantic relatively unmolested by German U-Boats. It was not a role that was necessarily anticipated. Prewar naval legislation had funded a battle fleet heavy in battleships. Instead, the commander of American naval forces in Europe, Admiral William S. Sims, forcibly argued for antisubmarine vessels. He vigorously supported the adoption of a convoy system, a much more efficient way of ushering ships and supplies overseas. The Navy also contributed to the building of a mine barrier across the North Sea to block German submarines from exiting and encircling the British home islands. While modest in scope when compared to the achievements and ships of the Royal Navy, the US Navy provided vital support to the war effort and mobilized to Europe relatively trouble free.[11]

World War One inaugurated a new dimension in warfare. For eons man had fought in two dimensions: on the land and on the sea. The perfection of human flight added a new dimension that came of age in the First World War—aerial warfare. The Wright Brothers may have secured their reputation in the United States, but as in other sectors, the Americans were woefully unprepared to wage a war in the air on their own. However, with help from the British and French, the Americans were able to build a fairly large force by the Armistice. Throughout most of the war, Americans flew European aircraft and were largely trained by the British and French air services.[12]

OVER THERE

When looking at the achievements of the AEF nearly a century after they deployed overseas, one can see that there were certainly issues and problems that dogged Pershing through the Armistice. Pershing's perspectives on how the Americans would contribute to victory were colored by his experiences. For Pershing, victory could not be attained through defensive warfare. The General postulated:

> It was my opinion that the victory could not be won by the costly process of attrition, but it must be won by driving the enemy out into the open and engaging him in a war of movement . . . . Therefore we took decided issue with the Allies and, without neglecting thorough preparation for trench fighting, undertook to train mainly for open combat, with the object from the state of vigorously forcing the offensive.[13]

Pershing's disconnect with the conditions of the front and the relative inexperience of the Americans certainly worked against constant success, but American units would continue to adapt to the changing circumstances in the last year of the war and emerge victorious, albeit at a high price.[14]

Pershing was also attempting to create an army, train it properly, and insert units into the front line to be exposed to the rigors of the Western Front, all the while steadfastly refusing to use his men as replacements for weakened French and British formations. For the sake of the coalition, some concessions were agreed to. British ships brought American divisions to France, in exchange for the British training them. Accelerating the number of troops going overseas upset deployment and training schedules, making it difficult to follow a strict formula to prepare American troops for combat. Moreover, the need for combat rather than supporting troops meant that all of the infrastructure required to support the AEF was also in disarray. These pell-mell deployments put men into the theater of operations, but they were ill-prepared to be thrown immediately into combat. Nevertheless, Americans entered the line.[15]

As more Americans joined the fight, the combat they experienced can be best understood as occurring in two stages. The first was our reaction to the German offensives from March to July 1918. With the success of the Russian Revolution, concluding with a separate peace with the Central Powers, tens of thousands of men could be re-deployed to the Western Front, renewing German fortunes and ending the war on their terms. In light of this crisis, Pershing relaxed his grip and allowed formations to be deployed where they were needed to stem the German tide. In May 1918, American forces attacked along various points of the large bulge created from the German push. One of the first actions was deploying courtesy units from the First Infantry Division at Cantigny in May 1918. To help blunt the German offensive that was threatening Paris, the Second and Third Infantry Divisions counterattacked at Belleau Wood. The German offensives of 1918 restored a degree of mobility to the battlefield that had

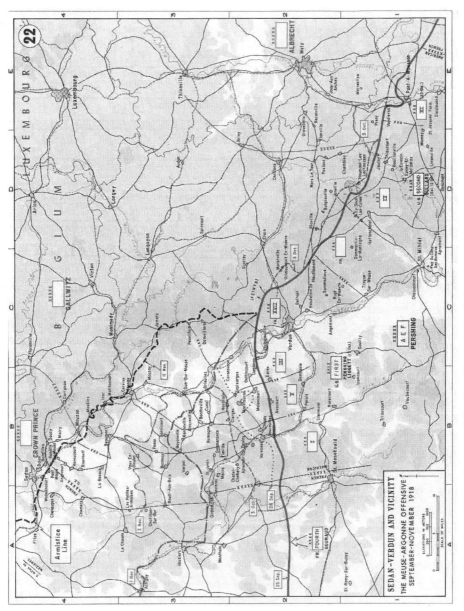

Figure 9.1   Map—Meuse-Argonne Offensive. *Source:* West Point Atlas

been missing since the closing days of 1914. In an effort to capture the desperation of the situation and the steadfastness of the Marines, the National Museum of the Marine Corps has created a vignette with a video presentation and artifacts related to this famous Marine moment. While this certainly helps visitors understand the accomplishments of the Marines and the chaos of the combat, depicting combat at this stage of the Great War is a challenge and difficult to accomplish. It does, however, serve as a corrective to the perception that the War was nothing but trenches and mud amid shattered trees and destroyed villages. Nevertheless, the exhibit helps dispel any romantic notions of warfare on the Western Front.[16]

The second stage of American participation was that of no longer reacting to German actions, but going on the offensive. Pershing sought to make a mark and commit the AEF to a series of relatively independent actions. The first was the reduction of the St. Mihiel salient in September 1918. A far more ambitious operation and the largest commitment of American troops during the war was a series of battles that began in late September and would continue until the Armistice. This was the so-called Meuse-Argonne Offensive. Attacking in hilly country and moving against powerful German defenses, the Americans bludgeoned their way across these dense German fortifications. Using a mix of veteran and green formations, in spite of impressive gains in the first week, the offensive stalled with high casualties. After reorganizing their lines, the Americans resumed the offensive, bringing in fresh troops. In tandem with French and German offensives to the north, German morale plummeted, breaking the fighting spirit of their troops. While it was not a pell-mell retreat, the Germans still had the capacity to inflict considerable casualties. The end was in sight.[17]

The end of the war came quickly. Wracked by revolution at home, facing intractable problems sustaining the civilian population because of the Allied blockade, the Central Powers collapsed. The speed of the collapse and the divergent views of the postwar world between the United States, Great Britain, and France led to a fractious peace process with little consensus among the victors. Woodrow Wilson pushed for his fourteen points, which were anchored on self-determination and collective security. Congress rejected Wilson's vision, leading to a separate peace with the Central Powers and leaving the job of enforcing the peace with the western European powers. The complete abdication of the United States and its insular foreign policy between 1920 and 1940 put a lasting peace in peril before the processes unfolded. The decade of the 1920s created a degree of stability that came to a halt with the onset of the world-wide depression in 1929. Burdened with the memories of the First World War and hobbled by poor economies, Britain and France lost the peace in the 1930s by failing to reign in or stop a resurgent Germany led by Adolph Hitler and his National Socialist party.[18]

From the point of view of both the victors and the defeated, the Great War as it came to be called was a cataclysm that stood alone. There was no other conflict yet experienced in modern times that could compare to the events of 1914–1918. In the war's immediate aftermath, it was thought by many that society could rebuild and create institutions that could resist the temptation of another destructive war. This was not to be. Germany was left with a disgruntled population whose fury would be channeled into world-wide conflagration with a level of violence and destruction that surpassed that of the first. If you had asked a representative sample of people in 1920 about the inevitability of another war, except for an ardent pessimist, the question would have been laughed at, in particular in the United States. Another war was by no means inevitable and until the mid-1930s at the earliest, these were heartfelt desires. Of course, we know now that it was a hollow promise; war would erupt again in Europe in 1939, and for the United States in 1941.

THE INTERWAR PERIOD

The period between the First and Second World Wars, beyond the realm of professional historians and buffs, is largely forgotten. The interwar period, the years between the First and Second World Wars, serves as a bridge between these two important events and provides insight into how the United States emerged victorious in 1945. Many of the officers, technologies, and ideas would emerge from the dark shadows of the interwar period.

The destruction of the Central Powers and the weakening of England and France left the United States with a great deal of economic and military power. The conscious choice made to reject an active role in the League of Nations and negotiate a separate peace signaled a withdrawal from the international stage. The United States would still be involved in various international efforts, notably the naval disarmament treaties of the 1920s and 1930s, but the military policy adopted in 1920 was a sign of retrenchment. The passage of the National Defense Act was one of the first attempts to create a coherent defense policy and was a reflection of the country's *zeitgeist* or mood. Rather than creating a large, expansible army of regular formations supplemented by universal military training to create a pool of manpower, the Congress enacted modest legislation. The final legislation created regular formations that would be supplemented in times of emergency by the National Guard, allowing for a mobilized regular army of 435,000 men. The regular army never achieved its legislated strength. For most of the interwar period, it remained at 125,000–150,000 men. It was certainly an appropriate expression of military policy coming after a brief but bloody experience on the Western Front.[19]

MEETING THE THREAT—THE US NAVY AND JAPAN

The US Navy was perceived as the first line of defense against a possible adversary. In spite of shrinking budgets and public apathy, the US Navy would emerge from the interwar period with a fleet that could meet the modern challenges of war. In 1916, Congress passed a massive naval construction bill for battle cruisers and battleships that would not be ready for service until after the War was over. Threatened by an ebullient United States, Great Britain was not willing to let go of its needs, triggering a naval arms race between the United States and Britain. With the German fleet out of the picture (it had surrendered its capital ships to the Royal Navy, but scuttled them in 1919) and the ending of the alliance between Britain and Japan, the British wanted to expand their fleet. Political and fiscal pressures led to the calling of the

Washington Naval Conference in 1921. At the conclusion of negotiations, the great powers agreed to reductions of capital ships. Using a ratio formula, the treaty allotted the United States and Great Britain 500,000 tons to Japan's 300,000 tons, creating a ratio of 5:5:3. Scrapping obsolete ships as well as some of the most modern that were still under construction, and limiting the construction of new fortifications in Japanese and American possessions in the central Pacific, this disarmament treaty was one of the most successful treaties of the twentieth century. The treaty, however, left Japanese and American admirals wondering if they still had the assets to defend their Pacific possessions, let alone the capital ships needed to defeat either side. There were further limits on heavy and light cruiser tonnage in 1930 that also affected the great powers. Treaties rather than a renewed naval arms race matched the country's mood. Naval disarmament was a prudent decision.[20]

The assumption that the primary adversary for the US Navy would be Japan-influenced war planning and how it would use the assets available to them. From the beginning of the twentieth century to the beginning of World War Two, (Japan) War Plan Orange (Japan) dominated naval thinking. While the plan evolved over time, the basic premise remained in place until the exigencies of the campaign in the Pacific had an effect. Anticipating a Japanese offensive across the central Pacific and cutting off the Philippines from direct reinforcement, an American counteroffensive would take the fleet across the central Pacific. Fleet actions would eliminate units of the Japanese Navy and secure bases as the United States advanced across the Pacific. It was assumed that a large naval battle would occur, either drastically inhibiting or destroying the Japanese fleet, allowing for the liberation of the Philippines and the siege of the Japanese home islands. The value of the Philippines declined until the entrance of the United States into the war when political considerations entered into the equation. While it was assumed that the battleship fleets would do most of the fighting, as the interwar period progressed, carrier-based aviation began to figure much more prominently than in the past.[21]

There is an axiom that innovation is often held up by those who hold on to tradition. The adoption of the aircraft carrier as a key component of the battle fleet took time as ideas and technology matured. Without the promise of air cover as they advanced across the Pacific made aircraft a valuable asset in terms of scouting. Naval aviators had a degree of independence from the battleship admirals, who understood the role of aircraft serving with the fleet in very narrow terms—as scouts for the battleships. Naval aviators around the world understood the inherent offensive potential that aircraft provided, allowing for innovation and experimentation. While there were bitter arguments over the utility of aircraft in fighting, by the mid-1930s, carriers had become a valuable asset and extension of the fleet's battle line. The other key to a successful campaign across the Pacific was securing bases. Beginning in the 1920s, the Marines began to explore how to use the Fleet Marine Force to serve the advance of the fleet. Experiments in Hawaii and the Caribbean explored landing techniques and technologies that would make a beach landing possible. In spite of budget issues and a fleet that did not have the necessary mix of capital ships and a logistic train to bring the war to Japan, the doctrines and technology that would allow for the US Navy to expand to meet that challenge were set by 1939–1940.[22]

THE PROMISE OF THE BOMBER

There is no other issue that generated more dogmatic ideas than strategic bombardment from the air. From a twenty-first-century perspective, there is certainly nothing novel about the airplane. It has been used in warfare for a century and air travel is as commonplace as taking the train was for our forebears. From the perspective of the 1920s and 1930s, the notion of warfare in a third dimension held for some prognosticators a promise—breaking the stalemates on the ground that defined combat in the First World War. Given what we know now, it is easy to dismiss the prophecies of airpower enthusiasts, but it was a precursor of things to come and becomes a necessary tool for having a dialogue with visitors on strategic bombardment and the application of airpower against civilian targets and populations. This is not a question of hardware, it is about ideas.

The Wright Brothers may have invented the airplane, but it came of age in the First World War. As soon as the war was over, European and American air power advocates pushed for the creation of independent air arms. The British air arm gained independence with the creation of the Royal Air Force in 1918 but in the United States, despite a great degree of independence, it was not until after the Second World War that complete independence from the Army was attained. One officer, William "Billy" Mitchell, was so vociferous in his complaints about not realizing the potential of strategic bombardment that he was court-martialed, which created a media event that was reminiscent of celebrity trials in our own century. The passage of the 1926 Air Corps Act conferred a degree of independence to the air arm, allowing the many notions of victory through air power to germinate and grow, leading to the comprehensive air campaign that began in World War Two.[23]

The impetus toward strategic bombing was the nexus between ideas and technology. Men like Billy Mitchell, Italian prognosticator Guilo Douhet, and the head of the RAF, Hugh Trenchard, captured the public's imagination with general notions of the utility of strategic bombardment in a future war. There was general recognition that in an industrialized war, the entire economy and the civilian workforce would be legitimate targets. Bombers could impede war-time production and depress civilian morale, leading to victory. The evolution of aviation technology, transitioning from canvas and wood to aluminum and higher-performance engines by the mid-1930s, allowed for the development of four engine bombers that could carry large bomb loads over the distances required to make strategic bombing a reality. In the United States, the development of what would become the Boeing B-17 and the Norden bombsight that provided a theoretical capability for pin-point strategic bombing quickly went from drawing boards to full-scale development. Theory became reality and developed into the chief doctrine of the Air Corps in the years immediately preceding the Second World War.[24]

FIGHTING THE NEXT GROUND WAR

The internal combustion engine provided motive power not only for airplanes, but also for tanks, automobiles, and trucks. The armored leviathans fielded by the British, French, and AEF, were like their counterparts in the air, were first generation vehicles that were prone to breaking down, time consuming to maintain, and not as practical as their inventors thought. Nevertheless, they stoked the imagination of many. Much like the theorists who dominated the strategic bombing debate, there were British writers in particular who saw the tank as the savior on the battlefield. American tank advocates agreed, but in the aftermath of the National Defense Act, the independent Tank Corps was disbanded.[25]

After observing British experiments with mechanization, the Secretary of War approved the creation of an Experimental Mechanized Force to study the needs of the Army during the next decade. A mixed force of tanks, armored cars, self-propelled artillery, and motorized infantry promised unparalleled mobility on the battlefield. While there was interest in moving toward a permanent mechanized force, budget priorities exerted themselves and nothing came of it. Based on experiments carried out in Great Britain, a small mechanized force was created to supplement the existing assets in the US Army. The experiment bore fruit as the 1920s gave way to the thirties. When Douglas MacArthur assumed office as Chief of Staff in 1930, he instituted a new policy that allowed every branch to mechanize. Rather than contravening the National Defense Act that had parceled out tanks to the infantry, cavalry experiments were conducted with combat cars. While there were some within the horse cavalry that lamented the loss of the horse, mechanized cavalry argued for maneuver rather than firepower as necessary for success. The infantry wanted tanks to accompany them, putting emphasis on staying power rather than speed. These internal struggles continued until the beginning of the war. It was the German victories with their so-called Blitzkrieg in the spring of 1940 that precipitated the merger of *all* tanks, whether in the cavalry or in the infantry, into an armored force. Heavily influenced by the cavalry, the United States emphasized mobility over protection and firepower, putting the Americans at a disadvantage when they met the Germans. Nevertheless, in spite of the challenges the Americans faced during the interwar period, the successes of American armor in the Second World War have their roots in the interwar period.[26]

THE NEW DEAL

Any discussion of the interwar period is, of course, dominated by the arrival of the Great Depression. Precipitated by the crash of the Stock Market in 1929, the consequences of the Great Depression were felt until the beginning of the Second World War, a decade later. With the election of Franklin D. Roosevelt into the White House, until the late 1930s every branch of the military experienced a drop in appropriations. They all struggled to preserve manpower with little left over to develop new technology. Regardless of the budget, the Army did gain invaluable experience in administering over the largest public relief campaigns of the New Deal—the Civilian Conservation Corps (CCC). With camps across the United States, the men enrolled in the CCC did conservation work on public lands across the country. Given the national scope of the program, the Army mobilized resources to support the camps, providing regular and reserve officers with valuable administrative and command experience at a time when training dollars were at a premium. While the Army was reluctant to take up this role, and fought any permanent connection with the CCC, it was one of the most visible efforts of public relief that the Army provided during the Great Depression. The CCC is a program that touched so many communities that it offers an opportunity for smaller museums and historical societies to talk about the role of the military in their local communities.[27]

On the opposite end of the spectrum was the Army's controversial role in the so-called Bonus March in 1932. Veterans of the AEF, many of whom were in desperate financial straits, wanted some compensation for their service during the Great War. When paying life insurance premiums while they were in the service, they had been promised a small cash bonus if the policy was never used. Unfortunately, the bonus was not to be paid out until 1945. Thousands of veterans marched on the nation's capital to pressure Congress into an early release of the bonus to help alleviate the suffering of veterans. A bonus bill passed in the House, but failed in the Senate. Tensions rose in the makeshift veterans' camps and further protests came to nothing. Worried over continued unrest and a cadre of Communist agitators wanting more violent action, political leaders in the capital wanted the Bonus Marchers out of town. As the police moved to evict marchers from downtown buildings, a marcher was killed, which escalated the tension. On July 28, 1932, President Herbert ordered the Army to disperse the marchers. By the evening, marchers had been cleared from downtown and were waiting to cross the Potomac to clear their camp. Army Chief of Staff Douglas

Figure 9.2 The Bonus March. *Source*: Library of Congress

MacArthur played a prominent role in the action, and in one of the most controversial decisions, he may have disobeyed orders from the President. He went ahead and cleared the camp, and went so far as to burn the camp down. It was a public relations disaster for Hoover and may have cost him the election. The veterans did get their bonus after more pressure and the memory of the incident would lead to the establishment of the GI Bill of Rights during the Second World War, providing veterans with benefits upon their leaving the service. Understandably worried over the implications of a massive protest in the nation's capital, MacArthur was, nevertheless, unrepentant about his decision. It was an indication of the desperation caused by the Depression, and is an incident that is little known by the American public. Thousands of veterans were moved to action, providing yet another event that allows local institutions to highlight a story of national importance.[28]

In spite of the challenges of a country prone to isolate itself from the international community and the problems associated with that, as international tensions mounted after 1937, more resources, further introspection, and a final reckoning in December 1941 would provide the proof that the United States was prepared to meet the challenges of the Second World War.

NOTES

1. John J. Pershing, *My Experiences in the World War*, Vol. 1 (New York: Harper & Row Publishers, 1931; reprint, Blue Ridge Summit: Tab Books, 1989), xvii.

2. Deaths are contemporary to the conflict. Does not include deaths that occurred while in uniform but not in a battle. The source is Leonard P. Ayres, *The War With Germany: A Statistical Summary* (Washington, DC: Government Printing Office, 1919), 119–22.

3. There are hundreds, if not thousands, of books that have been published on nearly every aspect of the First World War, too many to mention here. The only way, however, to understand the war in its totality is delving into some of the details of the war before April 1917. Solid overviews of the war are Michael S. Neiberg, *Fighting the Great War: A Global History* (Cambridge: Harvard University Press, 2005) and David Stevenson, *Cataclysm: The First World War as Political Tragedy* (New York: Basic Books, 2004). For a historiography of US sources, a good place to begin is Dennis Showalter, "The United States in the Great War: A Historiography," *Organization of American Historians Magazine of History* 17, no. 1 (October 2002): 5–13.

4. Access to ABMC interpretive materials can be found on their website: http://www.abmc. gov/. For an interactive timeline on World War One: http://www.abmc.gov/sites/default/files/ interactive/interactive_files/WW1/index.html.

5. For the National World War One Museum and the Liberty Memorial, please visit https:// theworldwar.org/. Carol Kammen, "Wilson's Ghost." *History News: The Magazine of the American Association for State and Local History* 69, no. 4 (Autumn, 2014): 3–4.

6. Arthur Link is the biographer of Woodrow Wilson. A summary of Wilson's views can be found in Arthur S. Link, *Woodrow Wilson: Revolution, Peace and War* (Arlington Heights: Harlan Davidson, 1979).

7. Link, *Woodrow Wilson*, 38–46, Justus D. Doenecke, *Nothing Less Than War: A New History of America's Entry into World War I* (Lexington: The University Press of Kentucky, 2011), Chapter 3. See also, Ernest R. May, *The World War and American Isolation, 1914–17* (Cambridge: Harvard University Press, 1959).

8. Link, *Woodrow Wilson*, 60–71; Doenecke, *Nothing Less Than War*, Chapters 9–10. The Zimmerman Telegram has been of interest to Americans since the publication of Barbara Tuchman's book, an interesting and compelling story that in the end did not really influence the decision-making process except to reinforce existing mistrust in German motives. See Barbara W. Tuchman, *The Zimmerman Telegram* (New York: Macmillan Publishing Company, 1966). For a revised and exhaustive look at the telegram and its effects on policy, see Thomas Boghardt, *The Zimmerman Telegram: Intelligence, Diplomacy, and America's Entry into World War I* (Annapolis: Naval Institute Press, 2012).

9. Allan R. Millett, "Over Where? The AEF and the American Strategy for Victory, 1917–1918," Kenneth J. Hagan and William R. Roberts, *Against All Enemies: Interpretations of American Military History from Colonial Times to the Present* (Westport: Greenwood Press, 1986), 235–39; Donald Smythe, *Pershing: General of the Armies* (Bloomington, IN: Indiana University Press, 1986), Chapters 1–3; Edward M. Coffman, *The War to End All Wars: The American Military Experience in World War I* (Madison: The University of Wisconsin Press, 1986), Chapter 2.

10. Coffman, *War to End All Wars*, 24–9; Mahon, *History of the Militia and the National Guard*, Chapter 11. The most complete account of the draft can be found in John Whiteclay Chambers II, *To Raise an Army: The Draft Comes to America* (New York: The Free Press, 1987).

11. Coffman, *War to End All Wars*, Chapter 4; Hagan, *This People's Navy*, 249–58.

12. Coffman, *War to End All Wars*, Chapter 7; Charles J. Gross, *American Military Aviation: The Indispensable Arm* (College Station: Texas A & M University Press, 2002), 29–36. For an excellent overview of the war in the air during World War One, see Lee Kennett, *The First Air War, 1914–1918* (New York: The Free Press, 1991).

13. Pershing, *My Experiences*, Vol. 1, 152.

14. The successes and failures of American arms have generated a great deal of literature. A representative voice in the sad state of American tactical doctrine is Timothy K. Nenninger. "Tactical Dysfunction in the AEF, 1917–1918" *Military Affairs* 51, no. 4, 177–81. For a more positive view of combat performance, see Mark E. Grotelueschen. *The AEF Way of War: The American Army and Combat in World War I* (New York: Cambridge University Press, 2007).

15. For insight into Pershing's thoughts on amalgamation, see Smythe, *Pershing: General of the Armies,* Chapters 8 and 13. For a counter against Pershing's actions, see David E. Trask, *The AEF and Coalition Warmaking, 1917–1918* (Lawrence: University Press of Kansas, 1993). One of the more fascinating topics of the AEF but one that is generally neglected is the immense effort and resources it took to keep the AEF supplied. While dated, a good place to start is Risch, *Quartermaster Support of the Army*, Chapters 14–15 and Huston, Sinews of War, Chapters 20–24.

16. For a concise overview of the battles of the AEF, see Millett, Maslowski, and Feis, *For the Common Defense*, 330–38 and Coffman, *The War to End All Wars*, Chapter 8. For the battles that shaped the AEF, see Allan R. Millett, "Cantigny, 28-31 May 1918" in Charles E. Heller and William A. Stofft, *America's First Battles, 1776–1965* (Lawrence: University Press of Kansas, 1986), 149–85; Douglas V. Johnson II and Rolfe and Rolfe Hillman, Jr., *Soissons, 1918* (College Station: Texas A & M Press, 1999). An indispensable reference book was published after the war by the American Battle Monuments Commission that is still useful today, *American Armies and Battlefields in Europe: A History, Guide, and Reference Book* (Washington, DC: Government Printing Office, 1938). The book can also be found online in the form of an Adobe PDF at http://www.abmc.gov/sites/default/files/publications/AABEFINAL_Blue_Book.pdf.

17. A tightly written account of the Meuse-Argonne can be found in Robert H. Ferrell, *America's Deadliest Battle: Meuse-Argonne, 1918* (Lawrence: University Press of Kansas,

2007). See also, Paul F. Braim, *The Test of Battle: The American Expeditionary Force in the Meuse-Argonne Campaign* (Shippensburg: White Mane Publishing, 1998).

18. Link, *Woodrow Wilson: Revolution, War and Peace*, 86–103. For the fight to ratify the Treaty, see Chapter 5; Stevenson, *Cataclysm*, Chapters 17–21.

19. Weigley, *History of the US Army*, 394–405; Robert K. Griffith, *Men Wanted For the United States Army: America's Experience With An All-Volunteer Army Between the World Wars* (Wesport: Greenwood Press, 1982), Chapter 1.

20. Hagan, *This People's Navy*, 259–74. See also, Thomas H. Buckley, *The United States and the Washington Conference, 1921–1922* (Knoxville: The University of Tennessee Press, 1970).

21. By far the most complete account of the navy's primary war plan can be found in Edward S. Miller, *War Plan Orange: The U.S. Strategy to Defeat Japan, 1897–1945* (Annapolis: Naval Institute Press, 1991).

22. Geoffrey Till, "Adopting the Aircraft Carrier: The British, American, and Japanese Case Studies," in Williamson Murray and Allan B. Millett, *Military Innovation in the Interwar Period* (New York: Cambridge University Press, 1996), 191–226. There's a great deal of literature on carrier aviation. For the origins of carrier aviation, see Charles M. Melhorn, *Two-Block Fox: The Rise of the Aircraft Carrier, 1911–1929* (Annapolis: Naval Institute Press, 1974). For a more international approach, see Norman Polmar, *Aircraft Carriers: A History of Carrier Aviation and its Influence on World Events* (Washington, DC: Potomac Books, 2009). For the development of Marine amphibious capabilities and doctrines, see Allan R. Millett, *Semper Fidelis: The History of the United States Marine Corps* (New York: Macmillan, 1980), Chapters 10 and 12.

23. Millet, Maslowski, and Fies, *For the Common Defense*, 345–49; David E. Johnson, *Fast Tanks and Heavy Bombers: Innovation in the U.S. Army, 1917–1945* (Ithaca: Cornell University Press, 1998), Chapters 3 and 7; Williamson Murray, "Strategic Bombing: The American, British, and German Experiences," in Williamson Murray and Allen R. Millett, ed., *Military Innovation in the Interwar Period* (New York: Cambridge University Press, 1996), 106–108. See also, James P. Tate, *The Army and Its Air Corps: Army Policy Toward Aviation, 1919–1941* (Maxwell Air Force Base: Air University Press, 1998), Chapters 1–4. A nice summary of the Billy Mitchell court martial and the issues surrounding the man and his crusade is Douglas Waller, *A Question of Loyalty* (New York: Harpers Collins, 2004).

24. Gross, *American Military Aviation*, 72–79. The development of air theory is often connected to its practice in the Second World War, which will be covered in the next chapter. For a discussion of the technical developments of strategic bombardment for the US Army Air Corps, see Stephan L. McFarland, *America's Pursuit of Precision Bombing, 1910–1945* (Washington, DC: Smithsonian Institution Press, 1995), in particular Chapter 4. For the moral dimensions of these ideas and their implications in the Second World War, see Michael Sherry, *The Rise of American Air Power: The Creation of Armageddon* (New Haven: Yale University Press, 1987), Chapter 2.

25. Robert S. Cameron, *Mobility, Shock and Firepower: The Emergence of the U.S. Army's Armor Branch, 1917–1945* (Washington, DC: Center of Military History, 2008), Chapter 1. See also, Dale E. Wilson, *Treat 'Em Rough: The Birth of American Armor, 1917–1920* (Novato: Presidio Press, 1989).

26. Timothy Nenninger, "Organizational Milestones in the Development of American Armor, 1920–1940," in George F. Hoffmann and Donn A. Starry, ed., *Camp Colt to Desert Storm: The History of U.S. Armored Forces* (Lexington: University Press of Kentucky, 1999), 36–66; Cameron, *Mobility, Shock and Firepower*, Chapters 2–7. There's a great deal of literature on the development of American armor in the interwar period. Other sources that are helpful in telling this story are M.H. Gillie, *Forging the Thunderbolt: History of the U.S. Army's*

Armored Forces, 1917–1945 (reprint, Mechanicsburg: Stackpole Books, 2006); George F. Hoffmann, *Through Mobility We Conquer: The Mechanization of the U.S. Cavalry* (Lexington: University Press of Kentucky, 2006). For motorization, see Norman M. Cary, Jr., "The Use of the Motor Vehicle in the United States Army, 1899–1939." Ph. D. diss., University of Georgia, 1980.

27. Charles W. Johnson, "The Army and the Civilian Conservation Corps, 1933–1942," *Prologue: The Journal of the National Archives* 4 (Fall, 1972): 139–56.

28. The most current and approachable work on the Bonus March is Paul Dickson and Thomas B. Allen, *The Bonus Army: An American Epic* (New York: Walker and Company, 2004). For the Army's role in the event, see John W. Killigrew, "The Army and the Bonus Incident," *Military Affairs* 26, no. 2 (Summer, 1962): 59–65. For works that give a flavor of life in the interwar army, see Lucian K. Truscott, Jr., *The Twilight of the U.S. Cavalry: Life in the Old Army, 1917–1942* (Lawrence: University Press of Kansas, 1989); Victor Vogel, *Soldiers of the Old Army.* (College Station: Texas A&M University Press, 1990) and Edward M. Coffman, *The Regulars: The American Army, 1898–1941* (Cambridge: The Belknap Press of Harvard University Press, 2004), Chapter 8.

Chapter 10

World War Two, 1941–1945

We are about to embark on a great crusade, toward which we have striven these many months. The eyes of the world are upon you. The hopes and prayers of liberty-loving people everywhere march with you. In company with our brave Allies and brothers-in-arms on other Fronts you will bring about the destruction of the German war machine, the elimination of Nazi tyranny over oppressed peoples of Europe, and security for ourselves in a free world.

Dwight D. Eisenhower[1]

World War Two is a popular subject, and in spite of the violence, destruction, and chaos it represents, the war continues to captivate the public. It is a topic that is not hidden in the historical time line, so resources abound in terms of telling either one story or many. Even seventy years after these events transpired, large museums and historical sites continue to captivate the public. The National Museum of World War Two in New Orleans, Louisiana, continues to expand from its humble beginnings as the National D-Day Museum. In 2015, Congress enabled Manhattan Project National Historical Park to protect the cultural resources and important stories related to the development of the Atomic Bomb. Perhaps we can now look at some of the more controversial issues generated by the War and have a rational and compelling conversation. Regardless of what you may think of the War, we are still living with the legacies of the greatest conflict of the twentieth century.

RESOURCES

Before delving into topics that may have local or national significance, it is vital to integrate our own national experiences into a wider, global context. There are hundreds of works available that speak to the campaigns in Western Europe, the Russian Steppes, the Mediterranean, and the Atlantic Ocean prior to December 1941, so a good place to start is in a broad overview. Gerhard Weinberg's *A World in Arms*, Allan R. Millett and Williamson Murray's *A War to be Won*, and Richard Overy's *Why the Allies Won* provide very competent overviews of the War before the United

States entered it.[2] The accomplishments of the United States and the other Western Allies are best understood in a global context. The relative success of the invasion of France in June 1944, for example, was made possible because of the huge sacrifices made by the Soviet Union. The Eastern Front consumed men and equipment in copious amounts, degrading the German's ability to respond to an invasion in France. Recognizing these contributions does not denigrate the United States' contributions, it puts them in their proper context.[3] Once one is grounded in the context of the War, there is a treasure trove of resources that tell the story of America's involvement in the world-wide struggle.

Moving from a global perspective to a singularly American one, there is no better place to start in gaining an appreciation of the commitment the country made to the War than the official histories published in the years after 1945. Of all of the series produced, the Army's so-called green books are the largest in terms of volume, and they are exhaustive. Yes, they are green. To date, there are 77 volumes divided between the campaigns in Europe and the Pacific, the various services, and other special studies. The volumes, as well as a reader's guide to the series, are available online, and are indispensable for a basic understanding of the role the US Army played around the world and at home during the Second World War.[4] The US Navy took a different approach. They commissioned Harvard-trained historian Samuel Eliot Morrison as a Lieutenant Commander in the US Navy reserves who then proceeded to research and write a fifteen-volume work on US Navy operations in the Second World War. They were published between 1947 and 1965 by Little, Brown and Company. As with the Army's Green Book series, the volumes cover both Europe and the Pacific, and while not as exhaustive as the green books, this series paints a compelling portrait of the accomplishments of the Navy.[5] Five volumes are devoted to the Atlantic; nine to the Pacific. Wesley Frank Craven and James Les Cate led the effort for the Air Force. Rather than serving as the primary authors of the seven-volume series, they enlisted a host of authors to write individual chapters. As with Morrison's books, they were published by the University of Chicago Press from 1948 through 1958; they were reprinted by the Office of Air Force History in 1983, and are currently available online.[6] Finally, the US Marines produced a five-volume series from 1958 through 1971 by several authors. It is available on the web through the historical division as well as other websites.[7]

TELLING THE STORY

The Second World War touched nearly every continent in one way or another. For a conflict that quite literally engulfed the world, how can we tell the story in a responsible and compelling manner that matches the mission of a small museum or historical society? Local and regional stories can be used to not only tell the story from a local perspective, but also provide insight and access into the wider stories of the home front and the fighting in the Atlantic, Pacific, Europe, and Asia. The Minnesota Historical Society took this approach in their exhibit, Minnesota's Greatest Generation. Rather than just another exhibit on the War, it focused not only on the war but also the decades before the war began and those after the end of the war. While the stories of the war defined the experiences of the men and women who participated, their stories

Figure 10.1 The Minnesota Historical Society's World War Two exhibit. *Source*: Author Photograph

continued to evolve. The veterans, their families, and children had led lives that went far beyond the experiences of the battlefields and the home front. Because of the exhibit's focus on the pre- and postwar periods, visitors who may not necessarily be drawn to a stand-alone exhibit on the War are hooked in. When the exhibit does talk about the War, it focuses on the home front as well as the fields of battle. It is a smart and effective technique to draw in multiple audiences to a "war" exhibit. The exhibit echoes the term that became fashionable several years ago in describing the World War Two generation as the "greatest" generation. While there is no doubt that these men, women, and families made many sacrifices that we certainly appreciate today, is it really right to label one generation's sacrifices greater than another's? That is up to every administrator and curator to decide, but it is a slippery slope when generalizations are used in this manner.

At the other end of the spectrum is the National World War Two Museum in New Orleans, Louisiana, which takes a different interpretive approach. Started as the D-Day Museum, it has since morphed into one of the largest private museums in the country devoted to telling the story of the War. Supported by corporate sponsors and attractions within the museum that make money, it operates at a different level of complexity and funding. Taking a comprehensive approach, its galleries put the American effort into an international context, while still focusing on American contributions. The museum succeeds by immersing the visitor in environments similar to those of the campaigns and employing interactive exhibits and video stations that use contemporary materials to put visitors within the context of those particular campaigns. While the museum operates on a scale that many smaller institutions cannot match, there are many practices that can be emulated at an appropriate scale by smaller organizations. For example, there is often a desire to tell the entire story of the War within the context of a small exhibit gallery. Using video stations, you can put the larger story on monitors, building the exhibit around the story that is most relevant to the mission and goals of the said institution. There is always a need for institutions like the National World War Two Museum, but for small museums, bigger does not mean better.[8]

PREPARATIONS FOR WAR

It was never foreordained that the United States would be engulfed in a world war. Much like his predecessor over twenty years earlier, Franklin D. Roosevelt had to temper his internationalist tendencies against the vicissitudes of domestic politics. It is far too easy to label US foreign policy as completely isolationist in the interwar period, but with the election of Franklin Roosevelt in 1933, it became evident that domestic issues were his focus. However, with the rise of a militant Japanese foreign policy and Hitler's Germany bent on a more expansive role in Europe, Roosevelt began to pay increasing attention to developments overseas. The Japanese invasion of greater China in 1937, the dismemberment of Czechoslovakia in 1938, and the German juggernaut's demolition of the armies of Western Europe in the spring of 1940 gradually eroded public resistance to greater vigilance. After the election of 1940, Roosevelt took bolder steps to protect American interests—initiating a peacetime draft and federalizing the National Guard, moving the Pacific Fleet to Pearl Harbor, pressing for Japanese concessions in China, and passing lend-lease legislation to help Britain's war effort. There was no conspiracy to drive the country toward war. Roosevelt was very cognizant of public opinion and driven to protect American interests while avoiding war. Actions beyond the President's control were what forced the issue. Regardless of these measures, it is fair to say that the country was still unprepared for the global responsibilities that the United States would assume after December 1941.[9]

When the Japanese attacked the American navy base at Pearl Harbor on the island of Oahu in the American territory of Hawaii, it was seen as a spectacular, perhaps even dastardly, attack on the Pacific Fleet. Tensions had been escalating for a long time, in particular in the aftermath of their invasion of greater China and the weakening of the European Asiatic Empires. Taking a calculated risk, disabling the American fleet in Hawaii, and neutralizing the Philippine Islands would put the Japanese in a position of strength. The subsequent attack on Pearl Harbor disrupted the Pacific Fleet, but only temporarily. By the spring and summer of 1942, American ground and naval forces blunted Japanese offensives into the Pacific, retaking the initiative.[10]

THE WAR IN EUROPE

With Germany's declaration of war on the United States on December 11, 1941, any reticence on the part of the public and the President over going to war evaporated.

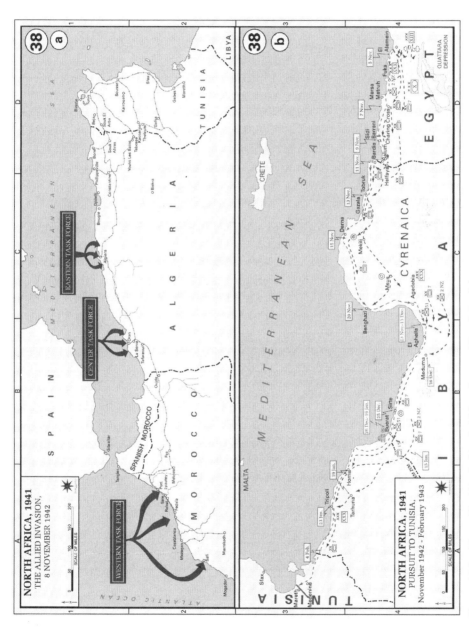

Figure 10.2 Map—The War in North Africa. *Source:* West Point Atlas

Roosevelt's problem was solved; a war in Europe involving the United States was on. From the outset, it was recognized that Germany must be defeated first. The question that dominated Allied discussions was: How? George C. Marshall, chairman of the American Joint Chiefs of Staff, wanted a direct strategy to deal with German power. The quicker the Allies could return to the continent, the better. Conditioned by the abysmal losses from the First World War and desiring to protect communication routes to India, the British were less than enthusiastic to pursue a direct approach. Regardless of Marshall's wishes, Americans were unprepared to invade the continent until 1944. Facing the political reality of getting Americans on the ground as soon as practicable, Roosevelt made the most prudent and politically expedient decision: putting Americans into North Africa and defeating German U-Boats in the Atlantic. With the entrance of the United States into the War, the one theater where the President could immediately devote resources to was winning the Battle of the Atlantic, which continued well into 1943.[11]

The invasion of North Africa in late 1942 marked the first opportunity for American troops, airmen, and sailors to go up against their German opponents. Overwhelming French collaborationists, the Americans fought a long campaign against a tough opponent. A German counteroffensive in February 1943, underscored how unprepared Americans were in light of German experience, but improved command arrangements and learning from mistakes allowed a combined British and American force to reduce the German bridgehead in North Africa and force the surrender of 275,000 Germans and Italians in May 1943. Several Allied conferences in the first half of 1943 reaffirmed the Germans' first strategy but postponed an invasion of the mainland until 1944. Buoyed by their success, the Allies opted for the invasion of Italy, first with the siege of the island of Sicily in July 1943, and followed two months later by an assault on southern Italy.[12]

The invasion of Sicily triggered the fall of Benito Mussolini's fascist government and would lead to an armistice between Fascist Italy and the Allies. With the fall of Sicily, there was a natural inclination to invade the Italian Peninsula. Americans reluctantly agreed but not before forcing the issue of the cross-channel invasion with the British, extracting a promise that the cross-channel invasion would be in 1944. Rather than making an amphibious end run closer to the top of the boot, the Allies bludgeoned their way up the peninsula with British landings at the toe of the Italian boot and Americans landing near Naples at Salerno. As the Allies advanced, the Germans held them, blocking the path to Rome. In an attempt to make an end run, there was a landing at Anzio in the spring of 1944 that nearly ended in disaster. Rome fell as the Allies landed in France, producing a hollow victory. Americans and British would remain in Italy until the end of the War, closing in on the top of the peninsula only as the War came to an end in the spring of 1945. There was no easy path when it came to defeating the Axis.[13]

The Normandy landings and the subsequent battle for France and pursuit to the border of Germany continue to capture the interest of historians and the imagination of casual followers of history. It was a stupendous achievement but not without controversies and issues. With the exception of the American landings at the beach code named Omaha, which were nearly repulsed, the Allied landings quickly knocked down Hitler's Atlantic Wall.[14] As the Germans attempted to contain the Allied

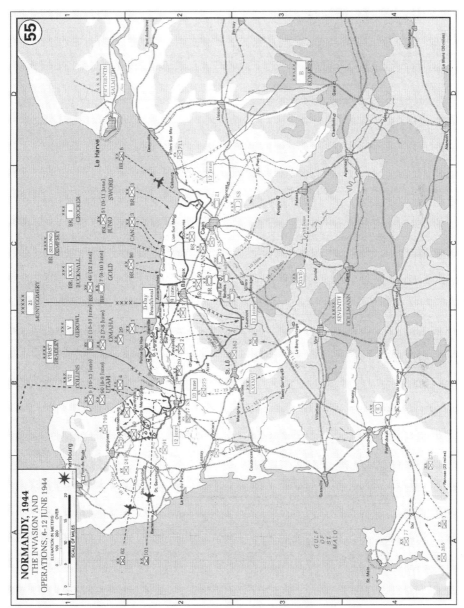

Figure 10.3   Map—D-Day, June 6, 1944. *Source:* West Point Atlas

advance, the subsequent battles for the bridgehead became a grinding slugfest, reminiscent of the battles of the First World War where advances were measured in yards. Obsessed with getting the invasion army ashore, the planners neglected to understand the difficulties of breaking out of the bridgehead. One of the lasting controversies that still echoes today is the continuing recriminations between the Americans and the British over who had a tougher and more complicated role. Regardless, the Americans broke through the German lines and swept through Brittany, trapping the Germans in a pocket that was closed slowly, causing more historical recriminations and allowing many Germans to escape. With subsequent landings in the south of France, named Operation Dragoon, the Germans' fate was sealed. By the fall, Paris had fallen and the Allies were butting up against the Netherlands and the German border. In an ill-fated attempt to create a breakthrough directly to the German industrial heartland, a massive airborne operation known as Market Garden was conducted in September 1944, which ended in failure.[15] With the thorough destruction of many French ports by the Germans and the inability of the British to open one of the largest ports in Europe at Antwerp, a logistical crisis developed as the fall transitioned to winter, halting the American offensive on the doorstep of Germany.

The halt of the Allied offensive on the borders of Germany ushered in the counterstroke known as the Battle of the Bulge. Continued logistical difficulties, weather, and the desperate need for a pause allowed the Germans to consolidate their defenses on the border and consider future steps.[16] Not content to rest, Hitler envisaged an offensive that would sweep through the Ardennes in December 1944, to the great port of Antwerp, cutting off the British from the Americans. In spite of the strategic surprise, a stubborn defense blunted the German penetration. Quick to respond, American army groups on either side of the German penetration pushed back, grinding up and destroying the last armored reserves the Germans had.[17] In spite of the Allied victory, the Battle of the Bulge was symptomatic of some of the most intractable issues regarding the conduct of the War that remain unresolved even seventy years after the end of the War.

History is a discipline that is always on the move as our understanding of the meanings behind the events continues to evolve. The commanding general in Europe, Dwight D. Eisenhower, had a difficult task. Success in the European theater depended upon balancing the needs and egos of the British and the Americans that answered to him. Delays in opening the second front in France, and problems dealing with Bernard Montgomery, the commanding general of British and Commonwealth forces in Europe, led to difficult debates over the prosecution of the War in Europe. Attempts to gamble by putting all of their resources in one push into Germany, Operation Market Garden, had failed. Eisenhower pursued a broad front strategy that demanded continual efforts across the entire front, making it difficult for the Germans to adjust their forces accordingly. While it meant that the line was weaker in some places than in others, leading to the initial success of German penetrations in the Battle of the Bulge, it was a prudent strategy. Since then, however, there has been a constant historical debate over the utility of this strategy. Seventy years later, there is still no consensus.[18]

Similarly, there is an interpretive sub-current that is a corollary to the narrow front/broad front debate over how the Americans in particular prosecuted the War. Many authors argue that, Americans bludgeoned their way across Europe, using firepower

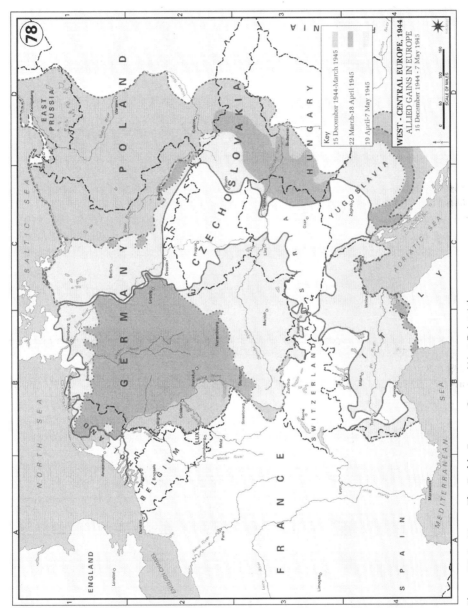

Figure 10.4   Map—The End in Europe. *Source:* West Point Atlas

and their material superiority to win the War in Europe. With strain between its roots as a constabulary force on the frontier where mobility was at a premium and the traditions of annihilation that emerged after the Civil War, there was a tension that emerged over the way the Americans fought that led to timidity and an over-reliance on firepower. As mentioned in the preface, there is a reaction to that, with others arguing that Americans did have the ability to operate toe to toe against their German opponents and win. Moreover, in spite of historical schizophrenia and decidedly inferior weapons, particularly tanks, the US Army was able to overcome those issues and make adjustments. The tension between both schools of thought, however, will more than likely never be resolved.[19]

With the period of rest and the defeat of the thrust in the Ardennes, the Germans had shot their bolt and the end was in sight. The last great barrier to the German heartland was the river Rhine. The Allies reached the left bank of the Rhine at the beginning of March and, in a very lucky break, found a relatively undamaged bridge at Remagen, allowing for a foothold on the opposite bank. Further crossings at other locations by the British and the Americans meant that by the end of the month, the last great natural barrier had been crossed. The Americans sprinted across central Germany, surrounded a large German Army in the industrial heartland of the Nazi Empire, the Ruhr, and reached the left bank of the Elbe toward the end of April, meeting advance elements of the Red Army. Decisions had been made previously to not advance on Berlin, creating recriminations that last to this day of selling out our eastern Allies, in particular Poland, for political expediency. With the suicide of Hitler and the surrender of the Germans, the War in Europe was over on May 7, 1945.[20]

THE HOME FRONT

Any discussion that involves the Second World War must touch on the home front. Unlike Great Britain and the Soviet Union, the United States was, with a few exceptions, left untouched by the ravages of war.[21] Parallel to its budding role in the First World War, the United States provided all of the Allies with raw materials, weapons, vehicles, and manufactured goods. Truly, the country was an arsenal of democracy. The mobilization of the country's economic resources for the war effort was unprecedented. Every sector of the economy was devoted to war work, touching even the smallest community. Individual households dealt with scarcities caused by rationing. Men and, in particular, women flocked to burgeoning war industries. Loved ones supported family members in the service overseas. Other households dealt with racism and discrimination and new opportunities. African-Americans volunteered and entered the draft, but served in segregated units or in labor battalions. Of course, some served in units that gained national renown, like the Tuskegee Airmen, but many others dealt with prejudice as they struggled to defeat racism at home as well as abroad. For those of Japanese descent, an executive order was given that displaced thousands of loyal citizens from communities along the West Coast to camps scattered across the United States. Ethnicity determined loyalty. While the camps were later dismantled and many Japanese Americans served in combat units and as translators, it was an act that effected the dreams and aspirations of a whole class of citizens. The role of women in the workplace certainly began a process of evolution that continued to move forward in the twenty-first century. This is a story that can be examined by even the smallest historical society; it is a story about people living with a national emergency of such a dimension, and it created lasting memories and stories that continue to be relevant.[22]

THE WAR IN THE PACIFIC

The War in the Pacific, unlike in Europe, was nearly an all-American theater of operations. There was also a racial component of the War that, admittedly, is difficult to measure and understand, but cannot be lightly dismissed. It was a bloody fight in which Japanese garrisons often fought to the last man, and pilots deliberately crashed their aircraft into ships, creating a weariness and tendency toward direct action as the War dragged on.[23]

In the aftermath of the attack on Pearl Harbor, the Japanese armed forces invaded all of Southeast Asia to the borders with India, the British possessions of Hong Kong and Singapore fell, including the Dutch East Indies, the Solomon Islands, and the American possessions of Guam and Wake Island. On the Philippines, Douglas MacArthur could not stem the Japanese onslaught, escaping as American forces were driven into a small peninsula near Manila and their island fortress of Corregidor. While many wanted to see MacArthur relieved after the Philippine disaster, he was a master of public relations, vowing to return to the Philippines to liberate them from Japanese oppression. With the ouster of the Americans from the archipelago, the Japanese threatened the remaining lines of communication with Australia, India, and the south Pacific. Moving toward Australia's tenuous connections with the United States, an American task force blunted the Japanese move at the Battle of Coral Sea, ending the immediate threat to the southern flank. Wanting to destroy the remaining American aircraft carriers and nullify American forces in the Hawaiian archipelago, the Japanese conceived an overly complex operation against the American garrison at Midway Island at the western end of the Hawaiian chain, as well an assault on several of the Aleutian Islands west of Alaska. Having compromised Japanese codes in June 1942, American naval aviation was able to stop the Japanese assault, sinking four of their invaluable carriers to the United States' one. The defeat at Midway put a stop to the Japanese advance and provided the Americans with their first opportunity to attack in the Solomon Islands and New Guinea.[24]

Unlike in Europe, where Eisenhower was deemed the Supreme Allied Commander, the Pacific Theater saw not one, but two efforts. Douglas MacArthur was the overall commander of the southwest Pacific and by 1943, Admiral Chester W. Nimitz became the commander in the central Pacific. The first opportunity to strike back came in the southwest Pacific in the Solomon Island Chain, beginning with Guadalcanal. From August 1942 until February 1943, American and Japanese land and naval forces contested these islands. MacArthur moved on to northwestern New Guinea, eventually hoping to isolate the major Japanese base at Rabaul on the northeastern tip of New Britain. As with Guadalcanal, these first offensives met the full brunt of Japanese forces and demonstrated the long learning curve in preparing to defeat Japan.[25]

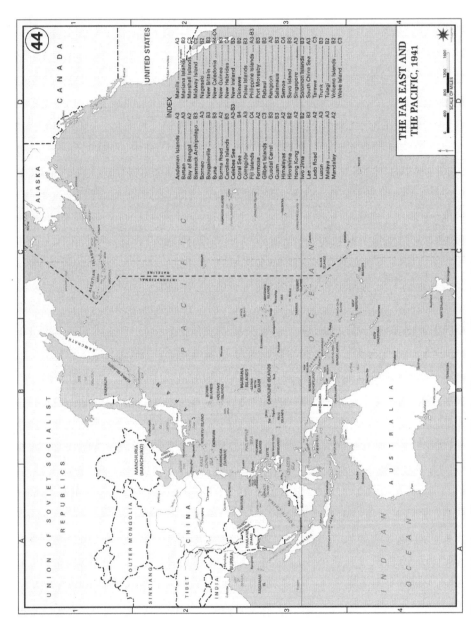

Figure 10.5   Map—The Far East and The Pacific. *Source:* West Point Atlas

After Guadalcanal was reduced, landings further up the Solomon chain including Bougainville Island occurred as well as other landings on the northeast and northwest coast of New Guinea. By the end of 1944, MacArthur had isolated the Rabaul base and nullified any remaining Japanese forces in New Guinea, allowing him to concentrate on the Philippines. The opening salvos of Nimitz's advance were in the Gilbert Island chain in November 1943, on a small coral atoll known as Tarawa. In a bloody slugfest, the Japanese contested every acre of the small atoll, exacting a huge toll on the Marines and soldiers assaulting the island. In an area that was about three square miles, the combat resulted in 1,000 dead and 2,000 wounded Americans, and nearly the entire Japanese garrison eliminated. Further raids by carrier aircraft and island assaults on Kwajalein and Eniwetok in early 1944 broke the defensive perimeter of the Japanese line encompassing the entire central Pacific.[26]

There is a visceral quality to the campaign against Japanese aggression in the Pacific that is very difficult to convey, even seventy years after these events. While the level of violence is repugnant to the average visitor, it is vital for the visitor to have an opportunity to understand not only the sacrifice, but also the cost. One of the places in the United States that focuses on the Pacific War is the National Museum of the Pacific War in Fredericksburg, Texas. Using the home of Admiral Chester Nimitz as an interpretive focus, the museum uses Nimitz as a lens to tell the story of the Pacific War. Using a variety of traditional techniques, dioramas, audio and video stations, panels, and large artifacts, the museum tells the story of the war from a decidedly American perspective. One of the more unique aspects of the museum is that it has a specially prepared backdrop to do reenactments of a "typical" fight between Americans and the Japanese. Volunteers use uniforms and equipment typical of what would have been found among Japanese and American soldiers. While the re-enactment certainly enlivens the visitor's senses, reenactments, regardless of the era, cannot recreate the emotion and violence of an island assault. Using a similar approach where the interpretive focus is a small part of the wider story, the visitor center for War in the Pacific National Historical Park on Guam tells the story of the War through the capture and liberation of the island. In each case, the visitors can absorb the entire exhibit or pick and choose the themes and subject matter that appeals to them. Moreover, it puts a large event on a more human scale by telling the story through the eyes of one of its leaders, Admiral Nimitz, or through the population of an island. It also gives the visitors the tools to understand the decisions that would lead to the final campaigns of the Pacific War.[27]

The breaking of Japan's defensive barrier in the central Pacific, combined with MacArthur's assaults in the southwest Pacific, set the stage for the crucial campaigns of the War. The isolation and nullification of Japanese garrisons in New Guinea provided a base for the jump to the Philippine Islands. Breaking the island fortresses in the Gilberts allowed for both the isolation of the key Japanese naval base on the island of Truk in the Caroline Islands and the capture of key airfields in the Marianas. Securing the Marianas would allow American bombers to reach the Japanese home islands and break their war economy. The Japanese contested the invasion and sent their remaining carriers to intercept the Americans. They failed, allowing MacArthur to invade the Philippines in the summer of 1944. In a bold but desperate stroke to stop the invasion, the remnants of Japan's carrier force lured American fleet carriers away from the invasion beaches. The Japanese surface fleet was meant to converge on American transports and sink them. They nearly succeeded, but the attacks were stopped, with great losses. The desperate defense also saw the beginnings of Japanese aircraft deliberately crashing onto American ships. Known as *Kamikazes* or divine wind, they harkened back to a time when a chance storm destroyed a Mongol fleet poised to invade Japan in 1271 and 1284. Invoking the past, the hope was that a similar action would spare the homeland from invasion. This was certainly an indication of the growing tenacity of the Japanese defenders and, perhaps, a hint of desperation. Undoubtedly, it was a portent of the final campaigns of the War.[28]

The end game of the Pacific War began in the spring of 1945; the capture of the islands of Iwo Jima and Okinawa was, in a sense, a rehearsal for what would be the final act of the Pacific War, the invasion of the Japanese homeland. Iwo Jima was the swan song of the Marine Corps' campaign across the Pacific. In March 1945, the Marines landed on the volcanic island. The landing was hotly contested, as was the entire island. Nearly the entire Japanese garrison of 21,000 died. The Marines lost 6,800 men; nearly 20,000 were wounded. Okinawa, part of the Ryukyu chain, pointed like an arrow to the southernmost home island of Japan, Kyushu. In June 1945, the invasion got underway, the largest of its kind in the Pacific. A tenacious defense, unrelenting kamikaze attacks, and the sorties of the Imperial Japanese Navy's flagship, the *Yamato*, made Okinawa, like Iwo, a bloody affair. Between the Navy, Army, and Marines, 12,000 were killed and 36,000 wounded. These numbers are important because they frame the most contentious historical debate of the Pacific—the invasion of the homeland and the dropping of two atomic weapons. The final act of the Pacific War is a complicated affair that cannot be understood without putting it into the wider context of strategic bombing.[29]

THE BOMBER ALWAYS GETS THROUGH

The veracity of strategic bombing has always generated a great deal of suspicion and controversy. Seen as a panacea for all that was wrong with the Western Front in the First World War, bombing did not live up to its pre-war reputation. While making a valuable contribution to the war effort, the bombing of civilians raised questions that we are still struggling with today. The assumptions made regarding the legitimacy of not only a country's war industries, but civilian populations as legitimate targets is a legacy with which we live in the Atomic Age. It is easy to cast moral judgments on policies and actions taken seventy years ago, but it is necessary to put them in a broader historical context.

Over the course of the War in Europe, the Americans and British diverged in how to achieve victory through the air—the British attacked at night and bombed wide swaths of Germany's urban and industrial areas, hoping to "de-house" workers, wreck infrastructure, and erode morale. The Americans bombed during the day, hoping for pin-point accuracy against specific industrial targets. Facing a determined foe, day and night, British and American bomber crews had some of the toughest jobs of the war.[30] Learning by doing, they conducted an air war that was a long and arduous campaign, and took place in several stages. The first stage was met with high losses and results that indicated neither a decline in industrial activity nor morale. Conditioned by the notion that the bomber would always get through, the *Luftwaffe* extracted a high cost. The second stage was the defeat of the *Luftwaffe* with the advent of fighter aircraft escorting bombers. By the spring of 1944, the Allies had won that contest and gained complete superiority over German skies. Only with a punishing assault on the German oil industry did it truly make an impact on the ability of the Germans to sustain military operations. Their operations were expensive to sustain in terms of both men and equipment—8,200 bombers and 3,900 fighters never made it home and 29,000 men died. At the other end of the bombing offensive, German civilian causalities perhaps topped 600,000. Given the butcher's bill for the air war, on both sides the key question anyone examining these issues has to ask is this: Was it worth it?[31]

The bombing of the economic, social, and cultural centers of the Axis powers can be understood from several points of view, all of which deserve equal consideration. Did strategic bombardment, as the pre-war airpower theorists speculated, single-handedly win the War? No. Was it a vital contribution to the eventual victory over the Axis powers? Yes. For the Germans, in particular, close to 60 percent of their fighter force was withdrawn from other fronts to defend the homeland. Tens of thousands of men and women staffed an extensive civil defense and anti-aircraft force that could have been devoted to either the Western or Eastern Fronts. Even though German war production rose as Allied bombing intensified, in the end the devastation of their petroleum industry and transportation network brought the German war machine to a halt. Was it necessary to unleash this aerial offensive on Germany? Probably. The Allies were often criticized by the Soviets for delaying the onset of a second front. Was it immoral to target these populations? It is an area that requires a great deal of thought. There was a useful military purpose to the campaign. In spite of the desire for spectacular, yet targeted, results, the so-called bomb in a pickle barrel was not going to happen. There was collateral damage that resulted in the deaths of thousands of civilians. Even if we are unable to label these as either moral or immoral actions, the deaths of civilians throughout the entire war lowered the bar in terms of providing the traditional immunity that civilians were accorded.[32]

As the air war in Europe reached its heights, the strategic bombardment against Japan got underway. The immense distances across the Pacific required a larger bomber. Developed by Boeing, the B-29 could carry a 2,000 pound bomb load over 7,000 miles. After teething development problems, it was deployed to China in the spring of 1944. The difficulties of sustaining an intense aerial bombardment from primitive airfields at the end of a long logistical chain proved to be a challenge. The capture of the Marianas Island chain provided bases that put B-29s in range of the Japanese home islands. High altitude raids against industrial targets proved ineffectual. With a change of leadership in the 20th Air Force, Curtis LeMay made the decision to change from high altitude to low altitude area bombing. The dispersed nature of the war industry and the relatively light construction of Japanese homes and businesses made fire-bombing an alternative to the approaches used in Europe, though in reality, it destroyed homes and killed the populace in unprecedented numbers. In March 1945, the first fire raid against Tokyo commenced. The resulting fire storm destroyed 250,000 buildings and killed an estimated 87,000 people. Additional fire raids in most of Japan's urban and industrial centers had devastating results. Moreover, an aerial mining campaign hindered the inter-island transportation system, affecting food distribution and further eroding the economy. As in Europe, the aerial campaign in Japan did not single-handedly win the War, but it was certainly instrumental in lowering the threshold for the use of an atomic weapon.[33]

With the end of the Okinawa campaign in June 1945, planning began for the invasion of the Japanese homelands. Plans were laid to land troops on Kyushu, the southern most of the home islands. The experiences at Iwo Jima and Okinawa indicated that the invasion would be bloody for soldier and civilian alike. It was not so much high casualties that made American leaders nervous as the difficulty of securing a victory in the home islands that forced the issue of using atomic weapons in conjunction with the strategic bombardment of the islands. Nevertheless, the ability to end the War quickly was in the hands of the Imperial Government. Certainly, a quick end of the War was difficult due to the American insistence on an unconditional surrender and the more bellicose members of the Emperor's government pressing for an armed struggle against the Americans. Only with the dropping of the bombs and the direct intervention of the Emperor did the War come to a close.[34] While an air and sea blockade may have prevented an all-out invasion, the end of the War in Europe meant that there was political pressure to end hostilities as quickly as time and resources would allow. The counterpoint to the military argument is that it was done with political and diplomatic justifications in mind. The invasion of Manchuria by the Soviet Union in August 1945 compelled the United States to use atomic weapons, not as a military necessity, but for political leverage against the Soviet Union, in particular since the Japanese, in the mind of revisionists, were all but defeated. In all fairness to both camps, there were undoubtedly both military and diplomatic considerations that led to President Truman's decision to move forward with the bomb.[35]

The dropping of two atomic weapons on Hiroshima and Nagasaki opened up the Atomic Age and changed everything. The end of the War made the United States, for a time, one of the most powerful nations on the face of the earth. As in previous conflicts, the country struggled to return to normalcy as the massive force of citizen soldiers returned to their civilian pursuits. In spite of the rush to peacetime, for the next fifty years the country would be locked in the throes of a Cold War with the Soviet Union. Although the United States endured two long wars in Asia, first in Korea and then in Vietnam, it never went to war with its nemesis, the Soviets. Even though World War Two was the most destructive conflict the world had yet witnessed, perhaps it was the end of an age of innocence. From that point forward, for better or for worse, the United States has carried the burden of policing the world on its shoulders.

NOTES

1. Carlo D'Este, *Eisenhower: A Soldier's Life* (New York: Henry Holt and Company, 2002), 526.

2. Gerhard Weinberg, *A World At Arms: A Global History of World War II* (New York: Cambridge University Press, 1994); Williamson Murray and Allan R. Millett, *A War To Be Won: Fighting the Second World War* (Cambridge: Belknap Press of Harvard University Press, 2000); Richard Overy, *Why The Allies Won* (New York: W.W. Norton & Company, 1995). See

also, H.P. Willmott, *The Great Crusade: A New Complete History of the Second World War* (New York: The Free Press, 1989). A bit long in the tooth, but still useful, is Gordon Wright, *The Ordeal of Total War, 1939–1945* (New York: Harper Torch Books, 1968).

3. In spite of the historical legacy of Stalin's regime, millions of Soviet soldiers and civilians lost their lives between 1941 and 1945. No matter how we rate our own martial prowess against the Germans, Soviet sacrifices must be recognized in the fight against Hitler's Germany. The best overviews can be found in the works of David M. Glantz, *Stumbling Colossus: The Red Army on the Eve of World War* (Lawrence: University Press of Kansas, 1998); *Colossus Reborn: The Red Army at War, 1941–1943* (Lawrence: University Press of Kansas, 2005); David M. Glantz and Jonathan House, *When Titans Clashed: How the Red Army Stopped Hitler* (Lawrence: University Press of Kansas, 1995).

4. The best place to understand the contents of the volumes and the sub-series is through the readers' guide. It is available online at Center of Military History website as an Adobe PDF: http://www.history.army.mil/html/books/011/11-9/CMH_Pub_11-9.pdf. The individual volumes are also available. The index page is http://www.history.army.mil/html/bookshelves/collect/usaww2.html.

5. There is a one-volume abridgement of the entire series, Samuel Eliot Morrison, *The Two Ocean War: A Short History of the United States Navy in the Second World War* (Boston: Little, Brown and Company, 1963).

6. The index page for the seven-volume series is http://www.afhso.af.mil/afhistory/factsheets/factsheet.asp?id=17871

7. The publications portal for the Marine Corps not only includes the History of U.S. Marine Operations in World War Two but also a host of other useful publications on the Marines. The portal can be found at https://www.mcu.usmc.mil/historydivision/Pages/Publications/Word_War_II_1939_1945.aspx.

8. For the National World War II Museum, please visit http://www.nationalww2museum.org/index.html.

9. The best place to begin with is one of the green book series, Mark Skinner Watson, *Chief of Staff: Prewar Plans and Preparations* (Washington, DC: Historical Division, Department of Army, 1950), Chapter 7; Lee Kennett, *G.I. The American Soldier in World War Two* (New York: Charles Scribner's Sons, 1987), Chapter 1; Griffith, *Men Wanted For the U.S. Army*, Chapter 7; Doubler, *Civilian in Peace, Soldier in War*, 195–201; Hagan, *This People's Navy*, 282–99. The impact of the 1941 maneuvers is well told in Christopher Gabel, *The U.S. Army GHQ Maneuvers of 1941* (Washington, DC: Center of Military History, 1991). See also, Waldo Heinrichs, *Threshold of War: Franklin D. Roosevelt and American Entry into World War II* (New York: Oxford University Press, 1988); Robert A. Divine, *Roosevelt and World War II* (Baltimore: The John Hopkins Press, 1969), Chapters 1 and 2.

10. The approach to the war with Japan and the attack on the naval base at Pearl Harbor has generated a tremendous amount of literature. The best overviews of the American war in the Pacific are Ronald H. Spector, *Eagle Against the Sun: The American War With Japan* (New York,: The Free Press, 1985), Chapters 1–4; Dorothy Borg and Shumpei Okomoto, *Pearl Harbor as History: Japanese-American Relations, 1931–1941* (New York: Columbia University Press, 1973). For the best single account of the attack on Pearl Harbor, see Gordon W. Prange, *At Dawn We Slept: The Untold Story of Pearl Harbor* (New York: Viking Press, 1981). For the Japanese Navy's perspective, see David C. Evans and Mark R. Peattie, *Kaigun: Strategy, Tactics, and Technology in the Imperial Japanese Navy, 1887–1941* (Annapolis: Naval Institute Press, 1997). The best single volume to look at the full range of blame for the Pearl Harbor attack is Gordon W. Prange, *Pearl Harbor: The Verdict of History* (New York: McGraw Hill, 1986). Also useful in looking at the dynamics of intelligence failure can be Barbara Wohlstetter, *Pearl Harbor: Warning and Decision* (Palo Alto: Stanford University Press, 1962).

11. The case for a direct Allied assault on the continent is made in Russell F. Weigley, *American Way of War*, Chapter 14. For an alternative explanation, see John Grigg, *1943: The Victory That Never Was* (New York: Hill and Wang, 1980). For a broad overview of American strategy, see Maurice Matlof and Edwin M. Snell, *Strategic Planning for Coalition Warfare, 1941–1942*. Reprint (Washington, DC: Center for Military History, 1999) [Available from Center of Military History website: http://www.history.army.mil/html/books/001/1-3/ CMH_Pub_1-3.pdf]. See also, Louis Morton, "Germany First: The Basic Concept of Allied Strategy in World War II," in Kent Roberts Greenfield, ed., *Command Decisions* (Washington, DC: Office of the Chief of Military History, n.d.), 3–38; Mark A. Stoler, *Allies and Adversaries: The Joint Chiefs of Staff, the Grand Alliance, and U.S. Strategy in World War II* (Chapel Hill: University of North Carolina Press, 2000). For a summary of the Battle of the Atlantic, see Murray and Millett, *A War to Be Won*, Chapter 10; Samuel Eliot Morrison, *Battle of the Atlantic: September, 1939–May, 1943* (Boston: Little, Brown, and Company, 1947).

12. The invasion of North Africa is ably told in Rick Atkinson, *An Army at Dawn: The War in North Africa, 1942–1943* (New York: Henry Holt and Company, 2002); the Army Green Book is George F. Howe, *Northwest Africa: Seizing the Initiative in the West*. For a look at the failures of American arms, see Martin Blumenson, "Kasserine Pass, 30 January–22 February, 1943" in Heller and Stoft, *America's First Battles*, 226–65. For a wider context, see Douglas Porch, *The Path to Victory: The Mediterranean Theater in World War Two* (Old Saybrook: Konecky & Konecky, 2004). For the invasion and reduction of Sicily, see Carlo D'Este, *Bitter Victory: The Battle For Sicily, 1943* (New York: Harper Perennial, 1991).

13. Weinberg, *A World At Arms*, 593–601. There are three separate volumes in the Army's Green Book series on the Italian campaign: Albert N. Garland and Howard M. Smith, *Sicily and the Surrender of Italy*; Martin Blumenson, *Salerno to Cassino*; and Ernest F. Fisher, *Cassino to the Alps*. All three are available at the Center for Military History website at http:// www.history.army.mil/html/bookshelves/collect/ww2-mto.html. See also, Rick Atkinson. *The Day of Battle: The War in Sicily and Italy, 1943–1944* (New York: Henry Holt and Company, 2007); Carlo D'Este, *Fatal Decision: Anzio and the Battle For Rome* (New York: Harper Collins, 1991).

14. For an overview of the campaign in northeastern Europe, including the invasion, see Rick Atkinson, *The Guns at Last Light: The War in Western Europe, 1944–1945* (New York: Henry Holt and Company, 2013). The list of books and films concerning D-Day is large and growing annually, containing too much to include here. The Army Green Book series has two volumes that deal with these campaigns, Gordon A. Harrison, *Cross Channel Attack* and Martin Blumenson, *Breakout and Pursuit*. The most helpful books for understanding D-Day are Stephen E. Ambrose *D-Day, June 6, 1944: The Climactic Battle of World War II* (New York: Simon and Schuster, 1994; Carlo D'Este, *Decision in Normandy*. Reprint (New York: Barnes and Noble Books, 1994); Russell A. Hart, *Clash of Arms: How the Allies Won in Normandy* (Norman: University of Oklahoma Press, 2001); Max Hastings, *Overlord: D-Day and the Battle For Normandy* (New York: Simon and Schuster, 1984); Craig Symonds, *Neptune: The Allied Invasion of Europe and the D-Day Landings* (New York: Oxford University Press, 2014). Two classics still worthy of consideration are John Keegan, *Seven Armies in Normandy: From D-Day to the Liberation of Pari* (New York: Penguin Books, 1994) and Cornelius Ryan, *The Longest Day, June 6, 1944* (New York: Crest Books edition, 1959). For the breakout from Normandy, see James Jay Carafano *After D-Day: Operation Cobra and the Normandy Breakout* (Boulder: Lynne Rienner Publishers, 2000) and Mark J. Reardon, *Victory at Mortain: Stopping Hitler's Panzer Counteroffensive* (Lawrence: University Press of Kansas, 2002).

15. The Army Green Book series devotes one volume to the invasion of Southern France, Jeffery J. Clarke and Robert Ross Smith, *Riviera to the Rhine*. A very approachable book in understanding Market Garden is the classic, Cornelius Ryan, *A Bridge Too Far* (New York,

NY: Simon and Schuster, 1974); see also, Guy LoFaro, *The Sword of St. Michael: The 82nd Airborne Division in World War Two* (Philadelphia: Da Capo Press, 2011), Chapters 15–19.

16. For the controversies and alternatives facing the Allies in the fall and winter of 1944, see Russell F. Weigley, *Eisenhower's Lieutenants: The Campaign of France and Germany, 1944–1945* (Bloomington: Indiana University Press, 1981), in particular, Part 4, 305–574. For insights into the battles of the frontier, see Robert Sterling Rush, *Hell in the Hürtgen Forest: The Ordeal and Triumph of an American Infantry Regiment* (Lawrence: University Press of Kansas, 2001); Keith Bonn, *When the Odds Were Even: The Vosges Mountains Campaign, October, 1944–January, 1945* (Novato: Presidio Press, 1994). There are two volumes in the Army's Green Book series that cover this period, Hugh M. Cole, *The Lorraine Campaign*, and Charles B. MacDonald, *The Siegfried Line Campaign*.

17. Given the circumstances of the Battle of the Bulge, it has attracted a great deal of attention. For an overview, see the Army's Green Book work on the bulge, Hugh M. Cole, *The Ardennes: Battle of the Bulge*. A well-illustrated, comprehensive account can be found in Jean Paul Pallud, *Battle of the Bulge, Then and Now* (London, UK: Battle of Britain Prints International, 1984). See also, Charles B. MacDonald, *A Time For Trumpets: The Untold Story of the Battle of the Bulge* (New York: William Murrow and Company, 1985).

18. For a contextual approach, see Weinberg, A World at Arms, Chapters 13–14. The debate between narrow versus broad is well captured in Carlo D'Este, *Eisenhower: A Soldier's Life*, Chapter 47. For the challenges facing the British, see Williamson Murray, "British Military Effectiveness in the Second World War" in Allan R. Millett, Williamson Murray, ed., *Military Effectiveness, Volume 3: The Second World War* (New York: Cambridge University Press, 2010), 90–135. For the alternatives to Eisenhower's actions, see John A. Adams, *The Battle For Western Europe, Fall 1944: An Operational Assessment* (Bloomington: Indiana University Press, 2010.

19. For an assessment of material superiority and its effect on how the United States and Allies fought, see John Ellis, *Brute Force: Allied Strategy and Tactics in the Second World War* (New York: Viking, 1990). For a more nuanced approach, see Weigley, *Eisenhower's Lieutenants*, 727–30. Revisionists include Michael Doubler, *Closing With the Enemy: How the GI's Fought the War in Europe, 1944–1945*; Peter R. Mansoor, *The GI Offensive in Europe: The Triumph of American Infantry Divisions, 1941–1945*; John Sloan Brown, *Draftee Division: The 88th Infantry Division in World War II* (Novato: Presidio Press, 1986); Michael R. Matheny, *Carrying The War to the Enemy: American Operational Art to 1945* (Norman University of Oklahoma Press, 2011); and James Jay Carafano, *GI Ingenuity: Improvisation, Technology, and Winning World War II* (Westport: Praeger Security International, 2006).

20. The Army's Green Book on the last campaign is Charles B. MacDonald, *The Last Offensive* (Washington, DC: Office of the Chief of Military History, 1973). See also, Derek S. Zumbro, *Battle for the Ruhr: The German Army's Last Defeat in the West* (Lawrence: University Press of Kansas, 2006) and Max Hastings, *Armageddon: The Battle For Germany, 1944–1945* (New York: Vintage Books, 2004).

21. With the exception of the occupation of two islands in the Aleutian Island chain and, of course, the Japanese attack on Pearl Harbor, the United States was largely untouched by the war. There were several incidents on the Pacific Coast where Japanese submarines and, later, balloon bombs came into the continental United States. For the campaign in Alaska, see Brian Garfield, *The Thousand Mile War: World War II in the Alaska and the Aleutians* (Fairbanks: University of Alaska Press, 1995). For attacks on the continental United States, see Bert Webber, *Silent Siege – II: Japanese Attacks on North American in World War II* (Medford: Webb Research Group, 1988) and Robert C. Mikesh, *Japan's World War II Balloon Bomb Attacks on North America* (Washington, DC: Smithsonian Institution Press, 1973).

22. There are several works that provide overviews of the Home Front: see John Morton Blum, *V Was For Victory: Politics and American Culture in World War II* (New York: Harcourt

Brace Jovanovich, 1976); Allan M. Winkler, *Home Front USA: America During World War II* (Arlington Heights, IL: Harlan Davidson, 1986). For a popular account covering innovations critical to the war, see Paul Kennedy, *Engineers For Victory: The Problem Solvers Who Turned the Tide in the Second World War* (New York: Harpers Collins, 2013). For a brief overview of the African-American experience, see Neil A. Wynn, *The African-American Experience During World War II* (Lanham: Rowman and Littlefield Publishers, 2010). For Japanese Internment, see Greg Robinson, *By Order of the President: FDR and the Internment of the Japanese-American* (Cambridge: Harvard University Press, 2001) and Dillon S. Meyer, *Uprooted Americans: The Japanese Americans and the WRA in World War II* (Tucson: University of Arizona Press, 1971).

23. The best single overview of the Pacific campaign remains Ronald H. Spector, *The Eagle Against the Sun: The American War With Japan* (New York: The Free Press, 1985). For the background of the Imperial Japanese Army and the challenges it faced, see Edward J. Drea, *Japan's Imperial Army: Its Rise and Fall, 1853–1945* (Lawrence: University Press of Kansas, 2009). The groundbreaking studies that laid the groundwork for understanding race and the Pacific War are John W. Dower, *War Without Mercy: Race and Power in the Pacific War* (New York: Pantheon Books, 1986) and Gerald F. Linderman, *The World Within War: America's Combat Experience in World War II* (New York: The Free Press, 1997), Chapter 4. See also, Alvin D. Coox, "The Effectiveness of the Japanese Military Establishment in the Second World War," in Millett and Murray, *Military Effectiveness, Vol. 3, The Second World War*, 1–44.

24. The Army and Navy's official histories of the war cover the Pacific thoroughly. The green Books series begins its Pacific campaign series with the fall of the Philippines with Louis Morton's *The Fall of the Philippines,* and Samuel Eliot Morrison's series includes several volumes on this critical period of the war, Volumes III, *Rising Sun in the Pacific, 1931–April, 1942* and IV, *Coral Sea, Midway, and Submarine Actions, May–August, 1942.* Supplementing these works are John B. Lundstrom, *The First South Pacific Campaign, December, 1941–June, 1942* (Annapolis: Naval Institute Press, 1976) and *The First Team: Pacific Naval Air Combat From Pearl Harbor to Midway* (Annapolis: Naval Institute Press, 1984). For Midway, see Craig L. Symonds, *The Battle of Midway* (New York: Oxford University Press, 2011). For the Japanese perspective, see Jonathan Parshall and Anthony Tully, *Shattered Sword: The Untold Story of the Battle of Midway* (Dulles: Potomac Books, 2005).

25. The green book series has two volumes on these campaigns, John Miller Jr., *The Guadalcanal: The First Offensive* and Samuel Milner, *Victory in Papua.* For the difficulties of the first campaigns in New Guinea, see Jay Luvaas, "Buna: 19 November 1942–2 January 1943: A 'Leavenworth Nightmare,'" in Heller and Stofft, *America's First Battles,* 186–225. For the battles in and around Guadalcanal, see Richard B. Frank, *Guadalcanal: The Definitive Account of the Landmark Battle* (New York: Random House, 1990).

26. Spector, *Eagle Against the Sun*, Chapter 12. See also, the Green book series, Philip A. Crowl and Edmund G. Love, *Seizure of the Gilberts and Marshalls* and Morrison's Volume 7, Aleutians, Gilberts and Marshalls, June 1942–April 1944. For an overview from the US Marine Corps perspective, see Allan R. Millett, Semper Fidelis: The History of the United States Marine Corps (New York: Macmillan Publishing, 1980), Chapter 14.

27. National Museum of the Pacific War, *Revised Interpretive Plan*, November, 2006, in the author's possession. The author took part in an exhibit evaluation team for the design of the War in the Pacific NHP visitor center. Rather than telling the entire story of the Pacific War in a small exhibit space, it was decided to use Guam as a focal point of the story.

28. Spector, *Eagle Against the Sun*, Chapters 19 and 22. There are four volumes in the Green book series that cover these campaigns, Philip A. Crowl, *Campaign in the Marianas*; Robert Ross Smith. *Approach to the Philippines*; M. Hamlin Cannon, *Leyte: The Return to the Philippines*; and Robert Ross Smith, *Triumph in the Philippines*. Morrison has several volumes in

his series, Volume 8, *New Guinea and the Marianas: March-August, 1944*; Volume 12, *Leyte, June, 1944–January, 1945*; and Volume 13, *Liberation of the Philippines, 1944–1945.* The battle of Leyte Gulf was the penultimate naval surface action of the war. To get a flavor of the various aspects of the battle, see James D. Hornfischer, *The Last Stand of the Tin Can Sailors: The Extraordinary Story of the U.S. Navy's Finest Hour* (New York: Bantam Books, 2005) and Anthony P. Tully, *Battle of Surigao Strait* (Bloomington: Indiana University Press, 2009).

29. Spector, *Eagle Against the Sun*, 493–503 and 532–40. Since Iwo Jima was a Marine operation, the last Green book of the Pacific War is Roy E. Appleman, James M. Burns, Russell A. Gugeler and John Stevens, *Okinawa: The Last Battle.* The last Morrison volume that covers the end game is Volume 14, *Victory in the Pacific.* A classic account of Okinawa is E.B. Sledge, *With the Old Breed at Peleliu and Okinawa* (Novato: Presidio Press, 1980).

30. Richard Overy, *The Bombing War: Europe, 1939–1945* (London, UK: Penguin Books, 2014), Chapters 1–4. To understand the origins of German air force doctrine and their lack of a strategic bombing force, a good place to begin is James S. Corum, *The Luftwaffe: Creating the Operational Air War, 1918–1940* (Lawrence: University Press of Kansas, 1997).

31. Kenneth P. Werrell, "The Strategic Bombing of Germany in World War II: Costs and Accomplishments," *The Journal of American History* 73, no. 3 (December, 1986): 702–13. The air war is as much a story of men and machines as it is of strategy and tonnage statistics. An introduction to the rigors of the bombing campaign can be found in Donald L. Miller, *Masters of the Air: America's Bomber Boys Who Fought the Air War Against Nazi Germany* (New York: Simon and Schuster Paperbacks, 2006).

32. Werrell, "Strategic Bombing of Germany," 709–713. For an approachable narrative on the air war as a whole, see Geoffrey Perret, *Winged Victory: The Army Air Forces in World War II* (New York: Random House, 1993). For the commitment to accuracy in American doctrine, see Conrad C. Crane, *Bombs, Cities and Civilians: American Airpower Strategy in World War II* (Lawrence: University Press of Kansas, 1993). For the moral dimension, see Ronald Schaffer, *Wings of Judgment: American Bombing in World War II* (New York: Oxford University Press, 1985).

33. Spector, *Eagle Against the Sun*, 487–94, 503–507; Schaffer, *Wings of Judgment*, Chapters 6 and 7. For an overview of the fire raids, see Kenneth Werrell, *Blankets of Fire: U.S. Bombers over Japan during World War Two* (Washington, DC: Smithsonian Institution Press, 1996).

34. There are many fine works that recount the last campaigns of the war and the provisional plans for invading the home islands. A sample includes Max Hastings, *Retribution: The Battle for Japan, 1944–45* (New York: Alfred A. Knopf, 2008); John Ray Skates, *The Invasion of Japan: Alternative to the Bomb* (Columbia: University of South Carolina Press, 1994); Richard B. Frank, *Downfall: The End of the Imperial Japanese Empire* (New York: Random House, 1999); D.M. Giangreco, *Hell to Pay: Operation DOWNFALL and the Invasion of Japan, 1945–1947* (Annapolis: Naval Institute Press, 2009).

35. For the alternative to the military explanations, see Gar Alperovitz, *The Decision to Use the Atomic Bomb and the Architecture of an American Myth* (New York, Alfred A. Knopf, 1995). See also, Kazuo Yagami, "Bombing Hiroshima and Nagasaki: Gar Alperovitz and His Critics," *Southeast Review of Asian Studies* 31 (2009): 301–307. For the development of the Atomic Bomb, see Richard Rhodes, *The Making of the Atomic Bomb* (New York: Simon and Schuster, 1986). The Army Green Book series also has a volume on the Manhattan Project, Vincent C. Jones, *Manhattan: The Army and the Atomic Bomb* (Washington, DC: Center of Military History, 1985).

Chapter 11

On The Brink

The Cold War, 1945–1973

In this uneasy age in which we live, strife abounds in many troubled parts of
the world. The weapons of modern warfare have become increasingly powerful
and numerous . . . . Despite continuing efforts to achieve and maintain peace, a
nuclear attack upon the United States remains a distinct possibility.

Protection in the Nuclear Age[1]

As a kid in Southern California, I remember seeing the prominent orange and yellow
fallout shelter signs that were on most of the large buildings in downtown Los Angeles. From a kid's perspective, I understood that a fallout shelter was akin to a bomb
shelter. While I was always curious as to what would be in the bowels of these buildings to protect us from this thing called fallout, I was blissfully unaware of the dangerous times we lived in. As a fifty-year old historian and interpreter, this is not history,
it is the reality I experienced. For the generation born after the fall of the Berlin Wall
and the disintegration of the Soviet Empire, these events are history, as ancient as the
Roman Empire or even World War Two for that matter. We are left with the challenge of acknowledging the stories and experiences of those who lived through these
momentous events, balanced against attempting to understand objectively the origins,
evolution, and meaning of these events. Can we honor both and still find the truth?

The Cold War, as the name suggests, never erupted into the equivalent of the Third
World War between the United States and the Soviet Union. Tensions escalated and
fell between the two super powers depending upon the crisis. How can we tell these
stories? Perhaps the best interpretive technique available is telling these stories from
a people perspective. Much like the wide range of experiences in the Second World
War, by putting these stories from the point of view of the participants and observers,
you get approachable history that is perhaps more relevant than a concentration of
stories at the top. Moreover, local stories will perhaps be a way to touch on the various aspects of how historians approach the Cold War, but in a more palatable manner.
Eric Leonard, Superintendent of Minuteman Missile National Historical Site in South
Dakota, is exploring that approach for the site: "Any interpretation of this period has
to directly relate to the person, place or thing being interpreted. Otherwise the themes
risk being so big and broad as to be unrelatable to the visitor."[2] As successful as local

stories can be in relating to visitors' interests, even these stories need to be placed in context with the larger events that dominate this era. What, then, is the Cold War?

THE COLD WAR EMERGES

It was not inevitable that the Soviets and Americans would move from being Allies to enemies. Given, however, the tensions between capitalism and communism and the way those ideologies manifested themselves through the personalities of the Soviet leader Stalin and President Harry S. Truman, it was difficult to see another outcome. The end of the war in Europe in 1945 ended the common goal for which the Allies had been fighting. As tensions developed and the world split, both countries looked after their own self-interests through the lenses of their own political organs, cultures, and societies. The devastation experienced by Soviet Russia in World War Two and their long history of invasions from the West drove the Soviet need for secure borders. Given the revolutionary ideology of Soviet style communism, the wretched shape of Europe, and the innate power that United States held with their atomic monopoly (until 1949 when the Soviets tested their first atomic weapon), it is no wonder there was a shift in attitudes.

Unwilling to let Europe and other countries fall into disarray, Truman made a stand known as the Truman Doctrine. The combination of revolutionary turmoil in Greece and France, the establishment of the Marshall Plan to rebuild the European economy, and the Chinese civil war ending in a communist victory led President Truman to make a bold statement against the spread of communism. Guided by the work of George F. Kennan who defined the problem as containing Soviet ambitions and given flesh through a policy document from the National Security Council, NSC-68, the United States committed itself to containing Soviet aggression within their borders. Containment became the policy of the United States. With both of the protagonists armed with nuclear weapons, there was a degree of reticence on both sides to engage in a full-on struggle, which could lead to a devastating nuclear exchange. Unlike in previous wars, where the United States could insulate itself in its splendid isolation, modern technology in the form of intercontinental ballistic missiles and jet-powered bombers put the United States at risk from Soviet nuclear weapons. Tensions would certainly rise throughout this time period, but with the capability to mutually destroy each other, after 1945 and until the fall of communism, most of the wars fought were through client powers—that is, North Korea and North Vietnam.[3]

The advent of the atomic era and the subsequent rise in tensions had an effect on the development of the United States' armed forces. In 1947, the National Security Act was enabled, abolishing the War Department for the Department of Defense, a single, theoretically unified department. The creation of an umbrella did not ameliorate the institutional angst over the future of the armed forces. Given what appeared to be the primacy of nuclear weapons, there were vicious institutional struggles over the budgeting for major weapon systems, in particular fleet carriers or strategic bombers. The canceling of a fleet carrier in favor of bombers briefly signaled the primacy of the Air Force in these struggles. As the decade of the 1950s unfolded, however, atomic weapons alone could not substitute for ground troops and ships as the country put containment to the test with the Korean War.[4]

The Korean War, seen within the context of its time, appeared to be a manifestation of the communist aggression against a legitimately elected, democratic government. Korea was a Japanese colony until 1945 when the Soviets and Americans occupied the northern and southern halves of the country. These divisions became permanent with a communist client state in the North and an elected government to the south. There is much more to the origins of the conflict than the standard narrative reveals. There were competing visions of what the country should become, and a bitter struggle akin to a civil war raged throughout the peninsula. Whether it was a civil war that the Americans intervened in or a conflict between two competing ideologies that truly represented a threat, there will probably never be agreement. The United States has supported the government of South Korea since the end of the war, but they were unprepared to meet the attacks of the North in June 1950. Unable to stem the tide, General Douglas MacArthur, with a UN mandate, was given command. Whatever American units were available in Japan attacked piecemeal until forced into a pocket on the southeastern part of the country. It appeared that South Korea would fall.[5]

MacArthur and his subordinates stopped the North Korean advance and planned a bold move to sever their overstretched supply lines with a landing at Inchon, just west of the capital, Seoul. MacArthur launched his bold attack in September 1950, when the Marines and a US Army division achieved complete surprise, breaking the spirit of the North Korean offensive and forcing a retreat from most of the south. The subsequent northern advance of UN troops in the fall of 1950 nearly broke North Korean resistance. As Allied columns reached the border between North Korea and China, the Chinese intervened. While the Chinese had been providing assistance to the North, MacArthur had ignored or downplayed the intelligence he was receiving. When the Chinese attacked, they pushed the Marines south in an epic retreat. The Chinese would continue attacking in January 1951, leading to the evacuation of Seoul as their advance surged southward. In the spring, the Allies would counterattack, settling the front line in the mountains north of Seoul, where the front line would remain until the end of the war. The spring of 1951 also saw the relief of Douglas MacArthur. The General advocated for more aggressive moves against China, which the President would not allow. These insubordinate activities were awarded with the General's relief by President Truman.[6] Even with a virtual monopoly on nuclear weapons, the United Sates continued with the war until 1953, when an armistice put a halt to the fighting, establishing a defacto border roughly following the 38th parallel.

At the moment, there is no American museum that concentrates on the story of the Korean War[7] but there is the Korean War Memorial on the National Mall in Washington, DC. For many years the War was brought into focus through the popular television program MASH, but in popular circles the War that raged on the Korean peninsula is often labeled as "unknown." While the country did not mobilize defense assets and war industries on the level of the Second World War, the use of general labels such as "unknown" might influence a visitor's understanding of this conflict as one that is not as important as other modern conflicts. Given the proximity of the Korean War to the end of the conflagration that was World War Two, its smaller scale seems to diminish its importance in the public's mind. Yet, it was the first test of the doctrine of containment, saw the resumption of the draft, and added the term limited war to the lexicon. Korea is by no means insignificant. As stated in previous chapters, a local focus through the lens of ordinary people allows small institutions to tackle large topics. For example, rather than providing the typical time line of what happened where and when, perhaps it would be more useful to approach the story of the war in Korea through special topics of local significance. In the fighting that raged up and down the Korean Peninsula, it was for the first time that the US Army fought with African-Americans integrated into frontline units. I cannot think of a better way to allow a special topic to tell the story of a larger event but at the same time serve as a means to diversify your institution's ties to the community.

THE NEW LOOK AND FLEXIBLE RESPONSE

In an age where nuclear weapons profoundly changed the formula for security, the leaders of the country in the 1950s and 1960s attempted to find a balance between the awesome but destabilizing power of nukes versus more conventional arms. Dwight D. Eisenhower was propelled into the White House in large part because of public dissatisfaction over the manner in which the war in Korea had been led. The Korean War may have ended with a temporary truce or armistice, but with the end of hostilities, Eisenhower took a unique approach to national security policy that capitalized on the destructive force of nuclear weapons and the challenges of the Cold War.

Believing in the efficacy of containment, Eisenhower did not want to relax against the ideological threat that the Soviets posed, but at the same time he did not want to create a large array of nuclear and nonnuclear or conventional forces to hem in the Soviet Union. In concert with the President's Secretary of State, A policy popularly known as the New Look came to symbolize Eisenhower's administration. Put simply, Soviet intentions would be deterred with the threat of nuclear weapons. The threat of nuclear annihilation was brought home with the development of a super bomb, popularly known as the hydrogen bomb. Tested in 1951 in the United States and in the Soviet Union a few years later, warheads became smaller, more destructive, and more numerous. In attempting to counterbalance Soviet propaganda and prevent the further spread of communism, the Eisenhower administration actively pursued covert operations to maintain friendly governments. In 1953 in Iran, and in Guatemala in 1954, the Central Intelligence Agency (CIA) was actively involved in removing legitimate governments. In spite of a clearly articulated strategy, reliance on nuclear weapons as a deterrent against all threats proved illusory.[8]

The New Look was less than successful in defusing crises that emerged during this period. In Asia, the French attempt to keep Indochina as part of its empire failed. In the aftermath of the Chinese Civil War, the nationalist government, installed on the island of Taiwan, clashed with the Communist Chinese over islands, escalating tensions. In the Middle East, Eisenhower intervened in Lebanon and stopped the British and French expedition against the Suez Canal. Moreover, after the death of the Soviet Leader Stalin in 1953, Eisenhower's attempt for a rapprochement with the Soviets ended in failure. The inauguration of the space race between the two countries and the U-2 incident, where an American spy plane was shot down over the Soviet Union and the pilot captured, raised tensions. In spite of a commitment to national liberation,

Eisenhower refused to intervene in the 1956 Hungarian Revolution, signaling the limits of the rhetoric of massive retaliation.[9]

Ultimately the fate of world lay in the hands of the two superpowers. With weapons of such raw destructive power, museums often fixate on the technology that made the weapons and delivered them. While many larger museums will devote a gallery or two to the Cold War, there are no US museums on the Cold War.[10] The US Air Force, which played a prominent role in projecting American power around the world, does have a substantial collection devoted to the Cold War years. The inventory of objects in their Cold War gallery alone include some of the largest aircraft in the Air Force.[11] Large objects have a way of appealing to most visitors, but are they enough? The equipment and stories of the men who flew these aircraft are no doubt interesting and compelling, but are they relevant to the widest array of visitors? Probably not. Objects become touchstones to greater narratives. While it is always important to recognize the basic information, these objects can serve as icons to larger stories. For example, the Air Force museum has a B-36 bomber on display. As a strategic bomber during the 1950s, its relevancy as an artifact is that it was the primary aircraft that would have been used to drop atomic weapons on the Soviet Union. The airplane, then, can serve as an icon to talk about the New Look in the Eisenhower administration or the challenges of making deterrence work. There are other installations around the country: as mentioned previously, Minuteman Missile National Historic Site and the sole remaining Titan Missile silo in Arizona offer very visceral experiences—access to what served as the frontline of the Cold War.

The election of John F. Kennedy as US President brought a thorough re-examination of policy and the movement away from Massive Retaliation to what was known as Flexible Response. As the term indicates, rather than relying on nuclear weapons, the Kennedy administration would apply an appropriate level of force around the world to address the perceived security issue. Like his predecessor, Kennedy did not reject the basic premise of containment, but he certainly thought of different methods to attain it. He recognized, particularly in an age of decolonization, that in a war between proxies of the Soviet Union and United States, nuclear weapons had no relevancy. Increasing the capacity to provide assistance in insurgencies with small teams of trainers and soldiers as well as enlarging American conventional forces were the chief differences between the policies of Eisenhower and the new President. Nevertheless, it was during Kennedy's administration that the nation came the closest to striking the Soviets over the island of Cuba.[12]

The Cuban Missile Crisis was, as the name suggests, about Soviet nuclear-capable missiles on the island of Cuba. Reacting against American intermediate range missiles ringing the Soviet Union, the Soviets, with the cooperation of the Castro regime in Cuba, moved to place similar missiles on the Caribbean Island. With the fall of the Cuban dictator to Fidel Castro, and his subsequent cozying up to the Soviets, this was not a welcome development. The failure to ferment a counter-revolution with a CIA-backed invasion at the Bay of Pigs was a black eye early in the Kennedy administration. Alarmed by the developments, the Americans blockaded Cuba and mobilized resources to forcibly remove the missiles if necessary. Tensions escalated. Rather than inflaming the situation, the Russians blinked first, agreeing to remove the missiles and, as it was later revealed, the United States did the same. With other incidents in Berlin, tensions did not ease. Moreover, with an emphasis on flexible response, such tensions may have provided the United States some impetus to intervene in Vietnam.[13]

THE FOREVER WAR: VIETNAM

A historical debate dichotomy that is ever present in the popular imagination and available literature between the Second World War and the War in Vietnam. The historical debate has raged between two opposing viewpoints. For some, the war was never a good match against US strategic interests, making a clear-cut victory impossible to achieve. Balanced against that approach is the fact that victory was in our grasp. The lack of will and a coherent military and political strategy prevented a victory from being achieved. Since the end of American involvement, there has been a struggle to understand the truth and provide a concrete legacy of what was seen at the time as America's longest war.

The amount of literature that has spawned in the aftermath of Vietnam is enormous, and ranges from historical monographs to novels. Although a majority of the monographs fall within the "unwinnable war" camp, there are a variety of points of view expressed. Good places to start are texts you would find in a college classroom—George C. Herring's *America's Longest War* (now in its fifth edition) paired with *Major Problems in the History of the Vietnam War*. These are concise overviews of the War. When paired with Stanley Karnow's *Vietnam: A History*, you get a fairly complete overview of the War. For every action, there is an equal and opposite reaction. Since the end of the War, there has been a current of historical thinking that argues that the War was winnable at various points in the timeline, "but if" only certain decisions had been made. An overview and critique of how so-called revisionists are rethinking the War can be found in Gary Hess' *Vietnam: Explaining America's Lost War*. How these views have an effect on scholarship can be seen in recent works on the commanding general of the American war effort in Vietnam, General William C. Westmoreland. Lewis Sorley, in his book *Westmoreland: The General Who Lost Vietnam*, places the blame of the War going poorly on the shoulders of Westmoreland. Rather than pursuing a counter-insurgency strategy that concentrated on nation building, he instituted a policy of attrition through firepower that failed in every respect. As a counter to Sorley's work, Gregory Daddis, in *Westmoreland's War: Reassessing American Strategy in Vietnam*, argues quite the opposite: that Westmoreland pursued a multilayered approach to a complex problem that has been properly addressed in the literature. As with all things, the truth lay somewhere in between.[14]

FRANCE AND THE UNITED STATES IN VIETNAM, 1945–1963

While it is always helpful to dissect a historical event to understand how and why decisions were made, given the passage of time between the past and the present, it is always difficult to truly reconstruct the tenor of the times in which these decisions were made. That being said, the involvement of the United States, first in assisting the French to keep their colony known as Indochina and, later, attempting to stabilize and support the

Republic of South Vietnam, can only be understood within the context of the Cold War. While the War as we know it is often defined as the period of direct American involvement, from around 1964 to 1973, the United States was involved one way or another since the end of the Second World War, first with France and later with South Vietnam.

The United States assisted France not out of altruism but out of a fairly narrow view of containing communism. Whether or not this was a correct assumption to be proceeding from can certainly be debated, but policy makers understood the challenge that Vietnam posed in narrow terms. The United States supported French efforts with financial and military aid until the French were defeated in 1954. On the eve of the French defeat at Dien Bien Phu, there were talks in the Eisenhower administration of intervention, but they went nowhere. An armistice agreement agreed to temporarily split the country in two and call for free elections to determine Vietnam's future. They never happened.[15]

Looking back in time, it seems that events were sliding inexorably toward war. In fact, with the establishment of the Republic of South Vietnam, there was a good-faith effort to build a viable nation. A Military Assistance and Advisory Group was established in the capital, Saigon, in an effort to build an army that could stand on its own. Ngo Dinh Diem emerged as the leader. Bolstered by American aid, to all appearances it looked as though the government would thrive. However, there was no tradition of popular democracy to build toward and Diem was paranoid, secretive, and felt no connection to the general population. With the establishment of the National Liberation Front or Viet Cong, Diem was beginning to face an insurgency from the North and, in spite of American aid, a military apparatus unwilling and unable to quell it. The challenge was how to build a cohesive and sustainable Vietnamese nationalism, democratic institutions, a strong economy, and a competent security apparatus with a less than successful regime. Diem chose to isolate himself from the populace and rule in an arbitrary and capricious way, bypassing the legislature and ruling by fiat. Beset by political difficulties and increasingly isolated, the United States may have encouraged those who were opposed to Diem to remove him. He was assassinated in a coup; three weeks later, Kennedy was shot in Dallas.[16]

The assassination of President Kennedy in Dallas in November 1963 nearly always triggers a sentiment over what might have been, which also reveals some of the most constant historical pitfalls in attempting to tell this story. There are many questions that just cannot be answered due to the President's death—how complicit was his administration in promoting the death of Diem? How much of a committed Cold Warrior was the President, and was he willing to entertain a negotiated settlement with the North? Did Kennedy have a cogent, long-term vision for the increasing involvement of the country in Vietnam? These are critical questions that can never be answered. When mounting an exhibit or creating public programming, while it can be fun and entertaining to delve into "what if" questions, in the end they are counterproductive and do not advance our understanding of the issues that Kennedy faced. Not only must we remember the other domestic and international pressures Kennedy had to address, but his decisions must also be evaluated on the basis of what we know, rather than by speculation. What we do know is that in the fall of 1963, Vietnam was facing a multitude of threats and it was up to Kennedy's successor, Lyndon B. Johnson, to figure things out.[17]

ESCALATION, 1963–1968

When Lyndon Johnson was sworn in as President on the flight back from Dallas, Vietnam became his problem. He continued to build the advisory capacity but was also given a pretext for direct intervention in the war against the North. Johnson was a skilled politician, having paid his dues in Congress before becoming Vice President. He was committed to social justice but cognizant of the Cold War. Unwilling to abide a South Vietnamese defeat on his watch, he appointed General William Westmoreland as commander of the military assistance command in Vietnam and continued to promote a robust Vietnamese response to the insurgency. In August 1964, it was reported (or perhaps not) that North Vietnamese torpedo boats had attacked a US Navy destroyer in the Tonkin Gulf. While the details remain fuzzy to this day, it gave Johnson the impetus he needed to get Congressional approval to expand the war. The so-called Tonkin Gulf Resolution gave the President the authority he needed. In the fall of 1964, he instituted a bombing campaign called Rolling Thunder against North Vietnamese targets to pressure the North and its supporters in the South to stop. In the New Year, Vietnamese insurgents attacked an American base, destroying American aircraft and killing American servicemen, which provided further justification to put American troops on the ground. Within two years of President Kennedy's death, then, Johnson committed himself to a war in South Vietnam to end the insurgency and stem the communist tide. Troop levels rose quickly so that by the end of 1967, over 480,000 men and women were serving in Vietnam.[18]

Given the preponderance of firepower that the Americans could bring to bear, as the American presence grew, General Westmoreland wanted to use force and overwhelming firepower to wear down the North Vietnamese and their Allies. Fixated on the body counts of the enemy more than nation building, he equated the rising body counts with victory. The Americans had unprecedented mobility with helicopters and could put men and equipment anywhere—except in North Vietnam. Not wanting to provoke a larger conflict with either China or the Soviet Union with an invasion of North Vietnam, American forces remained south of the 17th parallel. The first battles with the North Vietnamese occurred in 1965 in the Ia Drang Valley and would be followed by other operations throughout the country until the disruptions caused by the Tet Offensive of 1968. American units performed well against their Vietnamese adversaries, chalking up impressive victories. In spite of these victories, winning the War conclusively proved elusive.[19]

The decision to introduce ground forces and a comprehensive air campaign against North Vietnam, and the subsequent escalation of the conflict through 1968, is another critical juncture. While there is general agreement that President Johnson went to war without a clear plan in place to either decisively defeat North Vietnam or create a viable government, there is a chorus of contrarians that suggests a full application of force, that is, an invasion of North Vietnam, was a viable concept and the only way to win the War. To Johnson's credit, he did not want to create a wider conflict with China in particular. That possibility cannot be easily dismissed. These debates, however, are helpful in that they provide various perspectives in attempting to understand not so much the circumstances of American intervention as what was hoped to be accomplished beyond saving Vietnam. Mounting a large exhibit to answer these questions is

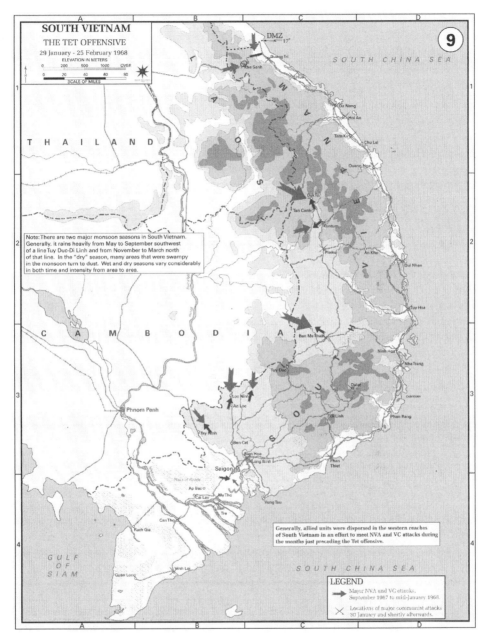

Figure 11.1 Map—The Tet Offensive. *Source*: West Point Atlas

beyond the resources of many institutions. Regardless, the focus on individual institutions or people who either fought in the War, agitated against it, or had no opinion otherwise can be used to simply ask the question of why a war in Vietnam?[20]

The pivotal point, perhaps even the most critical moment, of American involvement was what has become known as the Tet Offensive in early 1968. The leadership of North Vietnam hoped to precipitate a rebellion with coordinated attacks across the country. Playing on the expectations of the American and South Vietnamese governments, expecting a temporary cease fire for the Tet holiday, the North Vietnamese achieved complete surprise. As events unfolded, Viet Cong teams attacked cities, towns, and military bases across the country, including high-profile targets such as the American Embassy in the South Vietnamese capital of Saigon. In spite of the surprise, both the Americans and South Vietnamese responded, temporarily breaking the back of the insurgency. The events of Tet, however, proved to be an embarrassment for the Johnson administration and the tipping point for public opinion and Congressional support to begin to wane. The toll was so great that Johnson refused to take on another term and the resulting domestic turmoil rocked the country to its core. The assassinations of Martin Luther King, Jr. and Robert F. Kennedy, race riots throughout the country, and the chaos at the Democratic National Convention in Chicago precipitated the election of Richard M. Nixon and another four years of war.[21]

RICHARD NIXON AND THE SEARCH FOR PEACE

The election of Richard M. Nixon in the aftermath of Tet was due, in part, to his promise to end the War on his administration's terms. With mounting public protests and a restive Congress making a great deal of noise to end the War, Nixon forged ahead with his plans. Nixon and his Secretary of State Henry Kissinger wanted to withdraw from the War on their terms, providing an opportunity for the South Vietnamese government to survive on their own, without the help of thousands of troops. Known as Vietnamization, it was, as the term suggests, an attempt to strengthen the South Vietnamese government, its Army, and the connection with the people that is so critical for a popular democracy. It cannot be denied that progress was made in stabilizing the government. Had this emphasis on building a civil society occurred at the outset of nation building, the United States could have prevailed, a small but vocal group of historians contend. Unfortunately, it comes down to wishful thinking about what should have happened rather than what did occur. While civil institutions and the Army saw considerable progress in fighting the War on their own, the South Vietnamese Army performed unevenly once the Americans left. South Vietnamese political institutions, though greatly improved, still tended to be dominated by the military and more concerned about securing political power than promoting the needs of their constituents.[22]

In the aftermath of the Tet Offensive and the election of Richard Nixon, there was a struggle to find some closure to the war in Vietnam. From 1969 to 1972, President Nixon and Secretary of State Kissinger cajoled and threatened North Vietnam with intensive bombings and other diplomatic maneuvers to begin peace negotiations. By far the most controversial of their moves was the invasion of Cambodia in 1970. By disrupting North Vietnamese bases in Cambodia, Nixon and Kissinger hoped that it would take pressure off the South Vietnamese government, giving them more time to prepare for the eventual American withdrawal. While the invasion did provide some tangible military benefits, it only temporarily disrupted North Vietnamese logistical traffic and, instead, destabilized the struggling government of Cambodia. The invasion unleashed an avalanche of domestic protests, including the tragic and unfortunate events at Kent State University in Ohio in which four students died in protests. The

War was no closer to a conclusion and the Nixon administration continued to struggle to find an honorable peace.[23]

In spite of the disaster that Cambodia represented, the Nixon administration continued to draw down American forces. As American support spiraled downward, the North Vietnamese struck in the spring of 1972. The offensive failed but restarted peace talks.[24] The Nixon administration wanted two things—get the United States out of Vietnam and make certain South Vietnam remained viable. After fits and starts and compromising over issues, a peace deal was reached. The United States could point to a viable South Vietnamese government, yet it allowed North Vietnamese forces to remain in the South. The United States got its prisoners of war returned and promised to continue to support the South financially, even after the withdrawal of US troops. Unfortunately, it was not a lasting peace. The Watergate Scandal brought down the Nixon White House and Congress was no longer interested in bankrolling the South Vietnamese government. In 1975, a final North Vietnamese offensive swept through the South, ending the Republic of South Vietnam and leaving an unresolved question in American minds of whether or not the sacrifice was worth the cost.[25]

The question remains of how to effectively tell a story that still elicits strong views and for many is not so much a historical event, but just as current as ever. For many veterans, telling stories can only occur after the wounds of the past are healed. For many, regardless of where they fought, that may never happen, but to move forward in telling a story, perhaps the best strategy is commemoration. In 1982, the Vietnam War Memorial in Washington, DC, opened. With funds raised by the Vietnam Veterans Memorial Fund, an open design competition was held, which was won by Maya Lin. Her design generated a great deal of controversy when it was unveiled. Missing the typical celebratory style of grand memorials, it is a simple artistic statement that, over time, has become an accepted symbol of the chaos of the Vietnam War. Veterans and their families continue to leave objects at the memorial in tribute to fallen comrades and veterans who have passed on. It was an appropriate first step in talking about Vietnam, but for institutions that want to move beyond commemoration into history, challenges and opportunities still remain.[26]

There is an orthodoxy of sorts that presents the Vietnam War as unwinnable. Regardless of how ideological or nationalistic the political elites of North Vietnam may have been, they were fighting to unify the entire country. After decades of colonization by the French and occupation by the Japanese, let alone the enmity with China, the North Vietnamese played the long game. No matter how many causalities were inflicted by American firepower, the North Vietnamese could and did wait until the Americans grew tired of war and withdrew. Since the end of the War, a contrary voice to the orthodoxy has emerged, contending that the War could have and should have been won. These works are wishful thinking, but still offer a powerful counterpoint to the meaning of the War. There will never be agreement, but each viewpoint is valid and should be recognized when mounting exhibits or programs on the War. The first step the first step to finding common ground is to at least openly discuss the War on its own terms.

The opening of the Atomic Era in 1945 and the subsequent years after Hiroshima and Nagasaki produced, at best, a tenuous peace. The fleets of bombers that stood ready on dozens of airfields around the world; missiles in silos; and submarines prowling the oceans depths, all stood like silent sentinels. As uncomfortable as it is to think about, the mere presence of these weapons certainly deterred a nuclear exchange between the United States and Soviet Union. For many, these weapons created a degree of stability, and perhaps even peace, yet it was an uneasy one. Punctuated by wars in Asia, the United States, as it had done in the past, could fight limited wars that kept the violence contained, but not without creating a great deal of uncertainty over whether even these limited wars were worth the cost in blood and treasure in containing the perceived communist threat. The early Cold War provides a plethora of stories that touched the lives of most Americans, myself included. While some will argue that our recent past is not history, these events are still relevant to modern audiences and deserve our attention.

NOTES

1. Defense Civil Preparedness Agency. *Protection in the Nuclear Age* (Washington, DC: Department of Defense, 1977).

2. E-mail to author, February 25, 2015. In author's possession.

3. Millett, Maslowski, and Fies, *For the Common Defense*, 440–44 and Muehlbauer and Ulbrich, *Ways of War*, 414–20. A good place to start for the origins and maturation of the Cold War is John Lewis Gaddis, *The Cold War: A New History* (New York: Penguin Press, 2005) and *Strategies of Containment: A Critical Appraisal of American National Security Policy During the Cold War* (New York: Oxford University Press, 2005). A nice introduction to NSC 68 can be found in Ernest R. May, ed., *American Cold War Strategy: Interpreting NSC 68* (Boston: Bedford Books of St. Martin's Press, 1993). For a military history of these events that shaped the Cold War, see Jonathan M. House, *A Military History of the Cold War, 1944–1962* (Norman: University of Oklahoma Press, 2012).

4. As defense budgets fell and rose in the 1950s and early 1960s, interservice rivalry was rife and had an effect on how the Navy and Army adapted their missions, doctrine, and equipment for an ever changing fiscal and threat environment. For an overview, see Hagan, The People's Navy, Chapter 12; Ingo Trauschweizer, *The Cold War U.S. Army: Building Deterrence for Limited War* (Lawrence: University Press of Kansas, 2008) and Major Robert Doughty, *Leavenworth Papers No. 1: The Evolution of US Army Tactical Doctrine, 1946–1976* (Fort Leavenworth: Combat Studies Institute, 1979). The Doughty study is available online at http://usacac.army.mil/cac2/cgsc/carl/download/csipubs/doughty.pdf.

5. For alternative views on the origins of the Korean War, see Bruce Cummings, *The Origins of the Korean War: Liberation and the Emergence of Separate Regimes, 1945–47* (Princeton: Princeton University Press, 1981) and *The Origins of the Korean War: The Roaring of the Cataract, 1947–1950* (Princeton: Princeton University Press, 1990). Allan R. Millett, *The War For Korea, 1945–1950: A House Burning* (Lawrence: University Press of Kansas, 2005) and the companion volume, *The War For Korea, 1950–1951: They Came From the North* (Lawrence: University Press of Kansas, 2010) reject Cummings' interpretation. For an international outlook, see William Steuck, *The Korean War: An International History* (Princeton: Princeton University Press, 1995).

6. There are several places to find traditional military histories of American military developments in Korea. See Roy E. Appleman, *South to the Naktong, North to the Yalu (June–November, 1950)* (Washington, DC: Office of the Chief of Military History, 1961); Walter G. Hermes, *Truce Tent and Fighting Front* (Washington, DC: Office of the Chief of Military

History, 1966); Roy E. Appleman, *East of the Chosin: Entrapment and Breakout in Korea, 1950* (College Station: Texas A & M Press, 1987). For an analysis of the opening battle, see Roy K. Flint, "Task Force Smith and the 24th Division: Delay and Withdrawal, 5–19 July 1950," in Heller and Stofft, *America's First Battles*, 266–99. For background on the Marines, see Charles R. Smith, ed. US Marines in the Korean War (Washington, DC: History Division, US Marine Corps, 2007).

7. There is a group raising the necessary funds to build a Korean War National Museum in New York City, NY. They can be reached at http://kwnm.org/freedom-center/.

8. Gaddis, *Strategies of Containment*, 125–61; Millett, Maslowski, and Feis, *For the Common Defense*, 478–82; Samuel F. Wells, Jr., "The Origins of Massive Retaliation," *Political Science Quarterly* 96 (Spring, 1981): 31–52. See also, Charles C. Alexander, *Holding the Line: The Eisenhower Era, 1952–1961* (Bloomington: Indiana University Press, 1975), For a critique on the Eisenhower administration New Look, see Maxwell D. Taylor, *The Uncertain Trumpet* (New York: Harpers and Brothers, 1959).

9. Gaddis, *Strategies of Containment*, 162–96; Millett, Maslowski, and Feis, *For the Common Defense*, 482–96. Eisenhower was a gifted story teller and his memoirs give a flavor of the times. They are in two volumes, *Mandate for Change, 1953–1956* (New York, Doubleday and Company, 1963) and *Waging Peace, 1956–1961* (New York, Doubleday and Company, 1963). For an understanding of the evolution of strategic thought, vis-à-vis nuclear weapons, please see Bernard Brodie, *Strategy in the Missile Age* (Princeton: Princeton University Press, 1959) and Barry H. Steiner, *Bernard Brodie and the Foundations of American Nuclear Strategy* (Lawrence: University Press of Kansas, 1991).

10. A quick google search using the term, "Cold War Museum" on March 9, 2015 yielded one stand-alone museum. The Cold War Museum in Warrenton, Virginia, is currently raising money to convert a former US Army Security Agency Field Station into a museum devoted to telling the story of the Cold War.

11. The National Museum of the US Air Force at Wright-Patterson Air Force Base in Dayton, Ohio, (http://www.nationalmuseum.af.mil/) houses a B-36, a B-1, and a B-2 bomber. The newest gallery of the museum that is currently under construction will provide 244,000 square feet of exhibit space. For a concise overview of the role of the US Air Force in the 1950s and 1960s, see Charles J. Gross, *American Military Aviation: The Indispensable Arm* (College Station: Texas A & M Press, 2002), Chapter 4.

12. Gaddis, *Strategies of Containment*, 197–234.

13. There is a wide array of works related to the Cuban Missile Crisis, one of the most tension-filled events of the Cold War. Some helpful works include James A. Nathan, ed., *The Cuban Missile Crisis Revisited* (New York: St. Martin's Press, 1992) and James G. Blight and David A. Welch, *On the Brink: Americans and Soviets Examine the Cuban Missile Crisis* (New York: Hill and Wang, 1989). For a broader view of Kennedy's actions around the world, see Lawrence Freedman, *Kennedy's Wars: Berlin, Cuba, Laos, and Vietnam* (New York: Oxford University Press, 2002).

14. George C. Herring, *America's Longest War: The United States and Vietnam, 1950–1975*. Fifth Edition (New York: McGraw Hill, 2013); Robert J. McMahon, ed., *Major Problems in the History of the Vietnam War*. Third Edition (New York: Houghton Mifflin Company, 2003); Stanley Karnow, *Vietnam: A History* (New York: Penguin Books, 1984); Gary R. Hess. *Vietnam: Explaining America's Lost War* (Malden: Blackwell Publishing, 2009); Lewis Sorley, *Westmoreland: The General Who Lost Vietnam* (New York: Houghton Mifflin Harcourt Publishing, 2003); Gregory Daddis, *Westmoreland's War: Reassessing American Strategy in Vietnam* (New York: Oxford University Press, 2014).

15. Karnow, *Vietnam*, Chapters 3–4; Herring, *Longest War*, Chapter 1.

16. Herring, *Longest War*, Chapter, 2–3. For contemporary American accounts on the United States and South Vietnam during this time period, see David Halberstam, *The Best and the Brightest* (New York: Random House, 1972) and Frances FitzGerald, *Fire in the Lake: The Vietnamese and the Americans in Vietnam* (New York: Atlantic Monthly Press, Little, Brown, and Company, 1972). To understand the institutional side of the advising mission, there are two volumes that provide an overview of the program, Ronald H. Spector, *Advice and Support: The Early Years, 1941–1960* (Washington, DC: Center of Military History, 1985) and Jeffery Clarke, *Advice and Support: The Final Years: 1965–1973* (Washington, DC: Center of Military History, 1988).

17. Hess, *Vietnam: Explaining America's Lost War*, Chapter 3.

18. Herring, *Longest War*, Chapter 4. For an overview of the veracity of the Tonkin Gulf Incident, see Edwin E. Moise, *Tonkin Gulf and the Escalation of the Vietnam War* (Chapel Hill: University of North Carolina Press, 1996). There is a great of literature about the air war over North Vietnam and in the South. For a broad overview, see Ronald B. Frankham Jr., *Like Rolling Thunder: The Air War in Vietnam, 1964–1975* (Lanham: Rowman and Littlefield, 2005); for the moral aspects of the air war, see Mark Clodfelter, *Limits of Airpower: The American Bombing of Vietnam* (New York: The Free Press, 1989).

19. Herring, *Longest War*, Chapter 5. The battle at Ia Drang has garnered particular attention since it was the first clash between North Vietnamese regulars and the US Army. Overviews include George C. Herring, "The 1st Cavalry and the Ia Drang Valley, 18 October–24 October 1965" in Heller and Stoft, *America's First Battles*, 300–26; Lieutenant General Harold G. Moore (Ret.) and Joseph Galloway, *We Were Soldiers Once . . . . And Young: Ia Drang-The Battle That Changed the War in Vietnam* (New York: Random House, 1992). Although it is not exclusively focused on the combat experience in Vietnam, see Peter S. Kindsvatter, *American Soldiers: Ground Combat in the World Wars, Korea, and Vietnam* (Lawrence: University Press of Kansas, 2003) is a valuable source.

20. Hess, *Vietnam: Explaining America's Lost War*, Chapter 4. See also, Harry G. Summers, Jr., *On Strategy: A Critical Analysis of The Vietnam War* (Novato: Presidio Press, 1982). For other critiques of the decisions made and not taken, see Lewis Sorley, *A Better War: The Unexamined Victories and Final Tragedy of America's Last Years in Vietnam* (New York: Harcourt Brace and Company, 1999) and H.R. McMaster, *Dereliction of Duty: Johnson, McNamara, the Joint Chiefs of Staff and the Lies That Led to Vietnam* (New York: Harper, 1997).

21. Herring, *Longest War*, Chapter 6, Hess, *Vietnam: Explaining America's Lost War*, Chapter 7. For a contemporary account on Tet, see Don Oberdorfer. *Tet! The Turning Point of the Vietnam War* (New York: Doubleday, 1971). Khe Sanh was an iconic event for the Marines in Vietnam and has triggered an avalanche of literature. For the official Marine Corps histories of 1968, see Captain Moyers S. Shore II, USMC. *The Battle For Khe Sanh* (Washington, DC: History and Museums Division, Headquarters U.S. Marine Corps, 1969) and Jack Shulimson, Lieutenant Colonel Leonard A. Blasiol, U.S. Marine Corps, Charles R. Smith and Captain David A. Dawson, *U.S. Marine Corps. U.S. Marines in Vietnam: The Defining Year, 1968* (Washington, DC: History and Museums Division, Headquarters U.S. Marine Corps, 1997). A good overview can be found in John Prados and Ray W. Stubbe, *Valley of Decision: The Siege of Khe Sanh* (New York: Doubleday, 1991). See also, Ronald H. Spector, *After Tet: The Bloodiest Year in Vietnam* (New York: The Free Press, 1993).

22. Herring, *Longest War*, 271–88; Hess, *Vietnam: Explaining America's Lost War*, Chapter 8. After General Westmoreland moved to Washington, he was replaced by General Creighton Abrams; many revisionists say his attention to taking and holding ground and pacification were the formulas for success. Lewis Sorley is the loudest proponent of this school and is well represented in Lewis Sorley, *Thunderbolt. From the Battle of the Bulge to Vietnam*

and Beyond: General Creighton Abrams and the Army of His Times (New York: Simon and Schuster, 1992).

23. Herring, *Longest War*, 288–304. For an overview of the antiwar movement and its impact, see Charles DeBenedetti and Charles Chatfield, *An American Ordeal: The Antiwar Movement of the Vietnam Era* (Bloomington: Indiana University Press, 1990). For an overview of the Cambodian campaign, see John M. Shaw, *The Cambodian Campaign: The 1970 Offensive and America's Vietnam War* (Lawrence: University Press of Kansas, 2005).

24. The exact numbers are unknown, but the North Vietnamese Army suffered at least 100,000 casualties; the south also had well over 110,000 dead, wounded, or missing, Herring, *Longest War*, 309. For accounts on the Easter Offensive, see Dale Andrale, *Trial By Fire: The 1972 Easter Offensive, America's Last Vietnam Battle* (Lawrence: University Press of Kansas, 2001).

25. Herring, *Longest War*, 304–68; Kanow, *Vietnam*, Chapter 16. For the last years in Vietnam, see James H. Wilbanks, *Abandoning Vietnam: How America Left and South Vietnam Lost its War* (Lawrence: University Press of Kansas, 2004). For a perspective on the South Vietnamese Army and its struggles, see Robert K. Brigham, *ARVN: Life and Death of the South Vietnamese Army*. (Lawrence: University Press of Kansas, 2006).

26. Monumental Achievement: Our 2002 profile of architect Maya Lin that marked the 20th year of the Vietnam Memorial, Smithsonian Magazine. Accessed on May 15, 2015 from: http://www.smithsonianmag.com/arts-culture/monumental-achievement-71095571/?no-ist=&page=1.

Chapter 12

A World Undone

The Cold War and Beyond, 1973–Present

The way ahead will not be easy. It will require resolve, much hard work, and resilience . . . . There will be more reverses, horrific attacks, and acts of sabotage and intimidation. Nonetheless, we are determined to keep our shoulders to the wheel.[1]

Major General David H. Petraeus

As we move forward along the time line toward the present, any notion of historical analysis goes out the window. The perception of what war is has changed for many in the last decade as the United States struggles with groups that are not affiliated with sovereign states but are independent actors. Not only do perceptions change, but the immediacy of events also makes modern military history more akin to current events than "real" history. Everyone has an opinion, which makes it difficult to look at events objectively. There is simply not enough information and temporal distance for us to render an objective, historical judgment on contemporary events. These challenges do not mean that the stories that these events generate should be avoided. Modern stories are, at their basic level, connected to communities and people and should be shared.

Even though we no longer live in a world dominated by two superpowers, the issues of the Cold War of the 1970s and 1980s, and the more difficult world in the 1990s through today, allow us to craft many interpretive opportunities that, while perhaps not getting to the objective, historical truth, still allow us to connect to the audience in a provocative manner. As nuclear weapons became more powerful and accurate, the United States and the Soviet Union continued their dance in attempting to assert their power without triggering an international crisis.

THE COLD WAR ROLLS ON

The onset of the Vietnam War and its escalation diverted attention from the tensions with the Soviet Union and its satellites. With the election of Richard Nixon and the subsequent drawdown of American troops from Vietnam, increased attention was placed on a pragmatic approach in dealing with the Soviets and other Communist

powers. While still an anticommunist at heart, President Nixon played down ideological differences in deference to power and national interest. Attempting to overwhelm
the Soviet Union by simply building more weapons, in Nixon's estimation, would be
counterproductive. While willing to bargain, he did not abandon containment, but just
reimagined it. By "opening" China, Nixon could contain the Soviet Union, engage
with both communist countries, and come to a degree of accommodation without
surrendering his anticommunist credentials. The policy was known as détente and
proved successful in getting the Soviets to the bargaining table. The Strategic Arms
Limitation Treaty (SALT) and the antiballistic missile treaty (ABM) allowed for both
sides to retain substantial nuclear weapons without engaging in an out-of-control and
unproductive arms race. For this moment in time, Nixon and Kissinger succeeded in
bargaining with the Soviets. Yet, détente certainly did not curb tensions between the
superpowers around the world.[2]

Even though the United States was able to withdraw from Vietnam, tensions
between Soviet and American proxy states rose in the 1970s and 1980s to a level not
seen since the beginning of the Cold War. The decolonization of Africa and Asia in the
aftermath of the Second World War led to vicious civil wars across both continents,
beginning with China and continuing into the 1970s, particularly in Africa. As new
independent countries emerged from their colonial status, conflict would sometimes
ensue. In the Middle East, the tensions over an independent Jewish state also took
on overtones of superpower politics. The establishment of the state of Israel in 1948
inflamed passions across the Middle East and would lead to decades of conflict with
brush-ups in 1956, 1967, and 1973. With Soviet arms going to the Arab nationalist
governments and the Americans supporting the Israelis, the issues that began with the
partition of Palestine continue to be an open wound to this day, with no solution in
sight. The invasion of Afghanistan by the Soviet Union in 1979 would evolve into a
conflict that is often compared to the war in Vietnam. These conflicts demonstrated
that, just as in the 1950s, the dominant nuclear powers could deter direct war between
each other, but fight proxy wars on the fringes of their influence that would prove to
be costly extensions of the Cold War.[3]

In spite of these ideological struggles that took place between the Soviet Union and
the United States, with the end of the war in Vietnam, the American military apparatus
entered into a period of stagnation, introspection, and reinvention. As they had poured
money into field operations in the Vietnam War, their cyclical process of modernization slowed down considerably. By the mid-1970s, Congress was reluctant to pour billions of dollars into modernization, having just gone through a decades-long conflict.
As a result, the Army, Navy, Air Force, and Marines saw declining appropriations and
the cancelation of major projects. President Carter ended major weapons procurement,
in particular the B-1 Strategic Bomber and several ship programs, but laid the groundwork to modernize the nuclear deterrent with the MX Missile and Ohio class ballistic
missile submarines that would carry the Trident missile. This cycle would drastically
change at the beginning of the 1980s as events overseas began to exert themselves on
US policy, but, at the very least, the 1970s was a decade of adjustment.[4]

With the end of military commitments in Vietnam, the draft came to an end. For
the Army in particular, the transition from conscription to an all-volunteer force raised
questions over the ability to maintain a flow of manpower to meet existing needs.

The end of the draft forced the Army, in particular, to pay closer attention to different methods of filling their quotas. Women became a key component of maintaining force levels. While it would not be until the twenty-first century that many of the barriers to allowing women to serve in combat units would be lifted, the doors were opened for greater gender equality.[5] The end of the war in Southeast Asia also provided an opportunity to reconceptualize the missions of the armed services. There was movement away from thinking about counterinsurgency, such as that experienced in Vietnam, toward a more conventional conflict between the Soviet Union and United States and their allies from the North Atlantic Treaty Organization (NATO).

Once the United States ended its involvement in Vietnam, the natural question to ask was, "What's next?" After a decade of fighting a counter-insurgency, the Army in particular turned its attention to what had been a traditional Cold War mission—deterring a ground war in Europe. With the growing conventional or nonnuclear force capabilities of the Soviets in the 1960s and 1970s, and the simple fact that the number of Soviet troops outnumbered what NATO could bring to the field, the answer to the question was straightforward—find ways to slow down or stop a Soviet advance in Western Europe. The Army began to explore how to defeat the Soviets. There were various attempts in the 1970s to blunt the Soviet juggernaut. The key was destroying not the waves of tanks coming across the border, but what was behind them.[6]

A robust debate among the policy makers and officers created a new solution. The idea was to strike Soviet forces behind the front line, rather than attempting to actively defend against a possible Soviet armored assault. If the Soviets invaded the west, rather than simply defending a tenuous front, aggressively strike the invaders in the rear, and along their front, and on their flanks. The bywords for these guidelines, known as AirLand Battle, were initiative, agility, depth, and synchronization. Historian Robert Citino captures the essence of what was seen as a new formula for victory:

> The commander was to seize the initiative, shocking the enemy with the initial assault and not allowing him to recover. He was to think more rapidly than the foe . . . . He was to bring every part of the enemy force under attack at once . . . forcing the enemy to defend everywhere at once, never knowing which blow was the killing one . . . . Synchronization, with the attacker orchestrating fire, movement, and assault into one grand symphony of destruction, was the key to the new doctrine.[7]

With new weapon systems coming on line, in particular the M1 Abrams Main Battle tank, the M2/M3 Bradley Infantry Fighting Vehicle, and the AH 64 Apache Attack helicopter, as well as the beginnings of digital communication, commanders on the ground now had the tools and techniques to defeat an enemy that could field a ground force much larger than the US Army. It is fair to say, with a large dose of hindsight, that while the Soviets held the quantitative edge in sheer numbers of men under arms and vehicles pointed east, by the late 1980s and early 1990s, the United States held the qualitative edge. Thankfully, the two superpowers never went to war to test this doctrine, though it was the foundation of the plans that emerged in the aftermath of Iraq's invasion of Kuwait in 1990.

The development of this doctrine in the shadow of the disaster in Vietnam is a case study on how an institution grasps change. Visitors are often attracted to tangible things. Think of a typical art museum or an institution that is devoted to material culture. The objects become touchstones to larger, less tangible ideas. You can examine an idea in your mind, but you cannot engage it with your senses. Given these challenges, there are very few cultural institutions that talk about ideas and how they evolve. Throughout the histories of our military institutions, there has often been struggle with change, to the point that any of the armed forces' struggles to adapt to change becomes a cliché—tradition-bound and resistant to change. From the adoption of steam power to the machine gun, you can find plenty of examples that illustrate this point—the airplane, the tank, the aircraft carrier, etc. The evolution of the ideas leading to the operations manual that emphasized AirLand Battle shows a more robust organization that debated and embraced change. While it can be difficult to mount exhibits or programs that speak to ideas, perhaps the development of Army Doctrine can be used to, at the very least, spark conversations with visitors regarding change and ideas. While the Army struggled with new ideas, the Cold War continued.

The invasion of Afghanistan in December 1979, and the resulting fallout was the nadir of Soviet-American relations. In light of what appeared to be growing Soviet capabilities and adventurism, Jimmy Carter began raising defense budgets and boycotted the 1980 Summer Olympics taking place in Moscow. Unfortunately, the invasion of Afghanistan coincided with ongoing turmoil in Iran. The Shah of Iran, installed as the leader in the aftermath of a coup in 1953, was a staunch ally of the United States. With the country's northern border butting up against the Soviet Union, Iran was an import buttress against the Soviet Union. Unfortunately, the Shah's repressive regime laid the groundwork for the creation of a theocracy. In the turmoil of the revolution, radicals stormed the US embassy in Tehran in November 1979. US diplomats remained as hostages for over a year. Carter's attention was absorbed by the hostage crisis, to the detriment of his administration.[8]

The election of Ronald Reagan, an avowed Cold Warrior, would put this relationship on a different trajectory. Conditioned by his own anticommunism and optimism that the United States could prevail, Reagan proposed to rebuild the American defense infrastructure to challenge the Soviet Union. From a 600-ship Navy to new equipment in the Army and Air Force, he aggressively charged forward with ideas and equipment that had been gestating since the time before Reagan became President. With the ascension of Mikael Gorbachev to the leadership of the Soviet Union, the President was able to develop a relationship that led to substantive talks which eliminated intermediate nuclear weapons and pushed for reductions in their respective strategic arsenals. By the late 1980s, the Soviet Union was a giant with clay feet, and Gorbachev knew it. Within a few years of Reagan's leaving office, the Soviet Union was no more. Unable to sustain its planned economy and meet not only its domestic needs but also its huge security apparatus, the Soviet Union was on the brink of complete economic disaster. Reagan's achievement, however, came at a price that the United States is still dealing with. The raise in deficit spending to cover increased defense outlays, political scandals, in particular the arms deals with Iran that funded covert operations in Central America with illicit arms sales to Iran, and controversial moves in Central America would all taint Reagan's reputation and create fiscal issues in particular that we are still grappling with today.[9]

In spite of the progress that the Soviets and Americans made in rebuilding their relationship, trouble was brewing in the Soviet Empire. Throughout the 1980s and into the 1990s, the American public's perceptions, shaped by the media and information that was readily available from the government, painted a picture of a Soviet juggernaut that, at any time, could invade Western Europe. In fact, the Soviet economy was falling apart and their Allies on the periphery of the Soviet Empire were shedding their heavy-handed governments, putting the entire system in jeopardy. Unrest in the Baltic States, East Germany, Hungary, Czechoslovakia, and Romania led to dramatic changes in rule and rulers. With the fall of the Berlin Wall in 1990 and the subsequent dissolution of the Warsaw Pact, the Soviet Union seemed to indicate that the world had changed and the country could refocus on other security matters at hand.

The events of the 1970s, 1980s, and early 1990s are certainly within the realm of memories for many visitors. The question, however, becomes how to connect these events to the interests of the visitor. In many regards, these events and how they transpired are still relevant. The reports of the latest events around the world are not stand-alone events, but they are connected to much larger regional historical trends. The headlines that have dominated American media outlets since 2001 can only be understood in the wider context of everything from 1979 on, including rearming the branches of military and the unrest in the Middle East. News outlets reported stories that editors deemed important but they also directed their readers to issues of national importance. Even using speculative fiction on a possible Third World War could be useful in revealing the feelings of the audience at the time. Knowing what the public felt on the issues of their time will provide a basis to engage the audience in a compelling and revealing manner. One of the most effective interpretive techniques to connect the past with the present is a facilitated dialogue, where the visitor's interests guide the conversation. By framing the right questions, the events of the past are made relevant to modern audiences through guided conversations. It is far too difficult to mount an exhibit with events so fresh not only in the public's mind, but also in the memory of participants as well. While the stories of participants are compelling and remind modern audiences of the sacrifices of the men and women in uniform, it is not necessarily an objective look at the recent past. Facilitated dialogue, at least, allows audiences to understand their own feelings and perhaps make sense of these feelings as they relate to modern events.[10]

THE FIRST GULF WAR

The Soviet Union dissolved quickly. After years of repression, the Soviet satellites rebelled first, beginning with Poland in 1989 and ending with the dissolution of East Germany in 1990. As these key allies fell and ended their ties to the Soviet state, a storm of dissent was unleashed that created the conditions that would lead to the dissolution of the Soviet Union in December 1991. After nearly fifty years of tension, the Cold War was over. While there was euphoria for a peace dividend as well as a world that was safer than ever, the dissolution of the Soviet Union created new concerns that had not been imagined just a decade earlier.

In the aftermath of the fall of the Shah's regime, Saddam Hussein, the dictator of Iraq since 1979, went to war with Iran in a calculated move to take advantage of the chaos. Saddam's decision proved a costly mistake. Unable to pay the debts he incurred while battling Iran, he blamed Kuwait for driving down oil prices. Unable to negotiate a solution, Iraq invaded Kuwait on August 7, 1990. A decade previously, President Carter had made a pledge to defend the states in the Persian Gulf region, which became known as the Carter Doctrine and was carried over into the successive administrations. Uncertain if Saddam would continue his invasion into Saudi Arabia and their oil fields on the eastern shore of the Persian Gulf, President Bush condemned the Iraqi invasion and drew a line in the sand. Building an international coalition to stop and eventually turn back the invasion was now the task at hand.[11]

The operations in Kuwait took part in two stages: the first involved the immediate deployment of American and Allied forces to the Gulf to serve as a trip wire and obstacle to any incursions by Iraq into Saudi Arabia. This was Desert Shield. The second step included the invasion of Kuwait and destruction of Iraqi forces, known as Desert Storm. In the month following the invasion, US Army combat, support, and aviation units set aside for rapid deployment went to Saudi Arabia, and there was deployment of naval and air force assets as well. The United Nations condemned the invasion and imposed economic sanctions against Iraq until they unilaterally withdrew from Kuwait. The demand for withdrawal was unconditional. Given the size of the Iraqi Army that moved into Kuwait, there was an understanding that for the United States to successfully defend the Saudi border region, larger units that could stand up to the perceived Iraqi threat were necessary. This required the call up reserves to fill out the units being sent overseas, the first large scale deployment of the National Guard since the Second World War. As these units began coming to the Middle East in late summer and early fall of 1990, the situation continued to evolve and move from protecting Saudi Arabia to expelling the Iraqis from Kuwait.[12]

When Iraq invaded Kuwait, the international community turned to means other than war to isolate Saddam and force his army out of Kuwait through international economic sanctions. By November 1990, the Bush Administration moved toward finding the method and means to eject Iraqi forces out of Kuwait. Bringing combat, support, and command units from Europe, as well as mobilizing support and combat units from the National Guard, gave the commanding general of the coalition effort, Norman Schwarzkopf, a more robust force to not only shield Saudi Arabia but also eject Iraqi forces from Kuwait. The question was: How? A plan developed using a variety of coalition forces to flank Kuwait and envelop or surround the elite of the Iraqi Army, the Republican Guard, and destroy them. The Guard had direct ties to Saddam and was used to enforce his repressive regime. They were the best trained, had the most capable equipment, and demonstrated complete loyalty to the regime. Trapping them in Kuwait would allow for the coalition to destroy the most capable forces in Saddam's arsenal. A massive flanking maneuver and subsequent air campaign would pin the remaining Iraqi forces in Kuwait, presumably making them more prone to destruction.[13]

The campaign to recapture Kuwait occurred in two stages. The first was an air campaign that would degrade not only the forces occupying Kuwait, but also the communication and control infrastructure across Iraq. Using all of the weapons in the US arsenal, including the highly secret F-117 stealth fighter/bomber, the Iraqi air force was either destroyed or driven to Iran. The success of the air campaign created the conditions for the ground campaign that began on February 24 and came to an end

100 hours later.[14] The ground war was quick and forceful, but less than successful. Coalition forces attempted to encircle Republican Guard, but delays in closing the trap allowed Iraqi forces to escape. Although they were damaged, they had enough vitality to put down internal Iraqi revolts and keep Saddam in power for another decade. There was no interest or political support to unleash this diverse coalition across Iraq. The goal was freeing Kuwait and that is what occurred. Desert Storm was a vindication of the post-Vietnam reforms. In Desert Storm, the US Army demonstrated that it could apply "maneuver, firepower, attrition, and destruction into one potent and distinctly American package."[15] In light of what occurred a decade later and would continue throughout the first decades of the twenty-first century, one is left wondering how complete this victory was.[16]

Why focus on the events of the 1990s? Given the historical context that the First Gulf War provides for the events that we have experienced for the last decade, it certainly provides a touchstone for the audience to not only appreciate the stories of Desert Storm and Desert Shield, but also see connections between these events and the present. While they are still too recent to draw any firm historical conclusions, interpretive opportunities can still be created, allowing visitors, at the very least, to see connections between the past and the present and form their own conclusions. Desert Shield and Desert Storm seem to stand alone. In fact, in the background of what was going on in the deserts of Kuwait and Iraq, the Cold War was drawing to a close.

A BRAVE NEW WORLD: 1992–2001

The successes of the armed forces in the deserts of Kuwait and Iraq may have resulted in a pyrrhic victory, but they demonstrated the successful use of American arms. Had Saddam's invasion occurred just a few years later, the forces arrayed may have been different. Beginning with the Bush Administration and accelerating with the Clinton Administration was a reexamination of American defense needs. In spite of the antics of Saddam, the question of how much was enough drove policy makers. These questions are by no means new. Since the founding of the Republic, asking the question of how much defense capacity we need has been a constant for the last two centuries. Inevitably, after every substantial conflict, Congressional reviews and recommendations, as well as tradition, reduce the number of men under arms. In the 1990s, the President focused on domestic issues and weighed any use of military force against what would best serve the country, such as for humanitarian missions and where American force could make a difference without drawing the country into a long war. The missions that stand out are Haiti, Somalia, and a peacekeeping mission in Bosnia.[17]

Intervention in Somalia and the Balkans occurred with the best of intentions. In Somalia, after the country disintegrated from a viable nation state into chaos, help came from the United Nations to stave off a humanitarian crisis. It was deemed a success. Unfortunately, as forces drew down, warlords attacked. The bloody battle that Army Rangers and Special Forces fought in October 1993 was a well-publicized failure of the mission. The action proved to be a major embarrassment and gave the administration cold feet in terms of further humanitarian interventions, most notably

the genocide in the central African country of Rwanda in 1994, though in the same
year American soldiers landed in Haiti to put a halt to political violence.[18] The Clinton
Administration also brokered a peace deal between the factions of the Civil War in
Yugoslavia. The unwillingness of Serbia to halt their actions against innocent civilians
triggered a US response. In combination with a Bosnian ground offensive, US airpower
disabled the Serbian air defense system and their heavy weapons. Followed up by
an international peacekeeping force known by their acronym IFOR (Implementation
Force), they deployed in 1996 and remained in the war zone for a year. In 1999, unwilling to deploy thousands of combat troops to fully engage the Serbs, the United States
filled the void with airpower. While it could not wholly stop the violence, it contributed
to finding closure. While the American policy of nonintervention saved American lives,
the lack of consistent force allowed the Civil War to wage longer than it should have.[19]

2001–PRESENT: A WORLD TURNED UPSIDE DOWN

September 11, 2001, changed the world in which we live. The event was traumatic
and startling, much like other iconic events of the twentieth century; many people can
place themselves at the moment in time when they first heard about the events of September 11. I was living in Washington State, waiting for a ferry to take me to Seattle
when I heard a murmur among the commuters that a plane had flown into the World
Trade Center. After I got to my office, it became clear to me that this was a disaster
in the making. The live news coverage of the collapse of the Twin Towers, the subsequent attacks on the Pentagon, and the tragic ending to Flight 93 in a field in Pennsylvania left us all numb. What are the implications for the community of public history
professionals charged with collecting artifacts and oral histories related to these fateful
events? Anyone born prior to this moment has perhaps seen and heard of the ongoing
deployments and fighting in Iraq and Afghanistan. The inherent difficulty in talking
about these events is that they are in the realm of current events rather than history.
While contemporary events can be used to reflect upon the past, the controversies and
emotions that are tied up to modern deployments overseas present challenges in terms
of presenting programs and exhibitions concerning current events.

   In the aftermath of these attacks, the United States went to war against the groups
that had perpetrated these deeds and we are still feeling those results more than a
decade after September 11. Unlike the Vietnam War Memorial, built after the troops
came home, there were efforts to memorialize the victims of the terrorist attacks.
These memorials have been completed and certainly offer places not only to contem-
plate losses incurred during these tragic events, but also, in some cases, to think about
the appropriate response to such levels of violence. Since the attacks of September
11, memorials have been built at the Pentagon, at the site where Flight 93 crashed in
Pennsylvania (managed by the National Park Service), and at the site of the World
Trade Center in New York City. The museum and memorial in New York City has
garnered a great deal of attention in the museum world as they try to find their way
through this tragedy.

   Tragedy is the most difficult subject to interpret. Contemporary events, in particular,
generate images that are both compelling and disturbing, raising questions of what

is appropriate and what is not. Historical sites that interpret places of tragedy, be it a battlefield or the World Trade Center site, often require less rather than more interpretation. At times, the most appropriate technique is to say nothing and let the visitor process the event. These are challenges that can be met. The events of September 11, for the most part, took place in some of the busiest urban areas in the United States, and in New York City, there was a desire to create a fitting memorial and a place that told the story of the event. Created by a nonprofit institution, National September 11 Memorial & Museum at the World Trade Center Foundation, Incorporated, established in 2005, has a commemorative mission:

> The National September 11 Memorial Museum at the World Trade Center bears solemn witness to the terrorist attacks of September 11, 2001 and February 26, 1993. The Museum honors the nearly 3,000 victims of these attacks and all those who risked their lives to save others. It further recognizes the thousands who survived and all who demonstrated extraordinary compassion in the aftermath. Demonstrating the consequences of terrorism on individual lives and its impact on communities at the local, national, and international levels, the Museum attests to the triumph of human dignity over human depravity and affirms an unwavering commitment to the fundamental value of human life.[20]

The museum has a focus on the event and the people whose lives became part of this story. Given the proximity to the events of 2001, this is the most appropriate mission to pursue. Alice Greenwald, the director of the museum, acknowledges obstacles that are unique to this project: "intense public scrutiny, divergent expectations of what would be appropriate to present at such an emotionally charged site and the daunting responsibility to construct an exhibition narrative that would codify a history not yet written."[21] For all intents and purposes, the museum and the accompanying memorial has succeeded in this mission. The focus is on people and the costs of violence. As the events of September 11 move down the time line and we can begin to digest what happened, these museum and memorial spaces could serve as a space for dialogue and reflection to not only commemorate the events, but also leverage that into ways of preventing them from happening again. Planning, however, is one thing, and how the public accesses the museum and experiences it is something else. How does the staff deal with visitors who are offended by the narrative voice of the exhibit? If there is a focus on commemoration, do you charge a fee to offset costs or make entry to the museum free? If the focus of the story is the story of not only victims but also first responders, is it appropriate to have a gift shop? These questions are raised by users in social media and, although they are clearly in the minority, they raise important issues that have no easy answers. The time and effort required to plan and execute a meaningful exhibit come at the expense of operational issues that are either not considered or cannot be forecast until people start experiencing it.[22]

The events that led to American intervention in Iraq and Afghanistan are fraught with emotion, making it difficult to pull back and present the various points of view dispassionately. Everyone has an opinion, in particular concerning the decision to go to war with Iraq. For example, the title of journalist Thomas E. Ricks' book on the Iraq War is, simply, *Fiasco*. It is a point of view that many people can appreciate. The title telegraphs how he will tell his story. In the beginning of the second paragraph, in plain language, he lays out his argument, "The U.S.-led invasion was launched recklessly, with a flawed plan for war and a worse approach to occupation."[23] As easy as it is to counter and argue with our constituencies over the veracity of going to war, at the very least, we have to acknowledge that there is more than one answer to not only why we went to war but also how it was prosecuted. Given how politically charged the origins of the War are and what happened after the initial fall of Saddam's regime, it is admittedly difficult to acknowledge the full range of opinions without taking sides. In terms of telling the story, while the events of September 11 served as a catalyst for action, the roots of what occurred go back to previous administrations.

In the aftermath of 9/11, Afghanistan was harboring the leaders of the organization that planned and carried out the attacks on New York and Washington, DC. Known as *Al-Qaeda*, it had its roots in the Muslim groups in and outside of Afghanistan that engaged the Soviet invaders. Funded by the United States, these groups formed the backbone of the anti-Soviet resistance and would form the cadre of groups who would eventually embrace radical Islam and wreak havoc across the Middle East. The leaders of *Al-Qaeda* were given sanctuary by the ruling coalition in Afghanistan known as the Taliban, putting them in the target of the Bush Administration. As mentioned previously, the expulsion of Iraq from Kuwait and the lack of political will to conduct a full-scale invasion with the large coalition in 1991 left Saddam in power and empty promises of helping the regime's enemies rebel and overthrow his hated rule. While Presidents Bush and Clinton kept Saddam contained to wither on the vine, there was a minority of Republicans who wanted the United States to oust Saddam and give all Iraqis a chance for true democracy.[24]

One of the common refrains in the planning for American action in the Middle East was to keep it simple. While coalition partners would join the United States, it was not at the level or interest that was seen in Desert Shield and Desert Storm. The United States invaded with the resources at hand. The campaign in Afghanistan was relatively short and was accomplished mostly with American Special Forces. Beginning in October 2001, Operation ENDURING FREEDOM was able to displace the Taliban government in the nation's capital, Kabul, and several major population centers with assistance from Afghan resistance forces, supported by American air power. In the spring of 2002, Afghan and American forces attempted to besiege and capture the leadership of *Al-Qaeda* in the mountains along the northwestern border with Pakistan. In a hard-fought and confusing battle, *Al-Qaeda* and Taliban leaders and fighters escaped to return to fighting again. Concurrent with American actions across Afghanistan were operations in Iraq, which began in March 2003, diverting American and Allied resources to another part of the Middle East. Unwilling to spread American forces throughout the country, the country set aside the gains made in 2001–2002 until more resources could be devoted to keeping the peace and building a new Afghan government.[25]

The American adventure in Iraq, which, at the date of this writing, was still ongoing, has been the longest conflict overseas in the country's history. It has generated a great deal of controversy at home and abroad, thousands of casualties, and billions of dollars in costs, humanitarian assistance, and rebuilding of a broken country. There are many resources available that tell the story of this conflict, too numerous to include here, but the endnotes will include sources of interest. The events of September 2001 provided the necessary impetus to reexamine what some members of the Bush Administration saw as a problem that needed to be dealt with once and for all. While there was a more reliable connection between the regime in Afghanistan and the events that took place in 2001, a case had to be built to justify any intervention and regime change in Iraq.

There is no doubt that Saddam Hussein was an unsavory character. Smarting over the failure to bring Saddam's regime to an end in the 1990s, some in the George W. Bush Administration wanted to use American power to unseat Saddam. While not directly associated with state-sponsored terrorist groups, given the heavy use of chemical weapons in Iraq's war with Iran and Saddam's off-and-on-again nuclear program, the issue of Weapons of Mass Destruction (WMD) became the focus for unseating the regime. The administration built a case for justifying an invasion to rid the region of these WMDs. With very few in Congress or the press challenging the veracity of the evidence and claims, the administration built a case against Iraq. Thinking that after decades of oppression, the Iraqi people would welcome an American invasion as liberation, the administration planned the invasion on a shoestring budget and little attention was given to creating a civil society in postwar Iraq. Certainly, the forces sent to defeat the Iraqi Army were adequate since the Iraqi military never fully recovered from its defeat in Kuwait. In hindsight, it is unconscionable that so little effort was put into postinvasion planning.[26]

The invasion, named Operation IRAQI FREEDOM (OIF), began on March 20, 2003, with massive air strikes against political and military targets in Iraq. Much of the criticism of the invasion centered on a lean assault force and the naïve assumption that a large follow-on force would not be required to rebuild the country and create the political infrastructure to build a truly free and independent nation. Admittedly, the forces that were arrayed against the remains of Saddam's military might made quick work of the conventional forces at the dictator's disposal. British forces secured Iraq's only outlet to the Persian Gulf at Basrah, and Special Forces secured the western portion of the country. The 173rd Airborne Brigade Special Forces, with Kurdish assistance, secured the northern half of the country, ensuring the safety of the autonomous Kurdish region. The main effort came up the Tigris and Euphrates River Valley with two airborne divisions and two Marine divisions securing the heart of the country in what amounted to a dash to Baghdad. Saddam escaped but the capital came into American hands by April 9. Allied casualties were light and what had been a thorn in the side of the Bush Administration was gone. The hardest part of the job, however, was yet to come.[27]

The removal of Saddam Hussein and his regime was certainly a noteworthy victory, but perhaps it is worth considering that we won the War, but lost the peace. There is the old cliché that nature abhors a vacuum. Iraq in the aftermath of that invasion certainly illustrates that old axiom. Iraq's population is made up of three groups: the Kurds in the north, Sunni Muslims in the center, and Shiite Muslims in the remainder of the country. In terms of population, Shiites hold the majority, but Saddam, a Sunni, kept them oppressed during his regime. Suffice to say, sectarian violence grew. The Bush Administration appointed a coalition provisional authority to put the pieces of Iraq together again. To provide the country with a fresh start, the army and government were dissolved, releasing functionaries into the ranks of the disaffected and unemployed. These formed the core of an insurrection and they were joined by foreign fighters anxious to combat the American infidels, and from 2003 until 2007, a level of violence was created that was not anticipated in the postinvasion planning. Soldiers faced a different kind of enemy. Attacks by car bombs, random shootings, and a great deal of hostility from the local population made governing difficult and stretched American forces to their limits. A new coalition commander, David Petraeus, lobbied for more men and crafted a counter-insurgency strategy to rebuild the government, train a new army and police force, and battle the insurgents with a lighter touch than his predecessors. Petraeus appears to have succeeded in his strategy, known as the surge. By devoting resources to institution building and creating relationships with local tribesmen, American and government forces could contain the violence and use these new found relationships to build rather than tear down. Unfortunately, the damage had been done and the President was faced with few options. He had staked his administration on Iraq and could not readily leave until the problem was fixed. Petraeus created the conditions that, perhaps, made that possible.[28]

The rhetoric of the Presidential election of 2008 that propelled Barack Obama to the White House was a message built around responsible disengagement from long wars in both Iraq and Afghanistan. As these words are being put to paper, although the number of troops has declined and the army has transitioned from a combat mission to a training mission, Americans are still serving in the Middle East. In both countries, insurgents are challenging the legitimacy of the governments that the United States helped create. For historians, it is difficult to draw any firm conclusions. The issues these conflicts raise, be they the stories of the veterans struggling to fight in a complicated and trying war or those of the policy makers looking to solve the next crisis, are worth noting and should be discussed and talked about. The wars that we fight, the legacies they create, the institutions that they shape are as valid now as they were in our past. They should not be ignored or ridiculed. Military history still has value and provides focus on the issues of the present and those of the past.

NOTES

1. Rick Atkinson, *In the Company of Soldiers: A Chronicle of Combat* (New York: Henry Holt and Company, 2005), 305.

2 Gaddis, *Strategies of Containment*, Chapter 9; Muehlbauer and Ulbrich, *Ways of War*, 482–484. For an engaging narrative on the SALT Treaty, see John Newhouse, *Cold Dawn: The Story of SALT* (Washington, DC: Brassey's, 1989).

3. Gaddis, *Strategies of Containment*, Chapter 10; Millett and Maslowski, *For the Common Defense*, 570–576.

4. Muehlbauer and Ulbrich, *Ways of War*, 488–490; Hagan, *This People's Navy*, 380–382.

5. The transition to an all-volunteer force is covered in Beth Bailey, *America's Army: Making of the All-Volunteer Force* (Cambridge: Harvard University Press, 2009).

6. The post-Vietnam era to the end of the Soviet Union, in particular for the US Army, is an important time in terms of ideas. A broad overview of the issues at hand are well captured in Robert M. Citino, *Blitzkrieg to Desert Storm: The Evolution of Operational Warfare* (Lawrence: University Press of Kansas 2004), Chapter 5, 254–258. See also, Brigadier General Robert H. Scales, *Certain Victory: The U.S. Army in the Gulf War* (Washington, DC: Brassey's, 1994), 1–25. The importance of the 1973 Yom Kippur War is important in shaping what would become a renaissance in Army thinking. See Saul Bronfield, "Fighting Outnumbered: The

impact of the Yom Kippur War on the U.S. Army," *The Journal of Military History* 71, no. 2 (April, 2007): 465–498; Richard Lock-Pullan, "'An Inward Looking Time': The United States Army, 1973–1976," *The Journal of Military History* 67, no. 2 (April, 2003): 483–511.

7. Citino. *Blitzkrieg to Desert Storm*, 262.

8. For an overview of Jimmy Carter's Presidency, see Burton I. Kaufman and Scott Kaufman. Second Edition. *The Presidency of James Earl Carter* (Lawrence: University Press of Kansas, 2006). Carter's Secretary of Defense shared his views in Harold Brown, *Thinking About National Security: Defense Policy in a Dangerous World* (Boulder: Westview Press, 1983). For an overview of the Iranian hostage crisis, see Mark Bowden, *Guests of the Ayatollah. The Iranian Hostage Crisis: The First Battle in America's War with Militant Islam* (New York: Grove Press, 2006). While memoirs have to be used carefully, at least they capture the thoughts of the individual in question, see Jimmy Carter, *Keeping the Faith: Memoirs of a President* (New York: Bantam Books, 1982).

9. Gaddis, *Strategies of Containment*, Chapter 11; Millett and Maslowski, *For the Common Defense*, 576–589. For an overview of the Reagan defense buildup, see Daniel Wirls, *Buildup: The Politics of Defense in the Reagan Era* (Ithaca: Cornell University Press, 1992). For an overview of the use of military force from Vietnam to the beginning of the Reagan Administration, see Daniel P. Bolger, *Americans at War, 1975–1986: An Era of Violent Peace* (Novato: Presidio Press, 1988).

10. While dialogue is focused on what your visitors are feeling now, at least to get a "flavor" of how the issues of the time may have influenced the audience, looking at press coverage of contemporary issues may provide some insight. A representative sample of news reporting from the late 1970s and 1980s includes "Arming for the 21st Century." *Time*, May 23, 1977, 14–26; "The Navy Under Attack." *Time*, May 8, 1978, 14–24; "The Price of Power." *Time*, October 28, 1978, 24–33; "Arming for the '80s." *Time*, July 27, 1981, 6–21; Robert S. Dudney, "The New Army With New Punch." *U.S. News & World Report*, September 20, 1982, 59–62. Typical speculative fiction in the 1970s that told tales of a Third World War includes General Sir John Hackett, *The Third World War* (New York, NY: Macmillan Publishing, 1978).

11. Frank N. Schubert and Theresa L. Kraus, ed. *The Whirlwind War: The United States Army in Operations Desert Shield and Desert Storm* (Washington, DC: Center of Military History, 1995), 3–23. Helpful in understanding the war are Brigadier General Robert H. Scales, *Certain Victory: The U.S. Army in the Gulf War* (Washington, DC: Brassey's, 1994); Rick Atkinson, *Crusade: The Untold Story of the Persian Gulf War* (New York: Houghton Mifflin Company, 1993). A nice overview of conflict between Iraq and Iran can be found in Efraim Karsh, *The Iran-Iraq War, 1980–1988* (London, UK: Osprey Publishing, 2002).

12. Schubert and Kraus, ed. *The Whirlwind War,* Chapter 4.

13. Schubert and Kraus, ed. *The Whirlwind War,* Chapter 5; Scales, *Certain Victory*, Chapter 3. For a contemporary run-down of the land, air, and naval forces of the Iraqis and the coalition, Osprey Publishing, a well-known military history publishing house, made an effort to catalog and explain the equipment used, see Tim Ripley, *Land Power: The Coalition and Iraqi Armies* (London: Osprey Publishing ltd., 1991); Roy Braybrook, *Air Power: The Coalition and Iraqi Armies* (London: Osprey Publishing ltd., 1991); Peter Gilchrist, *Sea Power: The Coalition and Iraqi Armies* (London: Osprey Publishing ltd., 1991).

14. Millett, Maslowski, and Feis, *For the Common Defense*, 599–600 and 601–604; Citino, *Blitzkrieg to Desert Storm*, 282–284. For the air war, see Richard Hallion, *Storm Over Iraq: Air Power and The Gulf War* (Washington, DC: Smithsonian Institution, 1992); Diane T. Putney, *Airpower Advantage: Planning the Gulf Air War Campaign, 1989–1991* (Washington, DC: Air Force History and Museum Program, 2004). For the official Air Force report on the air war, see Thomas Keaney and Eliot A. Cohen, *Gulf Air Power Survey: Summary Report* (Washington,

DC, 1993), which can be found online at www.afhso.af.mil/shared/media/document/AFD-100927-061.pdf.

15. Citino, *Blitzkrieg to Desert Storm*, 290.

16. Schubert and Kraus, ed. *The Whirlwind War,* Chapter 8; Scales, *Certain Victory: The U.S. Army in the Gulf War*, Chapter 5. For the naval contribution, see Edward J. Marolda and Robert J. Schneller Jr., *Shield and Sword: The United States Navy and the Persian Gulf War* (Annapolis: United States Naval Institute, 2001). For the Marines, see Paul W. Westermeyer, *United States Marines in the Gulf War, 1990–1991: Liberating Kuwait* (Quantico: History Division, United States Marine Corps, 2014).

17. A concise overview of the Clinton years can be found in Millett, Maslowski, and Feis, *For The Common Defense*, 610–624.

18. By far the most well-known account of the conflict, serving as the inspiration for the movie of the same name, is Mark Bowden, *Black Hawk Down: A Study in Modern War* (New York: Atlantic Monthly Press, 1999). The US Army's Center for Military History has produced a concise overview of the intervention, see Richard W. Steward, *The United States Army in Somalia*. Available at http://www.history.army.mil/brochures/Somalia/Somalia.htm. The official after-action report for the debacle is *United States Forces, Somalia After Action Report and Historical Overview, 1992–1994* (Washington, DC: Center for Military History, 2003). Available at http://www.history.army.mil/html/documents/somalia/SomaliaAAR.pdf.

19. A concise overview of the Army's actions in Bosnia can be found in R. Cody Phillips, *Bosnia-Herzegovina: The US Army's Role in Peace Enforcement Operations, 1995–2004.* This publication is available on the Center for Military History website at http://www.history.army.mil/html/books/070/70-97-1/cmhPub_70-97-1.pdf. Since much of what was achieved was through air power, the US Air Force has compiled its analysis, see Colonel Robert C. Owen, USAF, ed. [Operation] *Deliberate Force: A Case Study in Effective Air Campaigning* (Montgomery, AL: Air University Press, 2000). For an institutional history of the Army as it continued to evolve to meet the challenges of this time period, see the important work of John Sloan Brown, *Kevlar Legions: The Transformation of the US Army, 1989–2005* (Washington, DC: Center for Military History, 2011).

20. Mission statement of the Museum, accessed May 16, 2015: http://www.911memorial.org/mission-statements-0.

21. "The Heart of Memory: Voices From the 9/11 Memorial Museum Formation Experience," *Museum*, May/June 2014: 28.

22. Social media provide anecdotal evidence of how visitors experience a museum or historical site. No organization should base management decisions on what is shared on social media, but social media do provide some insight into the visitor experience. Trip Advisor, a social media site that allows people to rate accommodations, local attractions, etc., has a page devoted to the 9/11 Memorial Museum. The majority of reviews are overwhelmingly positive. Those that are negative raise some operational issues, in particular cost and the gift shop. Trip Advisor accessed on May 16, 2015: http://www.tripadvisor.com/Attraction_Review-g60763-d1687489-Reviews-The_National_September_11_Memorial_Museum-New_York_City_New_York.html#REVIEWS.

23. Thomas E. Ricks, *Fiasco: The American Military Adventure in Iraq* (New York, NY: Penguin Books, 2006), 3.

24. Millett, Maslowski, and Feis, *For The Common Defense*, 638–640. A decade after the war began, the literature on Iraq overwhelms what is available for Afghanistan. Good places to start are Ahmed Rashid, *Taliban: Militant Islam, Oil and Fundamentalism in Central Asia* (New Haven: Yale University Press, 2000); Seth G. Jones, *In the Graveyard of Empires: America's War in Afghanistan* (New York: W.W. Norton, 2009).

25. Millett, Maslowski, and Feis, *For The Common Defense*, 640–650. The American military is digesting the lessons and issues of the campaign in Afghanistan and is already publishing histories of the campaign. For a brief overview of US Army operations in Afghanistan, see *Operation Enduring Freedom, March 2002–April 2005* available at http://www.history.army.mil/html/books/070/70-122-1/CMH_Pub_70-122-1.pdf. An in-depth study is Donald P. Wright, et al. *A Different Kind of War: The United States in Operation ENDURING FREE-DOM (OEF), October 2001– September 2005* (Fort Leavenworth: Combat Studies Institute Press, 2010) available at http://usacac.army.mil/cac2/csi/docs/DifferentKindofWar.pdf. The US Marines' contribution to the operation is told in Colonel Nathan S. Lowrey U.S. Marine Corps Reserve. *From the Sea: U.S. Marines in the Global War on Terrorism* (Washington, DC: History Division United States Marine Corps, 2011). Available at: http://www.mcu.usmc.mil/historydivision/Pages/Publications/Publication%20PDFs/FROM%20THE%20SEA.pdf. The U.S. Air Force contribution was reported from the RAND Corporation in Benjamin S. Lambeth, *Air Power Against Terror: America's Conduct of Operation Enduring Freedom* (Arlington: National Defense Research Institute, Rand Corporation, 2005). Available at http://www.rand.org/content/dam/rand/pubs/monographs/2006/RAND_MG166-1.pdf.

26. Millett, Maslowski, and Feis, *For The Common Defense*, 650–655. Some of the works, written by journalists, that help tell the countdown for the war can be helpful in understanding the dynamics of what was going on in the Bush Administration, see the aforementioned Thomas E. Ricks, *Fiasco: The American Military Adventure in Iraq* and Bob Woodward. *Bush at War* (New York: Simon and Schuster, 2002).

27. Millett, Maslowski, and Feis, *For The Common Defense*, 650–655; Muehlbauer and Ulbrich, *Ways of War*, 505–508. There are a large number of books about the campaign and the first twenty-four months of the war in Iraq. For analysis from journalists and historians, see Rick Atkinson, *In the Company of Soldiers: A Chronicle of Combat*; Michael R. Gordon and Lt. General Bernard E. Trainor, *COBRA II: The Inside Story of the Invasion and Occupation of Iraq* (New York: Pantheon Books, 2006). With US forces in Iraq for over a decade, official histories on nearly every aspect of the war are beginning to be released. Perhaps a good place to start is Colonel Gregory Fontenot, Lt. Colonel E.J. Degan, and Lt. Colonel E.J. Degan, *On Point: The United States Army in Operation Iraqi Freedom* (Fort Leavenworth: Combat Studies Institute, 2004). This can be found at http://usacac.army.mil/cac2/cgsc/carl/download/csipubs/OnPointI.pdf. The follow-up volume is Donald W. Wright and Colonel Timothy R. Reese, et al., *On Point II: Transition to the New Campaign: The United States Army in Operation Iraqi Freedom, May 2003–January, 2005* (Fort Leavenworth: Combat Studies Institute, 2008). This can be found at http://usacac.army.mil/cac2/cgsc/carl/download/csipubs/OnPointII.pdf. The US Marines played a prominent role and their historical arm has produced many publications dealing with the contributions of the Marines. The appropriate works can be found at http://www.mcu.usmc.mil/historydivision/Pages/Publications/The_Iraq_War_2003_2010.aspx.

28. Millett, Maslowski, and Feis, *For The Common Defense*, 660–672; Muehlbauer and Ulbrich, *Ways of War*, 508–513. See also, Thomas E. Ricks, *The Gamble: General David Petraeus and the American Military Adventure in Iraq, 2006–2009* (New York: Penguin Press, 2009); Fred Kaplan, *The Insurgents: David Petraeus and the Plot to Change the American Way of War* (New York: Simon and Schuster, 2013).

Epilogue

> Though the study of war is demanding, both intellectually and emotionally, we
> cannot afford to eschew or ignore it.
>
> Society for Military History White Paper[1]

When I was a teenager and my interests in military history were growing, my siblings
would poke fun at me, calling me a warmonger. I would robustly defend myself, say-
ing I was not, but as a teenager I really could not form a cogent counter-argument
against my brothers' labels. As I have matured as a historian, I am much better prepared to counter any off-the-cuff remarks that categorize the study of military history
as a synonym for the avocation of conflict. On the contrary, my lifelong interests have
provided ample evidence that war is something to assiduously avoid unless the conditions at hand require it. In graduate school at Temple University, I had the pleasure
of getting to know many officers who had enrolled in a Master's Degree Program in
preparation for teaching assignments at the United States Military Academy at West
Point. Some of them had seen service in Vietnam, others had attended West Point,
but all had chosen to make their career in the US Army. They treated their chosen
avocation with a great deal of professionalism. In hindsight, they were by far some of
the most thoughtful people I encountered in graduate school. They were very sober
individuals and approached the application of armed force with the respect that it
deserves. While the end result of any military action usually involves death, destruction, and sorrow, it also provides insight into who we are as people. It is a field that is
much more than the study of organized violence.

The Society for Military History published a white paper in 2014 that underlines
the importance of military history in the academy. While military history continues to
hold value in understanding the dynamics of war and combat, it also serves as a lens
that provides insight into our culture and the behavior of nations. It is now a more
inclusive field than a generation ago, and one in which we strive to understand the
human condition. In our own political system, an informed electorate should be able
to understand the complexities and responsibilities of going to war. Since 1787, the
United States has honored the notion of civilian control of the military. By implication,

as participants in the political process, we should take the responsibility of going to war seriously and with deliberate thought to guide our actions.[2] There is value, then, in exploring these topics within the realm of public history.

Public and academic historians have access to tools that help unlock the truth. For historians, the events, personalities, and actions of states provide the necessary information to find meaning. Similarly, the tools available to us as interpreters, when used appropriately, provide meaning to our visitors. With proper knowledge of our resources and our audiences, and the use of appropriate techniques, military history can be used to reveal meanings that all of us can identify with—life, death, survival, heroism, sacrifice, and loss. National Park Service historian John Hennessy captured the power of interpretation in the context of the sesquicentennial of the Civil War: "It is virtually impossible to come to these places [Civil War Battlefields] and be with someone who is a skilled communicator who can relate the stories and their meanings and not walk away and say, 'Holy Cow!'. It's not an education—it's a revelation about the human experience that was our war."[3] Regardless of the title of our positions or whether we work as paid staff members or volunteers, we owe it to the institutions we work for, and the audiences that we serve, to hold to these high standards.

One of the most contentious debates over the intersection between history, museums, and the knowledge of the audience occurred in the 1990s when the Smithsonian Institution's Air and Space Museum attempted to mount a permanent exhibit on the development and dropping of the Atomic Bomb. The centerpiece of the exhibit was to be a portion of the meticulously restored B-29 bomber that carried out the first mission, the Enola Gay. The planning process triggered a storm of protest over how the story of dropping the atomic bomb was to be told. Complicating the process, Congress interceded with public hearings that put the Smithsonian on the defensive. The designers wanted the exhibit to acknowledge the complexity of the decision to use atomic weapons in the Pacific, highlighting all of the scholarship done to that point. They wanted an exhibit to tell the story of why the bomb was used, commemorate the men and women who made it happen, and highlight the destruction of the bomb and, by implication, the strategic bombing campaign. However, instead of providing interpretive opportunities or meaning, it generated controversy and sowed distrust among stakeholders. Faced with heat from Congress, Air Force boosters, and veterans groups, the exhibit was canceled. While the controversy has to be understood in the wider context of the politics of the so-called culture wars of the 1980s and 1990s, it underlines the importance of understanding all of the elements of interpretation before moving forward with an exhibit of a program.[4]

If anything, the controversy over how to tell the story of the Enola Gay and its mission highlights the need to plan interpretive exhibits and programs with care and deliberation. While there will never be any sector of your public that is completely satisfied, a competent and compelling exhibit or program can be mounted in a completely responsible manner. In the end, it comes down to recognizing all of the elements of the interpretive equation that were laid out in the first chapter of this book. Engaging programs should be crafted with a complete knowledge of the resource. If an institution chooses to mount an exhibit on a controversial topic, it is the responsibility of the planners to completely understand all of the viewpoints of that particular topic, acknowledging the points of controversy and creating a narrative that can stand up to scrutiny. Second, the knowledge of the audience is critical in creating a voice that is consistent with the voice of the exhibit. The Enola Gay exhibit wanted to acknowledge the sacrifices and contributions of the air crews that mounted the air campaign by commemorating their actions. Yet, this voice was tempered by a narrative that acknowledged Japanese aggression as a trigger for the War in the Pacific and implied that the destruction wrought by the strategic bombing campaign in general and the dropping of an atomic weapon were also questionable. One particular audience narrative voice was challenged by another. There are always many stakeholders in a story. It is critical to acknowledge contrary points of view and, if possible, create an inclusive and transparent planning process that recognizes these voices. Finally, it is critical to choose the appropriate techniques to tell a story. The Enola Gay exhibit's centerpiece was a portion of the plane itself. What kind of messages does an artifact telegraph when you are telling a story of alternative viewpoints? Is it appropriate or not? Did the narrative of the exhibit clash with the meanings inherent in the object? The only way to understand this dynamic is to create evaluation mechanisms that allow test audiences to understand if a technique is appropriate or not.

Whether we work in a museum or a historical site, I think it is fair to say that we work in one of the few fields where one interaction can change a person's views, and perhaps the trajectory of his or her life. We certainly do not create meanings, but we have the power to connect people to something that can be meaningful in ways beyond measure. These connections may be as simple as making a decision to display a certain object, or the courage and conviction to preserve a historic site, or creating a well-crafted interpretive program. For example, seeing the piles of shoes on display in the United States Holocaust Memorial Museum humanized the victims of the Holocaust in such a profound and compelling manner that I will always carry the experience with me. If we move beyond the stereotypes of military history and use it as a medium to tell the stories of our communities and nation, it can be used as a touchstone to the things that we all care about. Moreover, a frank and honest approach to our military past can underline that going to war is something that should not be done lightly and without thought to the consequences of war, unintended or otherwise.

NOTES

1. Tami Davis Biddle and Robert M. Citino, "The Role of Military History in the Contemporary Academy: A Society For Military History White Paper," p. 1, accessed May 25, 2015 at http://www.smh-hq.org/whitepaper.html.

2. Ibid, 4–7.

3. Karen Jones, "A Sesquicentennial Evolution: National Parks Take a New Look at the Civil War," *Museum* (November/December, 2014): 59.

4. The Enola Gay controversy generated a great deal of literature. A helpful overview of the controversy can be found in the Journal of American History, which devoted nearly an entire issue to the controversy, David Thelen, ed. "History and the Public: What Can We Handle? A Round Table About History after the *Enola Gay* Controversy," *Journal of American History*, vol. 82 (December, 1995): 1029–44. See also, Edward T. Linenthal and Tom Engelhardt, *History Wars: The* Enola Gay *and Other Battles For the American Past* (New York: Metropolitan Books, Henry Holt and Company, 1996).

Bibliography

Abrahamson, James L. *American Arms for a New Century: The Making of a Great Military Power.* New York: The Free Press, 1981.

Adams, John A. *The Battle For Western Europe, Fall 1944: An Operational Assessment.* Bloomington: Indiana University Press, 2010.

Adler, Jerry et al. "Revisiting the Civil War: A Stunning Television Documentary Rekindles Enduring Passions." *Newsweek,* October 8, 1990, 58–64.

Alden, John D. *American Steel Navy: A Photographic History of the U.S. Navy from the Introduction of the Steel Hull in 1883 to the Cruise of the Great White Fleet, 1907–1909.* Annapolis: Naval Institute Press, 1972.

Alden, John R. *A History of the American Revolution.* New York: Knopf, 1969.

Alexander, Charles C. *Holding the Line: The Eisenhower Era, 1952–1961.* Bloomington: Indiana University Press, 1975.

Allen, Thomas B. "Remember the *Maine?*" *National Geographic,* February 1998, 92–111.

Alperovitz, Gar. *The Decision to Use the Atomic Bomb and the Architecture of an American Myth.* New York: Alfred A. Knopf, 1995.

Ambrose, Stephen E. *D-Day, June 6, 1944: The Climactic Battle of World War II.* New York: Simon and Schuster, 1994.

———. *Upton and the Army.* Baton Rouge: Louisiana State University Press, 1992.

Ambrose, Stephen E. *Band of Brothers. E Company, 506th Regiment, 101st Airborne. From Normandy to Hitler's Eagle Nest.* New York: Simon and Schuster, 1992.

American Battle Monuments Commission. *American Armies and Battlefields in Europe: A History, Guide, and Reference Book.* Washington, DC: Government Printing Office, 1938.

Anderson, Fred. *The War That Made America: A Short History of the French and Indian War.* New York: Viking, 2005.

———. *Crucible of War: The Seven Year's War and the Fare of the British Empire in North America, 1754–1766.* New York: Alfred A. Knopf, 2000.

———. *A People's Army: Massachusetts Soldiers and Society in the Seven Years' War.* Chapel Hill: University of North Carolina Press, 1984.

Andrale, Dale. *Trial By Fire: The 1972 Easter Offensive, America's Last Vietnam Battle.* Lawrence: University Press of Kansas, 2001.

Appleman, Roy E., James M. Burns, Russell A. Gugeler and John Stevens. *Okinawa: The Last Battle.* Washington, DC: Historical Division, 1948.

Appleman, Roy E. *East of the Chosin: Entrapment and Breakout in Korea, 1950*. College Station: Texas A & M Press, 1987.

———. *South to the Naktong, North to the Yalu June–November, 1950*. Washington, DC: Office of the Chief of Military History, 1961.

Atkinson, Rick. *The Guns at Last Light: The War in Western Europe, 1944–1945*. New York: Henry Holt and Company, 2013.

———. *The Day of Battle: The War in Sicily and Italy, 1943–1944*. New York: Henry Holt and Company, 2007.

———. *In the Company of Soldiers: A Chronicle of Combat*. New York: Henry Holt and Company, 2005.

———. *An Army at Dawn: The War in North Africa, 1942–1943*. New York: Henry Holt and Company, 2002.

———. *Crusade: The Untold Story of the Persian Gulf War*. New York: Houghton Mifflin Company, 1993.

Ayres, Leonard P. *The War With Germany: A Statistical Summary*. Washington, DC: Government Printing Office, 1919.

Bailey, Beth. *America's Army: Making of the All-Volunteer Force*. Cambridge: Harvard University Press, 2009.

Ballard, Michael B. *Vicksburg: The Campaign that Opened the Mississippi*. Chapel Hill: University of North Carolina Press, 2003.

Barsness, Richard W. "John C. Calhoun and the Military Establishment, 1817–1825." *The Wisconsin Magazine of History* 50, no. 1 (Autumn, 1966): 43–53.

Baucom, Donald R. *The Origins of SDI, 1944–1983*. Lawrence: University Press of Kanas, 1992.

Bauer, K. Jack. "The Battles on the Rio Grande: Palo Alto and Resaca de la Palma, 8-9 May, 1846." In Charles E. Heller and William A. Stofft, *America's First Battles, 1776–1965*. Lawrence: University Press of Kansas, 1986.

———. *The Mexican War, 1846–1848*. New York: Macmillan Publishing Company, 1974.

Beaver, Daniel R. *Modernizing the War Department: Change and Continuity in a Turbulent Era*. Kent: The Kent State University Press, 2006.

Beck, Larry and Ted Cable. *Interpretation For the 21st Century*. Champaign: Sagamore Press, 1998.

Beisner, Robert L. *From the Old Diplomacy to the New, 1865–1900*. Arlington Heights: Harlan Davidson, 1986.

Beringer, Richard, Herman Hattaway, Archer Jones and William N. Still, Jr. *Why The South Lost The Civil War*. Athens: University of Georgia Press, 1986.

Berton, Pierre. *War of 1812*. Anchor, Canada, 2011.

Black, Jeremy. "The North American Theater of the Napoleonic Wars, or, as it is Sometimes Called, The War of 1812." *Journal of Military History* 76 (October, 2013): 1053–66.

Blackburn, Marc K. "A New Form of Transportation, the Quartermaster Corps and the Standardization of the United States Army's Motor Trucks, 1907–1939." Ph.D dissertation, Temple University, 1992.

Blight, James G. and David A. Welch. *On the Brink: Americans and Soviets Examine the Cuban Missile Crisis*. New York: Hill and Wang, 1989.

Bloch, Marc. *The Historians Craft*, trans. Peter Putnam. New York: Vintage Books, 1953.

Blum, John Morton. *V Was For Victory: Politics and American Culture in World War II*. New York: Harcourt Brace Jovanovich, 1976.

Blumenson, Martin. "Kasserine Pass, 30 January-22 February, 1943." In Charles E. Heller and William A. Stofft, *America's First Battles, 1776–1965*. Lawrence: University Press of Kansas, 1986, 226–65.

————. *Salerno to Cassino*. Washington, DC: Office of the Chief of Military History, 1969.

————. *Breakout and Pursuit*. Washington, DC: Office of the Chief of Military History, 1961.

Bodle, Wayne. *The Valley Forge Winter: Civilians and Soldiers in War*. University Park: Pennsylvania State University Press, 2002.

Boghardt, Thomas. *The Zimmerman Telegram: Intelligence, Diplomacy, and America's Entry into World War I*. Annapolis: Naval Institute Press, 2012.

Bolger, Daniel P. *Americans at War, 1975–1986: An Era of Violent Peace*. Novato: Presidio Press, 1988.

Bonn, Keith. *When the Odds Were Even: The Vosges Mountains Campaign, October, 1944–January, 1945*. Novato: Presidio Press, 1994.

Boot, Max. *The Savage Wars of Peace: Small Wars and the Rise of American Power*. New York: Basic Books, 2002.

Borg, Dorothy and Shumpei Okomoto. *Pearl Harbor as History: Japanese-American Relations, 1931–1941*. New York: Columbia University Press, 1973.

Bowden, Mark. *Guests of the Ayatollah. The Iranian Hostage Crisis: The First Battle in America's War with Militant Islam*. New York: Grove Press, 2006.

————. *Black Hawk Down: A Study in Modern War*. New York: Atlantic Monthly Press, 1999.

Braim, Paul F. *The Test of Battle: The American Expeditionary Force in the Meuse-Argonne Campaign*. Shippensburg: White Mane Publishing, 1998.

Brasser, T.J. "Early Indian-European Contacts." In *Handbook of North American Indians, Vol. 4, History of Indian-White Relations*. Washington, DC: Smithsonian Institution, 1988, 78–88.

Braybrook, Roy. *Air Power: The Coalition and Iraqi Armies*. London: Osprey Publishing Ltd., 1991.

Breen, T.H. "English Origins and New World Development: The Case of the Covenanted Militia in Seventeenth-Century Massachusetts." *Past & Present* 57 (November, 1972): 74–96.

Brenckle, Matthew, Lauren McCormack and Sarah Watkins. *Men of Iron: USS Constitution's War of 1812 Crew*. Boston: USS Constitution Museum, 2012.

Brigham, Robert K. *ARVN: Life and Death of the South Vietnamese Army*. Lawrence: University Press of Kansas, 2006.

Brochu, Lisa and Tim Merriman. *Personal Interpretation: Connecting Your Audience to Heritage Resources*. Fort Collins: Interp Press, 2002.

Brodie, Bernard. *Strategy in the Missile Age*. Princeton: Princeton University Press, 1959.

Brodine, Charles E, Michael J. Crawford and Christine F. Hughes. *Interpreting Old Ironsides: An Illustrated Guide to the USS Constitution*. Washington, DC: Naval Historical Center, 2007.

Bronfield, Saul. "Fighting Outnumbered: The impact of the Yom Kippur War on the U.S. Army." *The Journal of Military History* 71, no. 2 (April, 2007): 465–98.

Brown, Harold. *Thinking About National Security: Defense Policy in a Dangerous World*. Boulder: Westview Press, 1983.

Brown, John Sloan. *Kevlar Legions: The Transformation of the US Army, 1989–2005*. Washington, DC: Center for Military History, 2011.

————. *Draftee Division: The 88th Infantry Division in World War II*. Novato: Presidio Press, 1986.

Browning, Robert S. *Two if by Sea. The Development of American Coastal Defense Policy*. Westport: Greenwood Press, 1983.

Buckley, Thomas H. *The United States and the Washington Conference, 1921–1922*. Knoxville, The University of Tennessee Press, 1970.

Burlingame, Michael. *Abraham Lincoln: A Life*. 2 vols., Baltimore: John Hopkins University Press, 2008.

Cameron, Robert S. *Mobility, Shock and Firepower: The Emergence of the U.S. Army's Armor Branch, 1917–1945.* Washington, DC: Center of Military History, 2008.

————. "Americanizing the Tank: U.S. Administration and Mechanized Development with the Army, 1917–1943." Ph.D. Dissertation, Temple University, 1994.

Cannon, Hamlin M. *Leyte: The Return to the Philippines.* Washington, DC: Office of the Chief of Military History, 1954.

Carafano, James Jay. *GI Ingenuity: Improvisation, Technology, and Winning World War II.* Westport: Praeger Security International, 2006.

————. *After D-Day: Operation Cobra and the Normandy Breakout.* Boulder: Lynne Rienner Publishers, 2000.

Carp, E. Wayne. *To Starve the Army at Pleasure: Continental Army Administration and American Political Culture, 1775–1781.* Chapel Hill: University of North Carolina Press, 1984.

Carter, Jimmy. *Keeping the Faith: Memoirs of a President.* New York: Bantam Books, 1982.

Cary, Norman M, Jr. "The Use of the Motor Vehicle in the United States Army, 1899–1939." Ph.D. Dissertation, University of Georgia, 1980.

Castel, Albert. *Decision in the West: The Atlanta Campaign of 1864.* Lawrence: University Press of Kansas, 1992.

Cave, Albert A. *The Pequot War.* Amherst: University of Massachusetts Press, 1996.

Center for Military History. *United States Forces, Somalia After Action Report and Historical Overview, 1992–1994.* Washington, DC: Center for Military History, 2003.

Chambers, John Whiteclay. *To Raise an Army: The Draft Comes to America.* New York: The Free Press, 1987.

Chambers, John Whiteclay. "The New Military History: Myth and Reality." *The Journal of Military History* 55 (July, 1991): 395–406.

Chernow, Ron. *George Washington: A Life.* New York: Penguin Books, 2010.

Citino, Robert M. *The German Way of War: From the Thirty Years' War to the Third Reich.* Lawrence: University Press of Kansas, 2005.

————. *Blitzkrieg to Desert Storm: The Evolution of Operational Warfare.* Lawrence: University Press of Kansas 2004.

Clark, Jason Patrick. "The Many Faces of Reform: Military Progressivism in the U.S. Army, 1866–1916." Ph.D. Dissertation, Duke University, 2009.

Clarke, Jeffery. *Advice and Support: The Final Years: 1965–1973.* Washington, DC: Center of Military History, 1988.

Clarke, Jeffery and Robert Ross Smith. *Riviera to the Rhine.* Washington, DC: Center of Military History, 1993.

Clary, David. *George Washington's First War: His Early Military Adventures.* New York: Simon and Schuster, 2011.

————. *Eagles and Empire: The United States, Mexico, and the Struggle for a Continent.* New York: Bantam Books, 2009.

Clendenen, Clarence C. *Blood on the Border: The United States Army and the Mexican Irregulars.* New York: Macmillan Publishers, 1969.

Clodfelter, Mark. *Limits of Airpower: The American Bombing of Vietnam.* New York: The Free Press, 1989.

Coffman, Edward M. *The Regulars: The American Army, 1898–1941.* Cambridge: The Belknap Press of Harvard University Press, 2004.

————. *The Old Army: A Portrait of the American Army in Peacetime, 1784–1898.* New York: Oxford University Press, 1986.

————. *The War to End All Wars: The American Military Experience in World War I.* Madison: The University of Wisconsin Press, 1986.

————. "The New American Military History." *Military Affairs* 48 (January, 1984): 1–5.

Cole, Hugh M. *The Ardennes: Battle of the Bulge*. Washington, DC: Office of the Chief of Military History, 1965.

———. *The Lorraine Campaign*. Washington, DC: Historical Division, Dept. of the Army, 1950.

Coles, Harry L. *The War of 1812*. Chicago: The University of Chicago Press, 1965.

Cooling, Benjamin F. *Forts Henry and Donelson: The Key to the Confederate Heartland*. Knoxville: University of Tennessee Press, 1987.

Cooper, Jerry M. "The Army's Search For a Mission, 1865–1890." In Kenneth J. Hagan and William R. Roberts, *Against All Enemies: Interpretations of American Military History From Colonial Times to the Present*. Westport: Greenwood Press, 1986.

Cooper, William J. *Jefferson Davis, American*. New York: Knopf, 2000.

Coox, Alvin D. "The Effectiveness of the Japanese Military Establishment in the Second World War." In Allan R. Millett and Williamson Murray, *Military Effectiveness, Vol. 3: The Second World War*. New York: Cambridge University Press, 2010, 1–44.

Cornish, Dudley. *The Sable Arm: Black Troops in the Union Army, 1861–1865*. Lawrence: University Press of Kansas, 1987.

Corum, James S. *The Luftwaffe: Creating the Operational Air War, 1918–1940*. Lawrence: University Press of Kansas, 1997.

Cosmas, Graham A. *An Army For Empire: The United States Army in the Spanish-American War*. Second Edition. Shippensburg: White Mane Publishing, 1994.

———. "San Juan Hill and El Caney, 1–2 July, 1898." In Charles E. Heller and William A. Stofft, *America's First Battles, 1776–1965*. Lawrence: University Press of Kansas, 1986.

Couvares, Francis G., et al. *Interpretations of American History*. Vol. 1. New York: Bedford/St. Martin's, 2009.

Cozzens, Peter. *Shenandoah, 1862: Stonewall Jackson's Valley Campaign*. Chapel Hill: University of North Carolina Press, 2008.

———. *The Shipwreck of Hopes: The Battles for Chattanooga*. Chicago: University of Illinois Press, 1994.

———. *The Terrible Sword: The Battle of Chickamauga*. Chicago: University of Illinois Press, 1992.

Crackel, Theodore J. *West Point: A Bicentennial History*. Lawrence: University Press of Kansas, 2002.

———. *Mr. Jefferson's Army: Political and Social Reform in the Military Establishment, 1801–1809*. New York: New York University Press, 1987.

Crackel, Theodore J. "The Battle of Queenstown Heights, 13 October 1812." In Charles E. Heller and William A. Stofft, *America's First Battles, 1776–1965*. Lawrence: University Press of Kansas, 1986, 33–56.

Crane, Conrad C. *American Airpower Strategy in Korea, 1950–1953*. Lawrence: University Press of Kansas, 2000.

———. *Bombs, Cities and Civilians: American Airpower Strategy in World War II*. Lawrence: University Press of Kansas, 1993.

Crane, Verner. *The Southern Frontier, 1670–1732*. Second Edition. Tuscaloosa: University of Alabama Press, 2004.

Crawford, Michael J. and Christine F. Hughes. *Interpreting Old Ironsides: An Illustrated Guide to the USS Constitution*. Washington, DC: Naval Historical Center, 2007.

Crowl, Philip A. and Edmund G. Love. *Seizure of the Gilberts and Marshalls*. Washington, DC: Office of the Chief of Military History, 1955.

Crowl, Philip A. *Campaign in the Marianas*. Washington, DC: Office of the Chief of Military History, 1955.

Cummings, Bruce. *The Origins of the Korean War: The Roaring of the Cataract, 1947–1950*. Princeton: Princeton University Press, 1990.

———. *The Origins of the Korean War: Liberation and the Emergence of Separate Regimes, 1945–47*. Princeton: Princeton University Press, 1981.

Cunliffe, Marcus. *Soldiers and Civilians: The Martial Spirit in America, 1775–1860*. Boston: Little Brown and Company, 1968.

———. *George Washington, Man and Monument*. New York: Mentor Books, 1958.

D'Este, Carlo. *Eisenhower: A Soldier's Life*. New York: Henry Holt and Company, 2002.

———. *Decision in Normandy*. Reprint. New York: Barnes and Noble Books, 1994.

———. *Bitter Victory: The Battle For Sicily, 1943*. New York: Harper Perennial, 1991.

———. *Fatal Decision: Anzio and the Battle For Rome*. New York: Harper Collins, 1991.

Daddis, Gregory. *Westmoreland's War: Reassessing American Strategy in Vietnam*. New York: Oxford University Press, 2014.

Daniel, Larry J. *Shiloh: The Battle That Changed the Civil War*. New York: Simon and Schuster, 1997.

Davis, William C. *Look Away! A History of the Confederate States of America*. New York: Free Press, 2002.

DeBenedetti, Charles and Charles Chatfield. *An American Ordeal: The Antiwar Movement of the Vietnam Era*. Bloomington: Indiana University Press, 1990.

Defense Civil Preparedness Agency. *Protection in the Nuclear Age*. Washington, DC: Department of Defense, 1977.

Dickson, Paul and Thomas B. Allen. *The Bonus Army: An American Epic*. New York: Walker and Company, 2004.

Divine, Robert A. *Roosevelt and World War II*. Baltimore: The John Hopkins Press, 1969.

Doenecke, Justus D. *Nothing Less Than War: A New History of America's Entry into World War I*. Lexington: The University Press of Kentucky, 2011.

Donald, David H. *Lincoln*. New York: Random House, 1995.

Doubler, Michael D. *Civilian in War and Peace – The Army National Guard, 1636–2000*. Lawrence: University Press of Kansas, 2003.

Doubler, Michael D. *Closing With the Enemy. How GIs Fought the War in Europe, 1944–1945*. Lawrence: University Press of Kansas, 1994.

Doughty, Robert. *Leavenworth Papers No. 1: The Evolution of US Army Tactical Doctrine, 1946–1976*. Fort Leavenworth: Combat Studies Institute, 1979.

Dower, John W. *War Without Mercy: Race and Power in the Pacific War*. New York: Pantheon Books, 1986.

Drea, Edward J. *Japan's Imperial Army: Its Rise and Fall, 1853–1945*. Lawrence: University Press of Kansas, 2009.

Eisenhower, Dwight D. *Mandate for Change, 1953–1956*. New York: Doubleday and Company, 1963.

———. *Waging Peace, 1956–1961*. New York: Doubleday and Company, 1963.

Eisenhower, John S.D. *So Far From God: The U.S. War with Mexico, 1846–1848*. New York: Random House, 1989.

Ellis, John. *Brute Force: Allied Strategy and Tactics in the Second World War*. New York: Viking, 1990.

Ellis, Joseph J. *His Excellency: George Washington*. New York: Vintage Books, 2004.

———. *Passionate Sage: The Character and Legacy of John Adams*. New York: W.W. Norton & Company, 2001.

———. *American Sphinx: The Character of Thomas Jefferson*. New York: Vintage Books, 1998.

Evans, David C. and Mark R. Peattie. *Kaigun: Strategy, Tactics, and Technology in the Imperial Japanese Navy, 1887–1941*. Annapolis: Naval Institute Press, 1997.

Faust, Drew Gilpin. *This Republic of Suffering: Death and the American Civil War*. New York: Vintage Civil War Library, 2009.

Fausz, J. Frederick. An "Abundance of Blood Shed on Both Sides": New England's First Indian War, 1609–1614," *The Virginia Magazine of History and Biography* 98, no. 1 (January, 1990): 3–56.

Ferling, John. *Struggle for a Continent: The Wars of Early America.* Arlington Heights: Harlan Davidson, 1993.

———. *A Wilderness of Miseries: War and Warriors in Early America.* Westport: Greenwood Press, 1980.

Ferrell, Robert H. *America's Deadliest Battle: Meuse-Argonne, 1918.* Lawrence: University Press of Kansas, 2007.

Fischer, David Hackett. *Washington's Crossing.* New York: Oxford University Press, 2004.

———. *Paul Revere's Ride.* New York: Oxford University Press, 1994.

Fisher, Ernest F. *Cassino to the Alps.* Washington, DC: Office of the Chief of Military History, 1977.

FitzGerald, Frances. *Fire in the Lake: The Vietnamese and the Americans in Vietnam.* New York: Atlantic Monthly Press, Little, Brown, and Company, 1972.

Fitzpatrick, David J. "Emory Upton and the Army of a Democracy," *The Journal of Military History* 77 (April, 2013): 463–90.

———. "Emory Upton and the Citizen Soldier," *The Journal of Military History* 65 (April, 2001): 355–90.

Flint, Roy K. "Task Force Smith and the 24th Division: Delay and Withdrawal, 5–19 July 1950." In Charles E. Heller and William A. Stofft, *America's First Battles, 1776–1965.* Lawrence: University Press of Kansas, 1986, 266–99.

Foner, Eric. *Reconstruction: America's Unfinished Revolution, 1863–1877.* New York: Harper & Row, 1988.

Fontenot, Gregory, Lt. Colonel E.J. Degan and Lt. Colonel David Tohn. *On Point: The United States Army in Operation Iraqi Freedom.* Fort Leavenworth: Combat Studies Institute, 2004.

Fowler, William M. *Rebels Under Sail: The American Navy during the Revolution.* Charles Scribner and Sons, 1976.

Frank, Richard B. *Downfall: The End of the Imperial Japanese Empire.* New York: Random House, 1999.

———. *Guadalcanal: The Definitive Account of the Landmark Battle.* New York: Random House, 1990.

Frankham, Ronald B. Jr. *Like Rolling Thunder: The Air War in Vietnam, 1964–1975.* Lanham: Rowman and Littlefield, 2005.

Frazer, Robert W. *Forts and Supplies: The Role of the Army in the Economy of the Southwest, 1846–1861.* Albuquerque: University of New Mexico Press, 1983.

Freedman, Lawrence. *Kennedy's Wars: Berlin, Cuba, Laos, and Vietnam.* New York: Oxford University Press, 2002.

Fussell, Paul. *Wartime: Understanding and Behavior in the Second World War.* New York: Oxford University Press, 1989.

Futrell, Frank. *The United States Air Force in Korea, 1950–1953.* Revised Edition. Washington, DC: Office of Air Force History, 1983.

Gabel, Christopher. *The U.S. Army GHQ Maneuvers of 1941.* Washington, DC: Center of Military History, 1991.

Gaddis, John Lewis. *The Cold War: A New History.* New York: Penguin Press, 2005.

———. *Strategies of Containment: A Critical Appraisal of American National Security Policy During the Cold War.* New York: Oxford University Press, 2005.

Gallagher, Gary W. *The Union War.* Cambridge: Harvard University Press, 2011.

———. *The Confederate War.* Cambridge: Harvard University Press, 1997.

Ganoe, William Addleman. *The History of the United States Army.* New York: D. Appleton-Century Company, 1942.

Garfield, Brian. *The Thousand Mile War: World War II in the Alaska and the Aleutians.* Fairbanks: University of Alaska Press, 1995.

Garland, Albert N. and Howard M. Smith. *Sicily and the Surrender of Italy.* Washington, DC: Office of the Chief of Military History, 1965.

Gates, John Morgan. *School Books and Krags: The United States Army in the Philippines, 1898–1902.* Westport: Greenwood Press, 1973.

Giangreco, D.M. *Hell to Pay: Operation DOWNFALL and the Invasion of Japan, 1945–1947.* Annapolis: Naval Institute Press, 2009.

Gilchrist, Peter. *Sea Power: The Coalition and Iraqi Armies.* London: Osprey Publishing Ltd., 1991.

Gildre, Richard P. "Defiance, Diversion, and the Exercise of Arms: The Several Meanings of Colonial Training Days in Colonial Massachusetts." *Military Affairs* 52 (April, 1988): 53–55.

Gillie, M.H. *Forging the Thunderbolt: History of the U.S. Army's Armored Forces, 1917–1945.* Reprint. Mechanicsburg: Stackpole Books, 2006.

Glantz, David M. *Colossus Reborn: The Red Army at War, 1941–1943.* Lawrence: University Press of Kansas, 2005.

———. *Stumbling Colossus: The Red Army on the Eve of World War.* Lawrence: University Press of Kansas, 1998.

Glantz, David M. and Jonathan House. *When Titans Clashed: How the Red Army Stopped Hitler.* Lawrence: University Press of Kansas, 1995.

Glatthaar, Joseph T. *General Lee's Army: From Victory to Collapse.* New York: Free Press, 2008.

———. *Forged in Battle: The Civil War Alliance of Black Soldiers and White Officers.* New York: Free Press, 1990.

———. *The March to the Sea and Beyond: Sherman's Troops in the Savannah and Carolina Campaigns.* New York: New York University Press, 1985.

Goldman, Theresa L, Wei-Li Jasmine Chen, David L. Larsen. "Clicking the Icon: Exploring the Meanings Visitors Attach to the Three National Capital Memorials." *Journal of Interpretation Research* 6, no. 1 (Summer, 2001): 3–30.

Gordon, Michael R. and Lt. Geneal Bernard E. Trainor. *COBRA II: The Inside Story of the Invasion and Occupation of Iraq.* New York: Pantheon Books, 2006.

Grady, Timothy Paul. *Anglo-Spanish Rivalry in Colonial South-East America, 1650–1725.* London, UK: Pickering and Chatto, 2010.

Graff, Alan D. *Bayonets in the Wilderness: Anthony Wayne's Legion in the old Northwest.* Norman: University of Oklahoma Press, 2004.

Grenier, John. *The First American Way of War: American War Making of the Frontier.* New York: Cambridge University Press, 2005.

Griffith, Paddy. *Battle Tactics of the Civil War.* New Haven: Yale University Press, 1987.

Griffith, Robert K. *Men Wanted For the United States Army: America's Experience With An All-Volunteer Army Between the World Wars.* Westport: Greenwood Press, 1982.

Grigg, John. 1943: *The Victory That Never Was.* New York: Hill and Wang, 1980.

Grimsley, Mark. *And Keep Moving On: The Virginia Campaign, May-June, 1864.* Lincoln: University of Nebraska Press, 1988.

Grinder, Allison L. and E. Sue McCoy. *The Good Guide: A Sourcebook for Interpreters, Docents, and Tour Guides.* Scottsdale: Ironwood Publishing, 1985.

Grodzinski, John R. "Opening Shots from the Bicentenary of the War of 1812: A Canadian Perspective on Recent Titles," *The Journal of Military History* 76 (October, 2012): 1187–1201.

Gross, Charles J. *American Military Aviation: The Indispensable Arm.* College Station: Texas A & M University Press, 2002.

Gross, Robert A. *The Minuteman and Their World.* New York: Hill and Wang, 1976.

Grotelueschen, Mark E. *The AEF Way of War: The American Army and Combat in World War I.* New York: Cambridge University Press, 2007.

Gruber, Ira D. "America's First Battle: Long Island, 27 August 1776." In *America's First Battles, 1776–1965*, ed. Charles E. Heller and William A. Stoft, Lawrence: University Press of Kansas, 1986.

Hackett, John. *The Third World War.* New York: Macmillan Publishing, 1978.

Hacker, J. David. "A Census-Based Count of the Civil War Dead," *Civil War History* 57, no. 4 (2011): 307–48.

Hagan, Kenneth J. *This People's Navy: The Making of American Sea Power.* New York: The Free Press, 1991.

Halberstam, David. *The Best and the Brightest.* New York: Random House, 1972.

Hallion, Richard. *Storm Over Iraq: Air Power and The Gulf War.* Washington, DC: Smithsonian Institution, 1992.

Ham, Sam H. *Interpretation: Making a Difference on Purpose.* Golden: Fulcrum Publishing, 2013.

———. *Environmental Interpretation: A Practical Guide For People With Big Ideas and Small Budgets.* Golden: Fulcrum Publishing, 1992.

Hamner, Christopher H. *Enduring Battle: American Soldiers in Three Wars, 1776–1945.* Manhattan: University Press of Kansas, 2011.

Hardin, Stephen L. *Texian Iliad: A Military History of the Texas Revolution.* Austin: University of Texas Press, 1994.

Harrison, Gordon A. *Cross Channel Attack.* Washington, DC: Office of the Chief of Military History, 1951.

Harsh, Joseph L. *Taken at the Flood: Robert E. Lee and Confederate Strategy in the Maryland Campaign, September, 1862.* Kent: Kent State University Press, 1999.

Hart, Russell A. *Clash of Arms: How the Allies Won in Normandy.* Norman: University of Oklahoma Press, 2001.

Hastings, Max. *Retribution: The Battle for Japan, 1944–45.* New York: Alfred A. Knopf, 2008.

———. *Armageddon: The Battle For Germany, 1944-1945.* New York: Vintage Books, 2004.

———. *Overlord: D-Day and the Battle for Normandy.* New York: Simon and Schuster, 1984.

Hattaway, Herman and Archer Jones. *How the North Won: A Military History of the Civil War.* Chicago: University of Illinois Press, 1983.

Heinrichs, Waldo. *Threshold of War: Franklin D. Roosevelt and American Entry into World War II.* New York: Oxford University Press, 1988.

Hennessey, John J. *Return to Bull Run: The Campaign and Battle of Second Manassas.* New York: Simon and Schuster, 1993.

Hermes, Walter G. *Truce Tent and Fighting Front.* Washington, DC: Office of the Chief of Military History, 1966.

Herring, George C. *America's Longest War: The United States and Vietnam, 1950–1975.* Fifth Edition. New York: McGraw Hill, 2013.

———. "The 1st Cavalry and the Ia Drang Valley, 18 October-24 October 1965." In Charles E. Heller and William A. Stofft, *America's First Battles, 1776–1965.* Lawrence: University Press of Kansas, 1986, 300–26.

Hess, Gary R. *Vietnam: Explaining America's Lost War.* Malden: Blackwell Publishing, 2009.

Hewes, James E Jr. *From Root to McNamara: Army Organization and Administration, 1900–1963.* Washington, DC: Center of Military History, 1975.

Hickey, Donald R. *The War of 1812: A Short History. Bicentennial Edition.* Chicago: University of Illinois Press, 2012.

———. *The War of 1812: A Forgotten Conflict.* Chicago: University of Illinois Press, 1990.

———. "American Trade Restrictions During the War of 1812," *The Journal of American History* 68 (December, 1981): 517–38.

———. "Federalist Defense Policy in the Age of Jefferson, 1801–1812," *Military Affairs* 45 (April, 1981): 63–70.

Higginbotham, Don. "The Military Institutions of Colonial America: The Rhetoric and Reality." In Don Higginbotham, ed. *War and Society in Revolutionary America: The Wider Dimensions of the Conflict.* Columbia: University of South Carolina Press, 1988.

———. "The Early American Way of War: Reconnaissance and Appraisal," *The William and Mary Quarterly*, 3rd Ser. 44 (April, 1987): 230–73.

———. *George Washington and the American Military Tradition.* Athens: University of Georgia Press, 1985.

———. *The War of American Independence: Military Attitudes, Policies and Practice.* Boston: Northeastern University Press, 1983.

Hill, Jim Dan. *The Minute Man in Peace and War. A History of the The National Guard.* Harrisburg: The Stackpole Company, 1964.

Hoffmann, George F. *Through Mobility We Conquer: The Mechanization of the U.S. Cavalry.* Lexington: University Press of Kentucky, 2006.

Hogan, David W. *225 Years of Service. The U.S. Army, 1775–2000.* Washington, DC: Center of Military History, 2000.

Hornfischer, James D. *The Last Stand of the Tin Can Sailors: The Extraordinary Story of the U.S. Navy's Finest Hour.* New York: Bantam Books, 2005.

Horton, James Oliver. "Slavery and the Coming of the Civil War: A Matter For Interpretation." In Robert K. Sutton, ed. *Rally on the High Ground: The National Park Service Symposium on the Civil War.* Fort Washington: Eastern National, 2001.

House, Jonathan M. *A Military History of the Cold War, 1944–1962.* Norman: University of Oklahoma Press, 2012.

Howarth, Stephen. *A History of the United States Navy, 1775–1998.* Norman: University of Oklahoma Press, 1991.

Howe, Daniel Walker. *What Hath God Wrought: The Transformation of America, 1815–1848.* New York: Oxford University Press, 2007.

Howe, George F. *Northwest Africa: Seizing the Initiative in the West.* Washington, DC: Office of the Chief of Military History, 1957.

Huntington, Samuel P. *The Soldier and the State: The Theory and Politics of Civil-Military Relations.* Cambridge: The Belknap Press of Harvard University Press, 1957.

Hutson, James A. *The Sinews of War: Army Logistics, 1775–1953.* Washington, DC: Office of the Chief of Military History, 1966.

Jamieson, Perry D. *Crossing the Deadly Ground: United States Army Tactics, 1865–1869.* Tuscaloosa: The University of Alabama Press, 1994.

Jennings, Francis. *Empire of Fortune: Crowns, Colonies, and Tribes in the Seven Years War in America.* New York: W.W. Norton, 1988.

———. *The Invasion of America: Indians, Colonialism, and the Cant of Conquest.* Chapel Hill: University of North Carolina Press, 1975.

Johnson, Charles W. "The Army and the Civilian Conservation Corps, 1933–1942," *Prologue: The Journal of the National Archives* 4 (Fall, 1972): 139–56.

Johnson, David E. *Fast Tanks and Heavy Bombers: Innovation in the U.S. Army, 1917–1945.* Ithaca: Cornell University Press, 1998.

Johnson, Douglas V. and Rolfe Hillman, Jr. *Soissons, 1918.* College Station: Texas A & M Press, 1999.

Johnson, Richard R. "The Search for a Useable Indian: An Aspect of the Defense of Colonial New England." *Journal of American History* 64 (December, 1977): 623–51.

Jones, Andrea K. "All Hands on Deck: Toward the Experience History Museum," *History News* (Spring, 2014): 18–22.

Jones, Archer. *Confederate Strategy From Shiloh to Vicksburg.* Baton Rouge: Louisiana State University Press, 1991.

Jones, Karen. "A Sesquicentennial Evolution: National Parks Take a New Look at the Civil War," *Museum* (November/December, 2014): 59.

Jones, Seth G. *In the Graveyard of Empires: America's War in Afghanistan.* New York: W.W. Norton, 2009.

Jones, Vincent C. *Manhattan: The Army and the Atomic Bomb.* Washington, DC: Center of Military History, 1985.

Jung, Patrick. *The Black Hawk War of 1832.* Norman: University of Oklahoma Press, 2007.

Kammen, Carol. "Wilson's Ghost," *History News: The Magazine of the American Association for State and Local History* 69, no. 4 (Autumn, 2014).

Kammen, Michael. *The Mystic Chords of Memory: The Transformation of Tradition in American Culture.* New York: Vintage Books, 1993.

Kaplan, Fred. *The Insurgents: David Petraeus and the Plot to Change the American Way of War.* New York: Simon and Schuster, 2013.

Karnow, Stanley. *Vietnam: A History.* New York: Penguin Books, 1984.

Karsh, Efraim. *The Iran-Iraq War, 1980–1988.* London, UK: Osprey Publishing, 2002.

Karsten, Peter. *The Naval Aristocracy: The Golden Age of Annapolis and the Emergence of Navalism.* New York: Free Press, 1972.

Kaufman, Burton I. and Scott Kaufman. Second Edition. *The Presidency of James Earl Carter.* Lawrence: University Press of Kansas, 2006.

Kaufmann, J.E. and H.W. Kaufmann. *Fortress America: The Forts That Defended America, 1600 to the Present.* Cambridge: Da Capo Press, 2004.

Keaney, Thomas and Eliot A. Cohen. *Gulf Air Power Survey: Summary Report.* Washington, DC: 1993.

Keegan, John. *Seven Armies in Normandy: From D-Day to the Liberation of Paris.* New York: Penguin Books, 1994.

Kennedy, Paul. *Engineers For Victory: The Problem Solvers Who Turned the Tide in the Second World War.* New York: Harpers Collins, 2013.

Kennett, Lee. *The First Air War, 1914–1918.* New York: The Free Press, 1991.

———. *G.I. The American Soldier in World War Two.* New York: Charles Scribner's Sons, 1987.

Ketchum, Richard M. *Saratoga: Turning Point of America's Revolution.* New York: Henry Holt and Company, 1997.

———. *Decisive Day: The Battle for Bunker Hill.* New York: Doubleday, 1974.

Killigrew, John W. "The Army and the Bonus Incident," *Military Affairs* 26, no. 2 (Summer, 1962): 59–65.

Kindsvatter, Peter S. *American Soldiers: Ground Combat in the World Wars, Korea, & Vietnam.* Manhattan: University Press of Kansas, 2003.

Kohn, Richard H. *Eagle and Sword: The Beginnings of the Military Establishment in America.* New York: The Free Press, 1975.

Konstam, Angus and Tony Bryan Illustrator. *Confederate Raider, 1861–1865.* Oxford, England: Osprey Publishing, 2003.

LaFeber, Walter. *The New Empire: An Interpretation of American Expansion, 1860–1898.* Ithaca: Cornell University Press, 1963.

Lambeth, Benjamin S. *Air Power Against Terror: America's Conduct of Operation Enduring Freedom*. Arlington: National Defense Research Institute, Rand Corporation, 2005.

Lapp, Derrick E. "Did They Really 'Take None But Gentleman'? Henry Hardman, the Maryland Line, and a Reconsideration of the Socioeconomic Composition of the Continental Officer Corps," *Journal of Military History*, 78 (October, 2014): 1239–61.

Larsen, David. *Meaningful Interpretation: How to Connect Hearts and Minds to Places, Objects, and other Resources*. Fort Washington: Eastern National, 2003.

Laurie, Clayton D. and Ronald H. Cole. *The Role of Federal Military Forces in Domestic Disorders, 1877–1945*. Washington, DC: Center of Military History, 1997.

Leach, Douglas Edward. *Roots of Conflict: British Armed Forces and Colonial Americans, 1677–1763*. Chapel Hill: University of North Carolina Press, 1986.

———. *Arms For Empire: A Military History of the British Colonies in North America, 1607–1763*. New York: The Macmillan Company, 1973.

———. *Flintlock and Tomahawk: New England in King Philip's War*. Woodstock: The Countrymen Press, 1958.

———. "The Military System of the Plymouth Colony," *The New England Quarterly* 24 (September, 1951): 342–64.

Lee, Wayne E. "Mind and Matter – Cultural Analysis in American Military History: A Look at the State of the Field," *Journal of American History* 93 (March, 2007): 1116–42.

Lee, Wayne E. "Early American Ways of War: A New Reconnaissance, 1600–1815," *The Historical Journal* 44, no. 1 (2001): 269–89.

Lepore, Jill. *The Name of War: King Phillip's War and the Origins of American Identity*. New York: Vintage, 1990.

Lewis, Emanuel Raymond. *Seacoast Fortifications of the United States: An Introductory History*. Missoula: Pictorial Histories Publishing Company, 1979.

Linderman, Gerald F. *The World Within War: America's Combat Experience in World War II*. New York: The Free Press, 1997.

———. *Embattled Courage: The Experience of Combat in the American Civil War*. New York: The Free Press, 1987.

Linenthal, Edward T. *Sacred Ground: Americans and Their Battlefields*. Chicago: University of Illinois Press, 1991.

Linenthal, Edward T. and Tom Engelhardt. *History Wars: The Enola Gay and Other Battles For the American Past*. New York: Metropolitan Books, Henry Holt and Company, 1996.

Link, Arthur S. *Woodrow Wilson: Revolution, Peace and War*. Arlington Heights: Harlan Davidson, 1979.

Linn, Brain M. *The Echo of Battle: The Army's Way of War*. Cambridge: Harvard University Press, 2007.

———. *The Philippine War, 1899–1902*. Lawrence: University Press of Kansas, 2000.

———. "The American Way of War Revisited," *Journal of Military History* 66 (April, 2002): 502–17.

———. *Guardians of Empire: The U.S. Army and the Pacific, 1902–1940*. Chapel Hill: The University of North Carolina Press, 1997.

LoFaro, Guy. *The Sword of St. Michael: The 82nd Airborne Division in World War Two*. Philadelphia: Da Capo Press, 2011.

Lock-Pullan, Richard. "'An Inward Looking Time': The United States Army, 1973–1976," *The Journal of Military History* 67, no. 2 (April, 2003): 483–511.

Lonetree, Amy. *Decolonizing Museums: Representing Native America in National and Tribal Museums*. Chapel Hill: The University of North Carolina Press, 2012.

Lowrey, Nathan S. *From the Sea: U.S. Marines in the Global War on Terrorism*. Washington, DC: History Division United States Marine Corps, 2011.

Lundstrom, John B. *The First Team: Pacific Naval Air Combat From Pearl Harbor to Midway.* Annapolis: Naval Institute Press, 1984.

Lundstrom, John B. *The First South Pacific Campaign, December, 1941–June, 1942.* Annapolis: Naval Institute Press, 1976.

Luvaas, Jay. "Buna: 19 November 1942–2 January 1943: A 'Leavenworth Nightmare.'" In Charles E. Heller and William A. Stofft, *America's First Battles, 1776–1965.* Lawrence: University Press of Kansas, 1986, 186–225.

Lynn, John A. "The Embattled Future of Academic Military History," *The Journal of Military History* 61 (October, 1997): 777–89.

———. *Battle: A History of Combat and Culture From Ancient Greece to Modern America.* Boulder: Westview Press, 2003.

MacDonald, Charles B. *A Time For Trumpets: The Untold Story of the Battle of the Bulge.* New York: William Murrow and Company, 1985.

———. *The Last Offensive.* Washington, DC: Office of the Chief of Military History, 1973.

———. *The Siegfried Line Campaign.* Washington, DC: Office of the Chief of Military History, 1963.

McFarland, Stephan L. *America's Pursuit of Precision Bombing, 1910–1945.* Washington, DC: Smithsonian Institution Press, 1995.

McKee, Christopher. *A Gentlemanly and Honorable Profession: The Creation of the US Naval Officer Corps, 1794–1815.* Annapolis: United States Naval Institute Press, 1991.

McMahon, Robert J. ed. *Major Problems in the History of the Vietnam War.* Third Edition. New York: Houghton Mifflin Company, 2003.

McMaster, H.R. *Dereliction of Duty: Johnson, McNamara, the Joint Chiefs of Staff and the Lies That Led to Vietnam.* New York: Harper, 1997.

McMurry, Richard M. *Atlanta 1864: Last Chance For the Confederacy.* Lincoln: University of Nebraska Press, 2000.

McPherson, James M. "The Rewards of Risk Taking: Two Civil War Admirals," *Journal of Military History,* 78 (October, 2014): 1225–37.

———. *Embattled Rebel: Jefferson Davis and Commander in Chief.* New York: Oxford University Press, 2014.

———. *War on the Waters: The Union and Confederate Navies, 1861–1865.* Chapel Hill: University of North Carolina Press, 2012.

———. *Tried By War: Abraham Lincoln as Commander in Chief.* New York: Penguin Books, 2008.

———. *For Cause and Comrades: Why Men Fought in the Civil War.* New York: Oxford University Press, 1997.

———. *Ordeal By Fire: The Civil War and Reconstruction,* Second Edition. New York: McGraw Hill, 1992.

———. *Abraham Lincoln and the Second American Revolution.* New York: Oxford University Press, 1990.

———. *Battle Cry of Freedom, The Civil War Era.* New York: Oxford University Press, 1988.

Mahon, John K. *History of the Militia and the National Guard.* New York: Macmillan Publishing Company, 1983.

———. *History of the Second Seminole War, 1835–1842.* Gainsville: University Press of Florida, 1967.

———. "Anglo-American Methods of Indian Warfare," *The Mississippi Valley Historical Review* 45 (September, 1958): 254–75.

Malone, Patrick M. *The Skulking Way of War: Technology and Tactics Among the New England Indians.* Baltimore: Johns Hopkins University Press, 1991.

Manning, Chandra. *What This Cruel War Was Over: Soldiers, Slavery, and the Civil War*. New York: Alfred A. Knopf, 2007.

Mansoor, Peter R. *The GI Offensive in Europe: The Triumph of the American Infantry Divisions, 1941–1945*. Lawrence: University Press of Kansas, 1999.

Marolda, Edward J. and Robert J. Schneller Jr. *Shield and Sword: The United States Navy and the Persian Gulf War*. Annapolis: United States Naval Institute, 2001.

Martin, James Kirby and Mark Edward Lender. *A Respectable Army: The Military Origins of the Republic, 1763–1789*. Arlington Heights: Harlan Davidson, 1982.

Matheny, Michael R. *Carrying The War to the Enemy: American Operational Art to 1945*. Norman: University of Oklahoma Press, 2011.

Matloff, Maurice and Edwin M. Snell. *Strategic Planning for Coalition Warfare, 1941–1942*. Reprint. Washington, DC: Center for Military History, 1999.

Matter, William. *If It Takes All Summer: The Battle of Spotsylvania*. Chapel Hill: University of North Carolina Press, 1988.

May, Ernest R. ed. *American Cold War Strategy: Interpreting NSC 68*. Boston: Bedford Books of St. Martin's Press, 1993.

———. *Imperial Democracy: The Emergence of America as a Great Power*. New York: Harcourt, Brace, 1961.

———. *The World War and American Isolation, 1914–17*. Cambridge: Harvard University Press, 1959.

Melhorn, Charles M. *Two-Block Fox: The Rise of the Aircraft Carrier, 1911–1929*. Annapolis: Naval Institute Press, 1974.

Merk, Frederick. *Manifest Destiny and Mission in American History*. New York: Vintage Books, 1966.

Meyer, Dillon S. *Uprooted Americans: The Japanese Americans and the WRA in World War II*. Tucson: University of Arizona Press, 1971.

Middlekauf, Robert. *The Glorious Cause: The American Revolution, 1763–1789*. New York: Oxford University Press, 1982.

Mikesh, Robert C. *Japan's World War II Balloon Bomb Attacks on North America*. Washington, DC: Smithsonian Institution Press, 1973.

Milner, Samuel. *Victory in Papua*. Washington, DC: Office of the Chief of Military History, 1957.

Miller, Darlis A. *Soldiers and Settlers: Military Supply in the Southwest*. Albuquerque: University of New Mexico Press, 1989.

Miller, Donald L. *Masters of the Air: America's Bomber Boys Who Fought the Air War Against Nazi Germany*. New York: Simon and Schuster Paperbacks, 2006.

Miller, Edward S. *War Plan Orange: The U.S. Strategy to Defeat Japan, 1897–1945*. Annapolis: Naval Institute Press, 1991.

Miller, John Jr. *Guadalcanal: The First Offensive*. Washington, DC: Historical Division, Dept. of the Army, 1949.

Miller, Nathan. *Sea of Glory: The Continental Navy Fights for Independence, 1775–1785*. New York: David McKay and Company, 1974.

Miller, Roger G. "Wings and Wheels: The 1st Aero Squadron, Truck Transport, and the Punitive Expedition of 1916." In *Air Power History* 42, no. 4 (Winter, 1995): 12–29.

Miller, Stuart Creighton. *"Benevolent Assimilation" The American Conquest of the Philippines, 1899–1903*. New Haven: Yale University Press, 1982.

Millett, Allan R. Peter Maslowski and William B. Feis. *For The Common Defense. A Military History of the United States from 1607–2012*. Third Edition. New York: Free Press, 2012.

Millett, Allan R. *The War For Korea, 1950–1951: They Came From the North*. Lawrence: University Press of Kansas, 2010.

————. *The War For Korea, 1945–1950: A House Burning.* Lawrence: University Press of Kansas, 2005.

————. "Over Where? The AEF and the American Strategy for Victory, 1917–1918." In Kenneth J. Hagan and William R. Roberts, *Against All Enemies: Interpretations of American Military History from Colonial Times to the Present.* Westport: Greenwood Press, 1986.

————. "Cantigny, 28-31 May 1918." In Charles E. Heller and William A. Stofft, *America's First Battles, 1776–1965.* Lawrence: University Press of Kansas, 1986.

————. *Semper Fidelis: The History of the United States Marine Corps.* New York: Macmillan Publishing, 1980.

————. "The Study of American Military History in the United States," *Military Affairs* 41 (April, 1977): 58–61.

Mindell, David A. *Iron Coffin: War, Technology, and Experience Aboard the USS Monitor.* Baltimore: John Hopkins University Press, 2012.

Moise, Edwin E. *Tonkin Gulf and the Escalation of the Vietnam War.* Chapel Hill: University of North Carolina Press, 1996.

Moore, Harold G. and Joseph Galloway. *We Were Soldiers Once . . . . And Young: Ia Drang- The Battle That Changed the War in Vietnam.* New York: Random House, 1992.

Morgan, Edmund S. *The Birth of the Republic, 1763–89.* Revised Edition. Chicago: University of Chicago Press, 1977.

Morrison, Samuel Eliot. Volume III, *United States Navy in World War Two: Rising Sun in the Pacific, 1931–April, 1942.* Boston: Little, Brown, 1948.

————. Volume IV, *United States Navy in World War Two: Coral Sea, Midway, and Submarine Actions, May–August, 1942.* Boston: Little, Brown, 1949.

————. Volume VII, *United States Navy in World War Two:* Aleutians, Gilberts and Marshalls, June 1942–April 1944. Boston: Little, Brown, 1951.

————. Volume VIII, *United States Navy in World War Two: New Guinea and the Marianas: March–August, 1944.* Boston: Little, Brown, 1953.

————. Volume XII, *United States Navy in World War Two: Leyte, June, 1944–Janaury, 1945.* Boston: Little, Brown, 1958.

————. Volume XIII, *United States Navy in World War Two: Liberation of the Philippines, 1944–1945.* Boston: Little, Brown, 1959.

————. Volume XIV, *United States Navy in World War Two: Victory in the Pacific.* Boston: Little, Brown, 1960.

————. *The Two Ocean War: A Short History of the United States Navy in the Second World War.* Boston: Little, Brown and Company, 1963.

Morton, Louis. "Germany First: The Basic Concept of Allied Strategy in World War II." In Kent Roberts Greenfield, ed. *Command Decisions.* Washington, DC: Office of the Chief of Military History, n.d.

————. "The Historian and the Study of War," *The Mississippi Valley Historical Review* 48 (March, 1962): 612–13.

————. "The Origins of American Military Policy," *Military Affairs* 22 (Summer, 1958): 75–82.

————. *The Fall of the Philippines.* Washington, DC: Office of the Chief of Military History, 1953.

Muehlbauer, Matthew S. and David J. Ulbrich. *Ways of War: American Military History from the Colonial Era to the Twenty-First Century.* New York: Routledge, 2014.

Murray, Williamson, "British Military Effectiveness in the Second World War." In Allan R. Millett, Williamson Murray, ed. *Military Effectiveness, Volume 3: The Second World War.* New York: Cambridge University Press, 2010, 90–135.

Murray, Williamson and Allan R. Millett. *A War To Be Won: Fighting the Second World War.* Cambridge: Belknap Press of Harvard University Press, 2000.

Murray, Williamson. "Strategic Bombing: The American, British, and German Experiences." In Williamson Murray and Allen R. Millett, ed. *Military Innovation in the Interwar Period.* New York: Cambridge University Press, 1996.

Nathan, James A. ed. *The Cuban Missile Crisis Revisited.* New York: St. Martin's Press, 1992.

Neiberg, Michael S. *Fighting the Great War: A Global History.* Cambridge: Harvard University Press, 2005.

Nenninger, Timothy K. "The Army Enters the Twentieth Century, 1904–1917." In Kenneth J. Hagan and William R. Roberts, *Against All Enemies: Interpretations of American Military History from Colonial Times to the Present.* Westport: Greenwood Press, 1986.

———. *The Leavenworth Schools and the Old Army: Education, Professionalism, and the Officer Corps of the United States Army, 1881–1918.* Westport: Greenwood Press, 1978.

———. "Tactical Dysfunction in the AEF, 1917–1918," *Military Affairs* 51, no. 4, (October, 1987): 177–81.

———. "Organizational Milestones in the Development of American Armor, 1920–1940," In George F. Hoffmann and Donn A. Starry, ed. *Camp Colt to Desert Storm: The History of U.S. Armored Forces.* Lexington: University Press of Kentucky, 1999.

Newhouse, John. *Cold Dawn: The Story of SALT.* Washington, DC: Brassey's, 1989.

Noe, Kenneth W. *Perryville: The Grand Havoc of Battle.* Lexington: University Press of Kentucky, 2001.

Oates, Stephen B. *To Purge This Land With Blood.* Second Edition. Amherst: The University of Massachusetts Press, 1984.

———. *Abraham Lincoln: The Man Behind the Myths.* New York: New American Library, 1984.

———. *With Malice Toward None: The Life of Abraham Lincoln.* New York: New American Library, 1977.

Oberdorfer, Don. *Tet! The Turning Point of the Vietnam War.* New York: Doubleday, 1971.

Overy, Richard. *The Bombing War: Europe, 1939–1945.* London, UK: Penguin Books, 2014.

———. *Why The Allies Won.* New York: W.W. Norton & Company, 1995.

Owen, Robert C. ed. [Operation] *Deliberate Force: A Case Study in Effective Air Campaigning.* Montgomery: Air University Press, 2000.

Pallud, Jean Paul. *Battle of the Bulge, Then and Now.* London, UK: Battle of Britain Prints International, 1984.

Palmer, Michael A. *Stoddert's War: Naval Operations During the Quasi War with France.* Chapel Hill: University of North Carolina Press, 1987.

Parshall, Jonathan and Anthony Tully. *Shattered Sword: The Untold Story of the Battle of Midway.* Dulles: Potomac Books, 2005.

Paterson, Thomas G, Garry Clifford J, Kenneth J. Hagan. *American Foreign Policy: A History to 1914.* Lexington: DC: Heath and Company, 1983.

Peckham, Howard H. *The Colonial Wars, 1689–1762.* Chicago: University of Chicago Press, 1964.

Perret, Geoffrey. *Winged Victory: The Army Air Forces in World War II.* New York: Random House, 1993.

Pershing, John J. *My Experiences in the World War*, Vol. 1. New York: Harper & Row Publishers, 1931. Reprint, Blue Ridge Summit, PA: Tab Books, 1989.

Polmar, Norman. *Aircraft Carriers: A History of Carrier Aviation and its Influence on World Events.* Washington: Potomac Books, 2009.

Porch, Douglas. *The Path to Victory: The Mediterranean Theater in World War Two.* Old Saybrook: Konecky & Konecky, 2004.

Potter, David M. *The Impending Crisis, 1848–1861.* New York: Harper and Row, 1976.

Prados, John and Ray W. Stubbe. *Valley of Decision: The Siege of Khe Sanh.* New York: Doubleday, 1991.

Prange, Gordon W. *Pearl Harbor: The Verdict of History.* New York: McGraw Hill, 1986.

———. *At Dawn We Slept: The Untold Story of Pearl Harbor.* New York: Viking Press, 1981.

Prucha, Francis Paul. *Broadax and Bayonet: The Role of the United States Army in the Development of the Northwest.* Reprint. Lincoln, NE: University of Nebraska Press, 1995.

———. "Andrew Jackson's Indian Policy: A Reassessment." In Francis Paul Prucha, ed. *Indian Policy in the United States: Historical Essays.* Lincoln: University of Nebraska Press, 1981, 139–47.

———. *The Sword of the Republic: The United States Army on the Frontier, 1783–1846.* Lincoln: University of Nebraska Press, 1969.

Putney, Diane T. *Airpower Advantage: Planning the Gulf Air War Campaign, 1989–1991.* Washington, DC: Air Force History and Museum Program, 2004.

Quarstein, John V. *The CSS Virginia: Sink Before Surrender.* Charleston: The History Press, 2013.

Radabaugh, Jack S. "The Militia of Colonial Massachusetts," *Military Affairs* 18 (Spring, 1954): 1–18.

Rafuse, Ethan S. *A Single Grand Victory: The First Campaign and Battle of Manassas.* New York: Rowman and Littlefield, 2002.

Rashid, Ahmed. *Taliban: Militant Islam, Oil and Fundamentalism in Central Asia.* New Haven: Yale University Press, 2000.

Reardon, Mark J. *Victory at Mortain: Stopping Hitler's Panzer Counteroffensive.* Lawrence: University Press of Kansas, 2002.

Rees, David. *Korea: The Limited War.* New York: St. Martin's Press, 1964.

Remini, Robert V. *Andrew Jackson.* New York: Harper Row, 1966.

Rhodes, Richard. *The Making of the Atomic Bomb.* New York: Simon and Schuster, 1986.

Ricks, Thomas E. *The Gamble: General David Petraeus and the American Military Adventure in Iraq, 2006–2009.* New York: Penguin Press, 2009.

———. *Fiasco: The American Military Adventure in Iraq.* New York: Penguin Books, 2006.

Rickey, Don Jr. *Forty Miles a Day on Beans and Hay: The Enlisted Soldier Fighting the Indian Wars.* Norman: University of Oklahoma Press, 1963.

Rickover, Hyman G. *How the Battleship Maine was Destroyed.* Second Edition. Annapolis: US Naval Institute Press, 1995.

Ripley, Tim. *Land Power: The Coalition and Iraqi Armies.* London: Osprey Publishing Ltd., 1991.

Risch, Erna. *Quartermaster Support of the Army: A History of the Corps, 1775–1939.* Washington, DC: Quartermaster Historian's Office, 1962.

Roberts, William R. "Reform and Revitalization, 1900–1903." In Kenneth J. Hagan and William R. Roberts, *Against All Enemies: Interpretations of American Military History from Colonial Times to the Present.* Westport: Greenwood Press, 1986.

Robertson, James I. Jr. *Stonewall Jackson: The Man, The Solider, The Legend.* New York: Macmillan and Company, 1997.

Robinson, Greg. *By Order of the President: FDR and the Internment of the Japanese-Americans.* Cambridge: Harvard University Press, 2001.

Royster, Charles. *A Revolutionary People at War: The Continental Army and American Character.* Chapel Hill: University of North Carolina Press, 1979.

Rush, Robert Sterling. *Hell in the Hürtgen Forest: The Ordeal and Triumph of an American Infantry Regiment.* Lawrence: University Press of Kansas, 2001.

Ryan, Cornelius. *The Longest Day, June 6, 1944.* New York: Crest Books edition, 1959.

————. *A Bridge Too Far.* New York: Simon and Schuster, 1974.

Satz, Ronald N. *American Indian Policy in the Jacksonian Era.* Lincoln: University of Nebraska Press, 1975.

Scales, Robert H. *Certain Victory: The U.S. Army in the Gulf War.* Washington, DC: Brassey's, 1994.

Schaffer, Ronald. *Wings of Judgment: American Bombing in World War II.* New York: Oxford University Press, 1985.

Scherbaum, Peggy Ann. *Handles: A Compendium of Interpretive Techniques to Help Visitors Grasp Resources.* Fort Washington: Eastern National, 2006.

Schubert, Frank N. and Theresa L. Kraus, ed. *The Whirlwind War: The United States Army in Operations Desert Shield and Desert Storm.* Washington, DC: Center of Military History, 1995.

Sears, Stephen W. *Chancellorsville.* New York: Houghton Mifflin, 1996.

————. *To the Gates of Richmond: The Peninsula Campaign.* New York: Ticknor and Fields, 1992.

————. *George B. McClellan: The Young Napoleon.* New York: Ticknor and Fields, 1988.

————. *Landscape Turned Red: The Battle of Antietam.* New York: Ticknor and Fields, 1983.

————. *Desert War in North Africa.* New York: American Heritage Publishing Co., Inc., 1967.

Sefton, James F. *The United States Army and Reconstruction, 1865–1877.* Baton Rouge: Louisiana State University Press, 1967.

Shaara, Michael. *The Killer Angels.* New York: Ballantine Books, 1974.

Sharp, Morrison. "Leadership and Democracy in the Early New England System of Defense." *American Historical Review* 50 (January, 1945): 244–60.

Shaw, John M. *The Cambodian Campaign: The 1970 Offensive and America's Vietnam War.* Lawrence: University Press of Kansas, 2005.

Shea, William L. and Earl J. Hess. *Pea Ridge: Civil War Campaign in the West.* Chapel Hill: University of North Carolina Press, 1992.

————. *The Virginia Militia in the Seventeenth Century.* Baton Rouge: Louisiana State University Press, 1983.

————. "The First American Militia," *Military Affairs* 46 (February, 1982): 15–18.

————. "Virginia At War, 1644–1646," *Military Affairs* 41 (October, 1977): 142–46.

Sherry, Michael. *The Rise of American Air Power: The Creation of Armageddon.* New Haven: Yale University Press, 1987.

Shore, Moyers S. *The Battle For Khe Sanh.* Washington, DC: History and Museums Division, Headquarters U.S. Marine Corps, 1969.

Showalter, Dennis E. "The United States in the Great War: A Historiography." *Organization of American Historians Magazine of History* 17, no. 1 (October, 2002).

————. "A Modest Plea for Drums and Trumpets," *Military Affairs* 39 (April, 1975): 71–4.

Shulimson, Jack, Lt. Colonel Leonard A. Blasiol, U.S. Marine Corps, Charles R. Smith and Captain David A. Dawson. *U.S. Marine Corps. U.S. Marines in Vietnam: The Defining Year, 1968.* Washington, DC: History and Museums Division, Headquarters U.S. Marine Corps, 1997.

Shy, John. "George C. Marshall Lecture," *The Journal of Military History* 72 (2008): 1033–46.

————. "The American Military Experience: History and Learning." In *A People Numerous and Armed,* revised edition. Ann Arbor: University of Michigan Press, Ann Arbor Paperbacks, 1990.

————. "Armed Force in Colonial North America: New Spain, New France, and Anglo-America." In Kenneth J. Hagan and William R. Roberts, ed. *Against All Enemies: Interpretations of American Military History from Colonial Times to the Present.* Westport: Greenwood Press, 1986.

Shy, John. "A New Look at Colonial Militia," *The William and Mary Quarterly* 20 (April, 1963): 175–85.

Singletary, Otis A. *The Mexican War.* Chicago: The University of Chicago Press, 1960.

Skates, John Ray. *The Invasion of Japan: Alternative to the Bomb.* Columbia: University of South Carolina Press, 1994.

Skelton, William B. *An American Profession of Arms: The Army Officer Corps, 1784–1861.* Lawrence: University Press of Kansas, 1992.

———. "The Army in the Age of the Common Man, 1815–1845." In Kenneth J. Hagan and William R. Roberts, ed. *Against All Enemies: Interpretation of American Military History from Colonial Times to the Present.* Westport, CT: Greenwood Press, 1986.

———. "The Commanding General and the Problem of Command in the United States Army, 1821–1841," *Military Affairs* 34 (December, 1970): 117–22.

Sledge, E.B. *With the Old Breed at Peleliu and Okinawa.* Novato: Presidio Press, 1980.

Smith, Charles R. ed. *US Marines in the Korean War.* Washington, DC: History Division, US Marine Corps, 2007.

Smith, Robert Ross. *Triumph in the Philippines.* Washington, DC: Office of the Chief of Military History, 1963.

———. *Approach to the Philippines.* Washington, DC: Office of the Chief of Military History, 1953.

Smythe, Donald. *Pershing: General of the Armies.* Bloomington: Indiana University Press, 1986.

———. *Guerilla Warrior: The Early Life of John J. Pershing.* New York: Charles Scribner's Sons, 1973.

Sommers, Richard J. *Richmond Redeemed: The Siege of Petersburg.* New York: Doubleday, 1981.

Sorley, Lewis. *Westmoreland: The General Who Lost Vietnam.* New York: Houghton Mifflin Harcourt Publishing, 2003.

———. *A Better War: The Unexamined Victories and Final Tragedy of America's Last Years in Vietnam.* New York: Harcourt Brace and Company, 1999.

———. *Thunderbolt. From the Battle of the Bulge to Vietnam and Beyond: General Creighton Abrams and the Army of His Times.* New York: Simon and Schuster, 1992.

Southard, John. "Beyond 'A Company, B Company' History: A Military History State of the Field," *The American Historian* (August, 2014): 20–23.

Spector, Ronald H. *After Tet: The Bloodiest Year in Vietnam.* New York: The Free Press, 1993.

———. *Eagle Against the Sun: The American War With Japan.* New York: The Free Press, 1985.

———. *Advice and Support: The Early Years, 1941–1960.* Washington, DC: Center of Military History, 1985.

———. "Military History and the Academic World." In *A Guide to the Study and Use of Military History.* Washington, DC: Center of Military History, US Army, 1982.

Sprout, Harold and Margaret Sprout. *The Rise of American Naval Power, 1776–1918.* Princeton: Princeton University Press, 1944.

Starkey, Armstrong. *European and Native American Warfare, 1675–1815.* Norman: University of Oklahoma Press, 1998.

Steele, Ian K. *Warpaths: Invasions of North America.* New York: Oxford University Press, 1994.

Steele, Matthew Forney. *American Campaigns.* Harrisburg: The Military Service Publishing Company, 1949.

Steiner, Barry H. *Bernard Brodie and the Foundations of American Nuclear Strategy.* Lawrence: University Press of Kansas, 1991.

Steuck, William. *The Korean War: An International History*. Princeton: Princeton University Press, 1995.

Stevenson, David. *Cataclysm: The First World War as Political Tragedy*. New York: Basic Books, 2004.

Stoker, Donald. *The Grand Design: Strategy and the U.S. Civil War*. New York: Oxford University Press, 2010.

Stoler, Mark A. *Allies and Adversaries: The Joint Chiefs of Staff, the Grand Alliance, and U.S. Strategy in World War II*. Chapel Hill: University of North Carolina Press, 2000.

Summers, Harry G Jr. *On Strategy: A Critical Analysis of The Vietnam War*. Novato: Presidio Press, 1982.

Symonds, Craig L. *Neptune: The Allied Invasion of Europe and the D-Day Landings*. New York: Oxford University Press, 2014.

———. *The Battle of Midway*. New York: Oxford University Press, 2011.

———. *Lincoln and His Admirals*. New York: Oxford University Press, 2008.

———. *Navalists and Anti-Navalists: The Navy Policy Debate in the United States, 1785–1827*. Newark: University of Delaware Press, 1980.

Taaffe, Stephen R. *Commanding the Army of the Potomac*. Lawrence: University Press of Kansas, 2006.

———. *The Philadelphia Campaign, 1777–1778*. Lawrence: University Press of Kansas, 2003.

Tate, James P. *The Army and Its Air Corps: Army Policy Toward Aviation, 1919–1941*. Maxwell Air Force Base: Air University Press, 1998.

Taylor, Maxwell D. *The Uncertain Trumpet*. New York: Harpers and Brothers, 1959.

Thelen, David, ed. "History and the Public: What Can We Handle? A Round Table About History after the *Enola Gay* Controversy," *Journal of American History* 82 (December, 1995): 1029–1144.

Tilden, Freeman. *Interpreting Our Heritage*. Fourth Edition. Chapel Hill: University of North Carolina Press, 2007.

Till, Geoffrey. "Adopting the Aircraft Carrier: The British, American, and Japanese Case Studies." In Williamson Murray and Allan B. Millett, *Military Innovation in the Interwar Period*. New York: Cambridge University Press, 1996, 191–226.

Tilley, John A. *The British Navy and the American Revolution*. Columbia: University of South Carolina Press, 1987.

Toll, Ian W. *Six Frigates: The Epic History of the Founding of the U.S. Navy*. New York: W.W. Norton & Company, 2006.

Tompkins, Frank. *Chasing Villa: The Story Behind the Story of Pershing's Expedition into Mexico*. Harrisburg: The Military Service Publishing Company, 1934.

Trask, David E. *The AEF and Coalition Warmaking, 1917–1918*. Lawrence: University Press of Kansas, 1993.

———. *The War With Spain in 1898*. New York: Macmillan Publishing, 1981.

Trauschweizer, Ingo. *The Cold War U.S. Army: Building Deterrence for Limited War*. Lawrence: University Press of Kansas, 2008.

Trautsch, Jasper M. "The Causes of the War of 1812: 200 Years of Debate," *Journal of Military History* 77 (January, 2013): 273–93.

Trudeau, Noah Andre. *Southern Storm: Sherman's March to the Sea*. New York; Harpers, 2008.

———. *Like Men of War: Black Troops in the Civil War, 1862–1865*. New York: Little, Brown, 1998.

Truscott, Jr. Lucian K. *The Twilight of the U.S. Cavalry: Life in the Old Army, 1917–1942*. Lawrence: University Press of Kansas, 1989.

Tuchman, Barbara W. *The Zimmerman Telegram.* New York: Macmillan Publishing Company, 1966.

Tucker, Spencer C. *Blue & Grey Navies: The Civil War Afloat.* Annapolis: Naval Institute Press, 2006.

Tully, Anthony P. *Battle of Surigao Strait.* Bloomington: Indiana University Press, 2009.

Utley, Robert M. *Frontier Regulars: The United States Army and the Indian, 1886–1891.* Lincoln: Bison Books, 1984.

———. *The Indian Frontier of the American West, 1846–1890.* Albuquerque: University of New Mexico Press, 1984.

Vogel, Victor. *Soldiers of the Old Army.* College Station: Texas A&M University Press, 1990.

Wallace, Willard M. *Appeal to Arms: A Military History of the American Revolution.* New York: Harpers and Brothers Publishers, 1951.

Waller, Douglas. *A Question of Loyalty.* New York: Harpers Collins, 2004.

Ward, Carolyn and Alan E. Wilkinson. *Conducting Meaningful Interpretation: A Field Guild for Success.* Golden: Fulcrum Publishing, 2006.

Washburn, Wilcomb E. "Seventeenth-Century Indian Wars." In *Handbook of North American Indians, Vol. 4, History of Indian-White Relations.* Washington DC: Smithsonian Institution, 1988, 89–100.

Watson, Mark Skinner. *Chief of Staff: Prewar Plans and Preparations.* Washington, DC: Historical Division, Department of Army, 1950.

Webber, Bert. *Silent Siege – II: Japanese Attacks on North American in World War II.* Medford: Webb Research Group, 1988.

Weigley, Russell F. *A Great Civil War: A Military and Political History, 1861–1865.* Bloomington: Indiana University Press, 2000.

———. *Eisenhower's Lieutenants: The Campaign of France and Germany, 1944–1945.* Bloomington: Indiana University Press, 1981.

———. *Towards an American Army: Military Thought from Washington to Marshall.* Westport: Greenwood Press, 1974.

———. *The American Way of War: A History of United States Military Policy and Strategy.* New York: Macmillan Publishing Co., 1973.

———. *The Partisan War: The South Carolina Campaign of 1780–1782.* Columbia: University of South Carolina Press, 1970.

———. *History of the United States Army.* New York: Macmillan Publishing Co., 1967.

Weinberg, Gerhard. *A World At Arms: A Global History of World War II.* New York: Cambridge University Press, 1994.

Wells, Samuel F Jr. "The Origins of Massive Retaliation," *Political Science Quarterly* 96 (Spring, 1981): 31–52.

Werrell, Kenneth P. *Blankets of Fire: U.S. Bombers over Japan during World War Two.* Washington, DC: Smithsonian Institution Press, 1996.

———. "The Strategic Bombing of Germany in World War II: Costs and Accomplishments," *The Journal of American History* 73, no. 3 (December, 1986): 702–13.

Westermeyer, Paul W. *United States Marines in the Gulf War, 1990–1991: Liberating Kuwait.* Quantico: History Division, United States Marine Corps, 2014.

Wilbanks, James H. *Abandoning Vietnam: How America Left and South Vietnam Lost its War.* Lawrence: University Press of Kansas, 2004.

Wiley, Bell Irwin. *The Life of Johnny Reb, The Common Soldier of the Confederacy.* Baton Rouge: Louisiana University Press, 1978.

———. *The Life of Billy Yank: The Common Soldier of the Union.* Baton Rouge: Louisiana State University Press, 1952.

Williams, T. Harry. *Lincoln and His Generals.* New York: Alfred A. Knopf, 1952.

Willmott, H.P. *The Great Crusade: A New Complete History of the Second World War*. New York: The Free Press, 1989.

Wilson, Dale E. *Treat 'Em Rough: The Birth of American Armor, 1917–1920*. Novato: Presidio Press, 1989.

Wilson, David K. *The Southern Strategy: Britain's Conquest of Georgia and South Carolina, 1775–1780*. Columbia: University of South Carolina Press, 2005.

Winders, Richard B. *Mr Polk's Army: The American Military Experience in the Mexican War*. College Station: Texas A&M University Press, 1997.

Winkler, Allan M. *Home Front USA: America During World War II*. Arlington Heights: Harlan Davidson, 1986.

Wirls, Daniel. *Buildup: The Politics of Defense in the Reagan Era*. Ithaca: Cornell University Press, 1992.

Wohlstetter, Barbara. *Pearl Harbor: Warning and Decision*. Palo Alto: Stanford University Press, 1962.

Woodward, Bob. *Bush at War*. New York: Simon and Schuster, 2002.

Wooster, Robert. *The American Military Frontiers: The United States Army in the West, 1783–1800*. Albuquerque: University of New Mexico Press, 2009.

———. *The Military and the United States Indian Policy, 1865–1903*. New Haven: Yale University Press, 1988.

Wright, Donald and Colonel Timothy R. Reese, et al. *On Point II: Transition to the New Campaign: The United States Army in Operation Iraqi Freedom, May 2003–January, 2005*. Fort Leavenworth: Combat Studies Institute, 2008.

Wright, Donald, et al. *A Different Kind of War: The United States in Operation ENDURING FREEDOM OEF, October 2001–September 2005*. Fort Leavenworth: Combat Studies Institute Press, 2010.

Wright, Gordon. *The Ordeal of Total War, 1939–1945*. New York: Harper Torch Books, 1968.

Wynn, Neil A. *The African-American Experience During World War II*. Lanham: Rowman and Littlefield Publishers, 2010.

Yagami, Kazuo. "Bombing Hiroshima and Nagasaki: Gar Alperovitz and His Critics," *Southeast Review of Asian Studies* 31 (2009): 301–307.

Zumbro, Derek S. *Battle for the Ruhr: The German Army's Last Defeat in the West*. Lawrence: University Press of Kansas, 2006.

Index

Index

About the Author

Born and raised in California, I developed a strong interest in history, which took me to the Pacific Northwest, where I earned a BA in history at the University of Puget Sound in Tacoma, Washington, in 1985. I continued my history education at Temple University in Philadelphia, Pennsylvania. Under the tutelage of Dr. Russell F. Weigley, I earned my Ph.D., with an emphasis on modern American military and diplomatic history. In 1996, I published my dissertation, "A New Form of Transportation, The Quartermaster Corps and Standardization of the US Army's Motor Trucks," through Greenwood Press.

In the summer of 1987, looking for a summer job, I became a seasonal park ranger at Independence National Historical Park in Philadelphia. Returning to the Northwest and settling in the Seattle area, while teaching at Green River Community College, I returned to the National Park Service as a permanent employee. In the intervening twenty-one years, I have served at the Seattle unit of Klondike Gold Rush National Historical Park, Nez Perce National Historical Park in Idaho and Mount Rainier National Park in Washington. I have also worked as a peer reviewer in the NPS interpretive development program since 2004 and have given presentations on the various aspects of historical interpretation at the American Association for State and Local History, the Western Museum Association and the National Association for Interpretation.